LEARNING to USE the INTERNET
an introduction with examples and exercises

Ernest Ackermann
Mary Washington College

FRANKLIN, BEEDLE AND ASSOCIATES INC.
8536 SW St. Helens Drive, Suite D
Wilsonville, OR 97070
(503) 682-7668

Contents

Preface

This book is written for all people who want to learn to use the Internet: People who want to use it in their work, people who want to use it in their studies, people who want to use it for recreation, people who want to use it for communication, and people who want to use it because they're curious to see what all the interest and hype concerning the Internet is about. The explanations, examples, and exercises have come from my experiences learning how to use the Internet and from teaching others in workshops and classes. The target audience is new or infrequent users of the Internet. It's designed for people who have a connection to the Internet and want to know *how* to use that connection in a productive and satisfying way to access services, resources, and information, and to communicate electronically with others. Why things work the way they do on the Internet is given some attention, but the focus is on learning how to use the Internet in a step-by-step manner. This book can be used by individuals learning on their own, or it can be used as a primary or supplemental textbook in courses dealing with the Internet.

The Internet is a vast collection of networks connecting over 1,000,000 computer systems and over 30 million individuals. Furthermore, it's growing at an astounding rate! Within the last few years it has become the focus of a great deal of commercial, governmental, and media attention. Its use, effects, and future have been featured in articles and broadcasts in major publications and on radio and television. Individuals in a variety of organizations and institutions regularly use it as a tool for communication, research, study, and recreation. Effectively using the services and resources on the Internet is recognized as an important asset for professionals in virtually every area of work or study.

Organization

The book is organized into four major sections:

❑ Introduction to the Internet and the three basic Internet services—e-mail, Telnet, and FTP—are covered in Chapters 1–4.

❑ Getting involved in discussion on the Internet through interest groups and Usenet news is covered in Chapters 5–6.

❑ Navigating and searching the Internet using Hytelnet, Archie, Gopher, WAIS, and the World Wide Web are covered in Chapters 7–11 and Appendix B.

❑ Ethical, legal, security, and social issues related to the Internet are covered in Chapter 12.

The book contains two appendices. One is a brief guide to using Unix for users who have access to the Internet through computer systems that use Unix as the operating system. The other focuses on Netscape Navigator, one of the most popular World Wide Web browers. A glossary of Internet terms is also included.

The chapters start with the basic services and cover others to match the development of Internet services over the past few years. Learning about the basic services first makes it easier and more rewarding to use more comprehensive tools. Each chapter is designed to take the reader through the steps necessary to make use of the tools needed to access the information and resources on the Internet. Chapters 2 through 10 deal with specific tools: e-mail, Telnet, FTP, interest groups, Usenet, Hytelnet, Archie, Gopher, and WAIS. Chapter 11 concentrates on the World Wide Web and how to access it through popular browsers Lynx and Mosaic. Another browser, Netscape Navigator, is covered in Appendix B. Chapter 1 serves as an introduction to and an explanation of the Internet. It also contains an overview of each of the services and tools covered in later chapters. In Chapter 12 we pay attention to the important issues regarding using the Internet.

All the chapters, except for the last, contain step-by-step examples to demonstrate using the tools and services. By following these and trying them out the reader/participant can gain some first-hand guided experience in using the Internet. Including these examples is a bit risky because of the dynamic nature of the Internet. Nothing is frozen in place, and it may be that when you work with these you'll see differences in the way information is displayed. Don't let that deter you. Using the Internet means you have to adapt to changes. Be persistent and use your skills to make accommodations to a changing environment. One of the things that makes the Internet exciting and vigorous is the way things are changing to make it more useful.

Each chapter contains several exercises to be used to explore the use of the tools and topics discussed in the chapter. Doing the exercises is an important part of learning how to use the Internet; the Internet is not a spectator sport. The exercises deal with topics drawn from a variety of areas, so someone doing the exercises can be exposed to many of the resources available on the Internet.

Several of the chapters contain a section dealing with proper Internet etiquette and acceptable and responsible uses of the Internet. Chapter 12 contains the most information on the subject, but rather than put all of that information in one chapter, it's dealt with in context in other chapters as well.

This book does not contain a catalog of resources on the Internet, but the exercises point you to many of the types of resources available. Also, many of the chapters provide ways to find out more about each topic and some general guides to resources on the Internet.

Supplemental Materials

An instructor's guide with answers to exercises and short quizzes for each chapter is available from the publisher. The author maintains a WWW page (**URL http://www.mwc.edu/ernie/ lrn-net.html**) and a Gopher directory (point your gopher to **gopher.mwc.edu**, choose **The Internet**, and then choose **Learning to Use the Internet**). Both of these contain links to the materials mentioned in the text.

Acknowledgments

This work wouldn't have been possible without the encouragement and support I received from my immediate and extended family. My wife Lynn has put up with my working on this book at all hours of the day and night for the past few months. I owe her a great debt of gratitude for her support and willingness to take up the tasks that are normally shared in our relationship and family. My older son Karl took time away from his studies at the Rhode Island School of Design and gave up his vacation time to prepare the illustrations that appear throughout the book. My younger son Oliver supported me throughout the project and did without my being around to be with him for the good part of this last year.

I want to express my appreciation to my colleagues at Mary Washington College who have worked with me throughout the years in preparing workshops on using the Internet, took the time to read some initial drafts of this work, and always seemed to be available to discuss issues related to using the Internet. These include Daphne Burt Carbaugh of the Campus Christian Community, Joseph Dreiss in the Art Department, Steve Greenlaw in the Department of Economics, John Reynolds in the Department of Computer Science, Gary Stanton in the Department of Historic Preservation, Neal Wyatt in the Library, Marsha Zaidman in the Department of Computer Science, and Paul Zisman in the Department of Education. I also owe a debt to my students who have given their support and have used a number of the exercises and examples.

The people at Franklin, Beedle, and Associates have been very supportive of this project and helped me greatly in preparing these materials. The ones I've worked the most closely with are Jim Leisy and Tom Sumner.

I also want to thank the following manuscript reviewers, whose contributions helped to make this a better book:

Roland Blasini	*Sheridan College*
Charlotte Thunen	*Foothill College*
James Frazier	*University of North Carolina, Charlotte*
Pauline Yeckley	*DeAnza College*
Kenneth Shaw	*Metropolitan State College*

Finally, I want to express my appreciation to the people who contribute to the Internet, in great and small ways. Some develop services, tools, and resources on the Internet. Their work in collecting, preparing, distributing, and otherwise making available resources and services continue to make the Internet an important, substantial, and invigorating place to learn and work. Almost all of their work has been geared to providing materials and tools to be shared in a cooperative manner. A great deal of people have helped me and many others by taking the time to answer questions and give their comments on the growth, development, and nature of the Internet and its uses. In the past the Internet has been shaped and has grown through the efforts of the people who use it. We all owe them a great deal of gratitude. As the Internet continues to grow and becomes a substantial part of modern society we can all add our efforts, imagination, ideas, and skills.

Ernest Ackermann
Department of Computer Science
Mary Washington College
ernie@mwc.edu

Contents

CHAPTER 4
Anonymous FTP: Retrieving Files from Other Computer Systems
94

CHAPTER 5
E-Mail Group Discussion: Discussion Lists, Interest Groups, Listserv, and Mailing Lists
122

CHAPTER 6
Usenet: Reading and Writing the News   141

CHAPTER 7
Hytelnet: Working on the Internet Using Telnet   175

CHAPTER 8
Archie: Locating Files to Retrieve by Anonymous FTP   192

CHAPTER 9
Gopher: Burrowing through the Internet   211

CHAPTER 10
WAIS: Searching Databases on the Internet   249

Introducing the Internet

Millions of people throughout the world use the Internet. They use it for communication with individuals and with groups to share information and ideas by electronic mail (e-mail). They use it to connect to other computer systems so they can look up information and retrieve files, documents, data, programs, and images. They use it to search for information on all sorts of topics in the arts, recreation, humanities, business, the sciences, and social issues. All this activity is possible because tens of thousands of networks are connected to the Internet and exchange information in the same basic ways. Furthermore, the Internet is growing at an astounding rate in terms of the number of users, the number of computer systems and networks making up the Internet, and the number of resources available. Through a single computer or terminal connected to a network which itself is connected to the Internet, users have access to a wide variety of services, tools, information, and other people.

This book is about learning to use the Internet in a productive and satisfying way. It's designed for new or occasional users. The text, examples, and exercises will take you through the basic tools, services, and methods used for working with the Internet. You'll see how to tap into the large collection of resources available on the Internet and how to communicate with any of the millions of other people using the Internet. You'll also learn a little bit about how the Internet works. To get the benefits of your Internet connection, you need to become familiar with the services and tools available and know about some of the major sources of information.

Chapter Overview

This chapter covers the basic information about the Internet and the concepts you need to get started making effective use of the Internet. The topics in this chapter include:

❑ A Description of the Internet

❑ How the Internet Works

❑ How the Internet Developed

❑ Explanation of Internet Domain Names and Addresses

❑ Your Internet Connection

❑ Proper Network Etiquette

This chapter ends with a detailed example of using the Internet to access information on a variety of topics. It's the first of many examples throughout the book. As you read the examples and follow along you'll get step-by-step instructions for using the services and tools on the Internet. Remember, though, that these examples reflect the Internet at the time of writing, but because of the dynamic nature of the Internet some things may not appear to you on screen as they do in this book. The Internet is not frozen in place, but don't let that deter you. Be persistent and use your skills to accomodate to a changing, but important, environment. Change is one of the things that makes the Internet exciting, vigorous, and useful.

Also, there are several exercises after the chapter summary. Do these to get practice using the Internet and to reinforce some of the concepts in the chapter. Now, let's get started!

A Description of the Internet

There are several ways to describe the Internet:

From a social point of view. The Internet is millions of people communicating, sharing ideas and information. They communicate electronically on a one-to-one basis or in groups.

From a practical, recreational, or commercial point of view. The Internet is a vast collection of information that can be searched and retrieved electronically. This collection includes advice on all sorts of topics, data, electronic texts, government information, images, museum exhibits, scholarly papers, software, and access to commercial activities. Tapping into these resources requires knowing which tools and services to use.

From a technical point of view. The Internet is a network of tens of thousands of computer networks. Together, the networks making up the Internet consist of over a million computer systems. These computers and networks communicate by exchanging data according to the same rules, even though the networks and computer systems individually use different technologies.

From a Social Point of View

Tens of millions of people throughout the world have access to the Internet. They use it to communicate with one another; they send and receive messages, some personal and some for wide distribution. Any individual on the Internet can communicate with anyone else on the

Internet. Each user has an electronic address and all users are equally accessible regardless of where they are. Since its beginnings, the Internet has been a place where people can communicate with others no matter where they are, their status, or their expertise. What's important is the quality of the communication, not where or who it comes from. It's not a place where people only read or see what others have done; two-way communication is welcomed, expected, and encouraged.

Many of the people on the Internet form personal or group relationships, or keep in touch with old friends. Electronic communication doesn't give you the opportunity to see someone and talk with them face-to-face, so you might think it's impersonal. Yet there is something very personal about writing to someone through e-mail. You type a message at the keyboard with an image in your mind of the person who'll receive the message. Users also share resources and information. It's satisfying knowing there are people around to answer questions and give help on almost any topic. It's also satisfying being able to share information you have. In some ways it's not surprising that there is so much communication and sharing on the Internet. At its technical basis, the Internet is a network, and networks are created to share resources.

People communicate on the Internet in a variety of ways:

Electronic mail (e-mail). This is a basic Internet service that allows individuals to communicate. It's the basis for how discussion or interest groups operate, and it can be used for access to other Internet services. E-mail is covered in Chapter 2, "Electronic Mail: The Basics about E-Mail."

Discussions in a group setting using e-mail. Some names for these groups are interest groups, Listserv, and mailing lists. Internet users join, contribute to, and read messages to the entire group through e-mail. Several thousand different groups exist; they're used to share opinions and experiences, ask and answer questions, or post information. These groups are covered in Chapter 5, "E-Mail Group Discussion: Discussion Lists, Interest Groups, Listserv, and Mailing Lists."

Group discussions, asking questions, and sharing information through Usenet (also known as Internet News). The messages are called articles and are grouped into categories called newsgroups. Individuals can read articles, reply to articles, and post articles to specific groups. The reply is either posted to the newsgroup or sent only to the original author. The communication here is from one computer system to another; it's available to individuals but isn't carried through their e-mail. Usenet existed before the Internet, but the news (as it's called) is often carried from site to site on the Internet. See Chapter 6, "Usenet: Reading and Writing the News" for information about using Usenet.

There is no organization or agency controlling activity on the Internet. Control is in the hands of individuals and local organizations, schools, or businesses. This allows for the formation of discussions, the exchange of ideas, and the spread of information in a free and open manner. The users come from a variety of countries and cultures, and this diversity and open two-way communication contribute to the Internet's utility and vigor. Some people describe the Internet as a form of anarchy, mainly because there isn't any central control. However, a number of laws apply to communications and activities on the Internet, local and regional network policies govern its use, and Internet-wide rules of etiquette and rules for acceptable behavior exist. The laws of one country or rules for one network can't be applied to everything that happens on the Internet. But, because communications often travel across several networks, local policies and laws can apply. Individuals have been arrested, sued for libel, or otherwise censured because of messages sent on the Internet. The people using the Internet themselves have a say in the way it's used. Inappropriate messages and practices are often met with a large number of complaints and protests, and sometimes result in the offenders losing access to the Internet. Some of these issues are discussed in detail in Chapter 12, "Issues: Ethical, Legal, Security, and Social."

The number of people gaining access to the Internet is growing at an astounding rate. If the number of users increases at the same rate as it was near the end of 1994, every person on earth will have Internet access by 2003! Most likely this isn't technologically possible, and there are a few countries the Internet doesn't touch. However, the Internet is a growing, vigorous, and valuable means for communication and interaction.

From a Practical, Recreational, or Commercial Point of View

There is a staggering amount of information on a wide variety of topics on the Internet. Some of it is practical; it can be used for business, research, study, and technical purposes. Users can access the services and information provided by professional organizations: documents, government information, data, on-line bibliographic searches, articles, publications, and software. There is an increase in the use of the Internet for commercial applications. This includes researching and using financial and economic data, business applications such as marketing and buying items of all types, and making services available for a fee. You can also use your access to the Internet for personal and recreational purposes. This includes getting information relating to your interests and hobbies, getting software and other items you'll find personally useful, and getting advice. Other types of information include travel recommendations and news, medical and health information, weather reports, entertainment listings, library holdings, museum exhibits, and sports news. You can tap into university and other libraries throughout the world, museums, commercial publications, software archives for many different types of computer systems, and databases of information dealing with topics such as art history, extragalactic data, literature, and molecular biology, to name a few.

Almost all of this information is shared free of any charges except what you pay to access the Internet, because sharing information and resources is at the basis of the Internet. Accessing some information or getting articles from recently published magazines does carry an extra charge. Conducting secure business transactions on the Internet, which includes charging for information, is becoming more commonplace. One of the fastest growing sectors of work on the Internet is in the area of commercial applications. As Internet use becomes more available and common, it's being viewed as a viable means of doing business and marketing.

You access the information or communicate with others on the Internet by using a collection of tools and services that give you access to people, information, and resources. There are three basic services:

Electronic mail (e-mail). An efficient and convenient means of user-to-user communication. See Chapter 2, "Electronic Mail: The Basics about E-Mail."

Telnet. Allows you to connect to and log into a remote computer. You can access any of the public services or tools at the remote site. Telnet can be used for access to libraries, databases, and other Internet services. It's described in Chapter 3, "Telnet: Access to Other Computers on the Internet."

FTP. Lets you transfer files from one computer on the Internet to another. FTP stands for File Transfer Protocol. Many systems on the Internet make archives or collections of files available through anonymous FTP. Its use is explained and demonstrated in Chapter 4, "Anonymous FTP: Retrieving Files from Other Computer Systems."

A number of other tools and services have been built to take advantage of these basic services, to make them easier to use, and to extend their use. Some of these tools are designed to search the Internet for resources.

Hytelnet. A collection of sites and services available through Telnet. The sites are arranged into categories based on the services they provide. Hytelnet also gives easy access to these sites. See Chapter 7, "Hytelnet: Working on the Internet Using Telnet" for details about using Hytelnet.

Archie. This service lets you search the archives of files accessible by anonymous FTP. You give the complete or partial name of a file and Archie returns the Internet address and location of files for you to use with anonymous FTP. Using Archie is discussed in Chapter 8, "Archie: Locating Files to Retrieve by Anonymous FTP."

Other services and tools concentrate on providing easier (more user-friendly) access to Internet resources along with some different ways of using the Internet.

Gopher. A menu-based document delivery system. An individual uses Gopher to access various types of information such as files, documents, address books, and images. Gopher also allows access to ftp, telnet, and searchable databases. All of this is done by selecting items from menus. See Chapter 9, "Gopher: Burrowing through the Internet" for details on using Gopher and using Veronica, a tool to search Gopher menus for resources throughout the Internet.

WAIS. Stands for Wide Area Information System. WAIS is discussed in Chapter 10, "WAIS: Searching Databases on the Internet."

The newer tools and programs provide a common method to access almost all the others. Having a single way to access all the Internet services means more than having one super-duper program or exceptional tool. You need those, but you also need a standard, Internet-wide way to indicate which service to use, which site to contact, and what to do at that site. The idea behind the World Wide Web (WWW) is just that, a single means of access to virtually everything available through the Internet: services, resources, tools, and information.

World Wide Web. This gives hypertext, even hypermedia, access to all varieties of resources and services on the Internet. There are several programs used to work with the Internet in this fashion including Lynx and Mosaic. These, along with tools for searching the WWW for resources, are discussed in detail in Chapter 11, "World Wide Web (WWW), Lynx, and Mosaic." Appendix B covers Netscape Navigator, another tool for searching the WWW.

The WWW isn't a tool, program, or service, but a way of viewing and accessing the Internet. Even with this view you need to know about the basic services you'll access.

From a Technical Point of View

The Internet is a network of tens of thousands of computer networks. Every network and every computer on these networks exchange information according to certain rules called *protocols*. It doesn't matter that the networks or the millions of computers that make up the networks use different technologies or are manufactured by different companies. When they use the same protocols they can exchange data or information. Two protocols used for working with the Internet are *Internet Protocol* or *IP*, and *Transmission Control Protocol* or *TCP*. You'll often see these mentioned together as *TCP/IP* when references are made to the software needed to make an Internet connection.

Each network and computer system on the Internet has an Internet address called an *IP address*. These IP addresses are numeric, like **123.45.67.321**. Each numeric address corresponds to a name called a *domain name* or *host name*, such as **chutney.engr.jackson.edu**. The term *host name* usually refers to the name of a specific computer, but it's still a domain name. The address is used to exchange information with, send e-mail to, or use an Internet service that involves another computer system.

Not all networks on the Internet have direct connections, but each network is connected to one or more other networks. That way there can be several paths from one system to another. One of the technical strengths of the Internet is that when some parts of it are unavailable for traffic, messages can still get through. When information is passed from one computer system to another, it's broken up into pieces called *packets*. Each packet contains the address of the sender, the address of the destination, and a portion of the total information to be sent. Packets from one system can be delivered to another system even if there is no direct connection between them. In fact, not all the packets have to take the same path. The emphasis is on delivering the packets, not on the connections between systems.

We can view the Internet as a large collection of computer systems that can exchange data. This capability comes from the hardware and software on individual computers and the hardware and software that allow networks to pass information. There doesn't have to be a direct connection from one site to another for them to communicate with each other. Each network has to be able to accept the information addressed to one of its own systems and be able to pass on information destined for other networks.

How the Internet Works

The Internet is a network connecting thousands of other computer networks. Each network on the Internet has a unique address, and the computer systems making up a network have an address based on the network's address. At a basic level the addresses are numeric, a sequence of four numbers (each between 0 and 255) separated by periods. An example is **192.65.245.76**. You don't need to memorize the addresses as numbers; they can also be specified as names such as **sage.myu.edu**. Each piece of information passed around the Internet contains the sender's address and the delivery address. As information is passed around the Internet each network decides whether to accept it or pass it on. Once information is accepted within a network, it's the network's job to get it to a specific computer system.

The Internet is designed so the computer systems within one network can exchange information with computers on other networks. The rules that govern this form of communication are called protocols. Using the same protocols allows different types of networks and computer systems to communicate with each other. Each needs to have the software and hardware in place so it can deal with information in the form specified by the protocols. This means a computer system or network has to be able to transform information from its own form into the form(s) designated by the protocols, transform information from the protocol's form to its own form, and be able to send and receive information in that form. Two protocols used are Internet Protocol (IP) and Transmission Control Protocol (TCP).

Packets of characters (bytes), like envelopes holding messages, carry information on the Internet. Using the IP protocol, a message consisting of no more than 1500 bytes or characters is put into a packet. Each packet has the address of the sender and the address of the destination. These addresses, mentioned above, are called IP addresses. You can think of a packet in the same way you think of a letter sent by a postal service. Using the TCP protocol a single large message is divided into a sequence of packets, and each is put into an IP packet. The packets are passed from one network to another until they reach their destination. At the destination the TCP software reassembles the packets into a complete message. If packets are lost or damaged, a request is sent out to resend them. It isn't necessary for all the packets in a single message to take the same route through the Internet, or for the same message to take the same route each time it's sent. This notion of a message naturally applies to e-mail, but is extended to apply to many of the other services on the Internet.

The Internet is a *packet-switched network*. The emphasis is on transmitting and receiving packets, rather than on connecting computer systems to each other. When Telnet is used, for example, it appears as if there is a direct connection between two computers on different parts of the Internet. However, it's a *virtual connection*; the two systems aren't directly connected to each other. In reality packets are being passed from one system to another. Passing information and implementing the Internet services with packets keeps one system from tying up the networks with a connection dedicated to a single program.

Many of the Internet services operate according to a scheme called *client/server*. A user on one computer system starts a program that contacts another (remote) computer system. The client is the program the user is running and the server is running on the remote system. The user gives commands to the client, which passes the information to the server. The server interprets those commands and returns information to the client, which passes the information to the user. Gopher is an example of this model. You start a Gopher session (actually you start a program named gopher on your system) and it contacts a computer system running a Gopher server. The information you see is passed from the server to the client. The commands you give are either used by the client to work with information on your system or passed from the client to the server. Usually, one server can deal with several clients. So a single Gopher server can handle requests from many client programs. All the server does is respond to individual requests from clients, and the clients take care of presenting the information to the user. All of this information is passed as packets between the server and the client.

The networks on the Internet use hardware or a device called a *router* to communicate with other networks. The router on a network accepts packets addressed to it and passes on packets addressed to other networks. Each computer system with a direct connection to the Internet has to have the hardware and/or software to allow it to work with packets. (Your access to the Internet may be of this type or you may be using a modem to tap into a system with direct access. In this case, you don't have a direct connection, but you're contacting one that does.) It's up to the individual computer systems to take care of sending and receiving packets.

Not all computer networks are part of the Internet. Some use a different technology or are strictly commercial networks. These can, however, exchange information with the Internet. This is done through a *gateway*, which allows different networks to communicate with each other. Systems connected through gateways usually can exchange electronic mail, but other Internet services may not be available.

How the Internet Developed

In the late 1960s the United States Department of Defense, through its Advanced Research Projects Agency (ARPA), funded research into the establishment of a decentralized computer network. From the beginning, some of the developers and researchers saw the advantages of a network in which computer systems of differing types could communicate. They also foresaw the development of a community from among the users of this network. The network was named ARPANET. It linked researchers at universities, research laboratories, and some military labs. The 1970s saw the further development of the ARPANET and the establishment of connections networks in other countries. There were a relatively small (fewer than 100) number of sites or hosts (computer systems) on these networks. In the early 1980s other networks, in the U.S. and elsewhere, were established.

In the late 1980s the National Science Foundation (U.S.) funded the development of a network (using the Internet protocols) named NSFNET to connect supercomputer centers in the United States. Many colleges and universities were encouraged to connect to that network. The number of sites increased rapidly; there were more than 10,000 sites in 1987 and more than 100,000 in 1989. Similar activity, although not on such a large scale, was taking place in other countries as well. This large worldwide collection of networks and computer systems communicating according to the same protocols has come to be what's called the Internet.

Usenet, the "User's Network," originated in 1979. It allowed people to share information in the form of articles arranged into newsgroups. Usenet was developed separately from the Internet, but programs and protocols for distributing articles on the Internet are readily available. A number of commercial networks and some others using technologies that can't be adapted to Internet protocols came into being in the 1970s and 1980s. Two examples are CompuServe, which charges users for connect time and other services, and BITNET, a network that linked many universities. Public access to the Internet has always been an issue. The Cleveland Free-Net, a community-based network, was also developed in the late 1980s to give Internet access to anyone with a computer and modem. Several other community groups have started free-nets and several have joined to form the National Public Telecommunications Network (NPTN).

The development and operation of ARPANET, NSFNET, and several other networks throughout the world was subsidized by government funds. These networks established *acceptable use policies*, which stated what type of activities were allowed on these publicly supported networks. These policies prohibited any purely commercial activities, and set the tone for a developing code of network ethics or etiquette. Commercial networks were also being developed, although under the acceptable use policies, they could not use the transmission links of the public networks. So for some time commercial activity on the major portion of the Internet in the United States was prohibited. However, in 1988 several commercial networks reached an agreement with NSFNET to allow their e-mail to be carried on NSFNET. That way a user on CompuServe or someone using MCImail could send a message to someone with an Internet address at a public institution such as a college or university. Likewise, messages could be sent from NSFNET to these private networks, but e-mail from one user on a private service couldn't be transported over NSFNET to another user on a private service.

In 1990 ARPANET ceased to exist as an administrative entity, and the public network in the U.S. was turned over to NSFNET. The Internet was growing at a remarkable rate and clearly becoming bigger than the public institutions wanted to manage or support. In the early 1990s commercial networks with their own Internet exchanges or gateways were allowed to conduct business on the Internet, and in 1993 the NSF created the InterNIC to provide services, such as registration of domain names, directory and database services to the Internet community, and information about Internet services. These services were contracted to the private sector.

The explosive growth on the Internet and the inclusion of commercial networks and services has been accompanied by an astounding increase in the population of Internet users. This increase includes users who are not part of an academic or research community. The Internet is reaching the size and importance of an infrastructure, a necessary underpinning of society. From a research project, the Internet has grown very rapidly into something that involves millions of people worldwide.

Explanation of Internet Domain Names and Addresses

Networks and computer systems on the Internet exchange data and communicate with each other. An address is assigned to each network, and each computer system within a network gets an address based on the network's address. These addresses are made up of a sequence of four numbers separated by periods, such as **192.65.245.76**. Each number is in the range of 0 through 255. Starting from the left the numbers in the address identify a network, and the number(s) on the right identify a specific host or computer system. For example, the network portion of the address **192.65.245.76** is **192.65.245** and the host portion is **76**. In this case the network can have 256 hosts (computer systems). On networks with more hosts, the last two or three groups of numbers are used for the host portion of the address. An address in numeric form is called an IP address. Information sent from one site on the Internet to another is divided into packets and each packet has the IP address of the sender and the IP address of the destination.

This numeric scheme of IP addresses works well for computer systems, but it's difficult (close to impossible) for people to remember, and type correctly, a sequence of four numbers for every Internet site they need to contact. Therefore, Internet sites also have names associated with them; for example, **jupiter.research.wonder.com** or **cs.greatu.edu**. The name is called a *domain name*. Like the numeric address, domain names are a sequence of words separated by periods. How many words? There are at least two, with three and four being more common, but there could be more. The most specific information, usually the name of a computer system or host, is on the left and you get more general information as you move to the right. This is the opposite of the arrangement of a numeric address.

The collection of networks making up the Internet is divided into groups called domains. The domains represent either a type of organization or a geographical location. For example, a site in the domain **edu** would be an educational institution, and a site in the domain **tx.us** would be in Texas in the United States. Each IP address (numeric address) is associated with one or more domain names. An address specified as a domain name is automatically converted to the IP address. The name of a specific computer system or host on a network is called a *fully qualified domain name*. Here's a dissected example:

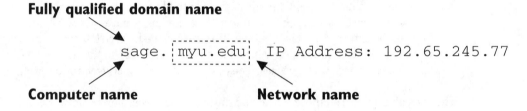

Table 1.1 lists domains by type of organization.

Domain	Type of Organization	Example: Name and IP address	
com	commercial organization	pipeline.netsurf.com	157.22.1.3
edu	educational institution	enuxsa.eas.asu.edu	129.219.30.12
gov	government (US)	csab.larc.nasa.gov	128.155.26.10
mil	military (US)	nic.ddn.mil	192.112.36.5
net	networks	ftp.sura.net	128.167.254.179
org	non-profit organization	gopher.eff.org	192.77.172.4

Table 1.1   Top-Level Domains

The geographical names representing a country or state are two letters long. Here's an example:

```
Fully qualified Domain Name: askhp.ask.uni-karlsruhe.de
Two-letter Domain Code:         de
Country:                        Germany
```

With hundreds of countries throughout the world, we can't list them all here. "FAQ: International E-mail accessibility," compiled by Olivier M.J. Crepin-Leblond, contains a list of two-letter country codes. The document is available by anonymous FTP from **rtfm.mit.edu** in the directory **/pub/usenet/news.answers/mail/**, and available on the WWW by using the URL **http://www.ee.ic.ac.uk/misc/country-codes.html**. Details on using anonymous FTP are in Chapter 4, and information about getting a document through a WWW browser is in Chapter 11.

A domain name can tell you something about the site or computer system you'll be contacting. If the domain name is geographical, you can identify the country and maybe more information about the locality. Let's look at the fully-qualified domain name **gopher.physics.utoronto.ca**. Starting from the left, **gopher** indicates this system might be a Gopher server, **physics** probably means this system is connected with the Physics Department, and **utoronto.ca** places the site at the University of Toronto, Canada. Except for Canada corresponding to **ca**, all of this was guesswork. There are no hard-and-fast rules for local names. However, you'd be making a good guess if you got mail from **somebody@lib.umich.edu** that the person was connected with the library at the University of Michigan.

Your Internet Connection

You're using a computer or a computer terminal to access the Internet. You know how to turn it on and get things set up so you can tap into the Internet. That's great! The details on doing these things vary depending on the type of computer and software you're using, and a number of other things. This book focuses on accessing the resources and services on the Internet after you're connected. If you need some help getting started or connected find a local expert, get in touch with the company or organization that's providing you with Internet access, or start reading the manuals. A number of good books cover the hardware and software issues of getting connected, and there's lots of good advice about that on the Internet.

There are essentially two different types of connections for accessing the services and resources on the Internet: an IP connection or dial-up access.

1. If the computer you're using has the hardware and software to be directly connected to a network on the Internet, that is, if it can send and receive packets according to the TCP/IP protocols, then we say you've got a *direct* or *IP connection* to the Internet. With an IP connection you've got access to all the services and resources on the Internet. If your computer can display images you'll probably take advantage of some of the graphical interfaces for using the Internet, although sometimes you'll use a text-based interface. Your computer either contains some hardware called a network card or network connection and there's a cable connected to your computer, or you use something called SLIP (Serial Line Internet Protocol). With SLIP you use a modem to call another computer, which gives you IP access.

2. You use a modem to call and log into another system. You don't have a direct connection to the Internet, but the system you've called does. This is sometimes called *dial-up* access or a *shell account*. You probably can access most of the services and resources on the Internet, but it's doubtful you'll have access to some of the graphical interfaces and certain types of World Wide Web browsers such as Mosaic. This sort of access is common for folks who dial into another system that's located where they work or go to school.

Both these types of connections are useful and they're available from any one of a number of private companies called *Internet providers*. The IP or SLIP connections are more expensive than dial-up access, but give more complete and sometimes faster access. There is one other crucial difference: The files you retrieve from and send out to the Internet are on the computer with the direct Internet connection. If you don't have an IP or SLIP connection, files have to be moved between the computer you're using and the one with a direct connection. For example, imagine you're using e-mail, you want to send a report to an associate, and the report is in a file on your hard drive. With an IP connection you include the file in a message you're composing. With the other type of access you have to *upload* the file first before it can be put into an e-mail message. (Upload means you have to transfer the file from your hard drive to the computer system you've accessed by a modem.) Likewise, suppose you want to save a message on your computer or print a message on the printer attached to your computer. If your computer has an IP or SLIP connection, just give the commands for saving or printing. If you have dial-up access, you probably have to save the message in a file on the system you're calling and then *download* it. (Download means transferring a file from the system you've called to the computer you're using.)

Proper Network Etiquette

The Internet connects networks throughout the world, and there isn't any one agency controlling it. People from many different countries, cultures, and backgrounds use it in an effective way. All this diversity along with no central control could lead to disorganized anarchy, a lack of concern for the effects of using resources at other computer systems, and an indifference to the feelings, opinions, and concerns of individuals. Any of these effects would not be tolerable and would detract from the utility, vigor, and richness of the Internet. It may seem too good to be true, but the users of the Internet generally behave in a way that protects individuals, fosters sharing information, and preserves Internet resources. This is because users realizing the benefits to individuals and to the group of maintaining the manner in which the Internet has developed and continues to grow.

Over the years organizations have developed policies, rules, and codes for acceptable behavior. Some of these are listed throughout the book and in the exercises for this chapter. We'll list a few here that you'll want to consider and think about as you use the Internet:

Resources and Services. The services and resources on the Internet are generally offered in a spirit of cooperation or sharing. They need to be used in the same manner. In many cases you'll be a guest, accessing resources on a remote computer system. Act like a good guest and respect needs and wishes of the host. This can mean limiting the amount of time you spend using a remote system, limiting the amount of disk space or other resources you might use on a remote system, and limiting your access to nonpeak times.

Individuals. There is strong support for individual rights, feelings, and opinions on the Internet. The users represent a wide range of opinions and values. Some folks may express opinions that aren't to your liking; some things may be offensive to you. Before making an immediate reply or taking instantaneous action, take a little time to consider your response. Treat others with respect and concern.

Example 1.1 — Accessing Information through Telnet and Gopher — 13

Copyrights. Material on the Internet is generally protected by copyright laws or treaties. Because something can be copied electronically and is easy to obtain doesn't mean it can be distributed without permission. Most of the information contains a copyright statement indicating that it can be distributed electronically and used for noncommercial purposes. This applies to text, images, and other types of information.

Commercial Activities. For a relatively long time, in terms of the history of the Internet, commercial activity wasn't allowed. That's not the case now, but still the Internet isn't wide open to marketing or commercial announcements. It's technologically possible to send an e-mail announcement of a product or service to thousands of people on the Internet. That type of activity has always been met with almost as many protests, thus wasting a lot of resources and generally doing more harm than good. Take some time to know the culture and expectations of Internet users before attempting any commercial activities.

The Law. Generally, laws governing espionage, fraud, harassment, libel, obscenity, and theft apply to messages and other activities carried on electronic networks. There have been several laws passed in the U.S. and other countries that appply specifically to electronic communications. There is a lot of freedom and openness on the Internet, but that doesn't mean it's beyond the rule of law.

Contribute to the Internet. The Internet is a network, and networks are created to share resources. When you have the opportunity to make something available to others on the Internet, do so. This includes helping others with questions, collecting and organizing information, and sharing your resources.

Example 1.1   Accessing Information through Telnet and Gopher

Throughout this book we'll show several examples of using the services and tools on the Internet. This one gets you started and shows some of the resources available. You'll see what to expect as you use the Internet, but remember that because the Internet is always changing, the menus and items here may be different when you go through the steps. Also, the commands you give to access an Internet service may be different from the ones here. The specific commands to start a service depend on the type of computer and software you're using. This example was constructed using Telnet on a Unix computer system.

In this example we'll use Telnet to access the Gopher server at the University of Michigan Library. Gopher is discussed in detail in Chapter 9. We'll choose an item from the menu that will take us to a menu of general reference resources. From there, we'll make our way to a collection of resources on the Internet, and then we'll let you explore on your own. When you use Gopher, you select an item from a menu by typing in its number or clicking on an item with a mouse, and then press Enter. Type **q** and press Enter at any time to quit this session.

We're using Telnet because everyone with any sort of connection to the Internet will be able to use Telnet. If you have access to Gopher then you can skip the first two steps using Telnet and start directly with starting a gopher session to **gopher.lib.umich.edu**.

Here are the steps we'll follow:

1. Start a Telnet session and connect to **una.hh.lib.umich.edu.**
2. Log in by typing **gopher** at the **login**: prompt.
3. Choose the item **General Reference Resources <Menu>** from the menu.
4. Choose the item **International Information <Menu>** from the menu.
5. Choose the item **Global** or **World-Wide Topics (From Gopher Jewels) <Menu>** from the menu and then Explore!
6. Press **q** to quit.

Feel free to explore other items on the menus. You can always go back to a previous menu by pressing **u** or the left arrow. Get help about what commands to use by pressing **?** or press **q** to quit. We're assuming you've logged into or started the system you use to connect to the Internet. Have a great time!

Start a Telnet Session and Connect to una.hh.lib.umich.edu

☞ **At the prompt, type** `telnet una.hh.lib.umich.edu` **and press** Enter.

Log in to or start up the software on the computer you use to access the Internet. The commands we've used in this example are the ones used on a Unix system. In this case, at the shell prompt ($ here but you may see %), type **telnet una.hh.lib.umich.edu** and press Enter. This shows how you might start any Telnet session; type **telnet** followed by the domain name of the site you want to contact and press Enter.

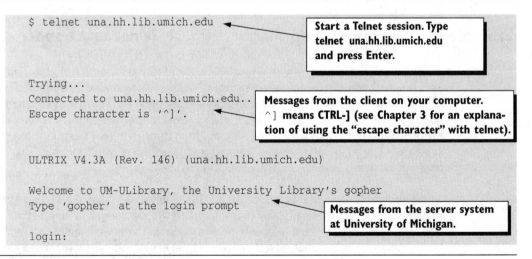

Figure 1.1   **Starting a Telnet Session**

Login by typing gopher at the login: prompt

☞ **To log in, type** `gopher` **at the** `login:` **prompt and press** Enter.

Example 1.1 — Accessing Information through Telnet and Gopher — 15

Figure 1.1 takes you up to the point where you get a **login:** prompt. The remote system is waiting for you to type in a log-in name. The instructions on the screen say to use the log in name **gopher**. Type **gopher** and press Enter. After that you'll see some information from the server about how some services are restricted to folks at University of Michigan. In this case, we're guests and would like to continue with access to everything that's open to the public. Press Enter one more time, as shown in Figure 1.2, to get to the main menu in Figure 1.3.

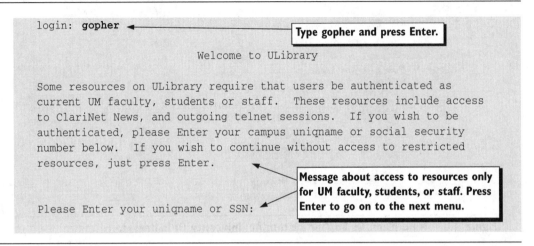

Figure 1.2   Login and Message About Access

At the bottom of Figure 1.2 you see the instruction to press Enter to continue. Do it! A display similar to the one in Figure 1.3 will appear in a short time. That's the Main Menu of the gopher system at University of Michigan Library. You'll probably see the arrow, →, pointing to the first item. The information at the top of the screen tells you what version of the client software you're using and the name of the server you're contacting. (If you started this example using Gopher instead of Telnet then you should have used a command such as **gopher gopher.lib.umich.edu** to start the Gopher session.)

Choose the item "General Reference Resources <Menu>" from the menu.

☞ **Type the number before** `General Reference Resources <Menu>` **and press** `Enter`.

The Main Menu, or any menu, on a gopher system contains a list of items. You select an item by using the down arrow key to position the arrow to the item you want or by typing in the number of the item and pressing Enter. If you're using a system that lets you use a mouse, point at the item you want to select and click on it.

```
                Internet Gopher Information Client v2.0.15
                      University of Michigan Libraries


        1.  About Using the ULibrary Gopher <Menu>
        2.  Contents of the ULibrary Gopher <Menu>
        3.  About Univ. Michigan Libraries and Information Resources <Menu>
        4.  News Services and Government Information <Menu>
        5.  Dissertations and Other Indexes <Menu>
    ->  6.  General Reference Resources <Menu>
        7.  Humanities Resources <Menu>
        8.  Science Resources <Menu>
        9.  Social Sciences Resources <Menu>
        10. Library Catalogs <Menu>
        11. Univ. Michigan Campus Information (GOpherBLUE) <Menu>
        12. Other Gophers and Veronica <Menu>
        13. What's New & Featured Resources <Menu>


    P Previous Page      M Go To Main Menu      ? Help Screen     D Download
    N Next Page          U Go Up A Menu         Q Quit            Page: 1/1
```

Figure 1.3   Main Menu Of Gopher System At University Of Minnesota

The line at the bottom of the screen points out that you can press **?** to get help or **Q** to quit the gopher session.

To get to what's shown in Figure 1.3 we pressed the down arrow key five times to get the arrow, →, opposite the item numbered **6**. Press Enter to select that item. Alternately, select the item by typing in **6** and pressing Enter. In any case the screen will show a menu similar to the one in Figure 1.4.

Choose the Item "International Information <Menu>" from the Menu

☞ **Type the number before** Internet Guides and Resources <Menu> **and press** Enter.

Now we'll have to go through one more menu before getting to a list of guides to the Internet going to have to go through a few more menus to get to a list of Internet resources kept at the Internet Network Information CEnter, as shown below.

```
                Internet Gopher Information Client v2.0.15
                        General Reference Resources


        1.  Academic Resources <Menu>
        2.  Biographical Information  <Menu>
        3.  British Library Online Information <Menu>
        4.  Dictionaries <Menu>
        5.  Directories: Phone, Place, Time & Weather Information <Menu>
        6.  Electronic Addresses (Email) Directories  <Menu>
```

Example 1.1 — Accessing Information through Telnet and Gopher —— 17

```
        7.  Electronic Serials <Menu>
        8.  Government & Non-Profit Group Information <Menu>
        9.  Grant, Foundation & Scholarship Information <Menu>
   ->  10.  International Information <Menu>
       11.  Internet Guides and Resources <Menu>
       12.  Occupational Outlook Handbook 1994-1995 <Menu>


P Previous Page      M Go To Main Menu      ? Help Screen      D Download
N Next Page           U Go Up A Menu         Q Quit             Page: 1/1
```

Figure 1.4   Menu Of General Reference Resources As Shown At University of Michigan Library

The line at the bottom of this menu includes the command **U** to go up a menu. Pressing **U** takes you back to the previous menu.

Choose the Item "International Information <Menu>" from the Menu

☞ **Type the number before** International Information <Menu> **and press** Enter.

The menu in Figure 1.4 shows the list of general reference resources available through the Gopher server at the University of Michigan Library. You see a variety of available resources. Choosing one of these items takes you to another menu. The menus could represent information and resources either on the computer systems at University of Michigan or on other Gopher servers anywhere on the Internet. We want to get to the resources dealing with International Information, so type **10** or use the down arrow to select item **10** and then press Enter. A menu similar to the one in Figure 1.5 will soon appear.

```
              Internet Gopher Information Client v2.0.15
                       International Information

        1.  Canadian Information Resources (M-Link) <Menu>
        2.  Famous International Documents <Menu>
        3.  Foreign (Non-U.S.) Country Information <Menu>
        4.  French Language Press Review <Menu>
   ->   5.  Global or World-Wide Topics (From Gopher Jewels) <Menu>
        6.  International Government Information (LC) <Menu>
        7.  International Information (M-Link) <Menu>
        8.  Radio Free Europe Daily Reports <Menu>
        9.  Treaties and International Agreements <Menu>
       10.  United Nations <Menu>
       11.  World Bank Information and Publications <Menu>
       12.  World Constitutions <Menu>
       13.  World Health Organization (WHO) <Menu>


P Previous Page      M Go To Main Menu      ? Help Screen      D Download
N Next Page           U Go Up A Menu         Q Quit             Page: 1/1
```

Figure 1.5   International Information as Shown at University of Michigan Library

Choose the Item "Global or World-Wide Topics (From Gopher Jewels) <Menu>" from the Menu

☞ **Type the number before** Global or World-Wide Topics (From Gopher Jewels) <Menu> **and press** Enter.

Figure 1.5 shows the menu for International Information at University of Michigan Library. Several of these items represent links to other Gopher servers in different parts of the world. To get to a menu of global or world-wide topics type **5** and press Enter. A menu similar to the one in Figure 1.6 will appear.

```
              Internet Gopher Information Client v2.0.15
               Global or World-Wide Topics (From Gopher Jewels)

  ->  1. Abbreviations for International Organizations (from CIA Fa.. <Text>
      2. Amnesty International Gopher <Menu>
      3. Ashoka - Innovators for the Public - The Meta Network <Menu>
      4. Catalog of Known Nuclear Explosions- OK. Geological Survey.. <Menu>
      5. CIA World Factbook 1993 (1994 ed.) - UM-St.Louis Gopher <Menu>
      6. CIESIN Global Change Information Gateway <Menu>
      7. Communications For A Sustainable Future <Menu>
      8. Current News From Around the Globe - Univ. System of Georg.. <Menu>
      9. Daily News - Free Internet Sources - NSTN's CyberMall <Menu>
     10. Domestic & International Agencies & Resources - UT-REENIC <Menu>
     11. Earthweb <Menu>
     12. Ejournal - World Politics Magazine <Menu>
     13. Foreign Currency Exchange Rates (current only) - Via U of .. <Text>
     14. Fourth World <Menu>
     15. Global Change Research Information Office (GCRIO) <Menu>
     16. Global Democracy Network <Menu>
     17. HungerNet - Brown University <Menu>


 P Previous Page      M Go To Main Menu      ? Help Screen      D Download
 N Next Page          U Go Up A Menu         Q Quit                Page: 1/4
```

Figure 1.6   Global or World-Wide Topics from University of Michigan Libraries

There's enough stuff listed in the menu in Figure 1.6 to keep anybody busy for a long time! Lots of things might be interesting at this point. You might want to start with the first item. By choosing it, you won't see another menu. Instead, a document will be displayed one screen at a time for you to read. The keystrokes to use for going to the next screen, previous screen, or back to the menu will be there on the screen. Some of the other items on the menu will take you to much more information and resources throughout the world. For example, the item "Daily News - Free Internet Sources - NSTN's CyberMall <Menu>" takes you to a menu of links to news reports from sources throughout the world.

The notation "Page: 1/4" at the bottom of Figure 1.6 lets you know this menu continues on to another screen. Press the spacebar to go to the next screen, and then press the Minus key or **P** to get to the previous screen. Now it's up to you to explore. Follow your interests. Eventually you'll have to end you session (Who knows? Maybe its time to eat!)

Press Q to Quit

☞ **Type** Q **or** q **to quit.**

——————————————————————————End of Example 1.1——————————————————————————

Summary

The Internet is used by millions of people throughout the world for communication, research, business, getting information, and recreation. To use it effectively you need to know how to use some of the services, tools, and programs that give access to its resources, and you need to know some of the sources of information on the Internet.

The Internet can be described in a variety of ways. It can be viewed in terms of the people who use it and the ways they communicate with each other to share information and ideas. It's also reasonable to look at it as a vast information system and source of information on all sorts of topics. From a technical point of view the Internet is a network of thousands of computer networks comprised of over a million computer systems. These networks and computers communicate with each other according to certain rules or protocols. The ones mentioned most frequently are the Internet Protocol (IP) and the Transmission Control Protocol (TCP). You'll often see them referred to together as TCP/IP.

There are a variety of tools and services used to access the Internet. Three basic services form the foundation for other Internet services:

❑ Electronic mail enables users to exchange messages electronically (Chapter 2).

❑ Telnet allows users on one computer to log in to and access services on another (remote) computer on the Internet (Chapter 3).

❑ FTP (File Transfer Protocol) enables users to copy files between computer systems on the Internet (Chapter 4).

Users can communicate one-on-one with e-mail, but there are facilities for group discussions:

❑ Interest groups, Listserv, or mailing lists make it possible for users to engage in group discussions focused on a specific topic by using e-mail (Chapter 5).

❑ Usenet or Internet News is a system for exchanging messages called articles arranged according to specific categories called newsgroups. Here the messages are passed from one system to another, not between individuals using e-mail (Chapter 6).

Other services and tools make it easier to use the basic services and are useful in finding resources on the Internet:

❑ Hytelnet helps users to use Telnet to access sites and computer systems on the Internet. The sites are arranged into categories based on the types of services they provide. This includes several hundred libraries, databases, Internet services, and other sources of information (Chapter 7).

❏ Archie is a service that helps search for files available by anonymous FTP (Chapter 8).

Some services have been developed to make access to the Internet easier and to allow for searching databases:

❏ Gopher is a menu-oriented system that gives access to documents, files, and other Internet services. Using Gopher allows you to focus on the information you want to retrieve rather than the services needed to access it. Gopher is very popular and there are thousands of Gopher sites around the world. A tool for searching for information available through Gopher is Veronica (Chapter 9).

❏ WAIS (Wide Area Information System) gives a uniform interface for searching databases. Several hundred databases can be searched in this way. WAIS is available through Telnet or Gopher systems (Chapter 10).

❏ World Wide Web or WWW gives you a uniform way of specifying what service to use, the site or host on the Internet where a resource is located, and the exact location of the resource. The World Wide Web attempts to unify access to services and resources on the Internet. An individual uses a WWW browser such as Lynx, Mosaic, or Netscape Navigator to access the Internet through the World Wide Web (Chapter 11 and Appendix B).

Each site on the Internet has a unique numeric address, called its IP address, and a corresponding name, called the domain name. Information is passed around the Internet in packets. Each packet contains information, the address of the sender, and the address of the destination. A message, commands, and the result of commands are divided into packets. The packets can take different paths through the Internet and it's up to the software at the destination to receive the packets and reassemble them. The emphasis is placed on the packets, not on the connections between systems. Users generally access sites by giving a domain name; the hardware and software convert a domain name to an IP address.

Many of the services operate according to a client/server model. A program called the client is started on one system and it contacts a program called the server at another computer on the Internet. The commands typed or given by a user are sent to the server by the client. The server sends a reply to the client, and the client presents the information to a user.

The Internet developed through projects sponsored by governments in the United States and elsewhere to allow researchers to communicate with each other and share results. The initial work began in the late 1960s. There has been a tremendous growth in the number of networks communicating according to the Internet protocols and the number of users accessing the Internet during the 1980s and 1990s. Now the Internet connects commercial, research, academic, and government networks throughout the world.

Users access the Internet in essentially two ways. One is through a direct (IP) connection either by having network hardware and software in their computers to implement TCP/IP protocols; using a modem and software called SLIP (Serial Line Internet Protocol). The other is through dial-up access, by using a modem to contact a system that has a direct connection. Many of the graphical interfaces to the Internet are available only through a direct connection, but it's possible to access most Internet services through a dial-up connection. You may also have to transfer files between the computer you're using and the computer you call if you don't have a direct connection to the Internet.

There isn't any central controlling agency which governs the activities on the Internet. However, a number of local laws, acceptable use policies, and codes of ethics adopted by most users help to make the Internet productive, useful, and exciting.

To use the Internet effectively you have to learn to use the services and tools described in this and following chapters. You need to remember you're sharing a resource that's spread throughout the world. There will be times when not everything works perfectly, and you'll need to practice using the Internet. In any case, be persistent and be ready to learn new things. You won't break or damage the Internet. It's a dynamic and vigorous place to learn, work, and enjoy yourself!

Exercises

Questions about Your Access to the Internet

1. What type of connection do you have to the Internet (IP, SLIP, or dial-up)? What are the charges for Internet access and who pays for them?

2. Write down the steps you have to follow to access the Internet.

3. What is the domain name and IP address of the system you use to contact the Internet?

4. What is your e-mail address?

5. What is the name, e-mail address, and phone number of someone you can contact when you have problems or questions about using the Internet?

6. What are the rules in your organization or on the network you use to access the Internet regarding proper usage and behavior on the Internet?

Getting Information about Using the Internet

This set of exercises focuses on accessing resources about the Internet listed at the Library of Congress. There are several ways to get to this information:

By Telnet:	Start a Telnet session with **marvel.loc.gov** and give **gopher** as a log in name. (Telnet is discussed in Chapter 3 and demonstrated in Example 1.1)
By Gopher:	Start a Gopher session with **marvel.loc.gov**. (Gopher is discussed in Chapter 8).
On the WWW:	Use the URL http://www.loc.gov and select the link LC MARVEL (WWW is discussed in Chapter 11)

7. Select the first item on the main menu to learn about LC Marvel. Read the **Welcome** document to learn a little about the Marvel Gopher server. Return to the Main Menu.

8. Select the item **Internet Resources** from the Main Menu. Then choose **Internet Guides, Policies, and Information Services/** and look in the section titled **Internet Organizations**. What can you find out about the Electronic Frontier Foundation? Write a short paragraph about the EFF. Go back to the menu **Internet Guides, Policies, and Information Services**.

9. From the menu titled **Internet Guides, Policies, and Information Services**, choose **Internet Documentation/**, then choose **Internet Documentation (RFC's, FYI's, etc.)/**, then **FYI's (For Your Information RFC's)/**, and finally **fyi9.txt**. Once you have it on the screen you'll see its title is "Who's Who in the Internet." Using the information there write a few sentences about one woman and one man listed. Now go back to the menu titled **Internet Resources**.

10. From the menu titled **Internet Resources** choose the item **Sales, Catalogs, and Commercial Services/**. How many items are listed? Explain which of these would be helpful to you.

11. Get a copy of the document **User Guidelines and Net Etiquette**, by Arlene Rinaldi. One way to retrieve is by using Gopher to the site **gopher.mwc.edu** and choosing **The Internet** from the main menu.
    a. What are the guidelines for using Telnet?
    b. What are the guidelines for using FTP?
    c. After looking at the entire document, compare the rules and guidelines there to the ones at your site.

LEARNING TO USE THE INTERNET

CHAPTER 2

Electronic Mail
The Basics about E-Mail

Electronic mail, or *e-mail*, lets you communicate with other people on the Internet. E-mail is one of the basic Internet services, and by far the most popular. You can use it for any type of conversation; it's a way to keep in touch with friends, get information, start relationships, or express your opinion. Much of the time you'll be exchanging messages in plain text form (like the words on this page) but you can also exchange files in special formats such as spreadsheets, files for word processors, images, or programs. You can use e-mail to join interest groups and access many other Internet services. You can send messages to anyone with an Internet address, and likewise you can receive e-mail from anywhere on the Internet. With over 30 million people having some sort of connection to the Internet you've got the opportunity to communicate with people nearby and around the world in a relatively quick and efficient manner.

You use a mail program on your computer to compose, send, and read e-mail. Once you compose (write) a message, it's sent in electronic form, usually passing through several other sites on the Internet. E-mail is held at its destination until the person to whom it's addressed reads it, saves it in a file, or deletes it. The recipient does not have to be logged in or using her computer for the e-mail to be delivered.

Most folks get their first exposure to the Internet by using e-mail, and they continue to use it regularly. It's a very convenient way to communicate with people, it's personal, and it seems everybody likes to get mail. Because e-mail is used so often, it's worth spending some time to learn about how it works and its capabilities. Some of these topics are covered in this chapter, and you'll learn about others later in the book.

Chapter Overview

Several different programs are used for e-mail. The one you choose may depend on a number of factors, not the least of which is what's available on your computer. Regardless of which you use you'll have to understand many of the following topics:

❑ How E-Mail Works

❑ Advantages and Limitations of E-Mail

❑ Understanding Internet E-Mail Addresses

❑ Dissecting a Piece of E-Mail: Headers, Message, Signature

❑ Finding Someone's Internet E-Mail Address

❑ Sending E-Mail from the Internet to Other Networks

❑ E-Mail Etiquette

❑ Working with Nontext Files

We'll also demonstrate using e-mail by working with two e-mail programs: *Mailx* and *Pine*. Mailx is a text-based, line-oriented program available on Unix computer systems. Pine is a full-screen e-mail program. The topics we'll cover include:

❑ Reading E-Mail

❑ Saving, Deleting, and Printing Messages

❑ Composing and Sending E-Mail

❑ Replying to a Message

❑ Printing Messages

❑ Working with an Address Book (Pine only)

❑ Working with Nontext Files (Pine only)

How E-Mail Works

Electronic mail lets you send messages and receive messages in electronic form. The person you communicate with could be any other user on the Internet, someone using the same computer system as you, or someone on a computer system thousands of miles away. The e-mail is transmitted between computer systems, which exchange messages or pass them on to other sites according to certain Internet protocols or rules for exchanging e-mail. You don't need to be concerned with many of the details, that's the computer's job. But you ought to know a little bit about the way e-mail works.

Sending e-mail is similar to sending something by a postal service. If you're sending a letter or a package to someone you follow these steps:

1. Write the letter or make up the package.
2. Put an address on it.
3. Put on the proper postage or pay the charges to send it.
4. Drop it off somewhere so it can be sent on its way and eventually delivered.

You don't care much about which methods are used to deliver it or what route it takes. You prepare what you want to send, address it, and hand it to the postal service or delivery company. You expect them to take care of the details of delivering the letter or package.

COMPOSE A MESSAGE...   ON A COMPUTER   SEND IT...   SO SOMEBODY ELSE CAN SEE IT ON THEIR COMPUTER

With e-mail you follow similar steps:

1. Start an e-mail program.
2. Give the address of where to send the e-mail.
3. Compose a message using that e-mail program.
4. Give a command to send the message.

You've probably noticed that we've left out the part about adding postage and paying charges. Individual users don't pay a per message fee for e-mail in many organizations—schools, companies—that have Internet access.

You use an e-mail program to address, compose, and send the message. E-mail programs are called *mail user agents*, because they act on the user's behalf. The user agent lets you prepare and send messages and also work with the mail you've received. The e-mail program acts as a go-between with you and computer systems, and the computer systems handle the details of delivering and receiving mail. Once again, you don't have anything to do with how mail is delivered.

Messages are sent from one site to another on the Internet in this way. When you compose your message it's all in one piece, but when it's sent out to the Internet, it's divided into several pieces called *packets*. The number of packets depends on the size of the message. Each of the packets contains, among other things:

❑   the e-mail address of the person who sent the mail, the sender

❑   the e-mail address of the person to receive the mail, the recipient

❑   between 1 and 1500 characters of the message

The packets are sent to the destination, passing through several Internet sites. Thousands of networks and millions of computers make up the Internet, and packets are passed from system to system. Each site accepts the packets addressed to it, but passes on the messages destined for another address. The packets can travel or arrive at their destination in any order and they don't all have to take the same path. When you communicate with a remote site, you may think you have direct connection, but that's usually not the case. At the destination the packets are collected and put in order, so the e-mail appears to be in the same form it was sent. If there are errors in the packets or if some are lost, the destination sends a request back to the source, asking for the message to be resent. All of this takes place according to *SMTP, Simple Mail Transfer Protocol*, the protocol the Internet uses to transport message between computer systems. SMTP uses *TCP, Transmission Control Protocol*, which provides a reliable means of communication. To put it all in a nutshell:

> *A message sent by e-mail is divided into packets, and the packets are sent (possibly by different paths and passing through different sites) to the destination where they are reassembled into the original message.*

Once a message is sent, it's put out on the Internet and usually delivered in a short time— minutes or seconds. But a few things could cause problems:

❑   **There are delays.** The computer system at the destination might not be accepting messages because it's down (not working) or too busy doing other things, or there is no path on the Internet to the destination—which usually means that some computer system or network is temporarily unavailable. If a message is delayed the program handling mail will try to send it at another time.

❑   **The mail can't be delivered to the remote site.** The system at the destination could be down for several days, or perhaps the address is wrong. Most programs handling e-mail try to deliver a message for at least three days. If it can't be delivered at the end of that time, you'll probably receive e-mail notifying you of the problem. If you type an address that doesn't exist, you'll be notified about that as well—usually pretty quickly.

❑   **The mail is delivered to the remote site, but can't be delivered to the recipient.** The local part of the address might be wrong; you'll get e-mail back about that. The recipient might have no more space left in his mailbox; either a disk is full or a quota (set by the system administrator) was exceeded. In this case you, the sender, may not be notified. After all, the mail was delivered to the remote site and the address is correct.

❑   **Other problems.** The person to whom you sent the message doesn't check to see if there is any e-mail, doesn't read the e-mail you sent, or accidentally deletes it. You may never know if any of these things happens. The most you can expect from an e-mail system is for it to notify the sender if there is some reason why the recipient could not receive e-mail.

When you read your e-mail, once again you use a program (a mail user agent) that helps you work with the messages you have waiting for you. On many systems you're told if you have e-mail when you log in, access the system you use to contact the Internet, or start your system. The e-mail messages can arrive at any time. They're added to a file that is part of a directory that holds all the e-mail for the system. The packets making up an e-mail message arrive at the system, they're assembled, and then added to the file for each user. That file is often called a *system mailbox*. It holds all the messages on the system addressed to you and only you can read your mail. If for some reason your mailbox gets scrambled, corrupted, or is changed so you can't read your mail, get in touch with the system administrator. On many systems all the users share the space allocated for the directory that holds e-mail. Usually there's enough space to hold a lot of messages, but it's important that you delete old e-mail messages and messages you've read so there's space to hold everybody's e-mail.

Advantages and Limitations of E-Mail

Advantages

E-mail has a number of advantages over some other forms of communication. It's quick, convenient, and nonintrusive.

❑ You can communicate quickly with anyone on the Internet. E-mail usually reaches its destination in a matter of minutes or seconds.

❑ The cost of communicating with someone has nothing to do with distance, and in many cases the cost doesn't depend on the size of the message. If you pay charges for e-mail, the cost is based on the number of messages, not where they're sent. Also, charges are often the same regardless of the size of the message. E-mail is a cost-effective way to communicate with friends, colleagues, or business associates regardless of where they are physically located.

❑ You can send letters, notes, files, data, or reports all using the same techniques. Once you learn how to use your e-mail program, everything is sent the same way.

❑ You don't have to worry about interrupting someone when you send e-mail. The e-mail is sent and delivered by one computer system communicating with the Internet. Although it is put into someone's mailbox, the recipient isn't interrupted by the arrival of e-mail.

❑ You can deal with your e-mail at a convenient time. You don't have to be interrupted when e-mail arrives, and you can read it or work with it when you have the time. Also, you can send it at a convenient time. It doesn't have to be written or sent at a time when you know the recipient will be available.

❑ You don't have to play phone tag or make an appointment to communicate with someone. Once again, the e-mail is sent when it's convenient for you, and it can arrive even when the person it's sent to isn't using her computer.

❑ You don't have be shy about using e-mail to communicate with anyone. E-mail isn't anonymous—each message carries the return address of the person who sent it—but you can write to anyone with an Internet address. Also, all the messages appear the same to the person who gets the e-mail. The messages are generally judged on what's in them, not where they're from.

Limitations

❑ E-mail isn't necessarily private. Since messages are passed from one system to another, and sometimes through several systems or networks, there are many opportunities for someone to intercept or read e-mail. Many types of computer systems have protections built in to stop users from reading other users' e-mail, but it's still possible for a system administrator to read the e-mail on a system or for someone to bypass the security of a computer system. This is discussed in more detail in Chapter 12.

❑ It's difficult to express emotion using e-mail. E-mail is, after all, a collection of words. When you communicate by e-mail, the recipient doesn't have the benefit of seeing your facial expressions or hearing your voice. You have to be careful with humor or sarcasm, since it's easy for someone to take your message the wrong way and interpret your words in a manner different from how you meant them.

❑ You can receive too much e-mail and you have to take the time to deal with it. You'll probably have some limit on the amount of space your e-mail can take up on the computer system you use. If you join an interest group (as described in Chapter 5) it's possible that you'll be flooded with messages that may be of little value or even offensive. You can receive "junk" e-mail in the same way you receive other types of junk mail. Some people see e-mail as an inexpensive way to market products or advertise. In any of these cases you may have to take active steps to delete the e-mail you receive and try to stop it from being sent to you in the first place.

❑ It's possible to forge e-mail. This is not common, but it is possible to forge the address of the sender. You may want to take steps to confirm the source of some e-mail you receive.

❑ Some e-mail systems can send or receive text files only. Many e-mail systems can deal with messages in text or character format only. If you want to send or receive images, programs, or files produced by word processing programs you have to go through some extra steps. However, some e-mail programs use *MIME* (Multipurpose Internet Mail Extensions) and can deal with messages in a variety of forms.

Although there are some drawbacks to using e-mail, it's still an effective and popular way to communicate.

Understanding Internet E-Mail Addresses

An e-mail address on the Internet usually has the form

```
local-address@domain-name
```

The local-address part is often the user's log-in name. That's followed by the character @, called the "at" sign. To its right is the domain name of the computer system that handles the e-mail for the user. Sometimes the domain-name portion is the name of a specific computer such as **oregano.mwc.edu**. It could be more general such as **mwc.edu**, and in this case the systems at the site **mwc.edu** handle delivering mail to the appropriate computer. The portions or fields making up the domain name are separated by periods (the periods are called *dots*).

Here are two examples:

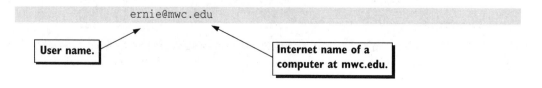

If you were going to tell someone the address you would say **ernie at mwc dot edu**. (Ernie is pronounced as a word, but mwc [em double-u see] and edu [e dee you] are pronounced as individual letters.)

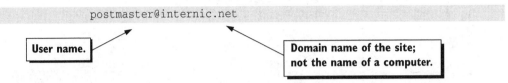

When you know someone's e-mail address you have an idea of their log-in name and the name of the Internet site they use. You should be able to send e-mail to **postmaster** at any Internet site. That's the address to use if you have questions about e-mail to or from a specific host or site, or general questions about a site. However, you may not get a quick response, since the person designated as "postmaster" usually has lots of other duties.

Sometimes you'll see or have to use addresses in the form

```
coco%jojovm.bitnet@brownvm.brown.edu
SMTP%jojo @great.place.com
IN%friener@more.money.us
```

In these cases the local address is handled by a gateway through the domain name to the right of the @. A gateway is a computer system providing e-mail transfers between the Internet and another type of network. For example, several gateways exist between the Internet and BITNET.

Dissecting a Piece of E-Mail: Headers, Message, Signature

One piece of e-mail has three main parts:

1. Headers
2. Message body
3. Signature

The *headers* are pieces of information that tell you and the e-mail system a number of things about a particular piece of e-mail. Each of these headers has a specific name and a specific purpose. You'll see some, but not necessarily all, of the headers each time you read a piece of e-mail. You don't have to fill in all of them. They're all generated and put in the proper form by the e-mail program you use.

Here is a list of the most common headers. Examples will be shown a little later.

Return-Path:	The address to use to reply to the e-mail
Date:	When the e-mail was sent
From:	The e-mail address of the sender
To:	The e-mail address of the recipient
Subject:	The subject of the e-mail

The *message body* or the *body of the message* is the content of the e-mail; what you send and what you receive. When you're sending e-mail to a computer system where your message will be interpreted by a computer program, you'll be given instructions to use specific words or phrases in the message body. One example of instructions like this is when you want to subscribe to or request a service from an interest group (discussed in detail in Chapter 5). Here's an example:

```
TO SUBSCRIBE (UNSUBSCRIBE): Send email message to:
                Majordomo@world.std.com
The body of the message should read: Subscribe (unsubscribe) rocks-and-fossils
```

The *signature* isn't a signed name but a sequence of lines usually giving some information about the person who sent the e-mail. It's optional and it is made up of anything the user wants to include. Usually a signature has the full name of the sender and some information about how to contact the person by e-mail, phone, or fax. Some signatures also contain a favorite quotation or some graphics created by characters typed from the keyboard. Since the signature (usually) is included with every piece of e-mail, you should make sure it's not too long. The longer it is, the more bytes or characters have to be sent, and so the more traffic to be carried on the Internet. It's fun to be creative and come up with a clever signature, but it ought to be limited to five lines.

You don't have to type in the signature each time. E-mail programs will automatically append the contents of a specified file to each outgoing message. The name of the file depends on the program you're using for e-mail. Some common names are **signature**, **.sig**, or **.signature**. Most e-mail programs allow you to specify what file to use as a signature, but you should check with a local expert about the precise name of the signature file.

Figure 2.1 shows an e-mail message dissected into its parts: headers, body, and signature.

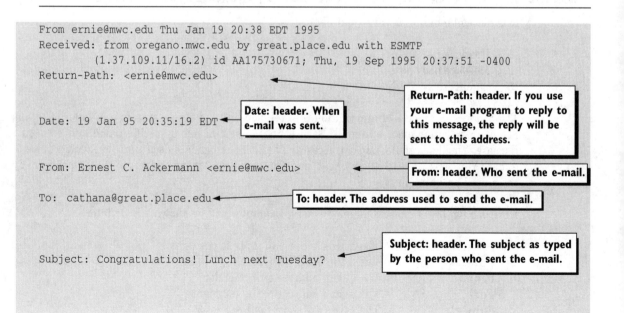

```
From ernie@mwc.edu Thu Jan 19 20:38 EDT 1995
Received: from oregano.mwc.edu by great.place.edu with ESMTP
        (1.37.109.11/16.2) id AA175730671; Thu, 19 Sep 1995 20:37:51 -0400
Return-Path: <ernie@mwc.edu>
```

Return-Path: header. If you use your e-mail program to reply to this message, the reply will be sent to this address.

```
Date: 19 Jan 95 20:35:19 EDT
```

Date: header. When e-mail was sent.

```
From: Ernest C. Ackermann <ernie@mwc.edu>
```

From: header. Who sent the e-mail.

```
To: cathana@great.place.edu
```

To: header. The address used to send the e-mail.

Subject: header. The subject as typed by the person who sent the e-mail.

```
Subject: Congratulations! Lunch next Tuesday?
```

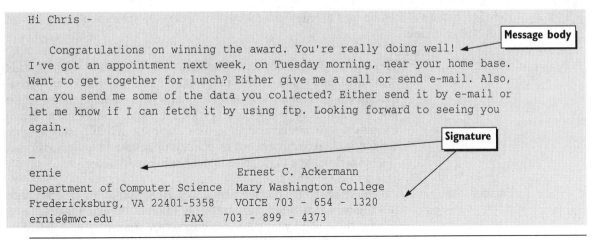

```
Hi Chris -

   Congratulations on winning the award. You're really doing well!
I've got an appointment next week, on Tuesday morning, near your home base.
Want to get together for lunch? Either give me a call or send e-mail. Also,
can you send me some of the data you collected? Either send it by e-mail or
let me know if I can fetch it by using ftp. Looking forward to seeing you
again.


—
ernie                       Ernest C. Ackermann
Department of Computer Science  Mary Washington College
Fredericksburg, VA 22401-5358   VOICE 703 - 654 - 1320
ernie@mwc.edu               FAX   703 - 899 - 4373
```

Message body

Signature

Figure 2.1   E-Mail Message Dissected

The e-mail you receive may include other headers as well as those shown in Figure 2.1. We wanted to show the major ones.

Finding Someone's Internet E-Mail Address

Once you get the bug of communicating by e-mail, you'll probably start to wonder about the e-mail addresses of your friends, and there may be other times you'll want to know someone's e-mail address. Some methods and services exist to help find e-mail addresses, but none of them are guaranteed to produce satisfactory results every time. A few of them will be covered in this section.

The problem with finding someone's e-mail address is that there is no central directory. If you were looking for someone's phone number, you'd either look in a phone book or call an information service. That approach usually works; everyone with a phone number usually receives a bill to pay for phone services, and even though there are lots of phone companies, each has up-to-date and readily available records. The situation on the Internet is much different. Many users don't pay any direct fees and there isn't any central agency that registers each user. Users are added and deleted by individual Internet sites; the decisions are made locally. There are times when it would be advantageous to have a directory of all Internet users and their e-mail addresses, but such a directory just doesn't exist.

Here are a few ways to find someone's e-mail address:

❑   Ask! Call or write to ask for an e-mail address. This is usually the easiest method.

❑   Check for an e-mail address on a resume, business card, or stationery.

❑   Look at the return address in the **From:**, **Return-Path:** or **Reply-To:** e-mail headers.

❑   Send e-mail to **postmaster@domain-name**. The person designated as postmaster will get back to you when she has the time available.

❑   Use an automated service. Several sites run services, on-line information databases, and Gopher systems that contain ways to find e-mail addresses.

Here is a list of a few automated services. It's followed by a detailed example of using the last on the list, NetFind.

WHOIS

This service gives information about registered domains on the Internet. It includes names and e-mail addresses of the administrative and technical contacts at those sites. It won't tell you about individual users, but can give you a starting point. This is useful if you're looking for an e-mail address at a particular domain or site. To access WHOIS, start a Telnet session with **rs.internic.net** or point your gopher to **rs.internic.net**. (Telnet is discussed in Chapter 3 and Gopher in Chapter 9.)

Phone books

Several Gopher sites provide *phone book services* allowing for searches of the names, e-mail addresses, and other information about users. To see some of these point your gopher to **gopher.tm.umn.edu**, and choose the item **Phone Books**. (Gopher is discussed in Chapter 9.)

Usenet-addresses server

The computer system called a *mail-server* at **rtfm.mit.edu** keeps a database of the e-mail addresses of people who've posted messages to Usenet. (Usenet is discussed in Chapter 6.) You can send a request to search the database by sending e-mail to **mail-server@rtfm.mit.edu** with **send usenet-addresses/name** in the body of the message. For **name** substitute one or more words separated by spaces to represent the name of the person whose e-mail address you are seeking. (For example, try the message **send usenet-address/ernest ackermann**.) You will get a reply by e-mail. How long you have to wait, an hour or two or longer, depends on the load on the system at **rtfm.mit.edu**.

NetFind

NetFind is an Internet program developed at the University of Colorado. You provide the name of the person you're looking for and some information about where they might be, and NetFind uses a number of different Internet services and programs to search for the e-mail address. The information could include a person's geographic location, the name of an organization, or portions of a domain name. It's best to be as specific as possible. NetFind is available through Telnet and a variety of other services that start a Telnet session. You can use Hytelnet (discussed in Chapter 7) to find the names and Telnet addresses of a number of NetFind locations or you can use Gopher (discussed in Chapter 9) to one of several Internet sites to access NetFind. An example using Telnet is given below. An example of using Gopher is to point your gopher to **gopher.mwc.edu**, choose **The Internet**, and then choose **Internet-wide e-mail address search (NETFIND)**.

Example 2.1   Using NetFind to Search for E-Mail Addresses

In this example we'll demonstrate using NetFind to search for an e-mail address. We'll use telnet to contact a site that provides NetFind services. A list of Telnet sites is available through Hytelnet (discussed in Chapter 7).

Example 2.1 — Using NetFind to Search for E-Mail Addresses —— 33

We'll search for the e-mail address of the author of this book. His name is Ernest Ackermann and the system he uses for Internet access is at Mary Washington College in Fredericksburg, Virginia. You don't necessarily need all this information to find someone's e-mail address, and we'll use only the two words Ernie and Fredericksburg. If this person were in Chicago it wouldn't be enough to use only Ernie and Chicago, because there are too many systems in Chicago for this to be useful. NetFind would ask us to choose at most three of the hundreds of sites listed there. In that case it would pay to be more specific and use more of the information in the search.

Here are the steps we'll follow:

1. Start a Telnet session with **ds.internic.net**.
2. Use **netfind** as the log-in name.
3. Choose the option to perform a search.
4. Enter the words **Ernie Fredericksburg**.
5. View the results.
6. Leave NetFind.

Let's get started!

Start a Telnet Session with ds.internic.net

☞ **At the prompt, type** `telnet ds.internic.net` **and press** Enter.

We're assuming you're already logged into a system that lets you start a Telnet session, and you have a system or command prompt on the screen. The prompt here is the character **$**; it may be different on the system you use. You type **telnet ds.internic.net** and press Enter as shown in bold in Figure 2.2. Once the Telnet session is established you'll get some messages on your screen, also shown in Figure 2.2.

```
$ telnet ds.internic.net
Trying...
Connected to ds.internic.net.
Escape character is '^]'.
            InterNIC Directory and Database Services


Welcome to InterNIC Directory and Database Services provided by AT&T.
These services are partially supported through a cooperative agreement
with the National Science Foundation.


First time users may login as guest with no password to receive help.


Your comments and suggestions for improvement are welcome, and can be
mailed to admin@ds.internic.net.


login:
```

> If things go wrong and you can't exit, press Ctrl-], and then enter quit to exit this session.

Figure 2.2   Starting a Telnet Session with ds.internic.net

Use netfind as the Log-in Name

☞ **Type the log-in name** netfind **and press** ⌈Enter⌉.

Figure 2.2 shows you what to expect when you start a Telnet session with **ds.internic.net**. Now you have to type the log-in name **netfind** and press Enter. Then you'll get a menu of **Top-level choices** to start the search as shown in Figure 2.3.

```
login:netfind
Last login: Wed Dec  7 14:16:41 from ix-nwk2-16.ix.ne
SunOS Release 4.1.3 (DS) #3: Tue Feb 8 10:52:45 EST 1994
**************************************************************************
              Welcome to the InterNIC Directory and Database Server.
**************************************************************************


I think that your terminal can display 24 lines.  If this is wrong,
please enter the "Options" menu and set the correct number of lines.
Top level choices:
        1. Help
        2. Search
        3. Seed database lookup
        4. Options
        5. Quit (exit server)
  →
```

Figure 2.3   Log-in Screen for NetFind

You need to make a choice here. When you try this example, choose option **1. Help** to get familiar with using NetFind.

Choose the Option to Perform a Search

☞ **Type** 2 **and then press** ⌈Enter⌉.

To perform a search, choose item **2. Search**. Type **2** and press Enter. You'll be prompted to enter a person's name and keys, as shown in Figure 2.4. The term *keys* refers to items that NetFind will use to locate information about the person, such as a city name, a name of a company, university or college, or a portion of the domain name.

Enter the Words Ernie Fredericksburg

☞ **Type** Ernie Fredericksburg **and press** ⌈Enter⌉.

Type **Ernie Fredericksburg**, as shown in bold in Figure 2.4, and press Enter.

```
Top level choices:
    1. Help
    2. Search
```

———————Example 2.1 — Using NetFind to Search for E-Mail Addresses——————— 35

```
        3. Seed database lookup
        4. Options
        5. Quit (exit server)
→2
Enter person and keys (blank to exit) -> Ernie Fredericksburg

Please select at most 3 of the following domains to search:
        0. fylinga.org.com (Flying A Organic Ranch, fredericksburg, virginia)
        1. mwc.edu (mary washington college, fredericksburg, virginia)
Enter selection (e.g., 2 0 1) -> 1
```

> Type 2 and press Enter to start the search. Then type in the person and keys to search.

Figure 2.4   Starting the NetFind Search, Entering Name and Key

After you enter the name and key(s), NetFind lists all Internet domains that match the key(s). In Figure 2.4 two sites are listed in Fredericksburg. If many were listed, you might want to start the search again to avoid choosing from so many. Since we know the person we're looking for is at Mary Washington College, type **1** and press Enter, as shown in Figure 2.4. NetFind then tries to find the e-mail address we're looking for. As shown in Figure 2.5, it will search through the computer systems at **mwc.edu** trying to find one with ernie as a registered user.

View the Results

☞ **Read the screen for results of the search.**

```
Domain search completed. Proceeding to host search.
—
( 1) SMTP_Finger_Search: checking host s850.mwc.edu
( 2) SMTP_Finger_Search: checking host server2.mwc.edu
( 3) SMTP_Finger_Search: checking host pcjohn.mwc.edu
( 4) SMTP_Finger_Search: checking host sta14.mwc.edu
( 5) SMTP_Finger_Search: checking host pcernie.mwc.edu


SYSTEM: s850.mwc.edu
        Login name: ernie                    In real life: ernest ackermann
        Bldg: B21 Trinkle
        Directory: /users/ernie              Shell: /bin/ksh
On since Dec  7 14:42:34 on ttyd2p1

FINGER SUMMARY:
- "ernie" is currently logged in from
  s850.mwc.edu, since Dec  7 14:42:34.
- The most promising email address for "ernie"
  based on the above finger search is
  ernie@s850.mwc.edu.

Continue the search ([n]/y) ? -> n
```

> NetFind uses a program called finger to check systems at mwc.edu. It looks for users with ernie in the log-in name or in the way they're registered on on those systems.

> NetFind lists all users with the name ernie. Only one was found in this search.

> This is NetFind's best guess at the e-mail address. It turns out to be ernie@s850.mwc.edu.

Figure 2.5   Results of NetFind Search

Near the bottom of the screen you'll see NetFind's best guess at the e-mail address. In this case it turns out to be an exact match! In some cases several addresses will be listed and you'll have to decide which to try. NetFind asks if you'd like to continue the search. If you type **y**, other systems at **mwc.edu** will be queried. Since the address has been found, you type **n** and press Enter. Just pressing Enter here also stops the search.

Leave NetFind

☞ **Press** n **and** Enter.

Press Enter, **then press** 5 **and** Enter.

After pressing **n** as shown in both Figure 2.5 and Figure 2.6, you'll get a prompt for another search. To leave NetFind press Enter, and you get the choices shown in Figure 2.6. Type **5** to quit and press Enter. That will let you leave NetFind and write e-mail to the address you just found.

```
Continue the search ([n]/y) ? -> n
Enter person and keys (blank to exit) ->
Top level choices:
        1. Help
        2. Search
        3. Seed database lookup
        4. Options
        5. Quit (exit server)
-> 5
Exiting Netfind server...
Connection closed by foreign host.
$
```

Figure 2.6   Leaving NetFind

─────────────End of Example 2.1─────────────

Sending E-Mail from the Internet to Other Networks

A number of other networks exchange e-mail with the Internet, but aren't part of the Internet. Some of these networks use technology and protocols that aren't compatible with the Internet, and some are private commercial networks. In any event, you may find occasions to exchange e-mail with people on different types of networks. It's not difficult; you need to know the proper form for an address. The e-mail addresses on these other networks may follow different rules or have a form different from Internet e-mail addresses. Once you know the right form for an address and send something off, the e-mail is routed on the Internet to a *gateway* system. A gateway is nothing more than a computer that allows for the exchange of e-mail between incompatible networks.

The most extensive list of ways to send e-mail from one network to another is "Inter-Network Mail Guide" currently maintained by Scott Yanoff (**yanoff@csd.uwm.edu**). It's available by anonymous FTP from **rtfm.mit.edu** in the directory **/pub/usenet/news.answers/mail**. Look for the file **inter-network-guide**. (FTP is explained in Chapter 4.) The guide is also available through the World Wide Web and its URL is **http://alpha.acast.nova.edu/cgi-bin/inmgq.pl**. (The World Wide Web is discussed in Chapter 11.) Table 2.1 lists ways to send e-mail from the Internet to several different networks.

Network	User Name or ID		Address from the Internet
America Online	My Buddy		mybuddy@aol.com
Applelink	buddy		buddy@applelink.apple.com
BITNET	buddy@site		buddy@site.bitnet
		or use	buddy%site.bitnet@cunyvm.cuny.edu
CompuServe	1234,897		1234.897@compuservecom
FidoNet	my buddy at 5:6/7.8		mybuddy@p8.f7.n6.z5fidonet.org
Genie	buddy		buddy@genie.geis.com
MCI Mail	My Buddy (123-5678)		1235678@mcimail.com
Prodigy	buddy		buddy@prodigy.com

Table 2.1   Sending Mail from the Internet to Other Networks

Note that if you're sending e-mail to a person on CompuServe, the comma in the CompuServe address is replaced by a period (.) in the address you use from the Internet. Here are two other examples. Suppose you want to send e-mail to someone who is known as Chris Athana on America Online. Use the address **chrisathana@aol.com**. Suppose a friend has a BITNET address of **cathana@abcVM.abc.edu**. Their address from the Internet would be **cathana@abcVM.abc.edu.bitnet** if your mail system can handle that correctly. You could also use an address such as the following:

cathana%abcVM.abc.edu.bitnet@cunyvm.cuny.edu.

E-Mail Etiquette

Writing to someone through e-mail is communicating with another person. You need to remember that the recipient will read it without the benefit of being with you and seeing your expressions or getting your immediate and considerate reactions. You need to say what you mean in a clear, direct, and thoughtful way. Here is a list of rules you should follow when writing e-mail.

❑ Choose the subject heading carefully. Make it brief, descriptive, and to the point. In many cases it's the first thing that will get a reader's attention or make the reader ignore your message.

❑ Be careful about spelling and punctuation. Try to follow the same rules you'd use if you were writing a letter or a memo. If you want to state something strongly surround it with asterisks (*) or write it all in uppercase, but don't take this too far. Some folks equate items in uppercase letters with shouting.

❑ Make your message as short as possible, but don't make it cryptic or unclear. Lots of users have to deal with disk quotas that limit the amount of e-mail they can receive. Keep the body of the message succinct. Limit a message to one or two screens.

❑ It's a good idea to include parts of an original message when you are writing a reply. It's not a good idea to include the entire original message. Include only the portions pertinent to your reply. Many e-mail programs allow you to annotate or include your remarks within the body of a message you've received. If you can't do that, summarize the original message and write a reply. For an example of this kind of correspondence, look ahead to Figure 2.27.

❑ Check the address when you compose a message or reply to a message you've received. Be sure it's going to the person(s) who ought to receive it. If the original message was sent to a group of people, such as a mailing list or interest group, be sure of the address you use so the reply goes to an individual or the entire group as necessary. It's embarrassing when e-mail is sent to a group but is meant for an individual.

❑ Be careful when using humor and sarcasm. The person reading the mail may misinterpret your remarks and you won't be around to immediately clear up a misunderstanding.

❑ Don't assume the e-mail is private. It's easy to forward e-mail, so the message you send could be shared with others.

❑ Take some time to consider what you will write. You can never be sure where the e-mail you write will end up. Also, if someone writes something that upsets you, don't react immediately. Perhaps you've misinterpreted the original message. You'll find you can usually give a better response if you take some time to think about it.

❑ Include a signature with all your e-mail. This ought to include your full name and some information about how to contact you by telephone or your mail address. Try to keep the signature to four or five lines.

Working with Nontext Files

Text files are sometimes called ASCII files. They contain only plain characters. All mail systems can send and receive text files. In fact, some are designed to do only that. Other types of information such as graphics, programs in the machine language of a computer, spreadsheets, compressed files, or files produced by a word processing program can't be sent unless the e-mail program uses MIME (Multipurpose Internet Mail Extensions) or the files go through a process call *encoding* before they're sent and *decoding* after they're sent. We'll be discussing the e-mail program Pine, which uses MIME, later in the chapter.

The programs *uuencode* and *uudecode* are commonly used to encode (before sending) and decode (after receiving) files. To send a nontext file, first encode it with a command similar to:

```
uuencode   filename filename > filename.out
```

This takes the contents of the file named *filename* and puts it in a form that can be sent by any e-mail program. The file *filename.out* has the original file in encoded form. The first line of the file **filename.out** will look something like:

```
begin 600 filename
M1G)O;2!N971W;W)K;7)K<R!U<;97-T-T'9I<F==;FEA+F5D=2!&<D@3F]V(#$X
```

The line **begin 600 filename** is a giveaway that this is an encoded file, which can be decoded by using uudecode. If a file like this is received as part of an e-mail message, first save it to a file, say **xyz**, and then decode it with the command:

```
uudecode xyz
```

That will create a file whose name is the same as the name in the first line of the encoded file.

To go through all the steps suppose a friend has a file named **eagle.gif** (it's an image of an eagle) and you'd like to have a copy of it. Also, suppose the image is in the public domain, so no copyright laws will be broken if you get a copy from your friend.

First your friend encodes the file using a command such as:

```
uuencode eagle.gif eagle.gif >eagle.cod
```

This puts the encoded information in the file named **eagle.cod**. The first line of that file will be something like:

```
begin 600 eagle.gif
```

Second, the file is sent to you by e-mail. Third, you receive the e-mail and save it in a file named **abc**. Name it anything you like! Finally, give the uudecode command as:

```
uudecode abc
```

You'll now have the file **eagle.gif** and you can view it if you've got a program that can display files like this. You can use these methods with all types of files.

Working with an E-Mail Program

We've talked about some general topics dealing with e-mail. In this section we'll look at two e-mail programs. There are lots of different e-mail programs and even the same programs have some differences depending on the environment in which they are used. Here we'll discuss using **mailx** and **pine**.

Mailx is common on many Unix computer systems. It's older and a bit more primitive than other e-mail programs available. However, many users have Internet access only through a *dial-up* or *shell account*. In these cases a modem calls a computer system, which uses the Unix operating system to get Internet access. The program which interprets your commands is called the shell, which is where the term *shell account* comes from. Mailx is completely line-oriented. This means you can deal with information on a single line only. You'll be able to see a list of e-mail messages and you can choose one to read, save, reply to, delete or print, but you can't move to different portions of a screen to enter information. This program is not the easiest to use, but you can do a lot with it.

Pine is a full-screen e-mail system. It's relatively easy to use to compose, read, and manage your e-mail messages. The commands you can use at any stage are always available on the screen, so you don't have to remember them, and on-line help is always available. Pine also has MIME (Multipurpose Internet Mail Extensions), so it's not limited to sending and receiving only text files. A MIME e-mail system can deal with messages that contain nontext items such as programs, images, spreadsheets, and documents to be used with word processing programs. Pine was developed by the Computing and Communications Group at the University of Washington.

Using Mailx

Mailx is a line-oriented e-mail program. Although you see information on several lines, such as a list of messages in your mailbox, the message you're composing, and the contents of a message you're reading, all the commands and actions take place on a single line. You work with e-mail on a message-by-message basis. In this section we'll go over some of the basic ways of using Mailx to work with electronic mail. The topics we'll cover are listed below.

❑ Starting and Leaving a Mailx Session.

❑ Reading E-Mail with Mailx

❑ Composing and Sending E-Mail with Mailx

❑ Replying to a Message with Mailx

❑ Saving, Deleting and Printing Messages with Mailx

If you're using mailx, you're most likely working on a Unix computer system. You'll either be at a terminal directly connected to the computer system or you'll access it through a modem or some other sort of communication device. To access your e-mail you first have to log in to the computer. You need to have a log-in name assigned to you and you also have to use a password. When you start you'll see a prompt similar to:

```
login:
```

You type in your user name or log-in name, press Enter, and then enter your password in the same way. The password won't show up on the screen. When you've typed in the correct information you'll probably get a message from the computer system giving information about the system or some notices. If you have e-mail waiting for you the system will notify you. It's up to you to act on it. In any case, once you log in successfully and have been notified about e-mail and other things, you'll be able to enter commands. You enter commands to start programs such as mailx on lines that have a command prompt or shell prompt. (A shell is a program that interprets your commands.) The prompt you see will most likely end with a **$** or **%**. We won't go into the differences here since they don't have much to do with e-mail. Figure 2.7 shows a user named mozart logging into a shell account on a Unix system.

```
login: mozart
password
********************************************************************
   Welcome to our computer system!
 >>> Special Announcement
    This system will not be available on Friday from 8:00AM to 1:00 PM.
    It's time for maintenance. Please plan accordingly.
********************************************************************
You have mail.
$
```

Figure 2.7   Logging In to a Unix Shell Account

Example 2.2 — Starting Mailx, Reading a Message, and Ending a Session ———————— 41

Example 2.2   Starting Mailx, Reading a Message, and Ending a Session

You'll want to start Mailx when you've mail to read. Here are the steps to follow:

1. Start a session by typing **mailx**.
2. Read a message.
3. Leave Mailx.

Type **mailx** and press Enter when you have a shell prompt. You'll see a list of messages for you to read or work with. To end or quit Mailx type **q** and press Enter. You can also end a Mailx session by typing **x** and pressing Enter. That ends the Mailx session without any changes being made to the mailbox, as if you didn't use Mailx at all. Figure 2.8 shows some examples.

```
You have mail.
$ mailx
mailx Revision: 70.7    Date: 92/04/16 15:39:44    Type ? for help.
"/usr/mail/mozart": 6 messages 5 new
     1 mozart@s850.mwc.edu  Thu Dec  8 08:06   13/352   a test
>N 2 jacson               Fri Dec  9 08:10   34/934   Art paper
 N 3 ernie@s850.mwc.edu   Fri Dec  9 19:13   22/707   Congratulations! Lunch?
 N 4 pclark@joj.com        Mon Dec  12 09:14  35/1253  phase 2
 N 5 apmills@green.hitech.org Mon Dec  12 09:54  101/5072  Why Invest in Info Tech?
 N 6 zebert@abc.edu        Mon Dec  12 11:15  56/2010  Bass (Guitar)
? q
Held 6 messages in /usr/mail/mozart
$
```

Figure 2.8   Starting and Ending a Mailx Session

Your messages are listed. You see who sent them, when they were sent, and the subject lines. New messages, the ones marked with N, arrived since you last used the command mailx. **/usr/mail/mozart** is the full name of the file holding your e-mail; it's sometimes called the *system mailbox*. When e-mail addressed to mozart is received and processed by the computer system it's stored in the system mailbox. The question mark **?** is a prompt from Mailx waiting for the next command. After typing **q** and pressing Enter, you see the message **Held 6 messages in /usr/ mail/mozart**. It says six messages, in this case all of them, were held in the system mailbox for mozart. The next time mozart uses Mailx those six will still be available.

Start a session by typing mailx

☞ **At the prompt, type** `mailx` **and press** Enter.

You start reading your e-mail by typing **mailx** and pressing Enter. Figure 2.9 is an example of a user named mozart doing that.

```
$ mailx
mailx Revision: 70.7    Date: 92/04/16 15:39:44    Type ? for help.
"/usr/mail/mozart": 6 messages 5 new
    1 mozart@s850.mwc.edu      Thu Dec  8 08:06   13/352    a test
U   2 jacson                   Fri Dec  9 08:10   34/934    Art paper
>N  3 ernie@s850.mwc.edu       Fri Dec  9 19:13   20/702    Congratulations! Lunch?
N   4 pclark@joj.com           Mon Dec 12 09:14   35/1253   phase 2
N   5 apmills@green.hitech.org Mon Dec 12 09:54   101/5072  Why Invest in Info Tech?
N   6 zebert@abc.edu           Mon Dec 12 11:15   56/2010   Bass (Guitar)
?
```

Figure 2.9   Starting to Read E-Mail with Mailx

A message line starting with **N** indicates new mail, e-mail that arrived since Mailx was last used. A message line starting with **U** indicates unread, but not new, e-mail. Mail previously read and kept in the system mailbox has neither an **N** nor a **U**. The character **>** before a message line marks the "current" message. That's the message to act on next. The question mark, **?**, on the last line is the command prompt indicating Mailx is waiting for the next command.

Read a message

☞ **To read a message, press** Enter**. To read any message, type the number of the message and press** Enter**.**

To read the current message press Enter. To read any message, type the number of the message and press Enter. The message you've read stays as the current message until you move on to another. When you choose a message to read it's displayed one screen at a time. A colon (:) will be at the bottom of the screen. You press Enter to see the next screen or **q** to get back to the **?** prompt from Mailx. The message list doesn't appear at this point. To see the list again type **h** and press Enter. Figure 2.10 shows going through those steps. We first press Enter to read the current message, number 4 in this case.

```
From ernie@s850.mwc.edu Thu Dec  8 09:13 EST 1994
Date: Fri, 9 Dec 1994 19:13:25 -0500
From: ernest ackermann <ernie@s850.mwc.edu>
Return-Path: <ernie@s850.mwc.edu>
To: mozart@s850.mwc.edu
Subject: Congratulations! Lunch Next Week?
Status: RO


Congratulations on your award! You're really doing well.


Are you available for lunch sometime next week? I'd like to see you
again and discuss some plans I have.


Let me know either by phone or e-mail
Ernest C. Ackermann
```

Example 2.2 — Starting Mailx, Reading a Message, and Ending a Session 43

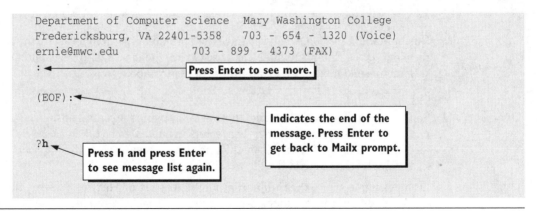

```
Department of Computer Science  Mary Washington College
Fredericksburg, VA 22401-5358    703 - 654 - 1320 (Voice)
ernie@mwc.edu           703 - 899 - 4373 (FAX)
:
```
Press Enter to see more.

```
(EOF):
```
Indicates the end of the message. Press Enter to get back to Mailx prompt.

```
?h
```
Press h and press Enter to see message list again.

Figure 2.10 Reading a Message with Mailx

Leave Mailx

☞ **Type** q **and press** Enter **to quit the Mailx session.**

At this point there are a number of things you can do, some of which we'll explain later. To get a list of all the commands to enter when you see the **?** prompt, type **?** and press Enter. If you end the Mailx session by typing **q** and pressing Enter, then any messages you've read will *not* be returned (unless you take special action) to the system mailbox. Instead they will be put into a file named **mbox** in your home directory, the directory you start with when you log in. To keep a message in the system mailbox type the mailx command *preserve* at the current message. You delete the current message so it's not saved anywhere by typing **d** and pressing Enter. It's up to you to decide what to do with messages. When you're done reading them press **q** to quit. The ones you've read and preserved will stay in the system mailbox and be available for reading the next time you enter the command mailx. The ones you've read and haven't preserved will be stored in the file *mbox* in your home directory.

———————————End of Example 2.2———————————

Reading E-Mail in Any File with Mailx

Typing the command **mailx** and pressing Enter reads mail from the system mailbox. However, any file containing e-mail can be read with Mailx. A good example of such a file is *mbox*. You type the command mailx, as at other times when you have a shell prompt, and you follow it with **-f file_name** where file_name is the name of the file holding the e-mail you want to read. For example,

```
mailx -f mbox
```

You use the same commands and methods to read e-mail from a file as when reading e-mail from the system mailbox.

Composing and Sending E-Mail with Mailx

Sending e-mail can be done in any of several ways:

❑ Type **mailx** followed by the address of the recipient, press Enter, and then compose (write) the message. Here is an example of starting to send a message to **mybuddy@great.place.edu**. We go over composing the message below:

```
$ mailx mybuddy@great.place.edu
```

❏ During a Mailx session, when you have the **?** prompt, type **m** followed by the address of the recipient, press Enter, and then compose (write) the message. Here is another example of starting to send a message to **mybuddy@great.place.edu**:

```
? m mybuddy@great.place.edu
```

❏ Send a prepared message (in a file) to someone by using the command mailx. Putting **-s** after **mailx** causes the next string (the characters in quotes) to be taken as the **Subject:** header for the message. You follow this by the Internet address of the recipient, then the character **<**, and finally the name of the file to send.

Here is an example where the **Subject:** header is **Report of Market Survey**, the address it's sent to is **mybuddy@great.place.com**, and the message is in the file named **report.txt**:

```
$ mailx -s "Report of Market Survey" mybuddy@great.place.com < report.txt
```

Composing the message within a Mailx session doesn't give you much flexibility in terms of typing the message. You work with only the current line and it's cumbersome to make modifications. You can compose the message using an editor on your system and put the message into a file. If you have a Unix shell account you might have to use the editor named *vi* (discussed in Appendix A), but that can be difficult to learn. As an alternative you can compose the message on another system, *upload* it, and then send it as a file. Sending a file is shown above.

Typing Mailx Followed by the Address of the Recipient

You can send e-mail by typing **mailx**, the address to which the e-mail is to be sent, and then pressing Enter. Once you do that you'll be prompted to enter a subject for the message. Type an appropriate subject and press Enter. The cursor will move to the next line and you're ready to start composing or typing the message. This is shown in Figure 2.11 where e-mail is going to be sent to the address **mozart@emperor.court.org** with the subject **Great Opera, Wolfgang!**

```
$ mailx mozart@emperor.court.org
Subject: Great Opera, Wolfgang!
```

Figure 2.11 Starting to Send E-Mail Using Mailx Followed by an Address

Now you type your message one line at a time, pressing Enter at the end of each line. You can use the backspace key on a line to make changes on that line, but you can't use the arrow keys to make changes to previous lines. To break off sending the message type Ctrl-C (hold down the Ctrl key, press the C key, and release them). See Figure 2.12.

```
Wolfgang,
        I saw the Magic Flute last night. It was wonderful!
How have you been feeling? You looked a little tired last night.
Take care of yourself and stay healthy.
Keep in touch.
```

Figure 2.12 Typing in a Message in Mailx

To include a file in the message (such as one holding a signature, as discussed above) type **~r** followed by the name of the file, shown in Figure 2.13. The numbers **4/172** give the number of lines and characters in the included file.

```
~r /users/ernie/.signature
"/users/ernie/.signature" 4/172
```

Figure 2.13 Including a File with E-Mail Using Mailx

To see what the message looks like type **~p** and press Enter. This is useful if you've included files. See Figure 2.14.

```
~p
───
Message contains:
To: mozart@emperor.court.org
Subject: Great Opera, Wolfgang!

Wolfgang,
          I saw the Magic Flute last night. It was wonderful!
How have you been feeling? You looked a little tired last night.
Take care of yourself and stay healthy.
Keep in touch.
Ernest C. Ackermann
Department of Computer Science  Mary Washington College
Fredericksburg, VA 22401-5358    703 - 654 - 1320 (Voice)
ernie@mwc.edu             703 - 899 - 4373 (FAX)
```

Figure 2.14 Displaying a Composed Message Using Mailx

To end the message and send it on its way, type a period (.) on a line by itself and press Enter as shown below. The shell prompt **$** will reappear.

```
.
$
```

During a Mailx Session

If you're using mailx to read or otherwise manage your e-mail you can send a message by typing **m** followed by an e-mail address and pressing Enter. You do this when you have the **?** prompt. Figure 2.15 is an example where a user named mozart has started reading his e-mail and decides to send a message to someone whose Internet address is **carolc@vienna.opera.com**.

```
$ mailx
mailx Revision: 70.7    Date: 92/04/16 15:39:44    Type ? for help.
"/usr/mail/mozart": 6 messages 2 new
    1 mozart@s850.mwc.edu     Thu Dec  8 08:06   13/352    a test
U   2 jacson                  Fri Dec  9 08:10   34/934    Art paper
    3 pclark@joj.com          Mon Dec 12 09:14   35/1253   phase 2
    4 apmills@green.hitech.org Mon Dec 12 09:54  101/5072   Why Invest in Info Tech?
>N  5 zebert@abc.edu          Mon Dec 12 11:15   56/2010   Bass (Guitar)
 N  6 ernie@mwc.edu Tue Dec 13 22:19   12/1234   Great Opera, Wolfgang!

? m carolc@vienna.opera.com
Subject:
```

Figure 2.15 Sending E-Mail while Using Mailx

The prompt for the **Subject:** header comes up after typing the address and pressing Enter. Composing and sending the message from this point is exactly the same as described in the previous section. The only difference is that after you type the period on a line by itself and press Enter, you'll see EOT (for *End of Transmission*) and get the **?** prompt again, as shown here:

```
.
EOT
?
```

Replying to a Message with Mailx

You reply to the current e-mail message by pressing either

❑   **R** (uppercase) to reply to the sender, the one listed in the *Return-Path:* header, or

❑   **r** (lowercase) to reply to the sender and everyone who received the message

E-mail can be sent to several addresses at once; it can be a group mailing. Including more than one e-mail address on a message that sends the mail to a group. For example, the command

```
mailx Ollie@oregano.mwc.edu mozart@emperor.court.org karl@mmedia.com
```

would send a message to three people. Replying to a group is useful when information needs to be shared. You always have a choice; be aware of the differences. It's easy to press **r** to reply, so remember that sends a reply to everyone who received the message.

The next example shows how this works. Suppose an e-mail message was sent by **ernie@mwc.edu** to three others as shown here:

```
$ mailx Ollie@oregano.mwc.edu mozart@emperor.court.org karl@mmedia.com
Subject:  Reminder: Group meeting Wednesday, 11:00 AM
Just a reminder: we have our group meeting on Wednesday at 11:00 AM.
I'm looking forward to hearing your presentations. Let me know if you're
having any difficulties. I'll treat for lunch after the meeting.
—
```

```
lynn
.
$
```

Suppose mozart types **mailx** and presses Enter. He reads a message and decides to reply in two ways: to everyone who received the message, and to the person who sent it. See Figure 2.16.

```
$ mailx
mailx Revision: 70.7    Date: 92/04/16 15:39:44    Type ? for help.
"/usr/mail/mozart": 6 messages 2 new
    1 mozart@s850.mwc.edu Thu Dec  8 08:06    13/352    a test
U   2 jacson               Fri Dec  9 08:10    34/934    Art paper
    3 pclark@joj.com        Mon Dec  12 09:14   35/1253  phase 2
    4 apmills@green.hitech.org Mon Dec  12 09:54 101/5072  Why Invest in Info
Tech?
>N 5 lynn@abc.edu          Thu Dec  15 14:15    17/121    Reminder: Group
Meeting Wednesday, 11:00 AM
?
Message  5:
From lynn@abc.edu Thu Dec  15 14:15 EST 1994
Return-Path: <lynn@abc.edu>
From: Lynn Aeschbach <lynn@abc.edu>
To: karl@mmedia.com mozart@emperor.court.org ollie@oregano.mwc.edu
Subject: Reminder: Group meeting Wednesday, 11:00 AM

Just a reminder: we have our group meeting on Wednesday at 11:00 AM.
I'm looking forward to hearing your presentations. Let me know if you're
having any difficulties. Ill treat for lunch after the meeting.
-
lynn
? r
To: lynn@abc.edu karl@mmedia.com mozart@emperor.court.org
ollie@oregano.mwc.edu
Subject: Re:  Reminder: Group meeting Wednesday, 11:00 AM

Looking forward to seeing all of you.
waM
.
EOT
?
```

Figure 2.16 Reply to Everyone Receiving a Message Using Mailx

Everything mozart needs to type is in boldface in Figure 2.16. After seeing the list of messages, he presses Enter to read the current message. He types **r** and presses Enter, which generates a response to everyone who received the message.

Replying only to the sender is shown in Figure 2.17. When mozart presses **R** a reply is generated to the address given in the *Return-path:* header.

```
? R
To: lynn@abc.edu
Subject: Re:  Reminder: Group meeting Wednesday, 11:00 AM

Thanks for the note, AND your offer to pay for lunch.

waM
.
EOT
?
```

Figure 2.17 Reply Only to Sender Using Mailx

Mozart types **R** and presses Enter. This creates a reply to the address of the person who sent the e-mail. The **To:** and **Subject:** headers are created automatically by Mailx. He then composes the message, typing each line and pressing Enter at the end of each line. Typing a period (**.**) as the first and only character on a line ends the message, **EOT** appears, and then the **?** prompt.

Saving, Deleting, and Printing Messages with Mailx

Saving, deleting, or printing must be done in a Mailx session. At a **?** prompt type the command **s file_name** to save the current message in the file named **file_name**, type **d** to delete the current message, **u** to undelete the current message (in case you change your mind), and **| lp** or **| lpr** to print the current message (this may be different on your system). Then press Enter.

The current message is the one marked with **>**. To make a message the current message, type its number at the **?** prompt.

When a message is saved to a file that already exists, it is appended to (added to the end of) the file. Otherwise a new file is created to hold the message.

When you give the command to delete a message it's removed from your mailbox when you quit the Mailx session. You can change your mind and type **u** to "undelete" the current message.

To print a message you need to use the vertical bar (**|**), known as the *pipe* character. The command for printing a file, which is what the message becomes until it's printed, goes to the right of the **|**. On some systems that command is **lp** and on others **lpr**. Ask a friend, a local expert, or read the system documentation to find out which command to use.

Using Pine

Pine (Program for Internet News and E-mail) is a program that lets users easily work with e-mail. The software was developed and is maintained by the Computing and Communications Group at the University of Washington. It's used in full-screen mode, it contains a relatively easy full-screen editor for composing messages, it has commands to save and organize messages into folders, it has a straight-forward way of keeping an address book of Internet addresses, and it allows for sending and receiving both text and nontext messages. The commands you use at each stage are on the screen, on-line help is available, and it's designed to be used without having a manual around to look up commands. Pine can also be used to read Internet News (discussed in Chapter 6), but here we'll focus on e-mail. The topics covered in this section include:

❑ Pine Main Menu

❑ Starting Pine and Leaving Pine

❑ Getting Help

❑ Reading E-Mail

❑ Saving Messages

❑ Deleting Messages

❑ Composing and Sending E-Mail

❑ Replying to a Message

❑ Forwarding E-Mail

❑ Working with Folders

❑ Working with an Address Book

❑ Printing Messages

❑ Working with Nontext Files

Pine Main Menu

When you use Pine you can always go to a screen called the main menu, and from there access any of Pine's major features. See Figure 2.18.

```
PINE 3.90   MAIN MENU                        Folder: INBOX  6 Messages


        ?     HELP              -  Get help using Pine

        C     COMPOSE MESSAGE   -  Compose and send a message

        I     FOLDER INDEX      -  View messages in current folder

        L     FOLDER LIST       -  Select a folder to view

        A     ADDRESS BOOK      -  Update address book

        S     SETUP             -  Configure or update Pine

        Q     QUIT              -  Exit the Pine program

    Copyright 1989-1994.  PINE is a trademark of the University of Washington.
? Help                      P PrevCmd                    R RelNotes
O OTHER CMDS L [ListFldrs] N NextCmd
```

Figure 2.18 Pine Main Menu

The last two lines on the screen in Figure 2.18 list the commands you can use to access Pine's major features. They're all single keystroke commands. If what you need isn't here, press **O** to see other commands or **?** for help. The commands you need for any portion of Pine are always displayed at the bottom of the screen. Pine has lots of on-line help. Press C to go to the portion of Pine where you can compose (write) and send a message. Pine includes a full-screen editor named *pico* (pine composer). The messages you work with when using Pine are either those in your system mailbox, or ones you've saved in a file. Pine refers to these files as *folders*, collections of e-mail messages. When you start Pine you'll be opening the folder named (by Pine) INBOX. This is your system mailbox where all incoming messages are delivered by the computer. You can, however, save e-mail in folders and use Pine to manage and read these folders. Pressing **A** takes you to the address book. Pine makes it easy to add, delete, and manage e-mail addresses. If you want to make any changes in the way Pine displays messages, prints messages, what file it uses for your signature, or other things, you do that by choosing Setup. Press **Q** to quit.

Example 2.3   Starting Pine, Reading a Message, and Ending a Session

How you start Pine depends on the way it's been set up on your computer system. On some systems you type **pine** and press Enter, on others you choose it from a menu, and on others start it by clicking on an icon. Once started Pine will display a list of the e-mail messages waiting for you. Figure 2.19 shows an example of starting Pine. In this case the program is started by typing **pine** and pressing Enter.

Start Pine

☞ **At the prompt, type** pine **and press** Enter .

```
$ pine

PINE 3.90    FOLDER INDEX                Folder: INBOX  Message 4 of 6

+    1   Dec  4 mozart              (299) a test
   A 2   Dec  4 Jacson             (847) Art paper
+    3   Dec  6 ernest ackermann   (669) Congratulations! Lunch Next Week?
+  N 4   Dec  7 Pete Clark         (5,087) Phase 2
   N 5   Dec  7 Alisa Mills        (825) Why Invest in Infotech?
   N 6   Dec  9 Zebert             (2,003) Bass (Guitar)



            [Folder "INBOX" opened with 6 messages]
? Help         M Main Menu  P PrevMsg     - PrevPage    D Delete     R Reply
O OTHER CMDS V [ViewMsg]   N NextMsg   Spc NextPage     U Undelete   F Forward
```

Figure 2.19 Starting Pine

Starting Pine lists the contents of the system mailbox, named **INBOX**. The current message, usually the oldest of the new messages, is highlighted, as shown in Figure 2.19. The top of the

Example 2.3 — Starting Pine, Reading a Message, and Ending a Session — 51

screen has the version number of the program (the higher the number, the newer the software) and the name of the open folder, which is a file containing e-mail. You'll see later how to save messages in folders. The last two lines at the bottom of the screen show commands you can use here. In this case they're all a single keystroke. To see commands other than the twelve listed here, press **O**. Pressing Enter performs the *default action*, the command surrounded by square brackets (**[ViewMsg]** here), for this screen. In this case you'll view or read the current message.

Reading E-Mail

Start Pine and you see a list of messages in your system mailbox, the folder named INBOX. Regardless of which folder you've opened you'll see a list of messages (if there are any). Each message is numbered and the listing also shows the date it was sent, the name of the sender, the number of characters in the message, and the subject. There's also a marking to the left of the message:

❑   **N** indicates it's a new message (one that hasn't been read)

❑   **+** means it was sent directly to you; the copy you have didn't result from your name being on a Cc: list or on a mailing list

❑   **A** means you've read and sent an answer or reply to the message

☞   **To read the current message (the one highlighted), press** Enter. **To read a different message, type the number of the message and press** Enter.

These three possibilities are shown in Figure 2.19.

Press Enter to view (read) the current message, the one highlighted. There are several ways to make another message the current message. Press the up/down arrow keys, type in the number of a message, press Enter. Press the spacebar or minus sign to go to another page of messages (if there is one), or press **N** or **P** to make the next or previous message the current message. Other commands are listed at the bottom of the screen as shown in Figure 2.19.

Viewing or reading a message shows it one screen at a time; press the spacebar to go to the next screen. The commands listed at the bottom of the screen tell you what to type to go to the next or previous screen, go to another message, get help, and a few other things we'll discuss later. Figure 2.20 is an example of the first screen of a message.

```
PINE 3.90   MESSAGE TEXT              Folder: INBOX   Message 4 of 6 21%

Date: Thu, 8 Dec 1994 09:13:25 -0500
From: Pete Clark <plark@joj.com>
To: mozart@s850.mwc.edu
Subject: Phase 2

   I've been thinking about our work on the first phase of the project and we
ought to take the same approach on the second phase. It seem to me we'll be
spending a lot of time away from our lab, and it will be better if we use an
approach we know will give some results without a lot of setup time.
```

```
     Sorry I haven't been able to get in touch with you sooner. It's been
hectic trying to write up our results, plan a wedding, and run a ranch at the
same time. Sometimes I wish I was the one running the lab. It seems so easy
from this distance!

     Here are some of the preliminary results. You can show them to Wendy, Bill,
and Jane, but please try to keep them from Hayden. I've got nothing against
him, just he's always talking to the wrong people when we're trying to keep
something to ourselves. Speaking of the wrong people - did you hear what
happened when Jane and Hayden went to the lake and met Bill there? OK, first
the results, then the rest of the story.

? Help          M Main Menu   P PrevMsg     - PrevPage     D Delete      R Reply
O OTHER CMDS V ViewAttch    N NextMsg    Spc NextPage    U Undelete    F Forward
```

Figure 2.20 Reading or Viewing a Message

To get back to the list of messages in the open folder press **I**. You can, in fact, give any of the commands you would if you were at the screen with the main menu—**?** for help, **L** to list your folders, **C** to compose a message, and so on.

Leave Pine

☞ **Type** Q **and press** ⌈Enter⌋.

☞ **When asked if you really want to quit, type** Y **and press** ⌈Enter⌋.

To leave Pine type **Q**. You'll see a line letting you know that the open folder (the file holding the e-mail messages listed on the screen) is being closed, and if you deleted or saved any messages, some messages are being deleted. If you only started Pine and read messages, you'd see something like Figure 2.21 near the bottom of the screen when you leave or quit Pine.

```
[Closing folder "INBOX". Keeping all 6 messages]
? Help          M Main Menu   P PrevMsg     - PrevPage     D Delete      R Reply
O OTHER CMDS V [ViewMsg]    N NextMsg    Spc NextPage    U Undelete    F Forward

Pine finished
```

Figure 2.21 Leaving Pine

—————————————————————**End of Example 2.3**—————————————————————

Getting Help

Pine has on-line help available regardless of which feature you're using. Press **?** (question mark) to see the help screen(s) at any time, except when writing or composing a message and saving a message. In that case press Ctrl-G, represented by **^G**, for help. (Ctrl-G means hold down the Ctrl key, press the G key, and release them both.)

There are specific commands to use for on-line help. As with other screens, the commands appear at the bottom of the screen. To save space, only the bottom of the screen is shown in Figure 2.22.

```
M Main Menu   E Exit Help        -    PrevPage    Y prYnt        B Report Bug
                                      Spc NextPage               W WhereIs
```

Figure 2.22 Commands for Viewing Help

These single keystroke commands are supposed to be self-explanatory, but we'll discuss a few of them. The Main Menu was discussed above. Press the spacebar (**Spc**) to go to the next page, and a dash or minus sign (**-**) to go to the previous page. Yes, you press **Y** to print a page. To look for a word or phrase in whatever you're viewing, press **W** (WhereIs), then type the word or phrase and press Enter.

Saving Messages

You save a message to a folder by typing **S**. The name of the folder is usually taken from the e-mail address in the **From:** header. You'll be prompted for the name of the folder before saving. Pressing Enter saves the message in the folder whose name appears in the brackets, as in Figure 2.23. If the folder already exists the message will be appended (added to) the folder; otherwise a new folder is created to hold the message. It's convenient saving messages in folders. You can save messages based on who they're from, or based on the subject matter of the message. Figure 2.23 shows the type of prompt Pine gives if we save message 5, as shown in Figure 2.19.

```
SAVE to folder [apmills] :
^G Help       ^T To Fldrs TAB Complete
^C Cancel     Ret Accept
```

Figure 2.23 Saving a Message to a Folder

The **^** represents the Ctrl key. For example, pressing Ctrl-C cancels the action and takes you back to what you were doing with Pine. Press Enter and Pine saves the message in the folder with the name it chose. You can type in a name and press Enter. You may want to press **^T** to see the names of folders you already have. You can type part of a name and press Tab to have Pine complete the name to match an existing folder. If you had only one folder, say **offers**, whose name starts with the letters **off**, you could type **off** here, press Tab, and the name **offers** would appear.

Once a message is saved it's marked to be deleted from INBOX. If you quit Pine the message will be deleted, but it has been saved. (You can press **U** to "undelete" a message.) It's a good idea to clean out your INBOX regularly. If your amount of e-mail is limited because of a quota, cleaning out your INBOX is mandatory!

Deleting Messages

Deleting messages is easy and necessary to keep the amount of e-mail in your INBOX and other folders under control. Just press **D** and the current message is marked to be deleted when you leave Pine. You can press **U** to undelete a message. You also get a chance to change your mind when you press **Q** to leave Pine. Here's the type of message you'd see if four files were marked to be deleted:

```
Expunge the 4 deleted messages from "INBOX"?
Y [Yes]
N No
```

If you type **Y** for yes or press Enter, the messages will be removed. You decide.

You can delete messages from INBOX or any other folder. You probably face some limit on the amount of space you're allowed for e-mail in INBOX or other folders. Think about deleting messages regularly. Take the plunge—expunge!

Composing and Sending E-Mail

Composing e-mail, at a minimum, involves:

❑   Setting the address of the recipient(s)

❑   Typing the message and/or including a file as part of the message body

❑   Giving the command to send the e-mail

Pine also allows several other optional commands or actions:

❑   Setting the address(es) for others to receive copies of the e-mail

❑   Sending a file as an attachment to the message (useful for sending non-text files)

❑   Including other headers as part of the e-mail

❑   Checking the spelling of the message

❑   Canceling or postponing the e-mail

You compose and send e-mail once you've started a Pine session by pressing **C** (for compose) any time you can enter a single letter command: reading mail, managing your folders, or working with an address book. If you start Pine by typing in pine and pressing Enter, you start to send e-mail to someone by typing Pine followed by the Internet address of the receiver. For example:

```
pine mozart@emperor.court.org
```

Regardless of which method you use you'll work with a screen similar to the one shown in Figure 2.24.

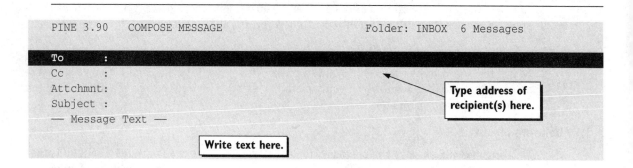

```
PINE 3.90    COMPOSE MESSAGE                    Folder: INBOX   6 Messages

  To     :
  Cc     :
  Attchmnt:
  Subject :
  — Message Text —
```

Type address of recipient(s) here.

Write text here.

```
Ernest C. Ackermann
Department of Computer Science   Mary Washington College
Fredericksburg, VA 22401-5358      VOICE 703 - 654 - 1320
ernie@mwc.edu              FAX    703 - 899 - 4373
```

> This is the signature for this user. By default, it's kept in the file .signature in the log-in directory. To change it, edit the file. On some systems, use the comand pico .signature to create/modify the signature. Check with a local expert to find what you should name your signature file.

```
^G Get Help   ^X Send      ^R Rich Hdr  ^Y PrvPg/Top ^K Cut Line   ^O Postpone
^C Cancel     ^D Del Char  ^J Attach    ^V NxtPg/End ^U UnDel Line^T To AddrBk
```

Figure 2.24 Composing E-Mail—Getting Started

The commands to use with the screen in Figure 2.24 are as shown at the bottom. The ^ before each characters represents pressing the Ctrl key. For example, ^G or Ctrl-G means get help; hold down the Ctrl key, press the G key, and release both to see the on-line help about composing a message. You can use the arrow keys or others to move about the screen. Read the on-line help to see a complete list of commands.

The initial screen has places for you to fill in the headers **To:** address(es) of primary receivers; **Cc:** address(es) where copies of the e-mail will be sent; **Attchmnt:** name(s) of files to attach to the message; **Subject:** what the message is about (make it brief and descriptive). You move from header to header by typing in the appropriate information and pressing Enter, or you can just press Enter or the down arrow key to skip a field. Separate multiple address with commas if you're sending the same e-mail to several people at the **To:** or **Cc:** headers. Use the **Attchmnt:** header to include files (text or nontext) with the message. You'll want to be sure the receiver can handle working with non-text files sent this way. The receiver's e-mail program has to include MIME (Multipurpose Internet Mail Extensions). Type the name of the file to include; Pine attaches it to the message. To attach several files use **^J**, as shown at the bottom of the screen.

The following line:

```
    66 Message Text 66
```

marks the beginning of the message body. As you move past that line you'll see the list of commands changes to:

```
^G Get Help   ^X Send      ^R Read File ^Y Prev Pg   ^K Cut Text   ^O Postpone
^C Cancel     ^J Justify   ^_ Alt Edit  ^V Next Pg   ^U UnCut Text^T To Spell
```

These are the commands to use while writing the body of the message. If you've got a signature file, it will be added automatically here. Check with your local experts or read your local documentation to see the precise name that file ought to have. (On many systems it's named **.signature**.) Type your message; Pine takes care of formatting it. You can use the arrow keys and others to go back to make modifications any time. While you're composing a message you're using an editor named *pico* (pine composer) that's included with the program. It's relatively easy to use and gives good results. You can include the contents of a text file by pressing Ctrl-R, typing in the name of the file, and pressing Enter. That's a way to include some previously prepared materials. Figure 2.25 shows a complete message.

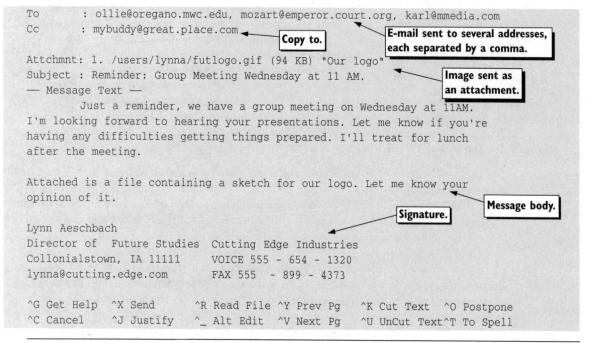

Figure 2.25 Composing E-mail—Complete Message

After composing, you can send the message, cancel it, or postpone it. The commands are at the bottom of the screen. When you give the command to send (**^X**) or cancel (**^C**) the message, you're prompted to confirm the action. When you give the command to postpone (**^O**) the message, Pine writes or puts the message to a folder of postponed messages, tells you it's writing it, and then returns to what you were doing when you gave the command to compose a message. The next time you compose a message, you're prompted to see if you'd like to go back to the postponed message(s).

Replying to a Message

You reply to the current message by pressing **R** for reply. You can reply while browsing the list of messages or while you're reading a message. When you press **R** you'll be asked if you'd like to include the original message in the reply as shown in Figure 2.26.

```
Include original message in Reply?
                Y Yes
^C Cancel       N [No]
```

Figure 2.26 Prompt to Include Original Message

Example 2.3 — Starting Pine, Reading a Message, and Ending a Session 57

Pressing **^C** (Ctrl-C) cancels the reply; you go back to whatever you were doing. In many situations, it's a good idea to include at least a portion of the original message so your reply can be read in context. This is particularly true if you're replying to a message that was sent to a group. Be sure to include only the relevant parts. The default action here, as shown in Figure 2.26, is *not* to include the original message. You must press **Y** to include the original message.

Assuming you don't cancel the reply, you may be asked several questions depending on the headers in the original message. At a minimum, you'll be asked if you want your reply to go to everyone on the list of addresses or only to the person sending the message, if the message was sent to several people. It's your choice; just be sure you don't send something to a group that you'd like to send to an individual. This can be embarrassing, especially if the reply is personal! The other questions you'll have to answer depend on the way Pine is set up, and we won't list all the possibilities here. You can press **^C** anytime to cancel the reply.

After you go through the questions, Pine will get the message ready for the reply. You'll see a screen similar to the one in Figure 2.24, except the **To:** address(es) will be filled in, the **Subject:** will be set to **Re:** followed by the subject of the original message, and if you said to include the original message, the original message will be on the screen. Now you work with composing a reply the same way you compose any message. You may want to delete lines from the original message and annotate (add your own statements) the original. Figure 2.27 shows what a user would see if he started a reply to everyone who received the e-mail in Figure 2.25.

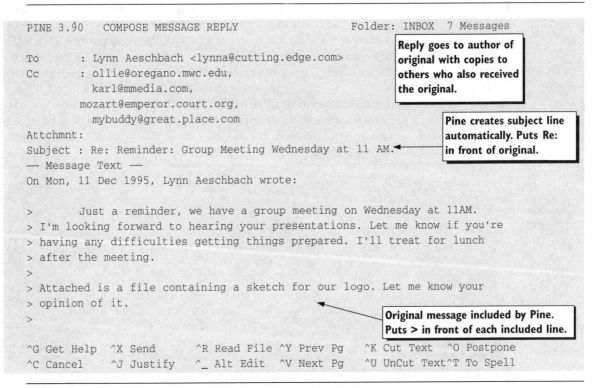

Figure 2.27 Reply to All Recipients—Include Original Message

At this point, you type/compose your reply, deleting lines from the original and including your own as you see fit. When it's complete you can send it off by pressing **^X** (Ctrl-X).

Forwarding E-Mail

Forwarding e-mail means passing the e-mail you've received on to another address. You can do this by pressing **F** for forward or **B** for bounce. They're related notions, but different.

When you press **B** for bounce, the current message is sent to another address, not as if it came from you, but as if it came from the person who sent it to you. Pine will ask you for an address to "bounce" or use to send the current message.

When you press **F** to forward e-mail, you're given the chance to add to the original message. You'll be working with a screen similar to the screen for composing a message, except the **Subject:** will be filled in with the subject of the original message followed by (**fwd**), any attachments to the original file will be listed, and the body of the message will include the message being forwarded.

Working with Folders

Pine stores e-mail into files called *folders*. Listing the messages in a folder shows you what Pine calls an index view of the folder. When you start Pine, you see the list of your e-mail messages in the folder INBOX. That's an index view of INBOX. Pine makes it relatively easy to arrange and work with e-mail in folders. When e-mail is saved, press **S** and give the name of a folder. The mail is put into a folder. This way you can save messages from an individual address or you can save messages any way you'd like. Once messages are in a folder you can work with them in *exactly* the same way you work with messages in your INBOX. You can go through a folder replying to, deleting, printing, forwarding, etc. the messages. Putting e-mail in folders keeps you from having to deal with a hundred or more different messages that aren't organized in any way.

To view your folders, press **L** for List Folders. You can do this at the main menu, or any time when you can give single keystroke commands (without Ctrl). Figure 2.28 is an example of the type of screen you'd see.

```
PINE 3.90    FOLDER LIST                        Folder: INBOX   7 Messages

INBOX                saved-messages       apmills           bwilliam
cathana              einstein             ernie             jacson
karen                listserv             mozart            postponed-msgs
rhoover              socrates             thodapp



? Help         M Main Menu  P PrevFldr    - PrevPage     D Delete     R Rename
O OTHER CMDS V [ViewFldr] N NextFldr  Spc NextPage    A Add
```

Figure 2.28 List Folders

The current folder is highlighted. The commands to use are at the bottom of the display as shown in Figure 2.28. You see that you can **D**elete a folder, **A**dd or create a new folder, or **R**ename a folder. To work with the messages in a folder, make it the current folder (press **P** and **N** to move from one folder to another on the screen) and then press **V** or Enter.

Working with an Address Book

Pine includes an e-mail address book that's an integrated part of the e-mail program. You can add addresses by typing them in or having the program take them directly from a message. You give each address an alias or short form so you can use the alias when you're composing or replying to a message, and you can go to the address book to retrieve an address whenever you want to compose, reply to, forward, or bounce e-mail. Furthermore, several addresses can be grouped together so you can send e-mail to all members of a group or organization. It's a good idea to keep frequently used addresses in the address book. That way you don't have to remember people's addresses or save messages and always reply to a previous message.

Adding Addresses

There are essentially two ways to add an address to the address book. One is to "take an address" from the current message and the other is to add it by typing it into the address book.

To "take an address" press **T** while browsing the list of messages or reading a message. Pine lists the address of the author of the e-mail and may list other addresses, such as the one in the **Reply-To:** header. Choose the one(s) you want to add to the address book. While selecting an address press **?** for on-line help. Once an address is selected press **T** to add the address to the address book. Pine then asks you to enter a nickname, a short name you'll be likely to remember for the address, and then it gives the full name of the person (as it appears in the **From:** header). You can change the full name if you'd like at this point. Pressing Enter shows the e-mail address that will be put in the address book. Once again you can change it here or press Enter to accept it. Pressing **^C** (Ctrl-C) at any of these steps cancels adding the address. If you go on, you'll get a message near the bottom of the screen notifying you the address has been added.

To add an address manually, press **M** to go to the main menu and then press **A** to go to the address book. All the addresses saved will be displayed, as shown in Figure 2.29. Press **A** to add an address. You'll be asked to enter a full name—last name, first name—for the address, then a single word nickname, and finally the e-mail address. You can press **^C** (Ctrl-C) to cancel the addition at any time. Pressing Enter after the last step adds the name to the address book. Addresses are listed in alphabetical order by last name.

```
PINE 3.90   ADDRESS BOOK            Folder: INBOX  Message 9 of 9
```

Nickname	Full Name	Internet Address
eca	Ackermann, Ernest	ernie@mwc.edu
binky	Ito, Burt	bito@coco.report.place.us
fba	Leisy, James	70217.3671@compuserve.com
cici	Mills, Alisa	apmills@green.hitech.org
pinebugs	Place to report Pine bugs	pine@cac.washington.edu
angie	Tonsoni, Angela	atonsoni@great.place.edu
z	Zebert	rhoover@garlic.mwc.edu

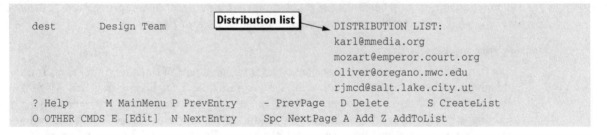

Figure 2.29 Address Book

Working with a Distribution List or Group Address. You can also create a *distribution list*, a list of addresses associated with a single nickname. That lets you send one e-mail message to a group. It's particularly useful if you regularly need to send or share e-mail with several people. To create a distribution list, first go to the address book (press **A** from the main menu) and press **S**. (All the commands you need are at the bottom of the screen.) Now you're prompted for a descriptive long name for the list. Type it and press Enter. Then you're prompted for a short nickname for the list, and then you need to enter the e-mail addresses one at a time, pressing Enter after each one. To stop adding names just press Enter without typing anything. Pine then adds the list to the address book. You can add to a distribution list by first highlighting it and then pressing **Z**. You'll be prompted to add e-mail addresses.

Deleting Addresses. Addresses can be deleted from the address book by first going to the address book (press **A** from the main menu), highlighting an address, and pressing **D** to delete an address. To highlight an address use the up/down arrow keys or follow the commands at the bottom of the screen. You'll be prompted if you want to delete that address. Press **Y** if want to delete it and **N** if you don't. You can use this to delete individual addresses from a list, delete a complete list, or delete a single address.

Using Addresses. You use the nickname you've assigned to an address when you want to use an address for sending, replying to, forwarding, or bouncing e-mail. Suppose, for example, you have an address in the address book with the nickname "binky," as in Figure 2.29. To send e-mail to this address, just type **binky** in the **To:** or **Cc:** field of a message you're composing. Pine will look up this address and fill in the Internet e-mail address associated with the nickname. You don't have to remember all the nicknames you've saved. While composing a message, press **^T** (Ctrl-T) and Pine will take you to the address book. You can then select an address by highlighting it and pressing Enter or **S** to select the address. Pine will put it in the place you left and then lets you continue.

Printing Messages. You press **Y** to print the current message. Why Y? Well, the letter P was already used (see Figures 2.22 and 2.28). The next question to ask is "Where is it printed?" It turns out the designers of Pine realized that you may want to print to different printers at different times. It could be you're working with your e-mail in your room and you'd like to print the messages to a printer attached to your PC, or you want to print to a printer connected to the larger system you're using (Pine assumes it's a Unix system), or you'd like to use a customized personal command for printing. This last one is useful to download messages to a personal computer from the system that receives your e-mail.

To set Pine to print to a specific printer, go to the main menu (press **M**), press **S** for setup, and press **P** for printer. You'll see a screen listing three possibilities. The first sets the print mechanism so Pine tries to print on a printer attached to your PC. This assumes you're using a program to communicate with the system holding your e-mail. This choice works with most communications programs, but not all. You'll have to try it. Press **1**, then press **Y** to try to print the current message. To print on a printer attached to a Unix computer system, press **2**. Once again press **Y** and check to see if it works. Finally, choose option **3** for your own printer command. When you do, the command for printing is displayed. You can use the command there or enter your own. If you want to download your messages from the system holding your e-mail to another computer, you'll have to know the commands for downloading, which are different in various environments. For example, to download using Kermit from a Unix system type the command **kermit -is - here**. Then when you enter **Y** to print, the system holding the e-mail will download the message by Kermit. You need to get your personal computer ready to accept a file transferred by Kermit. Check with your friends or local experts to find out how to do this effectively.

Working with Nontext Files

With Pine you can send and receive nontext files such as images, spreadsheets, files from a word processing program, compressed files, programs, and others. Pine includes these as MIME (Multipurpose Internet Mail Extensions) *attachments* to messages. They are sent along with a message, but aren't part of the message body. You need to be sure that your e-mail system can deal with MIME as well as the e-mail system receiving these messages. You may also need to have special software installed to work with the attachments once you receive them, for example, a program to view certain types of graphics files. Pine handles including and extracting a MIME attachment, but it doesn't provide any way to work with the files after they've arrived.

Sending nontext files. You send a nontext file by typing its name in the **Attchmnt:** header or by pressing **^J** (Ctrl-J) when you compose a message. In the latter case it's put alongside the **Attchmnt:** header along with any comments you want to write about it. You have to enter the exact name of the file including any directory information if it's not in your home directory. Some possible entries are **eagle.gif** or **/users/ernie/documents/report.doc**. Pine takes care of sending the attached file with your message.

Receiving nontext files. If one or more nontext files have been sent along with a message as attachments, they're listed alongside the **Attchmnt:** header when you're reading a message. An example of a message with nontext attachments is shown in Figure 2.30. Exactly what you do to get the attachments depends on which version of Pine you're using.

```
PINE 3.90    MESSAGE TEXT              Folder: INBOX  Message 8 of 9 73%

Date: Sun, 11 Dec 1994 18:36:24 -0500 (EST)
From: ernest ackermann <ernie@mwc.edu>
To: Mozart <mozart@oregano.mwc.edu>
Parts/attachments:
  1 Shown      8 lines  Text
  2           76 KB     File "rept.doc", "word processor output of the report"
  3  OK      129 KB     Image, "image for the report"
```

```
Here is my report with text in word processor format and an image for the
cover.

Ernest C. Ackermann
? Help        M Main Menu  P PrevMsg     - PrevPage     D Delete      R Reply
O OTHER CMDS V ViewAttch   N NextMsg     Spc NextPage   U Undelete    F Forward
```

Figure 2.30 Message with Nontext Attachments

You either view the attachments on the screen or save them in a file. Press **V**. The attachments are listed, and you can choose to work with them one at a time. You can view an attachment—which is what you might want to do if it's an image—only if the right programs are installed and configured on your computer. Check with your friends, local experts, or the documentation to see if that's possible. In any case select an attachment from the list and type **V** (again) to view it or **S** to **save** it. You should always be able to save it to a file and then work with it. You can use it with a program on the system you've saved it on, or you can download it or otherwise transfer it to a system that has the proper software (graphics program, word processor, spreadsheet program, etc.) to deal with it. You can get on-line help by pressing **?** (question mark).

Summary

Electronic mail, or e-mail, allows users on the Internet to communicate with each other electronically. Using an e-mail program, you can compose messages or write and then send them to any other Internet address. Using the same e-mail program you can read the messages you've received, save them to a file, print them, or delete them. You can also reply to a message. The e-mail program sends a reply to the address from which the original was sent, or forwards a message to another address. An e-mail message consists of three main parts: the *headers*, which contain information about the address of the sender, the address of the recipient, when the message was sent, and other items; the *message body*, which holds the text portion of the e-mail; and an optional *signature*, which holds information about the sender such as full name, mailing address, phone number, etc. The signature ought to be limited to four or five lines and can be put into a file so it's automatically included with each message.

Some e-mail programs allow only text (ASCII) files to be sent or received, and other e-mail programs include MIME (Multipurpose Internet Mail Extensions), which make it easy to send and receive nontext files. In the former case you have to use programs such as uuencode and uudecode to send and receive nontext items such as images, word processor documents, spreadsheets, programs, compressed files, etc. If the e-mail program has MIME you can include these nontext items as attachments to the message.

In order to send e-mail you have to give the Internet address of the recipient, compose or write the message, and then give a command to send it on its way. The message is broken up into packets, each containing the address of the sender and the address of the recipient, and the packets are routed through several sites on the Internet to the destination. The computer systems on the Internet handle the transmission and delivery of the e-mail. Once e-mail arrives at a site it's put into a system mailbox for an individual user. The person receiving the mail doesn't have to be using her computer to receive the e-mail.

E-mail is a convenient and efficient means of communication. However, all communication is by the text of the message, so you have to be considerate and be careful to communicate effectively, without misunderstandings. Since most users have a limited amount of space for their e-mail, be sure to get rid of unwanted or unnecessary e-mail and also be sure to send concise, appropriate messages to others. E-mail isn't necessarily private. Because it's transmitted electronically, there are several opportunities for someone to read your messages. It's relatively easy to forward copies of e-mail so a message sent to one person can be easily transmitted to others.

E-mail or Internet addresses usually have the form of **local-name@domain-name**. **Local-name** is often the log-in or user name of the person receiving the e-mail, and **domain-name** is the Internet name of the site or computer system receiving the messages. It's possible to send e-mail to addresses on networks not on the Internet. You need to know the proper form of an address to communicate with users on these networks. Gateways, computer systems that move e-mail from one network to another, exist to transfer mail between these different networks.

Finding someone's e-mail address isn't always easy. There is no central directory keeping a list of the e-mail address for everyone on the Internet. If you want to find someone's address, one of the best things to do is to call or write that person and ask for the e-mail address. There are a number of automated services to use to search for an e-mail address. These include WHOIS and NetFind. A query can be sent to a database of addresses of people who've posted articles to Usenet, and several Gopher servers provide directories for finding addresses.

Two e-mail programs are discussed in the chapter: Mailx and Pine. Mailx is common on Unix computer systems. It is a line-oriented, text-based e-mail program. Pine is a full-screen e-mail program with on-line help at every stage. It includes MIME, an address book for keeping frequently used e-mail addresses, and a number of other useful and convenient features.

Exercises

Questions About Your E-Mail

1. What is your e-mail address? What is the e-mail address of someone at your site to contact if you have questions or problems?

2. What is the name of the e-mail program you use? Does it have MIME (Multipurpose Internet Mail Extensions)? How do you send a nontext file?

3. Is there a quota or limit on your e-mail? What is it? What commands do you use to print messages?

Using E-Mail

4. Send e-mail to yourself reminding you about something you need to do in the next few days.

5. Read your e-mail and reply to at least one message.

6. Send a message, using multiple addresses, to at least three other people.

7. Using your e-mail program save a message to a file and print the same message.

8. If your e-mail program allows you to use a signature file, create a signature for yourself and test it by sending yourself a short message.

Finding E-Mail Addresses

9. Use the NetFind program to search for your own e-mail address. Now use it to search for the e-mail address of a friend.

10. Send e-mail to **mail-server@rtfm.mit.edu** with **send usenet-addresses/name** in the body of the message to try to find the e-mail address of a friend. How long did it take before you received a reply?

Accessing Other Internet Services through E-Mail

11. The document "Accessing the Internet by E-mail, Doctor Bob's Guide to Offline Internet Access" by "Doctor Bob" Rankin lists ways to access various Internet services by e-mail.
   a. Get a copy of the document either by anonymous FTP to **ubvm.cc.buffalo.edu**, **cd NETTRAIN**, and **get INTERNET.BY-EMAIL**, or by sending e-mail to **listserv@ubvm.cc.buffalo.edu**. If you use e-mail, leave the **Subject:** header blank and include only this line in the message body:

   GET INTERNET BY-EMAIL NETTRAIN F=MAIL

   b. After reading the document, list at least five Internet services you can access through e-mail.
   c. Following the instructions to retrieve a copy of the U.S. Declaration of Independence, get a copy through FTP by e-mail of the file **va.decl-of-rights**, at **ftp.eff.org** in the directory **pub/CAF/civics**.
   d. Follow the instructions for retrieving items from WWW and send e-mail to the address given to retrieve the list of recent Usenet articles from the newsgroup **comp.mail.mime**.
   e. Why would someone use e-mail to access the Internet services given in the document, rather than access the services directly?

Telnet
Access to Other
Computers on the Internet

When you are working on a computer connected to the Internet you are part of a system of networks composed of over one million computers. Networks are often designed to allow users on one computer in the network to access information or run programs on another computer on the network. The Internet allows for that possibility through the service named **Telnet**. The service was created so that an Internet user at one site (the local site) could access facilities, software, or data at another site (the remote site). When you use Telnet on your computer to contact another computer system on the Internet it's as if you are directly connected to the remote system. Naturally, you have to have permission to use the remote system. Some sites require a log-in name and a password, while others don't. There are thousands of sites on the Internet that allow almost anyone access to their computers through Telnet. We'll mention some sources on the Internet for finding lists of sites and services you can reach by using Telnet.

You use Telnet to contact a remote system by typing the command telnet followed by the domain name or Internet address of the remote site, or by starting the Telnet program (typing a command, clicking on an icon, highlighting a term in a menu, etc.) and then opening a session to a remote site. For example, to browse the list of items at the U.S. Library of Congress you type **telnet locis.loc.gov** and press Enter, or start the Telnet program and open a session to **locis.loc.gov**. You'll be connected to a computer system that allows access to the catalog of items at the library, and while you can't retrieve any of the items, you can search the holdings to find names of works on a particular subject, or create a bibliography. That site doesn't require a log-in name or password, but some do. For example, you can contact the Electronic Newsstand, which gives access to articles in several periodicals, by using **telnet enews.com** and giving the log-in name **enews**, and you can access the U.S. Space Shuttle Earth Observations Photographic Database by using **telnet sseop.jsc.nasa.gov** and giving the log-in name **photos** and the password **photos**.

You'll see that you always use Telnet in the same way to contact other systems. You give the telnet command from your computer system. Your system sends the appropriate information onto the Internet to access a remote site. Your local Telnet program is called a *client* and the remote Telnet program is called a *server*. The remote site will acknowledge your request to start a session by running a Telnet program, which acts a server responding to your requests. You send commands to get information from the server. You'll also be able to interrupt this client-server communication and send commands directly to your client. You may want to do this to quit the client program and thus close the connection with the server if your session with the server isn't going well.

There are some differences in the way you log into the various computer systems. You'll also find a great deal of variation in the computer systems you contact and the types of services they provide. Many of the computer systems are associated with libraries and allow you to search their on-line catalogs. These library systems have something in common in that you search by author, title, subject, or keyword. Otherwise the methods, techniques, and purposes differ from system to system. Remember you are a guest on another computer system, so follow the rules at the remote site. One good tool for finding your way around the Internet using Telnet is **Hytelnet**. We go over that program in detail in Chapter 7, "Hytelnet: Working on the Internet Using Telnet."

Chapter Overview

Some of the things you can do using Telnet are:

❏ Search the electronic card catalog of any one of hundreds of libraries

❏ Use databases on a large variety of topics such as agricultural information, food and nutrition, history, and extragalactic data

❏ Check weather reports

❏ Access other Internet services such as WAIS, Archie, and Gopher

Now that we've given a general overview of Telnet we'll go through some of the basic information you need to use Telnet, give some examples, and mention some ways of finding what's available. The topics we'll cover include:

❏ Using Telnet to Access a Remote System

❏ Telnet Commands

❏ Examples of Telnet Sessions

❏ What's Available with Telnet

Using Telnet to Access a Remote System

The command **telnet** allows you to log in to a remote computer. In essence this creates a virtual terminal session on the remote system as if you are directly connected to that system. In that way it's possible to share services and resources without having to move large amounts of data or programs from one site to another.

You begin a Telnet session with another site by starting Telnet on your computer and then supplying the name or address of the remote site. On some systems this means typing **telnet** followed by the domain name or the numerical IP address of the remote system. On other systems you start the Telnet program by typing a command, clicking on an icon, highlighting a term in a menu, etc., and then opening a session to a remote site. Once connected you may have to give a log-in name and password. In other cases you access a Telnet service on a remote system by using the command **telnet** with either the domain name or IP address followed by a number called a *port number*. This last form is used at some remote sites so an Internet user doesn't have to give a log-in name. The remote site automatically starts a program or service when your client makes the connection. Table 3.1 shows these three forms and includes an example of each.

General Form	Example
telnet domain-name	**telnet delocn.udel.edu**
telnet IP-address	**telnet 1128.175.24**
telnet domain-name port-number	**telnet wind.atmos.uah.edu 3000**

Table 3.1   Forms of Accessing Telnet Services

In other cases you start Telnet on your system and then use the command or option **open** to make the connection. For example,

```
telnet
open delocn.udel.edu
```

We'll use the **telnet domain-name** form in Table 3.1 above for the rest of this chapter.

A session starts soon after the server responds. Not everything goes smoothly all the time (you probably know that) and you may not be able to connect to a site using Telnet. You may have made a mistake typing the domain name, the site may be out of service (temporarily or permanently), or your Internet connection may be down. In those cases you'll get an informative message such as **Network Unreachable**, **Unable to connect to remote host: Connection Refused**, or **Unknown host**. Just hope the problem is temporary. Check your typing or your sources and give it another try.

To see what happens when you start a Telnet session, let's start a session by typing

```
telnet delocn.udel.edu
```

as shown in Table 3.1. You'll see these three lines. Pay close attention to the last one.

```
Trying.. .
Connected to delocn.udel.edu

Escape character is '^]' .
```

This is very important! ^] represents Ctrl-]. After you type it, you can give commands such as quit, to your client.

After Telnet makes the connection, all the information you see will be coming from the remote system. It's important to know how to take control of the situation and stop a Telnet session in case things go amiss. That is where the *escape character* comes into play. The notation ^] means you type the escape character by pressing both the Control (Ctrl) key and the] key. You do this by holding down the Ctrl key, pressing the] key, and then releasing them both. After you type Ctrl-] you'll see the prompt **telnet>** appear on the screen. That's a prompt from your client, and you can give a command to Telnet running on your system. One command the client understands is **quit**. You use that to terminate the session. You may want to do this in situations such as when

❑ You connect but don't know which log-in name or password to use,

❑ You can't figure out or don't remember the command(s) to give to the remote system to terminate or quit the session,

❑ You connect to a site that is very busy and very slow, or something goes wrong during the session.

THE USER STARTS A TELNET SESSION

AFTER THE CLIENT CONNECTS, ALL THE INFORMATION WILL COME FROM THE REMOTE SYSTEM

IT IS IMPORTANT TO KNOW HOW TO STOP A TELNET SESSION IN CASE THINGS GO AMISS

AFTER YOU TYPE CTRL-] YOU'LL SEE THE PROMPT TELNET> —TYPE Q TO QUIT

Telnet Commands

There are a number of commands you can use in a Telnet session. To display the list, first press **CTRL-]**, then you'll see the prompt **telnet>**, and then press **?**. Press Enter to get back to your Telnet session. The most commonly used command is **quit**, which terminates a session.

Example 3.1 — Starting a Telnet Session; Stopping a Session Using CTRL-] · 69

Example 3.1   Starting a Telnet Session; Stopping a Session Using CTRL-]

This example shows how to make a Telnet connection, and just as importantly, how to terminate the session. Although the instructions for terminating the session are displayed by the remote system, we'll use the escape character Ctrl-] to get the client's attention and give the Telnet command to halt the session. We'll use Telnet to connect to the Health Sciences Information Network, a library system on the Internet that contains the holdings of several health sciences libraries. After we look at a couple of screens, we'll type Ctrl-] and end the session.

The domain name of the site is **shrsys.hslc.org** (the IP address is **192.100.94.3**) and that site requires you to use the username **sal** to access the system. You can find information about the proper user names or log-in names and passwords through Hytelnet (Chapter 7). You can also find information about this from sources mentioned later in this chapter.

Here are the steps we'll follow:

1. Start a Telnet session with **shrsys.hslc.org**.
2. Use **SAL** as the log-in name.
3. Type Ctrl-] to send a command to your client.
4. Type **quit** to end the Telnet session.

Start a Telnet session with shrsys.hslc.org

☞ **At the prompt, type** `telnet shrsys.hslc.org` **and press** Enter.

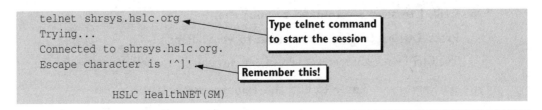

Figure 3.1   Starting a Telnet Session

Use SAL as the log-in name

☞ **When you see** `Username:` **type** `SAL` **and press** Enter.

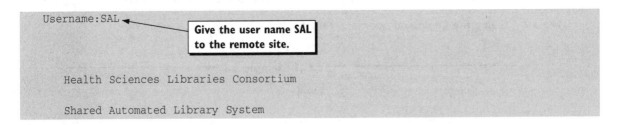

```
On-line Catalog — 2.3Copyright 1993, Data Research Associates, Inc.,
All rights reserved.

Instructions on how to search the catalog.
You may search the catalog by any of the following:

AUTHOR    To find authors, editors, conferences, corporate authors,
illustrators, etc.
          EXAMPLES: A=Freud Sigmund (type last name first)
                    A=American Medical Association

TITLE  To find a work by title.
          EXAMPLES: T=American Journal of Medicine
                    T=Principles of Surgery

SUBJECT   To find material using a subject heading. (Both LC and MeSH)
          EXAMPLES: S=Child Psychology
                    S=Osler William (type last name first)

KEYWORD   To search by a keyword (a word in the title, name,
etc.), type the command KEYWORD at the (>>) prompt.

Type your search below (or press N for more information) then press
(ENTER).
>>
```

Instructions on how to search the catalog.

This is where you would type a command to search the catalog. Instead, type Ctrl-] to give a command to your client. The Ctrl-] will not show up on the screen.

Type CTRL-] to send a command to your client

☞ Press **Ctrl**+] to give a command to your client.

The Ctrl-] won't show on the screen, but you should see **telnet>** appear.

Type quit and press Enter to end the Telnet session.

☞ **When you see** telnet> **type** quit **and press** Enter.

```
telnet> quit

Connection closed.
```

At the telnet> command, type quit to end the session.

Figure 3.2   Giving the Command quit to a Telnet Client

─────────── End of Example 3.1 ───────────

Example 3.2 — Searching for Information at PENpages — 71

In Example 3.1 you saw how to start and stop a Telnet session. We were connected to a library system and could have searched its catalog. In Example 3.2 we'll use Telnet to connect to PENpages, a text information service consisting of a wide variety of items submitted by Cooperative Extension experts and researchers throughout the United States. Example 3.2 demonstrates some methods of searching for information and shows some of the diversity of information and systems you can work with using Telnet.

Example 3.2   Searching for Information at PENpages

PENpages is an information service supported by the College of Agricultural Sciences at the Pennsylvania State University. This service has thousands of documents available on a wide variety of topics. These documents are contributed by experts from around the U.S. Much of the information deals with agricultural, consumer, and health issues. Here we'll use PENpages to demonstrate accessing and searching a database through the Internet.

We'll connect to PENpages by Telnet, using **telnet psupen.psu.edu**. PENpages asks you for a username. The username you use depends on whether you're in the United States. If you are in the U.S., use the two-letter abbreviation for your state; otherwise use **world**.

We're interested in learning about eating vegetables as it relates to health and nutrition. We'll search the database for items using the three keywords: *health*, *nutrition*, and *vegetables*. When this example was constructed, eight items were found. You may find more when you try it.

Here are the steps we'll follow:

1. Start a Telnet session with **psupen.psu.edu**.
2. Use **VA** as the username (we're logging in from Virginia; use the appropriate username for your location).
3. Press Enter to continue and select PENpages from the menu.
4. Select **Keyword Search** from the PENpages Menu.
5. Use **health** as the first keyword.
6. Narrow the search by using **nutrition** as an additional keyword.
7. Narrow the search even further by using **vegetable** as yet another keyword.
8. List the titles of the items found.
9. Exit PENpages.

There are other things you can do. You can display the documents you've found or search for others.

Start a Telnet Session with psupen.psu.edu

☞ **At the prompt type** `telnet psupen.psu.edu` **and press** Enter.

You'll be connected to a computer system at Penn State. That computer system prompts you for a log-in name or user name.

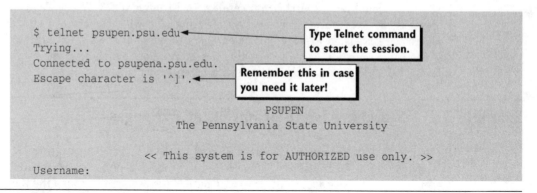

Figure 3.3   Connecting to PSUPEN by Telnet

Use VA as the username

☞ **Type** VA **and press** Enter.

PENpages expects you to use the two-letter abbreviation for your state if you're in the U.S.; otherwise use **world** as a username. Figure 3.4 shows the brief welcome screen after using the username VA; at the bottom you see the instruction to press Enter to continue.

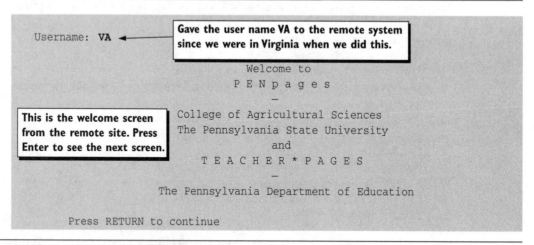

Figure 3.4   Welcome Screen at PENpages

Press Enter to Continue and Select PENpages from the Menu

☞ **Press** Enter **to go on to the next screen.**

☞ **Type** 1 **and Press** Enter.

Pressing Enter takes you to the screen shown in Figure 3.5. You select PENpages from that menu by typing its number and pressing Enter.

Example 3.2 — Searching for Information at PENpages — 73

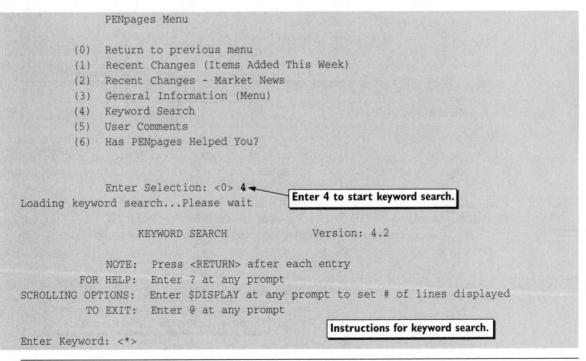

```
        PSUPEN System Menu              Main menu from PSUPEN.

    (0)  Logoff System
    (1)  PENpages              (19 documents added on  1-FEB-1995 )
    (2)  TEACHER*PAGES         ( 7 documents added on  1-FEB-1995 )



        Enter Selection:  1       Enter I to go to PENpages.
```

Figure 3.5   Main Menu from PSUPEN

Select Keyword Search from the PENpages Menu

☞ **Type** 4 **and press** ⎡Enter⎤.

Figure 3.6 shows the PENpages menu. We'll perform a keyword search of the items available, so type the number for keyword search and press Enter. Shortly, you'll see instructions about keyword searching and a prompt asking you to Enter a keyword.

```
        PENpages Menu

    (0)  Return to previous menu
    (1)  Recent Changes (Items Added This Week)
    (2)  Recent Changes - Market News
    (3)  General Information (Menu)
    (4)  Keyword Search
    (5)  User Comments
    (6)  Has PENpages Helped You?


        Enter Selection: <0> 4       Enter 4 to start keyword search.
Loading keyword search...Please wait

        KEYWORD SEARCH              Version: 4.2

        NOTE:  Press <RETURN> after each entry
    FOR HELP:  Enter ? at any prompt
SCROLLING OPTIONS:  Enter $DISPLAY at any prompt to set # of lines displayed
    TO EXIT:  Enter @ at any prompt
                                    Instructions for keyword search.

Enter Keyword: <*>
```

Figure 3.6   PENpages Menu and Start of Keyword Search

Use health as the First Keyword

☞ **At the** Enter Keyword : <*> **prompt type** health **and press** Enter.

☞ **At the** Enter keyword # or choice: <3> **prompt press** Enter.

PENpages prompts you to enter a keyword. We want items with the keyword *health*, so we type in **health** and press Enter. Any word or beginning part of a word could be entered here. After that, PENpages displays a list of keywords with an arrow pointing to the keyword you entered, or the word in its list closest to the keyword. Figure 3.7 shows the list for the keyword *health*.

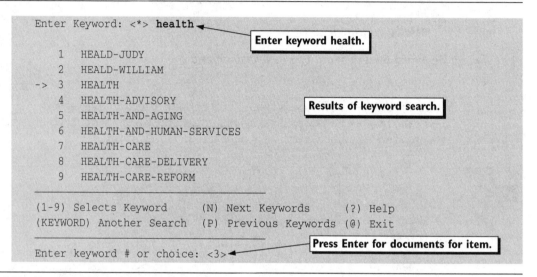

```
Enter Keyword: <*> health
                                        Enter keyword health.

      1   HEALD-JUDY
      2   HEALD-WILLIAM
 ->   3   HEALTH
      4   HEALTH-ADVISORY
      5   HEALTH-AND-AGING               Results of keyword search.
      6   HEALTH-AND-HUMAN-SERVICES
      7   HEALTH-CARE
      8   HEALTH-CARE-DELIVERY
      9   HEALTH-CARE-REFORM


 (1-9) Selects Keyword      (N) Next Keywords      (?) Help
 (KEYWORD) Another Search   (P) Previous Keywords  (@) Exit

                                        Press Enter for documents for item.
 Enter keyword # or choice: <3>
```

Figure 3.7   Result of Keyword Search

After displaying the keyword list, PENpages displays the menu shown at the bottom of Figure 3.7. You can use the keyword number from the list, choose another keyword, or exit. We're going to continue, so we press Enter for information about the documents with the keyword *health*.

PENpages displays the number of documents found and allows you to list titles, modify the search, show help information, or exit. For the keyword *health* PENpages found 723 documents! Choose option **R** to restrict the search. We'll enter other keywords to make the search more specific.

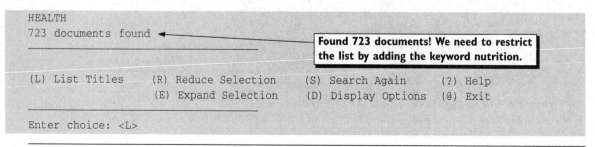

```
HEALTH
723 documents found
                                   Found 723 documents! We need to restrict
                                   the list by adding the keyword nutrition.

(L) List Titles      (R) Reduce Selection   (S) Search Again    (?) Help
                     (E) Expand Selection   (D) Display Options (@) Exit


Enter choice: <L>
```

Figure 3.8   Keyword Search: Number of Documents Found and Options

Example 3.2 — Searching for Information at PENpages—————————————— 75

Narrow the Search by Using nutrition as an Additional Keyword

☞ **At the** `Enter choice: <L>` **prompt type** R **and press** `Enter`.

☞ **At the** `Enter additional keyword to reduce selection: <*>` **prompt type** nutrition **and press** `Enter`.

☞ **At the** `Enter keyword # or choice: <3>` **prompt press** `Enter`.

You Enter **R** to reduce the selection, or narrow the search. The PENpages prompts for a word to use as an additional keyword. We typed nutrition and pressed Enter to select documents which contain nutrition as a keyword. These are selected from the group we've already found which contain health as a keyword. So we'll end up with fewer documents.

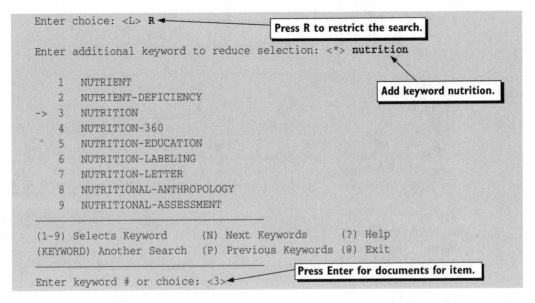

```
Enter choice: <L> R ◄          ┌──────────────────────────────┐
                               │ Press R to restrict the search. │
                               └──────────────────────────────┘
Enter additional keyword to reduce selection: <*> nutrition

     1   NUTRIENT
     2   NUTRIENT-DEFICIENCY       ┌──────────────────────────┐
 ->  3   NUTRITION                 │  Add keyword nutrition.  │
     4   NUTRITION-360             └──────────────────────────┘
     5   NUTRITION-EDUCATION
     6   NUTRITION-LABELING
     7   NUTRITION-LETTER
     8   NUTRITIONAL-ANTHROPOLOGY
     9   NUTRITIONAL-ASSESSMENT
_____

(1-9) Selects Keyword    (N) Next Keywords      (?) Help
(KEYWORD) Another Search (P) Previous Keywords  (@) Exit
_____
                          ┌────────────────────────────────┐
Enter keyword # or choice: <3> ◄ │ Press Enter for documents for item. │
                          └────────────────────────────────┘
```

Just as before, we'll get a list of keywords containing either the keyword we entered or words close to it. Nutrition is in the list so press Enter to see how many were found. It turns out to be 230, which is still a lot of documents to look through! We'll restrict the search further using the keyword vegetables.

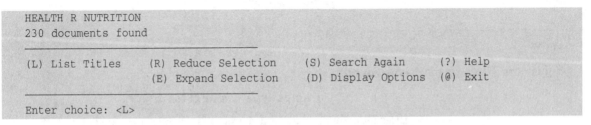

```
HEALTH R NUTRITION
230 documents found
_____

(L) List Titles    (R) Reduce Selection   (S) Search Again    (?) Help
                   (E) Expand Selection    (D) Display Options (@) Exit
_____

Enter choice: <L>
```

Narrow the Search Even Further by Using vegetables as Another Keyword

☞ **At the** `Enter choice: <L>` **prompt type** R **and press** `Enter`.

☞ **At the** `Enter additional keyword to reduce selection:<*>` **prompt type** `vegetables` **and press** `Enter`.

☞ **At the** `Enter keyword # or choice: <3>` **prompt press** `Enter`.

We use one more keyword to narrow the search and get to the documents that would be most appropriate.

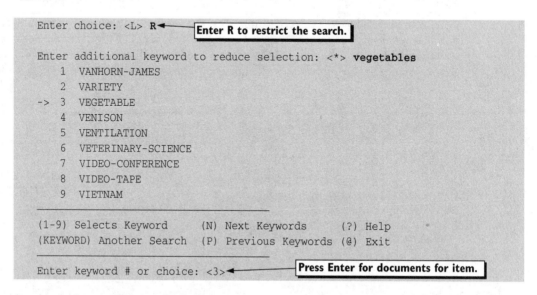

```
Enter choice: <L> R ◄─── [Enter R to restrict the search.]

Enter additional keyword to reduce selection: <*> vegetables
     1   VANHORN-JAMES
     2   VARIETY
 ->  3   VEGETABLE
     4   VENISON
     5   VENTILATION
     6   VETERINARY-SCIENCE
     7   VIDEO-CONFERENCE
     8   VIDEO-TAPE
     9   VIETNAM
  _____

  (1-9) Selects Keyword     (N) Next Keywords      (?) Help
  (KEYWORD) Another Search  (P) Previous Keywords  (@) Exit
  _____

  Enter keyword # or choice: <3> ◄─── [Press Enter for documents for item.]
```

Just as before, we'll get a list of keywords. This one doesn't contain the word we entered, vegetables, but vegetable is close enough. We can press Enter for the documents containing the keyword vegetable. Don't forget these are chosen from the other documents we've selected. So we ought to get documents that contain the keywords *health*, *nutrition*, and *vegetables*. As it turns out we have eight documents. That's a good number to deal with, and we'll list the titles in the next step.

```
HEALTH R NUTRITION R VEGETABLE
8 documents found
_____

(L) List Titles     (R) Reduce Selection    (S) Search Again    (?) Help
                    (E) Expand Selection     (D) Display Options (@) Exit
_____

Enter choice: <L>
```

List the Titles of the Items Found

☞ **At the** `Enter choice: <L>` **prompt type** L **and press** `Enter`.

Entering L lists the titles found by the keyword search. Figure 3.9 shows the list and the other information displayed.

Example 3.2 — Searching for Information at PENpages—————————— 77

```
Enter choice: <L> L ◄———————[Enter L to list titles.]
List of Titles
_____

HEALTH R NUTRITION R VEGETABLE

From: 17-NOV-1994     To:  7-JUN-1993          TOTAL DOCUMENTS: 8

   #                TITLE                          DATE
   1    ADA issues position on functional foods    17-NOV-1994
   2    Elec Food Rap:Progress Slow on Healthy People 2000  9-NOV-1994
   3    ICN2:Description of Nutr Status of Population(23p) 24-SEP-1994
   4    ICN:Promote Healthy Diets, Lifestyles Summary  30-AUG-1994
   5    Ideas for Better Living (August 1994)       2-AUG-1994
   6    Americans Want Good Nutrition and Good Taste  25-FEB-1994
   7    ICN:Scope/dimensions of nutr problems (27p.Ch.1)  1-SEP-1993
   8    Ideas for Better Living (June 1, 1993)      7-JUN-1993

_____

(N) Next Titles     (R) Reduce Selection    (S) Search Again    (?) Help
(P) Previous Titles (E) Expand Selection    (D) Display Options  (@) Exit
_____

Enter title # or choice: <N>
```

Figure 3.9   List of Titles Found through Keyword Search

There are a number of options at this point. You can view a document by typing its number and pressing Enter, you can start searching again, get some help, or exit the keyword search.

Exit PENpages

There are a few steps to go through to exit PENpages. That's because you go from the keyword search section back through the menus in Figure 3.5 and Figure 3.6.

☞ **At the** `Enter title # or choice: <N>` **prompt type** @ **and press** [Enter].

☞ **At the** `Enter Selection:<0>` **prompt type** 0 **and press** [Enter].

☞ **At the** `Enter Selection:` **prompt type** 0 **and press** [Enter].

```
Enter title # or choice: <N> @

          PENpages Menu
     (0)  Return to previous menu
     (1)  Recent Changes (Items Added This Week)
     (2)  Recent Changes - Market News
     (3)  General Information (Menu)
     (4)  Keyword Search
     (5)  User Comments
     (6)  Has PENpages Helped You?
```

```
        Enter Selection: <0> 0

        PSUPEN System Menu

    (0)  Logoff System
    (1)  PENpages              (19 documents added on   1-FEB-1995 )
    (2)  TEACHER*PAGES         ( 7 documents added on   1-FEB-1995 )


        Enter Selection:   0
```

─────────────────────End of Example 3.2─────────────────────

For Example 3.3 we'll use Telnet to reach a site that requires a port number. The port number is usually four or five digits and follows the domain name. When you start a Telnet session using a port number, you don't have to supply a username or password. The remote system starts the program you'll access as soon as the connection is made.

Example 3.3 uses Telnet to connect to a weather service. You can get the weather predictions for several cities in each state in the U.S., the Canadian provinces, Mexico, and several U.S. territories. The Internet weather service sites in the U.S. use a program called Weather Underground, originally written by Jeff Masters of the University of Michigan, to access weather information. There is also a weather service site available in Australia, although it doesn't use Weather Underground. The site we'll contact is in Alabama. You might want to connect with one that's geographically close to you to cut down on the amount of Internet traffic and to decrease the amount of time to wait for a response. Table 3.2 gives a list of sites.

Domain Name	Port Number	Site
madlab.sprl.umich.edu	3000	University of Michigan, Ann Arbor, MI
vicbeta.vic.bom.gov.au	55555	Bureau of Meteorology, Melbourne, Australia
wind.atmos.uah.edu	3000	University of Alabama, Huntsville, AL

Table 3.2   Weather Service Sites Available by Telnet

Example 3.3   Weather Forecasts; Telnet with a Port Number

We'll use the Telnet command with a port number to contact Weather Underground at the University of Alabama in Huntsville (see Figure 3.10). We can expect the service to start when Telnet makes the connection. No username, password, or command is needed. You can find several different types of weather information at a site like this one. For fun, let's suppose we're going to be going to Orlando, Florida, tomorrow and we'd like to check out the weather forecast.

Example 3.3 — Weather Forecasts; Telnet with a Port Number — 79

Here are the steps to follow:

1. Start a Telnet session with the Southeast Weather Underground at **wind.atmos.uah.edu 3000**
2. Go to the main menu and choose **Forecast and Climate Data for a U.S. City**
3. Choose the item from the **City Forecast Menu** that will display the three-letter city codes for a state
4. Enter **FL**, the abbreviation for Florida, see the list of codes for its cities, and note the code for Orlando.
5. Enter the three-letter code for Orlando to see the forecast
6. End the Telnet session.

Start a session with the Southeast Weather Underground at wind.atmos.uah.edu 3000

☞ **Type** `telnet wind.atmos.uah.edu 3000` **and press** Enter.

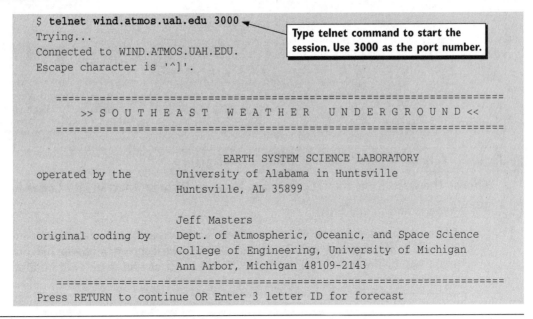

```
$ telnet wind.atmos.uah.edu 3000
Trying...
Connected to WIND.ATMOS.UAH.EDU.
Escape character is '^]'.


      ========================================================
            >> S O U T H E A S T   W E A T H E R   U N D E R G R O U N D <<
      ========================================================


                           EARTH SYSTEM SCIENCE LABORATORY
operated by the       University of Alabama in Huntsville
                      Huntsville, AL 35899


                      Jeff Masters
original coding by    Dept. of Atmospheric, Oceanic, and Space Science
                      College of Engineering, University of Michigan
                      Ann Arbor, Michigan 48109-2143

      ========================================================
Press RETURN to continue OR Enter 3 letter ID for forecast
```

Type telnet command to start the session. Use 3000 as the port number.

Figure 3.10 Starting a Telnet Session to Southeast Weather Underground

Go to the main menu and choose "Forecast and Climate Data for a U.S. City"

☞ **Press** Enter.

☞ **Type** 1 **and press** Enter.

At the prompt shown at the bottom of Figure 3.10 you press Enter for the next menu, or if you know the three-letter abbreviation for a city you can Enter it and see the forecast. We don't know or aren't sure of the proper code for Orlando, Florida, so we press Enter to get to the next menu (shown in Figure 3.11), and then Enter a **1** to get to the forecast menu.

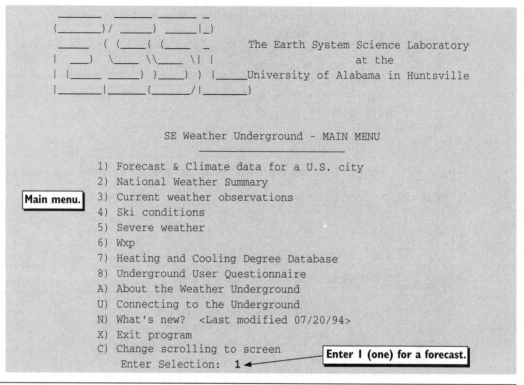

```
    _____   _____   _____  _
   (_____)/ _____) _____|_)
    _____  ( (____( (_____   _         The Earth System Science Laboratory
   | ____)  \_____ \\_____ \| |                      at the
   | |_____ _____) )____) ) |____University of Alabama in Huntsville
   |_____|_____(_____/ |_____)

                    SE Weather Underground - MAIN MENU
                    _____

              1) Forecast & Climate data for a U.S. city
              2) National Weather Summary
              3) Current weather observations
              4) Ski conditions
              5) Severe weather
              6) Wxp
              7) Heating and Cooling Degree Database
              8) Underground User Questionnaire
              A) About the Weather Underground
              U) Connecting to the Underground
              N) What's new?   <Last modified 07/20/94>
              X) Exit program
              C) Change scrolling to screen
                 Enter Selection:   1
```

Main menu.

Enter I (one) for a forecast.

Figure 3.11 Main Menu at Southeast Weather Underground

Choose the Item from the City Forecast Menu to Display 3-letter City Codes for a State

☞ **Type** 5 **and press** Enter.

The menu shown in Figure 3.12 contains several choices for forecast information for a city. Since we don't know the proper code for Orlando, Florida, we'll choose the option that gives the three-letter codes for cities in a selected state. We'll have to say the state we want also.

```
                           CITY FORECAST MENU
                           _____

              1) Print forecast for selected city
              2) Print climate data for selected city
              3) Long range forecasts
              4) Canadian forecasts
              5) Display 3-letter city codes for a selected state
              6) Display all 2-letter state codes
              M) Return to main menu
              X) Exit program
              ?) Help
              5
```

We want the forecast for Orlando, Florida, but don't know the 3-letter code for that city, so we Enter 5 to get codes of cities in Florida.

Figure 3.12 City Forecast Menu

Example 3.3 — Weather Forecasts; Telnet with a Port Number 81

Enter FL, the Abbreviation for Florida and Note the Code for Orlando in the Results

☞ **At the** `Enter 2-letter state code:` **prompt type** FL **and press** Enter.

Type in the two-letter abbreviation for a state, press Enter, and you'll see the list of codes for cities in the state. There are several for Florida, and the code for Orlando is **MCO**. Figure 3.13 shows the list of codes and also shows the **City Forecast Menu** appearing right after the list of cities.

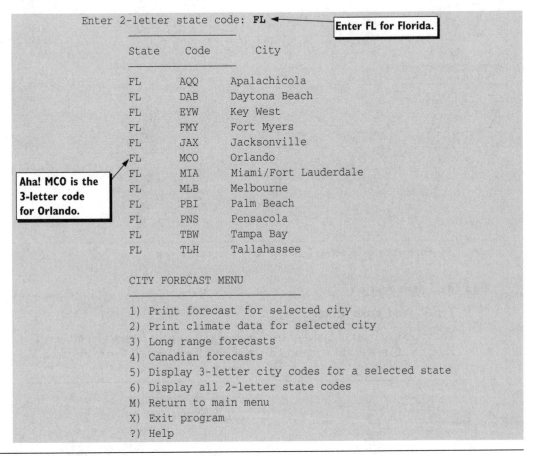

Figure 3.13 List of Three-letter Codes for Cities in Florida

Enter the Three-letter Code for Orlando to See the Forecast

First we need to choose **Print forecast for selected city** from the **City Forecast Menu**.

☞ **Type** 1 **and press** Enter.

Now we can Enter the code for Orlando and see the forecast.

☞ **At the** `Enter 3-letter city code:` **prompt type** MCO **and press** Enter.

After going through these steps, the forecast is displayed on the screen, as shown in Figure 3.14. The **City Forecast Menu** pops up again.

```
1

        Enter 3-letter city code:    MCO

TODAY...PARTLY CLOUDY. HIGH IN THE LOWER TO MID 70S. LIGHT WIND
BECOMING EAST5 TO 10 MPH.
TONIGHT...INCREASING HIGH CLOUDS. LOW IN THE MID TO UPPER 50S.
LIGHT SOUTH WIND.
SATURDAY...MOSTLY CLOUDY WITH A SLIGHT CHANCE OF SHOWERS. HIGH
IN THE MID TOUPPER 70S. SOUTH WIND 10 TO 15 MPH. CHANCE OF RAIN 20 PERCENT.


CITY FORECAST MENU
_____

1) Print forecast for selected city
2) Print climate data for selected city
3) Long range forecasts
4) Canadian forecasts
5) Display 3-letter city codes for a selected state
6) Display all 2-letter state codes
M) Return to main menu
X) Exit program
?) Help
```

Enter MCO.

Figure 3.14 Forecast for Selected City and City Forecast Menu

End the Telnet Session

☞ **Type** X **and press** Enter.

There are a number of choices here. You could look up the forecast for other cities, go back to the main menu, or exit the program. We're exiting here, but feel free to browse around some more.

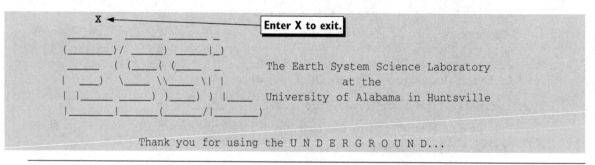

Enter X to exit.

```
        X

_____  _____ _____ _
(_____)/ _____) ____|_)
_____  ( (____( (____ _     The Earth System Science Laboratory
|  ___)  \____ \\____ \| |              at the
| |_____ _____) )____) ) |____ University of Alabama in Huntsville
|_____|_____(_____/|_____)

        Thank you for using the U N D E R G R O U N D...
```

Figure 3.15 Exiting Southeast Weather Underground

End of Example 3.3

Example 3.4 — Accessing Gopher through Telnet ⎯⎯⎯⎯⎯ 83

You can use Telnet to access several other Internet services. Some of the services or resources can be contacted by other means, but it's worth knowing about Telnet as an alternate approach if you need it. Everyone with access to the Internet can use telnet, but not all of these services are available everywhere. Table 3.3 gives ways of using these services through Telnet.

Service	How to Access by Telnet	Username	Also See Chapter
Archie	**telnet archie.ans.net**	archie	8
Gopher	**telnet consultant.micro.umn.edu**	gopher	9
WWW	**telnet lynx.cc.ukans.edu**	www	11

Table 3.3   Other Internet Services Available through Telnet

Example 3.4   Accessing Gopher through Telnet

In this example we'll enter **telnet consultant.micro.umn.edu** to start a Gopher session, as shown in Figure 3.16. That site is at the University of Minnesota, where Gopher was developed. At each stage of a Gopher session you'll see a menu of choices. Choose an item by entering its number. That will either display a document on your screen or take you to another menu. In addition to choosing an item number, press **u** to go to the previous menu, press the spacebar to go to the next screen if there is one, and press **q** to end the session. You can press **?** to get a list of all the commands. Example 3.4 shows how to start a Gopher session and then connect to other Gopher sites throughout the world. We'll connect to a Gopher site in Africa. More details about working with Gopher are discussed in Chapter 9.

Here are the steps we'll follow:

1. Start a telnet session with **consultant.micro.umn.edu** and use the log-in name **gopher**.
2. Choose the item from the main Gopher menu that will take us to other Gopher servers.
3. Choose the item from **Other Gopher Servers** menu that takes us to sites in Africa.
4. Choose the item which will connect to Rhodes University, South Africa.
5. End the Gopher session.

Start a Telnet Session with consultant.micro.umn.edu and Use the Log-in Name Gopher

☞ **At the prompt type** `telnet consultant.micro.umn.edu` **and press** ⌑Enter⌑.

☞ **At the** `login:` **prompt type** `gopher` **and press** ⌑Enter⌑.

☞ **At the** `TERM = (vt100)` **prompt press** ⌑Enter⌑ **or Enter your terminal type and press** ⌑Enter⌑.

After your client contacts the server at **consultant.micro.umn.edu** you'll be prompted for a log-in name. Follow the instructions on the screen and use the login name **gopher**. Figure 3.16 shows this.

```
$ telnet consultant.micro.umn.edu
Trying...
Connected to hole.micro.umn.edu.
Escape character is '^]'.
* * *   University of Minnesota * * *
     * * Public Gopher Access * *

Type 'gopher' at the login prompt

AIX Version 3
(C) Copyrights by IBM and by others 1982, 1993.
login: gopher

This machine is a public gopher client.

You are sharing this machine with many other people from all around
the internet.

To get better performance we recommend that you install a gopher
client on your own machine.  Gopher clients are available for
Unix, Macintosh, DOS, OS/2, VMS, CMS, MVS, Amiga, and many others

You can get these clients via anonymous ftp from boombox.micro.umn.edu
in the directory /pub/gopher

The Gopher Team thanks you!


TERM = (vt100)
Erase is Ctrl-H
Kill is Ctrl-U
Interrupt is Ctrl-C
I think you're on a vt100 terminal
Welcome to the wonderful world of Gopher!

Gopher has limitations on its use and comes without
a warranty.  Please refer to the file 'Copyright' included
in the distribution.

Internet Gopher Information Client 2.1 patch0
Copyright 1991,92,93,94 by the Regents of the University of Minnesota

Press RETURN to continue
```

Callouts:
- Enter telnet consultant.micro.umn.edu to start the session.
- Remember this in case you need it during the session.
- Log in with the name gopher.
- Messages from the remote system.
- Remote system is asking for the type of terminal you're using. Press Enter if you're using a vt100-type terminal. Otherwise enter your terminal type.

Figure 3.16 Using Telnet to Log in to a System That Gives Access to Gopher

——Example 3.4 — Accessing Gopher through Telnet—— 85

Choose the Item from the Main Gopher Menu to Take Us to Other Gopher Servers

☞ **Type** 8, **the number of the item "Other Gopher and Information Servers," and press** [Enter].

To explore an item on a Gopher menu you can type its number and press Enter. Chapter 9 gives other ways of selecting items.

```
            Internet Gopher Information Client v2.1.0
               Home Gopher server: gopher.tc.umn.edu

  ->    1.  Information About Gopher/
         2.  Computer Information/          ┌─────────────────────────────┐
         3.  Discussion Groups/             │ Main Gopher menu. Enter 8 to│
         4.  Fun & Games/                   │ connect to other Gopher servers.│
         5.  Internet file server (ftp) sites/ └─────────────────────────────┘
         6.  Libraries/
         7.  News/
         8.  Other Gopher and Information Servers/
         9.  Phone Books/
        10.  Search Gopher Titles at the University of Minnesota <?>
        11.  Search lots of places at the University of Minnesota  <?>
        12.  University of Minnesota Campus Information/

Press ? for Help, q to Quit                       Page: 1/1
```

Figure 3.17 Main Gopher Menu

Choose the Item from Other Gopher Servers Menu That Takes Us to Sites in Africa

☞ **Type** 4, **the number of the item that lists Gopher sites in Africa, and press** [Enter].

Figure 3.18 shows how this system keeps track of Gopher sites throughout the world. We're choosing Africa; Figure 3.19 shows the menu for Gopher sites in Africa.

```
            Internet Gopher Information Client v2.1.0
               Other Gopher and Information Servers

  ->    1.  All the Gopher Servers in the World/
         2.  Search All the Gopher Servers in the World <?>
         3.  Search titles in Gopherspace using veronica/
         4.  Africa/
         5.  Asia/
         6.  Europe/                     ┌──────────────────────────────┐
         7.  International Organizations/ │ After a short time you'll see a menu│
         8.  Middle East/                │ such as this one. Enter 4 to see a list│
         9.  North America/              │ of Gopher servers in Africa.  │
        10.  Pacific/                    └──────────────────────────────┘
        11.  Russia/
```

```
     12. South America/
     13. Terminal Based Information/
     14. WAIS Based Information/
     15. Gopher Server Registration <??>


Press ? for Help, q to Quit, u to go up a menu              Page: 1/1
```

Figure 3.18 Other Gopher and Information Servers Menu

```
              Internet Gopher Information Client v2.1.0
                                Africa

  ->     1.   African National Congress Information/
         2.   J.S.Gericke Library, University of Stellenbosch/
         3.   Proxima Research and Development Gopher Server/
         4.   RINAF project information service/
         5.   Rhodes University Computing Centre, Grahamstown, South Africa/
         6.   The Foundation for Research Development/
         7.   The Internet Solution/
         8.   The Internetworking Company of Southern Africa (TICSA)/
         9.   The Tunisian Gopher server/
        10.   Uniforum SA/               ┌──────────────────────────────┐
        11.   University of Natal (Durban)/  After a short time you'll see a │
                                         │ screen like this. Enter 5 to connect │
                                         │ to the server at Rhodes          │
                                         └──────────────────────────────┘
Press ? for Help, q to Quit, u to go up a menu              Page: 1/1
```

Figure 3.19 Menu of Gopher Sites in Africa

Choose the Item to Connect to Rhodes University, South Africa

☞ **Type** 5, **the number of the item for Rhodes University, and press** Enter.

After selecting Rhodes University, you'll see the first screen of the menu for that site, as shown in Figure 3.20.

```
              Internet Gopher Information Client v2.1.0
          Rhodes University Computing Centre, Grahamstown, South Africa

  ->     1.   About the Rhodes University Computing Services Gopher
         2.   Rhodes University/
         3.   Rhodes University - mail addresses and phone numbers
         4.   Rhodes University - email addressing
         5.   Rhodes University - 1994 examination results    ┌─────────────────────────┐
         6.   Rhodes University WWW Server <HTML>             │ Choose any item you wish. │
         7.   South African politics, culture and news/       │ You're connected to a server │
         8.   African Networking/                             │ at Rhodes University in   │
         9.   Local experiments with gopher - transient info/ │ South Africa.             │
        10.   Gopher Jewels/                                  └─────────────────────────┘
```

```
11. Information About Gopher/
12. Interesting services - after hours/
13. Interesting services - working hours/
14. Other Internet Gopher Servers/
15. Search Gopherspace with Veronica/
16. South African Rugby Information/
17. The CricInfo Cricket Database/
18. The Internet Hunt/
```

> Feel free to browse. We'll discuss Gopher in more detail in Chapter 9. For now, press q to quit. You'll be asked if you really want to quit.

```
Press ? for Help, q to Quit, u to go up a menu          Page: 1/1
```

Figure 3.20 Gopher Menu for Rhodes University

At this point, feel free to browse among items on this menu or go on to others. We're going to end this session by pressing **q** to quit. It won't show up on the screen.

End the Gopher Session

☞ **Type** q **and press** `Enter`.

☞ **Type** y **and press** `Enter`.

To end a Gopher session, you type the letter q. If it's in lower-case you'll be prompted to confirm your choice, as shown in Figure 3.21. If you use uppercase Q, the session ends without asking you for a confirmation.

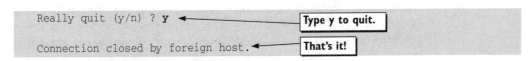

```
Really quit (y/n) ? y ◄            Type y to quit.

Connection closed by foreign host. ◄   That's it!
```

Figure 3.21 Confirm the Request to Quit a Gopher Session

———————————————————End of Example 3.4———————————————————

Finding What's Available with Telnet

Thousands of sites provide some form of Telnet service. You can use Telnet for all sorts of tasks including searching library catalogs, accessing databases, finding weather forecasts, and accessing government bulletin boards and databases in the U.S. A number of commercial services are also available by using Telnet. With so many interesting sites you can reach by Telnet, it's fortunate there are some information guides to tell you what's accessible. We'll discuss three sources of information. They all are excellent, and almost indispensable for anyone who uses the Internet regularly. The people who created and continue to maintain these items have performed a great service to the Internet.

1. "Special Internet Connections," compiled and maintained by Scott Yanoff (e-mail address: **Yanoff@alpha2.csd.uwm.edu**), is a list of sites that offer information and services on the Internet. The list is arranged by subject relating to the type of information or service; some topics are agriculture, fax via Internet, literature/languages/

books, and travel. The list is updated monthly. Not all of the items are accessible by Telnet. The list is available in a variety of ways; you may want to see other chapters in this book for some of the methods listed.

- ❏ Send e-mail to **inetlist@aug3.augsburg.edu**. You'll receive a copy of the list by e-mail.

- ❏ Check the newsgroup **alt.internet.services**. The list is posted monthly.

- ❏ Use anonymous FTP to **ftp.csd.uwm.edu**; then **get /pub/inet.services.txt**.

- ❏ Use Gopher to **gopher.csd.uwm.edu** and select **Remote Information Services**.

- ❏ On the WWW use the URL **http://www.uwm.edu/Mirror/inet.services.html**.

2. "Information Sources: the Internet and Computer-Mediated Communication," compiled and maintained by John December (e-mail address: **decemj@rpi.edu**), is a list of Internet sites that offer information and services. The document contains a wealth of information about accessing many types of information on the Internet. It comes with a table of contents, and is updated regularly. Not all of the items are accessible by Telnet. The list is available in a variety of ways; you may want to see other chapters in this book for some of the methods listed.

- ❏ Use anonymous FTP to **ftp.rpi.edu**; then **cd /pub/communications**. The document is available in several formats. To obtain the text version type **get internet-cmc.txt**.

- ❏ Use Lynx or Mosaic with the URL **http://www.rpi.edu/Internet/Guides/decemj/ icmc/internet-cmc.html**.

3. **Hytelnet**, which Peter Scott (e-mail: **aa375@freenet.carelton.ca**) compiled and maintains, is a program that allows users to reach a large collection of Telnet resources on the Internet. The software comes with an easy-to-use hypertext interface to the sites arranged under several categories. Virtually every library in the world that's on the Internet is listed. Some of the other categories are electronic books, databases and bibliographies, general bulletin boards, and network information services. Chapter 7, "Hytelnet: Working on the Internet Using Telnet" covers its use in detail. The software is available by anonymous FTP from **ftp.usask.ca** in the directory **/pub/hytelnet**.

If you don't have Hytelnet on your system, it's accessible through both Gopher and the World Wide Web (WWW). For Gopher, start a Gopher session with **liberty.uc.wlu.edu**, select **Explore Internet Resources** from the main menu, and then select **Choose Telnet Login to Sites (Hytelnet)**. To access it through the WWW use Lynx, Mosaic, or Netscape with the URL **http://www.cs.ukans.edu/hytelnet_html/START.TXT**.

Summary

Working on the Internet, you can use the command **telnet** to log in to other computer systems. When you make a connection through Telnet it's as if you're using a terminal directly connected to the remote site. You begin a Telnet session with another site by starting Telnet on your computer and then supplying the name or address of the remote site. On many systems this means entering a command such as:

```
telnet domain name                    example: telnet nih-library.nih.gov
telnet IP address                     example: telnet 137.187.166.250
telnet domain name port-number        example: telnet wind.atmos.uah.edu 3000
```

In other cases you start Telnet on your system and then use the command or option **open** to make the connection. For example,

```
telnet
open nih-library.nih.gov
```

Some Telnet sites require you to supply a log-in name and a password, others only a log-in name, and some sites don't require either. Remember that the remote site provides Telnet access as a service and generally at no expense to you. So respect any requests they make about using their system, and restrict your access to nonpeak hours when possible.

When you give the command or start a Telnet session, a version of Telnet runs on your computer to contact the remote system. When the remote system is contacted, it will execute a Telnet program as well. The Telnet that's running on your system is called the client and the Telnet that's running at the remote site is called the server. Some things to note are:

❑   You are communicating with a server on a host through your client.

❑   Most of the messages you'll see during a Telnet session come from the server.

❑   Use **^]** to get to your client. This is useful if you get lost or stuck or don't know how to log out. **^]** means Ctrl-]. Hold down the key labeled Ctrl, press the key labeled], and then release them. When you do that during a Telnet session you'll see the prompt **telnet>**. That's your client talking! Type **quit** when you see **telnet>** to terminate a session.

❑   If the host isn't available you might see the message **Unknown Host**, or **Unable to connect to remote host: Connection Refused**.

Several thousand sites allow Telnet connections. Many offer unique services and few generalizations can be made about using them. Hytelnet, discussed in Chapter 7, provides a means for finding and reaching many of these sites. Some lists of Telnet-accessible sites available on the Internet are given in this chapter.

Exercises

Telnet with Port Numbers—Weather, Subways, Sports Schedules, Chemistry

In this group of exercises you'll be able to use Telnet with a port number, so a log-in name or password isn't necessary.

1.   Example 3.3 showed how to use Telnet to find the weather forecast for Orlando, Florida.
     a.   Use Telnet to contact a weather service to find the forecast for a city near you.
     b.   Find the current weather forecast for Melbourne, Australia.

2. In this exercise you'll use Telnet with a port number, so a log-in name or password isn't necessary. Find the subway route you need to follow to get from a given location to another in Paris and do the same thing for a subway route in Boston. Impossible? Not if you use Telnet to contact the Subway Navigator. To do that, use **telnet METRO.JUSSIEU.FR 10000** or **telnet 134.157.0.132 10000**. Once you're connected, choose either French or English as the language used for the menus.
   a. Choose France/Paris as the city and find the subway route from *Notre-Dame de Lorette* to *Champs Elysees*. Which lines (trains) should you take? Which stops will you pass through? Where do you change trains? How long will it take?
   b. Now answer the same questions for the route from the airport to the Fenway area in USA/Boston.

3. The sports schedules for the National Basketball Association (NBA), National Hockey League (NHL), and Major League Baseball (MLB) are available on-line through Telnet. To find the schedule for

   NBA, use **telnet culine.colorado.edu 859**
   NHL, use **telnet culine.colorado.edu 860**
   MLB, use **telnet culine.colorado.edu 862**

   Use Telnet to answer each of these:
   a. What are the next three scheduled games for the Houston Rockets? (Basketball)
   b. What are the next three scheduled games for the Montreal Canadiens? (Hockey)
   c. What are the next three scheduled games for the New York Yankees? (Baseball)

4. You probably know the periodic table was devised to classify the known chemical elements. The table is available by using **telnet CAMMS2.CAOS.KUN.NL 2034**. Once you connect, take some time to get familiar with the menu; it helps you display and move about the periodic table. You return to that menu by pressing **?**.
   a. Use the information from the periodic table to determine the atomic weight, atomic number, boiling point, melting point, and natural state of sodium. Its chemical symbol is Na. (*Hint:* Press **i** when the symbol for Sodium, Na, is highlighted.)
   b. Do the same for chlorine, chemical symbol Cl.
   c. What is the common name for the compound that is formed from sodium and chlorine, NaCl? (*Hint:* Press **d** when the symbol for Chlorine is highlighted.)
   d. What's the effect of liquid chlorine on the skin? What's the effect of breathing chlorine gas? *Look this up—don't try it!*

Using Telnet to Access Gopher

5. Use Telnet to access the Gopher server at the University of Minnesota. In Example 3.4, you saw how to connect to a Gopher server in Africa. This time, connect to the Gopher server at Mary Washington College in Fredericksburg, Virginia. Once there you'll see the item **The Internet** on the first menu; select that item. Select the item **Internet Guides** from the next menu. Now you should be able to view the documents by Yanoff and December that were referred to in this chapter. (*Hint:* Look at **inet.services.txt** and **internet-cmc.txt**.) See if you can figure out how to get a copy of either list sent to

you by e-mail. (That will be discussed in Chapter 9, "Gopher: Burrowing through the Internet.")

6. The Electronic Newsstand is accessible through Telnet at **enews.com**. The required log-in name is **enews**. It's a virtual newsstand and similar to a real newsstand in that you can browse through several publications. Once you connect you'll be using a Gopher menu system. (Gopher is discussed in Chapter 9, "Gopher: Burrowing Through the Internet.") When you select an entry for a specific periodical, you'll be able to look at the table of contents for the current issue. Choose the item that leads you to the titles arranged by subject and look at the table of contents for a periodical in each of these categories: literature and science. After looking at each, send yourself a copy by e-mail.

Using Telnet to Search Libraries and Databases

7. You've got to do some research on Beethoven's works. Your challenge is to come up with a list of five or more references—author, title, call number—that deal with Beethoven's chamber music. Probably any book about Beethoven will contain the topic, but the references you find ought to be specific to chamber music. Luckily the Beethoven Bibliography Database is accessible by Telnet. Here's how to reach it. First telnet to **sjsulib1.sjsu.edu**. Use **lib** when you're prompted for a log-in name; select **D** on the main menu; then select Beethoven Bibliography Database. You'll want to do a search by subject, a search by keyword, or perhaps a search by genre.

8. You can reach libraries throughout the world by using Telnet. In some cases the instructions for searching are in the language of the host country; others also carry instructions in English. In this exercise you'll be doing some searching at a library in Chile. The topic is the aurora (a luminous meteoric phenomenon), also known as polar lights, so it's appropriate to see what a library in Chile might have on the topic.

   Use Telnet to contact the Universidad de Concepcion with **telnet cisne.bib.udec.cl**. Give **opac** for a log-in name, and select a terminal type (use vt100 if you don't know your terminal type). You'll see the question *FUE LEGIBLE LA PRUEBA DE LA PANTALLA? (S/N).* Enter **s**. You should see a menu of choices. Do you feel comfortable working with the menus in Spanish? One choice will allow you to set the menus in English. Regardless of what language you choose, come up with three references to items dealing with the type of aurora mentioned above. Which are currently checked in and available?

9. The National Institutes of Health Library in Bethesda, Maryland, makes its catalog available through Telnet; use **telnet nih-library.nih.gov**. No password is required to log in. Once you're connected you'll see a menu such as:
   A > AUTHOR
   T > TITLE
   S > SUBJECT
   C > CALL #
   W > WORDS in the title
   V > VIEW your circulation record
   I > Library INFORMATION
   D > DISCONNECT

    a. Search the catalog for books or journals whose author has the same last name as yours. If nothing meets that criterion, search for items by an author whose name is close to yours. The catalog system will let you know what is close. Write down the title, author, and call number of three items whose author's name matches these criteria.

    b. Suppose you need to do some research on the topic of AIDS. Do a subject search and report the title, author and call number of five items.

    c. Do a word search on the topic of AIDS and report back the title, author, and call number of five items different from the ones you reported in part b.

10. The National Technology Transfer Center's Online System is called Business Gold. It contains information on new technologies and business opportunities that has come about from research and development sponsored by the U.S. government. After working through this exercise, you'll see how to retrieve some of this information.

    a. Start a Telent session to Business Gold using **telnet iron.nttc.edu**, and when you see the prompt **login:** type visitor and press Enter. (You may be asked to enter your e-mail address; do it.) Soon you'll see a first screen which describes Business Gold and tells the types of things accessible through this service. List a few.

    b. Press Enter to get a menu of **Current News** and **Business Gold Database Access**. Select an item from the **Current News** section dealing with Environmental Technology. After you make the selection, a list of items will appear. What's in the list?

    c. Choose an item and another menu will appear. You may have to go through another menu or two, but you'll eventually be able to select and display a document. Which one did you select?

    d. You can get a copy of a document you're viewing by sending it to yourself by e-mail. Be sure you're viewing a document and press **M** to mark a document. After you've marked it press **D** to download it. (This lets you get a copy of the document.) A window will pop up on your screen giving you a few options. Press **E** to e-mail the document to yourself.

    e. Get yourself back to the main menu, and then choose the option **L** to logoff.

11. Contact two databases to search for information on the topic *absolute pitch*, the capability some people have to identify or produce musical tones exactly. The two databases are the Music and Brain Information Database and CAIRSS (Computer-Assisted Information Retrieval Service System) for Music.

    a. Use Telnet to find at least three references on the topic of absolute pitch at the Music and Brain Information Database. Contact that site by Telnet to either **MILA.PS.UCI.EDU** or **128.200.29.81**. Give the log-in name **mbi** and the password **nammbi**. After you log in you'll see the prompt TERM = (vt100). If your terminal type is not VT100, give it here; otherwise press Enter. Instructions will follow. Take notes so you'll be able to search the database.

Note: To search the database, select **(1) Search MBI Database** and then press the space bar after the "mbi" source is seen highlighted.

```
            MBI Main Menu
            (1)   Search MBI Database
            (2)   News, Notices, Items of Interest
            (3)   Information about the MuSICA system
            (4)   Help
            (5)   Exit/Logout
       Enter the number of your selection:
```

You will search the database by using a service named WAIS, which is covered in Chapter 10, "WAIS: Searching Databases on the Internet." The instructions for the commands you use at MBI will be on the screen, or you'll be told how to get help. Use absolute pitch as the keyword. When you find items make note of the references—title, author, and other pertinent information—and since you're using WAIS, you'll be able to send the items you select to yourself via e-mail. Figure out how to do this.

b.   Now search the CAIRSS for Music database of music research literature for references on the same topic—absolute pitch or absolute. To contact that site, use Telnet to **utsaibm.utsa.edu**. At the prompt **TS> ! VT100,3278**, press Enter. At the screen with **UTSA** in large letters, type **library** and press Enter, then select local, and then select **CMUSC.A.I.R.S.S. FOR MUSIC**. Now perform a subject search and a keyword search on the topic *absolute pitch*. Report on a total of five references taken from both searches.

Anonymous FTP
Retrieving Files from
Other Computer Systems

A wealth of information is stored in files available to anyone on the Internet. In fact, one of the primary reasons for creating the Internet was so that researchers could exchange ideas and results of their work. One basic Internet service is designed to copy files from one computer system to another. Its name is FTP, which stands for *file transfer protocol*. FTP is precisely the tool or service you want to use when you need to retrieve a file quickly. It's most effective when you know the exact location—file name, directory name, and Internet name of the remote computer system—of a file. It lets you retrieve files from a large number and variety of computer systems.

Chapter Overview

In this chapter we'll look at how to use FTP to retrieve copies of files from another site on the Internet. You'll see how to use *anonymous FTP*, which allows you to retrieve files without being a registered user on another computer system. The topics we'll cover are:

❑ Connecting to an Anonymous FTP Site and Retrieving Files

❑ Common ftp Commands

❑ Working with Different File Types

❑ Reading and Understanding Citations to FTP Resources

❑ Sources of Information about ftp and FTP Archives

❑ E-Mail Access to FTP Archives

FTP was created at a time when most Internet users had a fair amount of experience using computers so it doesn't provide very much in the way of a user-friendly interface. Other tools or services may be better to use for browsing or searching. You'll also want to look at Chapter 8, "Archie: Searching for Files Available by Anonymous FTP." Archie is a service that searches through the names of the millions of files available by anonymous FTP to let you know where to get the file you want.

Connecting to an Anonymous FTP Site and Retrieving Files

You use one of the basic Internet services, FTP, to transfer files from one Internet site to another. Working on your computer you give the command **ftp** along with the domain name of another system. This sets up a connection between the two, so files can be copied by following proper procedures. As you give commands the remote system responds.

Anonymous FTP allows you to retrieve files that are publicly available from another computer system on the Internet. Naturally the other computer has to be set up to allow for this. Systems that allow anonymous FTP sessions are called *anonymous FTP sites* and the collection of files they make available are called *FTP archives*. Anonymous FTP isn't meant to be a tool for browsing. It is, however, very effective and relatively easy to use if you know the complete location of a file on the Internet. The term *complete location* means the exact name of the file, the directory it's stored in, and the domain name of the site at which it's located. For example, a copy of the United Nations Charter is in the file named **un_charter.txt** in the directory **/cpsr/privacy/privacy_international/international_laws** at **cpsr.org**. With just a few commands, you can retrieve and copy it to your computer system.

You access an anonymous FTP site by giving the command **ftp** followed by the domain name or address of the remote system. Once ftp makes the connection to the FTP site you will be prompted to enter a user name. Enter the user name **anonymous**—that's where the term anonymous FTP comes from. Next you'll be prompted for a password. Proper network etiquette requires you to give your e-mail address as the password. Most anonymous FTP sites keep a log of users. In rare cases you'll have to use the password **guest**.

While you are in an FTP session you can expect to see some responses from the remote system. These responses could be the remote system prompting you for information, displaying information to let you know it's working, or responding to your commands. The behavior of the ftp program on your system may be slightly different from what you see here. We've constructed the examples so that they don't take advantage of special features available at some anonymous FTP sites but not others.

The ftp program running on your computer system is called a *client*. The remote system is also running an ftp program called a *server*. The commands you type are passed by your program, the client, to the remote system. At the remote site the server program receives the commands, interprets them, and sends responses to your client. The following figure depicts the relationship between the client and the server.

| THE CLIENT REQUESTS FILES | THE REMOTE SYSTEM PROMPTS THE CLIENT FOR MORE INFORMATION... | ...AND RESPONDS TO THE CLIENT'S DEMANDS | FURTHER TRANSAC- TIONS ARE AVAILABLE |

Example 4.1   Using ftp to Retrieve a File

Example 4.1 uses anonymous FTP to access the Internet site **nic.merit.edu**, a site that hosts a variety of information about the Internet. You will use anonymous FTP to retrieve the file named **READ.ME**. Here are the steps to follow:

1. Start the session.

☞ **Type** `ftp nic.merit.edu` **and press** Enter.

☞ **Type** `anonymous` **and press** Enter.

☞ **Type your e-mail address and press** Enter.

2. Retrieve the READ.ME file.

☞ **Type** `get read.me` **and press** Enter.

3. End the session.

☞ **Type** `quit` **and press** Enter.

The file named **READ.ME** contains information about contacting that site and others using anonymous FTP, e-mail, and Gopher. You'll find a similar file at many anonymous FTP sites. The file states policies, means of access, and what's available. The file isn't always named **READ.ME**; in some cases it is named **README**, **00readme**, **index**, or something similar. (You'll see how to list the files and directories available in Example 4.2.) Here is the complete example. The items you type are underlined and explained on the right in boldface; the actual user name here is mozart.

```
ftp nic.merit.edu                        Enter the ftp command
Connected to nic.merit.edu.
220 nic.merit.edu FTP server (SunOS 4.1) ready.
Name (nic.merit.edu:mozart): anonymous   Enter user name anonymous
```

Example 4.1 — Using ftp to Retrieve a File

97

```
331 Guest login ok, send ident as password.
Password:                                    Enter your e-mail address as
                                             a password

230 Guest login ok, access restrictions apply.
ftp> get READ.ME                             Give command to retrieve or
                                             get the file READ.ME

200 PORT command successful.
150 ASCII data connection for READ.ME (192.65.245.76,4619) (16622 bytes).
226 ASCII Transfer complete.
16979 bytes received in 6.16 seconds (2.69 Kbytes/s)
ftp> quit                                    Quit or exit ftp program
221 Goodbye.
```

Let's take a detailed look at the previous session:

```
ftp nic.merit.edu
```

You enter the command **ftp**, which starts the ftp program on your computer. It then notifies the system at **nic.merit.edu** that you wanted to start an FTP session with that computer system.

```
Connected to nic.merit.edu.
220 nic.merit.edu FTP server (SunOS 4.1) ready.
```

These are responses from the FTP server, which works to satisfy FTP requests at **nic.merit.edu**.

```
Name (nic.merit.edu:mozart): anonymous
```

You are prompted to enter a user name. You enter **anonymous** so you can gain access to publicly available files.

```
331 Guest login ok, send ident as password.
Password:
```

This is a response from the server letting you know it's OK to log in as **anonymous** and then a prompt for the password. The term **ident** means that the system is expecting you to type your e-mail address.

```
230 Guest login ok, access restrictions apply.
```

This indicates the login is successful. Some systems allow access only at certain times or limit the number of public sessions.

```
ftp> get READ.ME
```

You issue the command **get**, allowing you to retrieve a file. For this command to work properly there has to be a file named **READ.ME** on the remote system. Be careful that the spelling, punctuation, and case of the letters exactly match the name of the file you want to retrieve.

Notice the prompt **ftp>**. This is coming from the ftp program running on your system. When you see this prompt it means that your system is ready for another ftp command.

```
200 PORT command successful.
150 ASCII data connection for READ.ME (192.65.245.76,4619) (16622 bytes).
226 ASCII Transfer complete.
16979 bytes received in 6.16 seconds (2.69 Kbytes/s)
```

This is another series of responses from the system sending you the file.

❏ The first indicates that your command **get READ.ME** was understood.

❏ The second says that a connection has been made between the two computer systems. The file **READ.ME** will be sent in ASCII or text form, and a total of 16,622 bytes will be transferred.

❏ The third and fourth tell you the transfer is complete, how long it took, and the rate of transfer.

```
ftp> quit
```

You give the command **quit**, which terminates the FTP session.

```
221 Goodbye.
```

Finally you get a response from the server at the remote site and you're all done.

Synopsis of ftp Commands Used in Example 4.1

Command	Meaning and Example
get	This command retrieves a file from the anonymous FTP site. In this example it was used as **get READ.ME**. The file named **READ.ME** is transferred from the remote site to your computer. It will have the same name on your system. The command's general form is **get remote-file-name local-file-name**. The **local-file-name** is optional. If we had used **get READ.ME README.TXT**, the file would have been transferred as before, but its name on your system would be **README.TXT**.
quit	This command ends the current anonymous FTP session.

──────────────────────**End of Example 4.1**──────────────────────

Once a file is transferred it resides in the current directory on your local system. You can treat it as you would any other file. The file **READ.ME** contains some useful information, so it would be a good idea to either view it on the screen or print it. Different sorts of files are available at FTP archives. Some may contain plain text, some might be programs ready to run, some might be files produced by a specific word processor, and others might be images that need a special viewing program. Although you have a file in your possession, you don't necessarily own the information. Don't distribute a file unless the author gives permission.

Information in anonymous FTP archives is stored in files that are arranged in directories. Each directory can hold files and other directories. You need to know how to get a list of the files and directories at an anonymous FTP site. Example 4.2 shows how to do this.

Example 4.2   Working with Files and Directories

In Example 4.1 you used anonymous FTP to get the file **READ.ME** at **nic.merit.edu**. In this example we'll learn how to look through the directories at an FTP archive site, show ways to identify files and directories, and how to move from one directory to another. This is important to know when the file you want to retrieve is stored in a subdirectory of the top directory at an

Example 4.2 — Working with Files and Directories ———————— 99

FTP site or when you want to browse through an archive to find files that might interest you. When you work along with this example by entering the commands yourself you'll see some of the same messages as in the previous example. Here are the steps to follow:

1. Start an anonymous FTP session with **nic.merit.edu**.
2. List the names of files and directories at the top level.
3. Look at the contents of a few directories.
4. Go to the directory **introducing.the.internet** with the file named **access.guide**.
5. Display the name of the current directory.
6. Retrieve **access.guide**.
7. Quit the FTP session.

You Enter	Explanation
ftp nic.merit.edu	Use the command ftp to contact the site **nic.merit.edu**
anonymous	Use the user name **anonymous**
your.email.address	Give your e-mail address as a password to use anonymous FTP to retrieve a file
dir	List the names of the files and directories in the current directory
dir resources	List the contents of the directory named **resources**
dir introducing.the.internet	List the contents of the directory named **introducing.the.internet**
cd introducing.the.internet	Change to the directory **introducing.the.internet**
pwd	Display the name of the current directory
get access.guide	Retrieve the file named **access.guide**
quit	Use the ftp command **quit** to stop using ftp

Start an Anonymous FTP Session with nic.merit.edu

☞ **Type** ftp nic.merit.edu **and press** Enter.

☞ **Type** anonymous **and press** Enter.

☞ **Type your e-mail address and press** Enter.

```
ftp nic.merit.edu                        Give the command ftp
Connected to nic.merit.edu.
220 nic.merit.edu FTP server (SunOS 4.1) ready.
Name (nic.merit.edu:mozart): anonymous   Enter user name anonymous
331 Guest login ok, send ident as password.
Password:                                Enter your e-mail address as a
                                         password
230 Guest login ok, access restrictions apply.
```

List the Names of Files and Directories at the Top Level

☞ **Type** dir **and press** Enter.

For this step you're going to use the ftp command **dir**. It lists the names of files and directories in the current directory and gives other information about them. Some of the more important pieces of information are the entries in the first, fifth, and last columns.

Figure 4.1 shows a partial list of the items in the current directory. You'll see a sequence of letters and dashes in the first column. If the first character is a dash (-) the entry is the name of a file. But if the first character is the letter **d** then the entry is a directory. You can retrieve files with the command get. Directories contain other files and directories, and you usually can't retrieve a directory with a simple **get**. The fifth column tells you the size in bytes or characters of the item. The last column tells you its name. In order to conserve space we won't list all the items that appear in the directory.

```
ftp> dir                          Use the ftp command dir to list the contents
                                  of the current directory
200 PORT command successful.
150 ASCII data connection for /bin/ls (192.65.245.76,4046) (0 bytes).
total 63
-rw-r--r--  1 nic     merit      22565 Apr 12 20:22 INDEX
-rw-r--r--  1 nic     merit      16622 Apr 12 20:23 READ.ME
drwxr-sr-x  2 nic     merit        512 Sep 15  1992 acceptable.use.policies
drwxr-sr-x  4 nic     merit        512 Oct 31 20:59 conference.proceedings
drwxr-sr-x  3 nic     merit        512 Apr 12 20:05 conferences.seminars
dr-xr-sr-x  2 root    staff        512 Aug  6  1993 dev
drwxr-sr-x  9 nic     merit        512 Nov 30 22:37 documents
drwxr-sr-x 11 nic     merit        512 Mar 25 22:35 internet
drwxr-sr-x  3 nic     merit        512 Nov 30 21:04 internet.tools
drwxr-sr-x  2 nic     merit       1024 Mar 11 12:03 introducing.the.internet
drwxr-sr-x  5 nic     merit        512 Apr 19 19:38 k12.michigan
drwxr-sr-x  7 nic     merit        512 Oct 14  1993 newsletters
drwxr-sr-x  7 nic     merit        512 Jan 10 17:53 nren
drwxr-sr-x 13 nic     merit        512 Apr  5 15:35 nsfnet
drwxr-sr-x  2 omb     omb          512 Sep 10  1993 omb
drwxr-sr-x  5 nic     merit        512 Mar 17  1993 resources
drwxr-sr-x  4 nic     merit        512 Jul 26  1993 statistics
226 ASCII Transfer complete.
```

Figure 4.1   Partial List of Items in Current Directory

You see there are two files and several directories

Look at the Contents of a Few Directories

☞ **Type** dir resources **and press** Enter.

☞ **Type** dir introducing.the.internet **and press** Enter.

To see the entries in a directory give the command dir followed by the directory name. You'll look at two of them in Figure 4.2.

Example 4.2 — Working with Files and Directories ————— 101

```
ftp> dir resources          Use the command dir to display the directory
                            resources
200 PORT command successful.
150 ASCII data connection for /bin/ls (192.65.245.76,4055) (0 bytes).
total 1469
-rw-r--r--  2 nic      merit       2265 Mar 17  1993 INDEX.resources
-rw-r--r--  3 nic      merit       1403 Mar  3  1991 bibliography.txt
drwxr-sr-x  2 nic      merit        512 Mar 17  1993 cruise.dos
drwxr-sr-x  2 nic      merit        512 Mar 17  1993 cruise.mac
-rw-r--r--  6 nic      merit     263640 Aug 14  1991 cwis.ps
-rw-r--r--  2 nic      merit      61740 Apr 11  1991 hitchhikers.guide
-rw-r--r--  6 nic      merit     434555 Aug 14  1991 libs.ps
drwxr-sr-x  2 nic      merit        512 Jul 15  1992 user.profiles
-rw-r--r--  3 nic      merit     492397 Mar 24  1992 zen-draft.ps
-rw-r--r--  3 nic      merit     183742 Jul 13  1992 zen-draft.txt
226 ASCII Transfer complete.

ftp> dir introducing.the.internet       Use the command dir to display the
                                        directory introducing.the.internet
200 PORT command successful.
150 ASCII data connection for /bin/ls (192.65.245.100,1709) (0 bytes).
total 1594
-rw-r--r--  1 nic      merit       4754 Mar 22 23:36  INDEX.introducing.the.internet
-rw-r--r--  1 nic      merit      15659 Mar 22 23:33 access.guide
-rw-r--r--  5 nic      merit      98753 Mar 11 11:49 answers.to.new.user.questions
-rw-r--r--  1 nic      merit       1966 Jan 26  1993 how-to-get.companion
-rw-r--r--  1 nic      merit       3047 Aug 26  1993 how-to-get.cruise
-rw-r--r--  1 nic      merit      11182 Aug 19  1993 how-to-get.resource.guide
-rw-r--r--  1 nic      merit     245636 Apr 15 17:07 information.sources
-rw-r--r--  1 nic      merit      12265 May 28  1993 internet.basics.eric-digest
-rw-r--r--  3 nic      merit      27089 Mar  3  1993 internet.books
-rw-r--r--  1 nic      merit      70586 Apr 15 17:07 internet.tools.summary
-rw-r--r--  5 nic      merit       7116 May 27  1993 intro.internet.biblio
-rw-r--r--  1 nic      merit      91214 Jul 28  1992 intro.to.ip
-rw-r--r--  5 nic      merit      71176 Jan 14  1993 network.gold
-rw-r--r--  5 nic      merit     104624 Jan  7  1993 users.glossary
-rw-r--r--  5 nic      merit      27811 May 27  1993 what.is.internet
-rw-r--r--  5 nic      merit      95238 Aug 19  1990 where.to.start
-rw-r--r--  3 nic      merit     492397 Mar 24  1992 zen.ps
-rw-r--r--  3 nic      merit     183742 Jul 13  1992 zen.txt
226 ASCII Transfer complete.
```

Figure 4.2   Entries in Directories resources and introducing.the.internet

Go to the Directory introducing.the.internet that Contains the File Named access.guide

☞ **Type** `cd introducing.the.internet` **and press** Enter.

When you displayed the contents of the directory **introducing.the.internet**, the name of the file **access.guide** was listed.

```
ftp> cd introducing.the.internet          Use the command cd to change or move
                                           to the directory introducing.the.internet
250 CWD command successful.
ftp>
```

Display the Name of the Current Directory.

☞ **Type** `pwd` **and press** Enter.

When you change directories, check the name of the current directory. This helps you make sure you're where you want to be. Use the command **pwd**, which stands for *print working directory*.

Command	Meaning and Example
dir	List the contents of a directory. You used it in two ways: **dir** to display the contents of the current directory, and **dir introducing.the.internet** to list the items in a subdirectory (**introducing.the.internet**) of the current directory. Giving the name of a directory after **dir** lists its contents.
cd	Change or move to another directory. You used the command **cd introducing.the.internet** to change or move to the directory. In general you use it as **cd** followed by a directory name. For example, **cd /resources/ cruise.mac** would change your current directory to **/resources/cruise.mac**.
pwd	Display the name of the current directory.

————————————————————End of Example 4.2————————————————————

In a similar manner you would give the commands below to retrieve the file **answers.to.new.user.questions** in the directory **introducing.the.internet** by anonymous FTP from **nic.merit.edu**.

```
ftp nic.merit.edu
anonymous
<type your e-mail address>
cd introducing.the.internet
get answers.to.new.user.questions
quit
```

Before going on here's a brief way to get a copy of the file mentioned earlier that contains the United Nations charter.

Example 4.2 — Working with Files and Directories — 103

```
ftp cpsr.org
anonymous
<type your e-mail address>
cd /cpsr/privacy/privacy_international/international_laws
get un_charter.txt
quit
```

Tips for Browsing

There are a couple of things you can do to make it easier to peruse directory listings or look at the contents of files:

Pause the screen display. When you enter the ftp command **dir** the names of the files and directories in the current directory are displayed on your screen. If there is more than one screen they may be displayed so quickly that you don't get a chance to look at all of them. On many systems you can press Ctrl-S (press the key labeled Ctrl and while holding it press the **S** key) to pause the screen display. After you've read it press Ctrl-Q to continue the listing.

Browse a file. Before you can look at the contents of a file it generally needs to be transferred to your computer system. You can use the command **get** together with a program on your local system to read the file one screen at a time. If the program named **more** or **pg** is on your computer then you can read a file by using one of these commands:

```
get the.file |more   or   get the.file |pg
```

Be careful about the spacing. There has to be at least one space after the file name and *no* space after the vertical bar character |. This doesn't get you a copy of the file, but after you look at it you can decide whether you want to transfer it to your system.

The two examples we've looked at give a fair amount of detail about using FTP. There are a few other issues we need to consider before leaving this chapter.

❑ The commands you can use during an FTP session. We'll look at the ones that are most commonly used.

❑ Retrieving different types of files—ASCII or binary. Files contain different types of information. Some are plain text; others are documents produced by a word processing program, programs that you can run on your computer, and images. You may have to give a special command to retrieve files that aren't plain text.

❑ Working with compressed files and several files combined into one file. Many FTP archive sites store files in a compressed format. Once you retrieve a file in that form you have to uncompress it or separate the collection of files.

❑ Reading references to FTP sources. We look at the terminology used to give a reference to a file at an archive site. You need to be able to decipher a reference or citation to a file available by anonymous FTP.

Common ftp Commands

There are a large number of commands you can use in an FTP session. To get a list of all of them type **?** or **help** during an FTP session. The next example shows how to do this.

Example 4.3   Listing Commands and Retrieving Help in an FTP Session

Example 4.3, shown in Figure 4.3, demonstrates how to list all the ftp commands and also how to get the help that ftp provides about a command. You'll see that the help messages displayed are terse. Here are the steps to follow:

1. Start an anonymous FTP session. (Any FTP site will do; we use **ftp.loc.gov**, U.S. Library of Congress, just for variety. You may want to examine some of the directories while you're there.)

☞ **Type** ftp.loc.gov **and press** ⎡Enter⎤.

☞ **Type** anonymous **and press** ⎡Enter⎤.

☞ **Type your e-mail address and press** ⎡Enter⎤.

2. Give the ftp command **?** to list all commands.

☞ **Type** ? **and press** ⎡Enter⎤.

3. Give the ftp command **help** followed by the name of a command to see a little more information.

☞ **Type** help get **and press** ⎡Enter⎤.

☞ **Type** help mget **and press** ⎡Enter⎤.

4. Quit the FTP session.

☞ **Type** quit **and press** ⎡Enter⎤.

```
ftp ftp.loc.gov                              ftp to Library of Congress
Connected to rs7.loc.gov.
220 rs7 FTP server (Version 4.9 Thu Sep 2 20:35:07 CDT 1993) ready.
Name (marvel.loc.gov:mozart): anonymous     Enter user name anonymous
331 Guest login ok, send ident as password.
Password:                                    Enter e-mail address as a password
230 Guest login ok, access restrictions apply.
Remote system type is UNIX.
Using binary mode to transfer files.
ftp> ?                                       Type ? to get help
Commands may be abbreviated.  Commands are:

  !          debug        mget      pwd        status
  $          dir          mkdir     quit       struct
```

```
account      disconnect    mls          quote         system
append       form          mode         recv          sunique
ascii        get           modt         ime reget     tenex
bell         glob          mput         rstatus       trace
binary       hash          newer        rhelp         type
bye          help          nmap         rename        user
case         idle          nlist        reset         umask
cd           image         ntrans       restart       verbose
cdup         lcd           open         rmdir         ?
chmod        ls            prompt       runique
close        macdef        proxy        send
cr           mdelete       sendport     site
delete       mdir          put          size
ftp> help get                          Show help message for
                                       the command get

get receive file
ftp> help mget                         Show help message for
                                       the command mget

mget   get multiple files
ftp> quit                              Quit or exit ftp program
221 Goodbye.
```

Figure 4.3   Ftp Commands and Using Help

──────────────────────────────End of Example 4.3──────────────────────────────

You probably won't use most of the commands you see, and several of them do the same thing. For example, both commands **?** and **help** provide a list of commands or give help about a command. The following is a guide to some of the more common things you do in an FTP session.

Working with Directories

> To: **list files in current directory**   Type: **dir**

You'll see a sequence of letters and dashes to the left of each listing. If the first letter is "d," the listing is a directory.

> To: **display the name of the current directory**   Type: **pwd**

The name of the current directory will be displayed.

> To: **move or change to another directory**   Type: **cd directory-name**

Change the current directory to the one following cd, for example, **cd /pub**. To change to the parent or directly above the current directory use **cd ..**

Retrieving Files

> To: **retrieve a file**   Type: **get file-name**
>   **get remote-file-name local-file-name**

Copy a file from the FTP site to your computer. The characters you type for file-name must be exactly as they appear (including upper- or lowercase) in the directory listing. In the second form you copy a file from the FTP site and give it another name on your system. For example, **get access.guide guide.txt** copies the file named **access.guide** from the remote system to a file named **guide.txt** on your computer.

To: **retrieve a group of files**   Type: **mget pattern**

The files in the current directory at the FTP site whose names match the pattern are eligible to be copied to your system. You'll be asked whether you want to copy each eligible file. The "pattern" isn't an exact name but includes the characters **?** or *****, which act as "wildcard" characters to make the match. A **?** matches a single character while ***** matches any collection of characters. Suppose an anonymous FTP site has files named **eagle**, **eagle.txt**, and **eagle.gif**. If you type **mget eagl*** you'll be able to copy all those files to your system. If you type **mget eagl?** you can copy only the file **eagle**. Also, the command **mget *.gif** will allow you to copy all the files whose names end with **.gif**. The command **mget** is also useful when you don't want to type the complete name of a file.

Changing Modes of File Transfer

To: **switch to binary mode**   Type: **binary**

Set to binary mode for transferring nontext files. You have to use this to transfer files that contain executable programs, compressed files, files produced in some word processor formats, and others. This is done automatically if the FTP site is a UNIX system.

To: **switch to ASCII mode**   Type: **ASCII**

Set to ASCII mode for transferring files that contain only plain text. These are files that contain only printable characters.

Ending or Quitting an FTP Session

To: **end an ftp session**   Type: **quit** or **bye**

Example 4.4   Retrieving "how-to" Guides for E-Mail, FTP, and Telnet

The anonymous FTP archive site at **nic.sura.net** contains several how-to guides for working with the basic Internet services. In this example you will retrieve three of the guides from the directory **/pub/nic/network.service.guides** using many of the commands above. As you do this example you'll see several descriptive messages from the FTP site that are not included here to conserve space. The example is shown in Figure 4.4.

Here are the steps to follow:

1. Start an anonymous FTP session with **nic.sura.net**.

☞ **Type** `ftp.nic.sura.net` **and press** `Enter`.

☞ **Type** anonymous **and press** Enter.

☞ **Type your e-mail address and press** Enter.

2. Use the ftp command **cd** to change to the directory **pub/nic/network.service.guides**.

☞ **Type** cd pub/nic/network.service.guides **and press** Enter.

3. Use the ftp command **pwd** to display the name of the current directory.

☞ **Type** pwd **and press** Enter.

4. Use the ftp command **mget how.to*** to get the names of files that begin with **how.to**.

☞ **Type** mget how.to* **and press** Enter.

5. As each file name is displayed type **y** for the first three to retrieve them and **n** so you don't retrieve the fourth one.

☞ **Type** y **and press** Enter.

☞ **Type** y **and press** Enter.

☞ **Type** y **and press** Enter.

☞ **Type** n **and press** Enter.

6. Quit the FTP session.

☞ **Type** quit **and press** Enter.

Now to go through these step by step. As you work through this example, your screen will look similar to the following:

```
ftp nic.sura.net                          Enter the ftp command
Connected to nic.sura.net.
220 nic.sura.net FTP server (Version 2.0WU(10) Fri Apr 9 15:43:49 EDT  1993) ready.
Name (nic.sura.net:mozart): anonymous     Enter user name anonymous
331 Guest login ok, send your complete e-mail address as password.
Password:                                 Enter e-mail address as a password
230-
230 Guest login ok, access restrictions apply.
ftp> cd pub/nic/network.service.guides    Change to directory
                                          /pub/nic/network.service.guides

250 CWD command successful.
ftp> pwd                                  Display name of current directory
257 "/pub/nic/network.service.guides" is current directory.
ftp> mget how.to*                         Request files whose names
                                          begin with "how.to"

mget how.to.email.guide? y                Type y to confirm the selection
200 PORT command successful.
```

```
150 Opening BINARY mode data connection for how.to.email.guide (12759 bytes).
226 Transfer complete.
12759 bytes received in 3.31 seconds (3.76 Kbytes/s)
mget how.to.ftp.guide? y                    Type y to confirm the selection
200 PORT command successful.
150 Opening BINARY mode data connection for how.to.ftp.guide (6327 bytes).
226 Transfer complete.
6327 bytes received in 2.31 seconds (2.68 Kbytes/s)
mget how.to.telnet.guide? y                 Type y to confirm the selection
200 PORT command successful.
150 Opening BINARY mode data connection for how.to.telnet.guide (2818 bytes).
226 Transfer complete.
2818 bytes received in 0.98 seconds (2.81 Kbytes/s)
mget how.to.use.vi.guide? n                 Type n; don't retrieve that file
ftp> quit
221 Goodbye.
```

Figure 4.4   Using the ftp Command mget to Retrieve Files

————————————————End of Example 4.4————————————————

Working with Different File Types

ASCII and Binary

You can transfer files during an FTP session in one of two modes: *ASCII* or *binary*. You use ASCII mode to transfer files that are in text or ASCII format. That means the files contain plain printable text. All of the examples we've looked at so far dealt with text files. You may know that information is stored in a computer as a string of 1s or 0s. A sequence of eight 1s or 0s is called a **byte**, and a file is a collection of bytes. In an ASCII or text file each byte represents a character that we can view as text: letters, numerals, punctuation, and spaces.

In order to retrieve nontext files you need to send the command **binary** to the FTP site. Once you give the command **binary** it is in effect for the rest of the FTP session unless you give the command **ascii**. To transfer nontext files you give the ftp command **binary** before copying them. Files containing executable programs aren't text files because the bytes in a program don't represent characters, they represent instructions in a particular computer's machine language. Files in the native form for most word processors aren't text files because the information to indicate some of the characteristics of the document, such as font and style, is not represented by printable or ASCII characters. Several other types of files aren't text files. You can often tell by the last few letters of the name. Files whose names end with a dot (.) followed by **arc, exe, gif, gz, jpeg, lzh, sit, Z, zip**, or **zoo** are compressed files and you need to retrieve them using binary mode. Three examples are:

/mac/misc/medical/education/asthmaeducation.cpt.hqx at **archive.umich.edu**
/pub/work/fedwork.zip at **handicap.shel.isc-br.com**
/CLR/multiling/chinese/Dictionary/ecd.exe at **clr.nmsu.edu**.

Example 4.5 — Using ftp Commands binary and ascii 109

You can transfer files in either mode; in other words, ftp doesn't complain about it or stop you. However, you won't be able to use the file if it's copied without using the correct mode. If you happen to be using a Unix system and the remote system is also a Unix system, this isn't a problem. Files of either type are copied faithfully without your having to take any action. If the archive site isn't supported by a Unix system you have to be more careful. Remind yourself: If the file you want to transfer consists of text, give the command **ascii** before you give the command **get**, otherwise give the command **binary** before using **get**.

Example 4.5   Using ftp Commands binary and ascii

To demonstrate the use of the ftp commands **binary** and **ascii**, you'll retrieve an English-Chinese dictionary program, **ecd.exe**, and **ecd.doc**, which gives some information about the program. The program is designed to run on a MS-DOS computer system and won't work on others. The dictionary program and supporting files are contained in **ecd.exe**, which is also an example of a self-extracting archive. You bring the file to your computer system and type **ecd**. It expands and separates into the files necessary to support the dictionary. As before some responses from the ftp site are left out to conserve space, but take care to read them when you try Example 4.5, which is shown in Figure 4.5.

Here are the steps to follow:

1.   Start the session.

☞ **Type** ftp crl.nmsu.edu **and press** [Enter].

☞ **Type** anonymous **and press** [Enter].

☞ **Type your e-mail address and press** [Enter].

2.   Change to the **/CLR/multiling/chinese/Dictionary** directory and list the contents.

☞ **Type** /CLR/multiling/chinese/Dictionary **and press** [Enter].

☞ **Type** dir **and press** [Enter].

3.   Change to binary transfer mode.

☞ **Type** binary **and press** [Enter].

4.   Retrieve the file **ecd.exe**.

☞ **Type** get ecd.exe **and press** [Enter].

5.   Change to ASCII transfer mode.

☞ **Type** ascii **and press** [Enter].

6.   Retrieve the file **ecd.doc**.

☞ **Type** get ecd.doc **and press** [Enter].

7.   End the session.

☞ **Type** quit **and press** [Enter].

As you work through this example, your screen will look similar to the following:

```
ftp crl.nmsu.edu                          Start ftp session with crl.nmsu.edu
                                          Connected to crl.nmsu.edu
220-   Computer Research Laboratory Anonymous FTP
220-
220-Anonymous FTP users: Note that all transfers are logged.  If you
220-do not agree with this policy, then please disconnect.
220-                    Welcome to the FTP Archives of
220-             The Consortium for Lexical Research
220-        ftp site: clr.nmsu.edu [128.123.1.33]
220-
220-Change to the directory CLR.
220-The file "README.clr.site" is a helpful place to start.
220-
220-Materials only for CLR members are in the directory "members-only".
220-
220-For comments or additional information on CLR: lexical@crl.nmsu.edu.
220-
220 crl FTP server (Version 2.1WU(3) Fri Oct 8 15:08:25 MDT 1993) ready.
Name (crl.nmsu.edu:mozart): anonymous       Enter user name anonymous
331 Guest login ok, send your complete e-mail address as password.
Password:                                   Enter e-mail address as a
                                            password

230 Guest login ok, access restrictions apply.
Remote system type is UNIX.
Using binary mode to transfer files.
ftp> cd /CLR/multiling/chinese/Dictionary   Use cd to change to directory
                                            /CLR/multiling/chinese/Dictionary

250 CWD command successful.
ftp> dir                                    Type dir to list contents of
                                            current directory

200 PORT command successful.
150 Opening ASCII mode data connection for /bin/ls.
total 458
-rw-r--r--   1 139      124          1123 Feb 23 16:28 ecd.doc
-rw-r--r--   1 139      124        454529 Feb 23 16:29 ecd.exe
226 Transfer complete.
ftp> binary                                 Type binary to switch to
                                            binary transfer mode

200 Type set to I.
ftp> get ecd.exe                            Use get to retrieve the file
                                            ecd.exe

200 PORT command successful.
150 Opening BINARY mode data connection for ecd.exe (454529 bytes).
226 Transfer complete.
454529 bytes received in 120.43 seconds (3.69 Kbytes/s)
```

Example 4.5 — Using ftp Commands binary and ascii

III

```
ftp> ascii                              Type ascii to switch to ASCII
                                        transfer mode

200 Type set to A.
ftp> get ecd.doc                        Use get to retrieve the file
                                        ecd.doc

200 PORT command successful.
150 Opening ASCII mode data connection for ecd.doc (1123 bytes).
226 Transfer complete
1153 bytes received in 0.72 seconds (1.57 Kbytes/s)
ftp> quit                               Leave ftp program
221 Goodbye.
```

Figure 4.5   Using binary and ascii during an FTP Session

The program **ecd.exe** is shareware. If you retrieve it and find it useful, the author expects to be paid a relatively small amount for the time and work involved.

—————————————————————End of Example 4.5—————————————————

Compressed Files

Some files are stored in compressed form. This saves space and also reduces the time to transfer files. (Some programs such as PKZIP, used on MS-DOS systems, or StuffIt, on Macintosh systems, allow for the grouping or archiving of a collection of files, with the entire collection compressed.) These files must be transferred using the command **binary** since they are not text files. Once you get them to your system you have to use a program that expands them for use on your system.

You need to know the proper program to run to undo the compression. Usually the last character or last few characters of the file name indicate the program used to construct the compressed file or archive. The letters at the end of a file name following a dot (.) are called the *file extension* portion of the file name. In the file named **mrcry20.zip**, **zip** is the file extension. If the name of the file ends with **.zip** then some form of the program PKZIP was used to create it. The program you use to return the file to its original form depends on what type of computer system you're using. On a Unix system you'd use the program UNZIP, on a DOS system you'd use PKUNZIP, and on a Macintosh system you'd use ZipIt. The next paragraph mentions resources for dealing with compressed files. Several different forms of compression are used, and we can't list them all here. Some tips for dealing with compressed files are:

❑   The last few letters of a file name are often the clue that the file is in compressed form.

❑   Give the command **binary** before using the command **get** to retrieve a file.

❑   Find someone locally who can help you with compressed files.

❑   Use anonymous FTP to get copies of these files to read about the compression formats used.

File	Site	Directory
faq	**rtfm.mit.edu**	**/pub/usenet-by-group/news.answers/ftp-list**
compression	**ftp.cso.uiuc.edu**	**/doc/pcnet**

There are many different compression schemes and each has a corresponding program to compress a file or undo the compression. One good source of information on this topic is the file **compression** maintained by David Lemson, available by anonymous FTP from **ftp.cso.uiuc.edu** in the directory **/doc/pcnet**. The file contains a table including the name of a compression scheme, the extension attached to the name of a compressed file (you use this to know the program to use to uncompress it), and the names of the compression programs for several different types of computer systems. It also gives sources on the Internet for the compression programs. Two anonymous FTP sources for many of the compression programs are **archive.umich.edu** (University of Michigan) and **garbo.uwasa.fi** (University of Wasa, Helsinki, Finland). At **archive.umich.edu** look in the directories **msdos/compression** and **mac/util/compression**. The latter directory contains the file **00index.txt**, which explains each of the programs at the archive. At **garbo.uwasa.fi** the directories **pub/mac/arcers**, **pub/pc/arcers**, and **pub/unix/arcers** are good places to look for information and sources dealing with compression.

Example 4.6   Retrieving a Compressed File and Compression Program

In this example, shown in Figure 4.6, you'll retrieve a compressed file as well as a program for uncompressing it. These files contain programs for MS-DOS computer systems. The programs are also shareware. That means you're free to use them on a trial basis, and the authors expect to be paid if you think the programs are useful.

To set the scene for this example, suppose that you need a program to do some math calculations including solving equations and graphing. You've been told a good program for doing this is in the file **mrcry209.zip** in **/pc/math** at **garbo.uwasa.fi**. You recognize by its name that the file is compressed and after doing some reading you know that you need a copy of PKUNZIP. As before some responses from the FTP site are left out to conserve space.

The steps in this example are as follows:

1. Start an anonymous FTP session with **garbo.uwasa.fi.**

☞ **Type** `ftp garbo.uwasa.fi` **and press** [Enter].

☞ **Type** `anonymous` **and press** [Enter].

☞ **Type your e-mail address and press** [Enter].

2. Use the ftp command **cd** to change to the directory **/pc/math**.

☞ **Type** `cd /pc/math` **and press** [Enter].

3. Use the ftp command **binary** to switch to binary transfer mode.

☞ **Type** `binary` **and press** [Enter].

4. Use the ftp command **get** to retrieve the file **mrcry209.zip**.

☞ **Type** `get mrcry209.zip` **and press** [Enter].

5. Use the ftp command **cd** to change to the directory **/pc/arcers**.

Example 4.6 — Retrieving a Compressed File and Compression Program ——— 113

☞ **Type** `cd /pc/arcers` **and press** Enter.

6. Use the ftp command **get** to retrieve the file **pkz204g.exe**.

☞ **Type** `get pkz204g.exe` **and press** Enter.

7. Quit the FTP session.

☞ **Type** `quit` **and press** Enter.

As you work through this example, your screen will look similar to the following:

```
$ ftp garbo.uwasa.fi                    Start ftp session with garbo.uwasa.fi
Connected to garbo.uwasa.fi.
220->
220-> Welcome to Garbo ftp archives at the University of Vaasa, Finland!
220-
220 garbo FTP server (Version wu-2.4(5) Fri Apr 22 11:42:44 EET DST 1994) ready.
Name (garbo.uwasa.fi:mozart): anonymous Enter user name anonymous
331 Guest login ok, send your complete e-mail address as password.
Password:                               Enter e-mail address as a password
230->
230-> There are currently 32 users connected to our archives (max 100)
230-
230 Guest login ok, access restrictions apply.
ftp> cd /pc/math                        Use cd to change to directory /pc/math
250- /pc/math Mathematical programs
250-
250- Highlights:
250- mrcry*.zip  Equation solver based on Borland's Eureka.  Excellent.
250-
250 CWD command successful.
ftp> binary                             Type binary for binary transfer mode
200 Type set to I.
ftp> get mrcry209.zip                    Use get to retrieve the file mrcry209.zip
200 PORT command successful.
150 Opening BINARY mode data connection for mrcry209.zip (296952 bytes).
226 Transfer complete.
296952 bytes received in 491.76 seconds (0.59 Kbytes/s)
ftp> cd /pc/arcers                      Use cd to change to directory /pc/arcers
250- /pc/arcers MsDos archiving (compression) programs
250-
250- If you do not already have it, you'll need the self-extracting
250- pkz204g.exe to handle the zipped files you download from Garbo.
250-
250 CWD command successful.
ftp> get pkz204g.exe                     Use get to retrieve the file pkz204g.exe
```

```
200 PORT command successful.
150 Opening BINARY mode data connection for pkz204g.exe (202574 bytes).
226 Transfer complete.
202574 bytes received in 267.96 seconds (0.74 Kbytes/s)
ftp> quit                              Leave ftp program
221 Goodbye.
```

Figure 4.6   Retrieving a Compressed Archive and a Compression Program

The next few steps don't have to do with FTP, but they provide an example of what needs to be done to make the files you've retrieved usable.

1. Get the compression program ready to run. The file **pkz204g.exe** can be run directly on an MS-DOS computer system, because its name ends with **.exe**. You may want to move it to a special directory. When it's in place type **pkz204g** and press Enter. You'll see that this is a self-extracting archive—as the program executes it will uncompress and create the necessary programs.
2. Apply the compression/uncompression program to the compressed file. In this case type **pkunzip mrcry20.zip** to extract the necessary files.
3. Work with the uncompressed files. It's a good idea to first read any file that contains a user guide or other documentation. After that you can run the program by typing **mercury** and pressing Enter.

Archived Files

Sometimes files are collected together in an archive format. This is useful when several related files need to be treated as a unit. The compression program PKZIP from Example 4.6 does exactly that. Other popular programs are BinHex and Stuffit for Macintosh systems, shar and tar for Unix systems, and gzip for Unix, MS-DOS, and Macintosh systems.

Common File Extensions

Table 4.1 explains some common file extensions and notes where the compression is for specific computer systems.

Extension	Transfer Mode	Explanation
.arc	binary	The file is in compressed mode. May also be a collection of files in an archive. Usually from a DOS system. Use a version of arc to unarchive the file(s).
.gif or **.jpg**	binary	The file contains an image. You'll need a viewing program to see the image.
.gz	binary	The file is in compressed mode using gzip.
.Hqx	binary	The file is in compressed or archived mode for a Macintosh. Use BinHex to uncompress.
.lzh	binary	The file is in compressed mode using some variation of the LHarc compression scheme.

.ps	ascii	The file is in PostScript form, to be viewed or printed. Be sure you can view or print PostScript.
.shar	ascii	This is a shell archive, usually from a Unix system. Use **sh** to unpack the files.
.sit	binary	This was compressed for a Macintosh using the program StuffIt or the shareware version StuffItLite.
.tar	binary	This is a collection of files archives with the program tar, often found on Unix systems. Use **tar xvf file-name** to unarchive **file-name.tar**.
.txt or **.text**	ascii	The file is in text format.
.uue	ascii	This is in ASCII or text format so it can be sent as e-mail. It contains information that isn't in text form. Need **uudecode** to convert to proper form.
.Z	binary	This was compressed using the Unix program named compress. You can use versions of compress or uncompress for various types of systems.
.zip	binary	This was compressed and archived using pkzip or some variation. Often used on DOS systems. Could also contain a collection of files.

Table 4.1   Common File Extensions

Reading and Understanding Citations to FTP Resources

In order to retrieve a file by anonymous FTP you need to know three things:

1. The name of the anonymous FTP site
2. The name of the directory that holds the file
3. The name of the file

Several forms of notation are used to specify this information. An informal method might be a reference from an e-mail message from a friend:

```
"I found the summary of the proceedings from the conference Technology,
Scholarship, and the Humanities. Its available by anonymous ftp at ftp.cni.org
in summary.txt, in the directory /CNI/documents/tech.schol.human."
```

In this case:

1. The anonymous FTP site is **ftp.cni.org**.
2. The directory is **/CNI/documents/tech.schol.human**.
3. The file is **summary.txt**.

To retrieve the information you would enter:

```
ftp ftp.cni.org                        Start FTP session
anonymous                              Give user name anonymous
                                       Give e-mail address as the
                                       password
cd /CNI/documents/tech.schol.human     Change to the directory
get summary.txt                        Retrieve the file
quit                                   End the FTP session
```

A more formal way to write a citation to a file available by anonymous FTP is with a **Uniform Reference Locator** or **URL**. A URL for the file mentioned above would be

```
ftp://ftp.cni.org/CNI/documents/tech.schol.human/summary.txt
```

or

```
file://ftp.cni.org/CNI/documents/tech.schol.human/summary.txt
```

1. The name of the FTP site follows the three characters ://.
2. The name of the directory starts with the first single / and goes up to but not including the last /.
3. The name of the file follows the last /.

The general form for this is:

```
ftp://name-of-ftp-site/directory-name/file-name
```

or

```
file://name-of-ftp-site/directory-name/file-name
```

You can also use a URL to refer to a directory by putting a / as the last character in a URL. For example,

```
"the papers from the conference Technology, Scholarship and the Humanities are
in ftp://ftp.cni.org/CNI/documents/tech.schol.human/papers/"
```

Sources of Information about ftp and FTP Archives

Here is a list of files (available by anonymous FTP) that are useful in working with ftp:

ftp://ftp.cso.uiuc.edu/doc/pcnet/compression

A chart to use as a guide for working with compressed files. Also contains the locations of various compression programs.

ftp://rtfm.mit.edu/pub/usenet-by-group/news.answers/ftp/faq
ftp://ftp.mwc.edu/internet.info/ftp/faq

Anonymous FTP Frequently Asked Questions (FAQ) List. Frequently asked questions *and* answers, about anonymous FTP. Very useful.

ftp://rtfm.mit.edu/pub/usenet-by-group/news.answers/ftp/

A large collection of names of anonymous FTP sites along with a topical description list of the files they have. The name given here is a directory. The list is in nine separate files.

ftp://ftp.bio.indiana.edu/help/bitnet-ftp.help

Gives step-by-step instructions for using anonymous FTP by e-mail. Useful for users who have only e-mail access to the Internet. Originally written for BITNET users.

E-Mail Access to FTP Archives

You can access anonymous FTP sites using e-mail, which is particularly useful if your only access to the Internet is by e-mail. You send a message that contains ftp commands to an address on the Internet. That address represents a computer program, which will convert your e-mail into ftp commands and then mail the results back to you. An address for e-mail access to ftp is **ftpmail@decwrl.dec.com**. Send an e-mail message that contains only the word **help** to that address to get a list of all the commands you can use to access ftp by e-mail.

We've seen before how to retrieve via anonymous FTP the file specified as **ftp://nic.merit.edu/ introducing.the.internet/answers.to.new.user.questions**. You type the following:

```
ftp nic.merit.edu
anonymous
<type your e-mail address>
cd introducing.the.internet
get answers.to.new.user.questions
quit
```

To get the same file by e-mail send the following e-mail message to **ftpmail@decwrl.dec.com**:

```
connect nic.merit.edu
ascii
chdir introducing.the.internet
get answers.to.new.user.questions
quit
```

You'll get an e-mail response to let you know that your request has been received and accepted. If you've made a mistake in the commands you'll get a copy of the help file explaining all the commands you can use. To get a copy of the help file send e-mail to **ftpmail@decwrl.dec.com**, with **help** as your entire message.

You'll receive the file(s) you've requested by e-mail. It may take from a few minutes to several hours or days to receive your file. The returned file may be broken into parts; there is a maximum size of 64K bytes for one e-mail message by ftpmail. If the file you want needs to be retrieved in binary mode you can choose the means by which it will be sent through e-mail: either uuencode or btoa. These programs encode the information in the file so that it can be sent via e-mail. You'll have to use either **uudecode** or **xbtoa** to decode the files once you receive them. Decide which to use based on what is available on your computer system.

There are other ftpmail servers you can use. A list is in the file **ftp://rtfm.mit.edu/pub/usenet-by-group/news.answers/ftp/faq**.

Summary

We've looked at using the command **ftp** to copy files from anonymous FTP archives to your computer system. When you want to retrieve a file by anonymous FTP you need to know

❑ the name of the file

❑ the name of the directory that holds the file

❑ the Internet name of the anonymous FTP site hosting the file

You also need to know if the file contains only plain text or if it's in some other form. If it's a text file, it can be transferred in ASCII mode. Otherwise you need to give the ftp command **binary** before you copy it to your system. If the archive site is a Unix system, you don't have to worry about setting the transfer mode.

Here are the steps you follow to retrieve a file:

1. Start session with the command **ftp** followed by the name of the anonymous FTP site.
2. Give the user name **anonymous** when the remote site prompts for name.
3. Give your **e-mail address** when the remote site prompts for password.
4. Use the ftp command **cd** to change or move to the directory that holds the file.
5. Give the command **ascii** or **binary** to set the transfer mode.
6. Use the ftp command **get** to retrieve the file.
7. Give the ftp command **quit** to end the FTP session.

Be careful that the names you type are correct in terms of upper- or lowercase letters, spelling, and punctuation. Citations or references to files available by anonymous FTP are often given as a **URL** or **Uniform Resource Locator** in the following form:

```
ftp://name-of-ftp-site/directory-name/file-name
```

To make the steps concrete we'll retrieve two files noted as:

```
ftp://ftp.eff.org/pub/Net_info/gender_in_networking.paper
ftp://ftp.eff.org/pub/Publications/CuD/Papers/gender-issues.gz
```

You enter

ftp ftp.eff.org	Step 1
anonymous	Step 2
your.e-mail.address	Step 3
cd /pub/Net_info	Step 4
ascii	Step 5—optional for Unix systems
get gender_in_networking.paper	Step 6
cd /pub/Publications/CuD/Papers	Step 4
binary	Step 5—optional for Unix systems
get gender-issues.gz	Step 6
quit	Step 7

Other ftp commands you are likely to use are:

dir   Display the contents of the current directory

help or **?**   List available ftp commands or get help on a specific command, as in **help mget**

mget   Retrieve a collection of files. The characters ***** or **?** match portions of a name. Use ***** to match any sequence of characters and **?** to match a single character. Examples: **mget eag*.gif** or **mget eagle?.gif**

Files or collections of files are often stored in compressed form. You retrieve them with a binary transfer and then you need to use another program to uncompress and separate them.

Remember that anonymous FTP sites are supported as a service to Internet users. Individual sites may have policies that limit or restrict access depending on time of day or number of users. Respect the policies and wishes stated at anonymous FTP sites.

Exercises

Retrieving files containing information for FTP users

1. This exercise gives you the chance to retrieve the **Readme** files at a few sites and see a sampling of what's available on the Internet.

    Retrieve and read each of the following files:
    a. **/pub/README at ftp.loc.gov**
        URL **ftp://ftp.loc.gov/pub/README**
    b. **/pub/README at lajkonik.cyf-kr.edu.pl**
        URL **ftp://lajkonik.cyf-kr.edu.pl/pub/README**
    c. **/pub/mac/00README at ftp.primate.wisc.edu**
        URL **ftp://ftp.primate.wisc.edu/pub/mac/00README**
    d. **/pub/Graphics/00README at princeton.edu**
        URL **ftp://princeton.edu/pub/Graphics/00README**

2. This chapter listed two sources for the Anonymous FTP Frequently Asked Questions (FAQ) List. (**URL ftp://rtfm.mit.edu/pub/usenet-by-group/news.answers/ftp-list/faq**, and **URL ftp://ftp.mwc.edu/internet.info/ftp/faq**.) Retrieve a copy of that document from one of those sources. Read it and save it.

3. The file **ftp-primer.txt** in the directory **/info-mac/comm/info** at **sumex-aim.stanford.edu** (URL **ftp://sumex-aim.stanford.edu/info-mac/comm/info/ftp-primer.txt**) has a lot of useful information about using FTP. Get a copy of the file and read it. What did it tell you about FTP that you didn't know?

4. a. Retrieve the file **netiquette.txt** from **nic.sura.net** in the directory **/pub/nic/InternetLiterature**.
    b. What does that document have to say about FTP? List the rules it contains regarding anonymous FTP.

Using ftp through e-mail

5. This chapter shows you how to use e-mail to retrieve a file from an anonymous FTP archive.
    a. Use that method to retrieve the file mentioned in Exercise 4.
    b. Write down the time you sent the e-mail message. When you receive a reply, check the **Received:** header to see when the file was received by your systems. How long did it take to get a file this way?

Finding files and directories

6. The lyrics and chords to several songs by The Beatles are in the directory **/ftp/mirrors/ uunet/doc/music/guitar/b** at **unix.hensa.ac.uk.**. Use anonymous FTP to retrieve one of the songs. (If that site is too busy try **ftp.uu.net** and look in the directory **/pub/doc/ music/guitar/b**.)

7. a. Write down the steps necessary to retrieve the file named **health-care.Z** from the directory **/usenet/news/answers/dogs-faq** at **ftp.uu.net**.
    b. Retrieve the file. It is compressed. If you have a program that can uncompress it, do so now. You can get a version of it in uncompressed form from either **rtfm.mit.edu** in the directory **/pub/usenet-by-group/news.answers/dogs-faq**, from **grasp1.univ-lyon1.fr** in the directory **/pub/faqs/dog-faq**, or from **mrcnext.cso.uiuc.edu** in the directory **/pub/faq/usenet-by-group/ news.answers/dogs-faq**.
    c. A similar file, dealing with health care for cats, exists. Can you find it?

8. Using just a few sentences for each, describe the contents of the directories at the anonymous FTP sites listed below.
    a. URL   **ftp://saul5.u.washington.edu/pub/user-supported/virtual-worlds**
    b. URL   **ftp://quartz.rutgers.edu/pub/nyc**
    c. URL   **ftp://locust.cic.net/pub/Sports/Baseball**

9. Interested in music? Several anonymous FTP archives have a directory named **music**.
    a. Describe the contents of the directory **/pub/music** at **ftp.uwp.edu**.
    b. Compare the contents of **pub/uunet/doc/music** at **unix.hensa.ac.uk** (an alternate site is **ftp.uu.net** in the directory **/pub/doc/music**) with the directory in Part a.

The Internet and Resources on the Internet

10. Retrieve a copy of the file **ftp://nic.merit.edu/introducing.the.internet/ answers.to.new.user.questions**. Using that file write a one- or two-sentence answer to each of the following questions:
    a. What is the difference between the Internet and an internet?
    b. What is an advantage to the Domain Name System (DNS)?
    c. What is Archie?
    d. How is Archie different from ftp?
    e. What is Gopher?

11. Retrieve a copy of **ftp://life.anu.edu.au/pub/medical/ medical_resources_on_internet**.
    a. List three Listserv lists that are interesting to you.
    b. List three anonymous FTP sites mentioned in the document.
    c. List three electronic journals listed in the file.

12. Start an anonymous FTP session with **gatekeeper.dec.com** and go to the directory **/pub/recipes**.
    a. Use the command **mget** to retrieve all the files whose names start with **choc**.
    b. Use the command **mget** to retrieve only those files whose names contain the string **rice**, but don't retrieve any files whose names indicate that the recipe has to do with pecans or gumbo.
    c. Retrieve five recipe files whose names contain a **z**.
    d. Create a menu for a dinner using the recipes in this directory.

Projects

13. The Electronic Frontier Foundation maintains an anonymous FTP site at **ftp.eff.org**. The directory **/pub/eff/Issues** contains several directories holding files relating to censorship, copyright, and privacy.
    a. For each of those three topics, find two files that would be useful to someone wanting to do research in that area.
    b. Pick one of those topics and, using only the resources at **ftp.eff.org**, write a short report.

14. The FTP archive site asked **ftp.loc.gov** is maintained by the Library of Congress. In Exercise 1 you were to retrieve the file **README** from the directory /pub and read it.
    a. Using information in the file named **README**, what is in the directory **/pub/ exhibit.images**?
    b. Retrieve the file **ftp://ftp.loc.gov//pub/exhibit.images/vatican.exhibit/ WARNING**. How does it limit the use of the files in that directory?
    c. A description of the images in the collection for the exhibit "Rome Reborn: The Vatican Library and Renaissance Culture" is in the directory **ftp://ftp.loc.gov/pub/ exhibit.images/vatican.exhibit/**. Retrieve the file **README** from that directory to see how the exhibit is arranged within the directory.
    d. After reading it go to the directory **/pub/exhibit.images/vatican.exhibit/exhibit/ g-nature**. Retrieve the file **Nature.txt** and at least one of the files containing an image. View the image. (If you don't have the software to view an image on your system, you can find several at **ftp://ftp.loc.gov//pub/exhibit.images/ vatican.exhibit/viewers**.)

E-Mail Group Discussion
Discussion Lists, Interest Groups, Listserv, and Mailing Lists

You already know that electronic mail allows you to communicate with other users on the Internet. It's natural that people with a common interest should form groups to discuss issues, share information, or ask questions related to a common topic or theme. The groups go by different names: discussion lists, interest groups, Listserv, or mailing lists. In this chapter we'll use the term *interest group* or *list* to refer to any of these types of groups. You'll find there are over 6,000 different lists covering a wide range of topics.

All communication within an interest group is carried on by e-mail. A user joins or subscribes to a group and then shares in the discussions of the group. A message sent to the group is usually broadcast via e-mail to all members of the group. So these discussions are public. There is an exception; some groups are *moderated* and a message sent to the group is first routed to the person serving as moderator. (The moderator either sends the message on to the group or takes some other action.) Some groups are very large, with thousands of subscribers, and some are very diverse, with members throughout the world. If you subscribe to an active group you can expect many e-mail messages per day. You'll find members at all levels of experience.

Being a member of an interest group means that you can join in discussions, ask questions, help others with questions, make announcements related to the group, or just see what others are talking about. You don't have to respond to every message; you can use your e-mail system just to read or even ignore some of the discussions. It's usually a good idea just to read messages when you first join a group so you can get an idea of the general tone and level of the discussion. Some folks use the term *lurking* to describe the behavior of observing the discussions. Lurking is just fine; it may be exactly what you want.

Discussions in the interest group should be carried on in a polite and civil manner. Occasionally someone gets upset about what someone else has written, and sends a message to the group that insults, scolds, berates, or is downright nasty about the author of the original message. This type of message is called a *flame*. To keep things from getting out of hand users sometimes need to be reminded to calm down or tone down their remarks. When you're ready you can send a message to the group (this is called *posting* a message), reply to the individual author of a message, or send a reply to the group. Replying to the group means your message goes to everyone on the list.

Most of the management of a list, tasks like adding new members or subscribers, removing members who choose to leave or *unsubscribe* from a list, and other tasks, is handled automatically by software (a collection of one or more computer programs) running on the computer that serves as the host system for the list. This software maintains the files associated with the list and responds to commands from the membership. As a member of a list you usually can retrieve archives or collections of past discussions, get a list of the current members, and ask that the mail of the list be sent to you in one packet, called a *digest,* at regular intervals instead of getting each message individually. All of these functions or other requests for service are handled by commands you send to an e-mail address, called the *administrative address*, which passes the command on to the software managing the list. Since these requests are satisfied automatically by a computer program, the requests need to be in a specific form that can be understood by the software.

When you're a member of a list you need to know two addresses, and you need to know when to use them:

1. The address of the list, sometimes called the *list address* or *group address*. This is the address you'll use to communicate with the list. When you send e-mail to this address, the mail is delivered to all members of the list.
2. The address to request services from or give commands to the manager of the list. This address is sometimes called the *administrative address* of the list. Most lists are automatically managed by software, such as Listserv or Listproc, so the commands are executed automatically by software. Some lists are maintained and managed entirely by individuals or groups of users. These services or commands allow you to subscribe, unsubscribe, receive messages in digest form, retrieve a list of members, request archives, etc. This administrative address is the same address you use to join or subscribe to the list.

It's easy to make a mistake and confuse the two. If you send a request to the list that should have gone to the other address, a member of the list will usually remind you of the correct address. If you send a message that's passed on to the managing software but was meant for the members of the list, you'll usually get a reply back indicating the message wasn't in the proper form.

The following figure shows the relationship among you, the list or group, and the software managing the list.

REQUESTS FOR SERVICES, SUCH AS
JOINING A GROUP, ARE SENT TO THE
ADMINISTRATIVE ADDRESS

ONCE YOU JOIN, MESSAGES FOR THE GROUP ARE SENT
DIRECTLY TO THE LIST ADDRESS

Chapter Overview

In this chapter we'll cover the details of working with lists:

❑   How to Join a List

❑   How to Communicate with and Contribute to the List

❑   How to Leave a List

❑   How to Request Services from the Software that Manages the List

❑   How to Find the Names and Addresses of Lists

❑   Proper Etiquette or Behavior Within an Interest Group

❑   Internet Sources of Information of Interest Lists

There are five prevalent types of software used to maintain interest groups: Listserv, Listproc, Mailbase, Mailserv, and Majordomo. We'll concentrate on them in the sections below. These systems all allow the same kinds of services, and we'll mention differences between them. You can usually tell which software manages the list by looking at the administrative address, the address you use to subscribe to the list. For example, if the address is **mailserv@coco.site.edu** (a fictitious address), Mailserv is being used. The type of software maintaining the list is chosen when the list is created; it isn't a decision each member can make. You generally don't need to worry about which software maintains the list, but you should be aware of the differences. Some lists aren't managed by software; all functions and services are dealt with by one or more administrators. In these cases most of the commands you'll send to the administrative address will be in ordinary prose form—real sentences! You can usually get help from other members of the list, and you'll get some instructions about using the services of a list when you join.

How to Join a List

In order to join a list you need to send e-mail to the administrative address for the list. The e-mail should contain the word **SUBSCRIBE** and the name of the list. For most lists you also need to include your full name (first name last name), unless you're subscribing to a list that's managed by Majordomo. Here are some interest lists on the Internet. You can tell the type of software used to administer the list from the administrative or list address.

List name:	BIRDCHAT
Administrative address:	**listserv@arizvm1.ccit.arizona.edu**
List address:	**BIRDCHAT@arizvm1.ccit.arizona.edu**
Brief description:	Discussions related to birding, birding activities, and birding experiences. This list deals with wild birds; please, no messages dealing with pets.
To Join:	Send e-mail to **LISTSERV@arizvm1.ccit.arizona.edu** with the message **subscribe BIRDCHAT Your Full Name** For example: **subscribe BIRDCHAT Chris Athana**

List name:	PHOTO-L
Administrative address:	**listproc@csuohio.edu**
List address:	**PHOTO-L@csuohio.edu**
Brief description:	Unmoderated open noncommercial discussion of all aspects of photography.
To join:	Send e-mail to **listproc@csuohio.edu** with the message **subscribe PHOTO-L Your Full Name** For example: **subscribe PHOTO-L Chris Athana**

List name:	SOFC
Administrative address:	**mailbase@mailbase.ac.uk**
List address:	**SOFC@mailbase.ac.uk**
Brief description:	Discussions related to solid oxide fuel cells.
To join:	Send e-mail to **mailbase@ mailbase.ac.uk** with the message **subscribe SOFC Your Full Name** For example: **subscribe SOFC Chris Athana**

List name:	CADUCEUS-L
Administrative address:	**mailserv@beach.utmb.edu**
List address:	**CADUCEUS-L@beach.utmb.edu**
Brief description:	A discussion group dedicated to anything dealing with the history of health sciences.
To join:	Send e-mail to **mailserv@beach.utmb.edu** with the message **subscribe CADUCEUS-L your full name** For example: **subscribe CADUCEUS-L Chris Athana**

List name:	F-COSTUME
Administrative address:	**majordomo@lunch.engr.sgi.com**
List address:	**F-COSTUME@lunch.engr.sgi.com**

Brief description:	Concentrates on design, motivation and execution of fantasy costumes.
To join:	Send e-mail to **majordomo@lunch.engr.sgi.com** with the message **subscribe F-COSTUME**

Note: Some versions of Majordomo software don't allow you to include your full name as part of the request to join the list. You do have the option of including your e-mail address. If you subscribe to a Majordomo list and include your full name, it may be OK. If not, you'll receive some automatically generated e-mail indicating that the version of Majordomo couldn't understand your request. Try again with a message in the form subscribe name-of-list.

Regardless of the type of list, remember you're not writing something for another person to read. You're giving a command to some software and the command has to be in a specific form. Also, you don't have to supply your e-mail address. Since you've sent e-mail to the administrative address, your e-mail address is part of the message. The software that manages the list takes your name and address and adds them to the list of members.

What Happens Next?

You ought to receive a response from the software managing the list within a few minutes, hours, or maybe a day or two. That is, of course, provided you've used the proper address and the list still exists. If the address isn't correct you'll probably have your mail returned as undeliverable or you'll get e-mail saying that the list doesn't exist at the site. But if you have used the proper address you'll get a response saying either you've succeeded in subscribing to the list or you've made some error in the message you sent to the administrative address. If there is some error then look up the address once more and try again.

Let's assume you've succeeded in subscribing to the list, and you've received e-mail about the list. In some cases you'll be asked to confirm your request to join or subscribe, but in most cases you'll receive an immediate e-mail message welcoming you to the list. SAVE THE WELCOME MESSAGE! It usually contains important information about leaving or unsubscribing from the list, and other commands to use to request services from the software that manages the list. It also tells you how to get more information. Once again, SAVE THAT MESSAGE! You'll probably want it and need it sometime in the future.

Figure 5.1 is a sample of the type of message you'll receive. It's from Listserv and it's for the fictitious list BOBOOTN. (The name was chosen just to demonstrate the message you might receive from the software managing the list.) You'll get a different but similar type of e-mail message from other list software. In any case, SAVE THAT MESSAGE!

```
Subject:     Your subscription to list BOBOOTN
To: Chris Athana <cathana@nice.place.edu>
Reply-To:  BOBOOTN-Request@listspot.coco.EDU

Dear networker,

Your subscription to list BOBOOTN (BOBO's on the Net) has been accepted.
```

Subscription has been accepted!

The next paragraph contains information about leaving the list.

You may leave the list at any time by sending a "SIGNOFF BOBOOTN" command to LISTSERV@LISTSPOT.BITNET (or LISTSERV@LISTSPOT.ABC.EDU). Please note that this command must NOT be sent to the list address(BOBOOTN@LISTSPOT.ABC.EDU)but to the LISTSERV address (LISTSERV@LISTSPOT.ABC.EDU).

Administrative address.

List address.

The amount of acknowledgment you wish to receive from this list upon completion of a mailing operation can be changed by means of a "SET BOBOOTN option" command, where "option" may be either "ACK" (mail acknowledgment), "MSGACK" (interactive messages only) or "NOACK".

Contributions sent to this list are automatically archived. You can obtain a list of the available archive files by sending an "INDEX BOBOOTN" command to LISTSERV@LISTSPOT.BITNET (or LISTSERV@LISTSPOT.ABC.EDU). These files can then be retrieved by means of a "GET BOBOOTN filetype" command, or using the database search facilities of LISTSERV. Send an "INFO DATABASE" command for more information on the latter.

Please note that it is presently possible for other people to determine that you are signed up to the list through the use of the "REVIEW" command, which returns the network address and name of all the subscribers. If you do not wish your name to be available to others in this fashion, just issue a "SET BOBOOTN CONCEAL" command.

More information on LISTSERV commands can be found in the LISTSERV reference card, which you can retrieve by sending an "INFO REFCARD" command to LISTSERV@LISTSPOT.BITNET (or LISTSERV@LISTSPOT.ABC.EDU).

Virtually,

How to get more information.

The LISTSERV management

Figure 5.1   Welcome Message from LISTSERV—Very Important!

How to Communicate with and Contribute to the List

Send e-mail to the list address if you want all the members of the list or group to receive it. Don't send e-mail meant for the members of the list to the administrative address. E-mail that's sent to the list address is either sent to all members of the list, or sent to a moderator who may or may not distribute the message to the rest of the group.

One other address you may need is the address of the *list owner* or *moderator*. You'll probably get that address with your "welcome to the group" e-mail. Write to the owner or moderator when you have questions about the nature of the list, if you think something is wrong with the list, or to volunteer to help the moderator.

Some lists allow you to send a message to the list only from the same address you used to join or subscribe to the list. That is a strict policy; some users access the Internet from a network of systems and they may not always be using a system with the same address. If you have problems sending or posting a message to a list, trying posting a message from the address you used to subscribe to the list.

Sometimes you may want to send a reply to a message you've received from a member of the list. You can send e-mail that either goes to everyone in the group or only to the one who originated the message. The program you use for e-mail will allow you to *reply* to a message. If you reply to a message from the group it will be sent to all the members of the group. You'll have to decide whether to reply to the list or to the individual. It's not OK to respond to the list when you meant to respond to the individual. You will most likely be reminded by other members of the list that you made a mistake. If you see a message on the list that was obviously meant for an individual, you might want to send a gentle reminder to the person who made the mistake.

How can you tell if a message came from a list or from an individual? Look at the e-mail headers **Reply-To:**, **From:**, or **To:**. Each e-mail message carries with it a collection of *headers* that include information about who will receive the reply (**Reply-To:**), who sent the message (**From:**), and to whom the message was sent (**To:**). If an e-mail message has the header **Reply-To:**, the address after **Reply-To:** is the address your e-mail program uses when you choose the reply option or operation. You find the address of the person who sent the original message by looking at the header **From:**. You can also look at the header **To:** to see if the e-mail was sent to all members of the list or especially to you. Figure 5.2 shows the pertinent information.

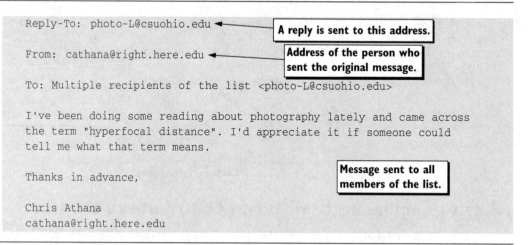

Figure 5.2   Example Message to an Internet Group

Here are two responses. The first is the proper type of response that ought to go to either the individual sending the original message (**cathana@right.here.edu**) or to the entire list. Since the response might benefit everyone on the list it's appropriate to reply to the list.

```
The term "hyperfocal distance" usually means the closest distance that's in
focus when the lens is focused at infinity. You can get more information about
```

```
this term and others you might be interested in by reading
Photographic_Lenses_FAQ , in the directory /pub/usenet-by-group.rec.photo, at
rtfm.mit.edu. Its available by anonymous ftp. Here is the URL
ftp://rtfm.mit.edu/pub/usenet/rec.photo.help/Photographic_lenses_FAQ
```

This next response should be sent only to the person who sent the original message (**cathana@right.here.edu**), *definitely not* to the entire list. Chris may appreciate the message, but other members won't.

```
Chris,

    How are you? I haven't heard from you in a while. Send me some e-mail
and I'll give you the answers to all your questions.

J. Richmond - richster@far.away.com
```

How to Leave a List

To leave or unsubscribe from a list send e-mail to the *administrative address*. The message needs to have the name of the list you want to leave since several lists may be managed by the same software at a site. The name of the list is represented by LIST-NAME below. In most cases you need to send the e-mail message to leave or unsubscribe from the same Internet address you used to join the list. If you have difficulty leaving a list, write to the list owner or moderator. Remember to unsubscribe or leave by sending e-mail to the administrative address, *not* the list address.

In the case of Listserv and Listproc you send the message:

```
unsubscribe LIST-NAME
```

In the case of Mailbase you send the message:

```
Leave LIST-NAME
```

If Mailserv or Majordomo is being used to manage a list, you may have to include your e-mail address, if you gave it when you joined the list or if you're leaving from different address. Send either the message:

```
unsubscribe LIST-NAME
```

or

```
unsubscribe LIST-NAME YOUR-CURRENT-E-MAIL-ADDRESS
```

Here is how to leave each of the lists mentioned before. We're assuming the Internet address was used for subscribing or joining the list.

List name:	BIRDCHAT
Send e-mail to:	**listserv@arizvm1.ccit.arizona.edu**
Message:	**unsubscribe BIRDCHAT**

List name:	PHOTO-L
Send e-mail to:	**listproc@csuohio.edu**
Message:	**unsubscribe PHOTO-L**

List name: SOFC
Send e-mail to: **mailbase@ mailbase.ac.uk**
Message: **leave SOFC**

List name: CADUCEUS-L
Send e-mail to: **mailserv@ Beach.UTMB.Edu**
Message: **unsubscribe CADUCEUS -L**
         or **unsubscribe CADUCEUS -L cathana@right.here.edu**

List name: F-COSTUME
Send e-mail to: **majordomo@lunch.engr.sgi.com**
Message: **unsubscribe F-COSTUME**
         or **unsubscribe F-COSTUME cathana@right.here.edu**

Requesting Services from the Software that Manages a List

Lists and interest groups generally offer a number of services to their members. In some cases all the messages to a list are archived or saved so members can retrieve them at any time. Lists generally also allow a member to specify the way she receives mail from the group, such as one at a time or in digest form. We'll explain some of the services a list provides as well as the commands used to get the services. All the commands are sent by e-mail to the administrative address. That way the commands may be detected by the software that manages the list. Sending a command to the list generally does nothing except to have several members of the list reply with reminders that the commands were sent to the wrong address.

Getting Help and a List of All Commands

Send a simple message:

```
HELP
```

to the administrative address and you'll receive, again by e-mail, a list of all the commands you can use with the list. This works for any type of software managing a list. Some lists also provide a reference card, really e-mail, that explains all the commands. If the managing software is Listserv send the command:

```
INFO REFCARD
```

to any system that supports Listserv. From the example in the previous sections you could send that message to **listserv@arizvm1.ccit.arizona.edu**. Another site is **listserv@bitnic.educom.edu**. If you subscribe to a list managed by Mailbase, you'll be sent a reference card along with other messages welcoming you to the list.

Getting a List of Subscribers

To find out who else has subscribed to a list or check the name and e-mail address you used to subscribe to a list, send a command to the administrative address. Some lists don't allow their membership to be made public; most lists allow each member to specify whether to make her name and e-mail address available. Table 5.1 gives the commands to use to get a list of subscribers (if available). Substitute the name of the list for *LIST-NAME* and send the command to the administrative address. You'll see that almost all will understand the command **REVIEW**.

List Type	Command
Listproc	REVIEW *LIST-NAME*
	or RECIPIENTS *LIST-NAME*
Listserv	REVIEW *LIST-NAME*
Mailbase	REVIEW *LIST-NAME*
Mailserv	SEND/LIST *LIST-NAME*
Majordomo	WHO *LIST-NAME*

Table 5.1   Getting a List of Subscribers

Hiding Your Name from the List of Subscribers

You can keep your name and e-mail address from appearing on the list of subscribers if the list type is Listproc or Listserv. This is similar to having an unlisted telephone number. In Table 5.2 substitute the specific list name for *LIST-NAME* and send the command as e-mail to the administrative address for the list.

List Type	Command
Listproc	SET *LIST-NAME* CONCEAL YES
	SET *LIST-NAME* CONCEAL NO—use this to make your name visible again.
Listserv	SET *LIST-NAME* CONCEAL
	SET *LIST-NAME* NOCONCEAL—use this to make your name visible again.

Table 5.2   Hiding Your Name from the List of Subscribers

Temporarily Suspending Messages

There may be times you want to suspend receiving messages from a list, perhaps times you go on vacation or are away from the Internet for some time. You want to remain a member of the list, but you don't want any mailings. (Of course you can unsubscribe to suspend messages, but then you have to join again to start receiving messages.) You substitute the specific name of the list for *LIST-NAME* in Table 5.3 and send the command to the administrative address. This service isn't supported with Mailserv or Majordomo.

List Type		Command
Listproc		SET *LIST-NAME* MAIL POSTPONE
	use	SET *LIST-NAME* MAIL to receive messages again.
Listserv		SET *LIST-NAME* NOMAIL
	use	SET *LIST-NAME* MAIL to receive messages again.
Mailbase		SUSPEND MAIL *LIST-NAME*
	use	RESUME MAIL *LIST-NAME* to receive messages again.

Table 5.3   Suspending Messages

Switching to Digest Mode

Switching to digest mode means you'll receive messages in a single daily or weekly mailing. Some people prefer this so they can work with messages from a group all at once, instead of receiving several messages during a day. It also helps to identify messages that come from one group. Mailbase and Mailserv don't provide this service. Table 5.4 shows the command(s) to use with each of the other types of lists. You substitute the name of a specific list for *LIST-NAME* and send the command by e-mail to the administrative address.

List Type		Command
Listproc		SET *LIST-NAME* MAIL DIGEST
	use	SET *LIST-NAME* MAIL ACK to cancel digest mode
Listserv		SET *LIST-NAME* DIGEST
	use	SET *LIST-NAME* MAIL to cancel digest mode
Majordomo		SUBSCRIBE *LIST-NAME*-DIGEST
		UNSUBSCRIBE *LIST-NAME*
	use	SUBSCRIBE *LIST-NAME*
		UNSUBSCRIBE *LIST-NAME*-DIGEST to cancel digest mode

Table 5.4   Switching to Digest Mode

Majordomo requires two commands, both included in the same message. The first subscribes to the list in digest mode. The second removes your name as a user to receive the messages as separate mailings.

Getting a List of Archived Files

Many lists are *archived*, which means that collections of past messages are kept so they can be retrieved by members. Some lists also keep collections of frequently asked questions (with answers) about the topics discussed on the list and other files useful to the group members. To get a list of the names of the files in a group's archives send e-mail containing the command:

```
INDEX LIST-NAME
```

to the administrative address for the list (except for Mailserv). Substitute the name of a specific list for *LIST-NAME*. For example, to get the archives for the list **F-COSTUME**, send the message:

```
INDEX F-COSTUME
```

to **majordomo@lunch.asd.sgi.com**.

If the list is managed by Mailserv software, send the command:

```
INDEX
```

to the administrative address.

Retrieving a File from the Archives of a List

You can retrieve any of the files in the list's archives by sending a command to the administrative address. The previous section described how to get a list of files; you might see something on the list you'd like to retrieve or someone tells you about a file that's kept in some list's archives.

You either use the command GET or the command SEND to retrieve a file from an archive (depending on the type of software that manages the list). Include the name of the list and the name of the file. Table 5.5 lists the commands to use for each type of software, and also includes an example. Substitute the specific name of a list for *LIST-NAME* and the specific name of a file for *FILE-NAME*. Remember to send your commands to the administrative address for the list.

List Type:	Listproc
Command:	GET *LIST-NAME FILE-NAME*
Example:	**GET PHOTO-L PHOTO-L.Sep-25**
List Type:	Listserv
Command:	GET *FILE-NAME FILE-TYPE LIST-NAME* F=MAIL
Example:	**GET AOU91 TXT BIRDCHAT F=MAIL**
	Listserv software also requires you to specify the type of the file, *FILE-TYPE*. This file type appears in the list of files in the archive.
List Type:	Mailbase
Command:	SEND *LIST-NAME FILE-NAME*
Example:	**SEND SOFC 04-1994**
List Type:	Mailserv
Command:	SEND *FILE-NAME*
Example:	**SEND HIST_MED.RESOURCES**
List Type:	Majordomo
Command:	GET *LIST-NAME FILE-NAME*
Example:	**GET F-COSTUME TOPICS**

Table 5.5   Retrieve a File

How to Find the Names and Addresses of Lists

There are thousands of interest groups, discussion groups, or mailing lists on the Internet. How do you find lists that match your needs or interests? You're likely to hear about some lists from the folks you correspond with on the Internet, you'll also see lists mentioned if you read Usenet news (Chapter 6), or you'll see some mentioned in other things you read.

There are many ways to use the services on the Internet to find the names, addresses, and descriptions of lists. Discussion lists, Listserv, and the other types of lists existed before the Internet became as popular or available as it is today. Also, some of these lists existed on other networks. Over the years a number of groups and individuals have kept "lists of lists." These lists are available on the Internet and you can get any of them through e-mail or other Internet services. The addresses of these collections of lists and the services used to retrieve them are given in the section "Internet Sources of Information of Interest Lists" below. In this section we'll talk about three ways to find the names and address of lists using Internet services.

1. Search the names of all Listserv lists by e-mail.
2. Use Gopher to search for lists.
3. Use programs and services available on the World Wide Web to search for lists.

Search the Names of All Listserv Lists by E-Mail

You can search through the names of all Listserv lists by using e-mail. Sending the command:

```
LISTS GLOBAL
```

to any Listserv site will return a list of *all* Listserv lists. This is likely to be more than you want to deal with; there are thousands of entries. You can search for a keyword by sending the command:

```
LISTS GLOBAL /KeyWord(s)
```

To search for all lists that deal with education, for example, send the command:

```
LISTS GLOBAL /education
```

in an e-mail message to **listserv@bitnic.educom.edu**. You can include more than one word after the /. To search for lists dealing with agricultural education send the command:

```
LISTS GLOBAL /agricultural education
```

Note: You can send the command *lists* to other types of list management software systems as well. For example, to see the lists available through Majordomo at **world.std.com**, send e-mail to **majordomo@world.std.com** with the message **LISTS**.

Use Gopher to Search for Lists

To use Gopher for searching, first start a Gopher session. (Gopher is discussed in Chapter 9.) Now you've got to do a little sleuthing. You're looking for a menu entry similar to **Electronic Lists (E-Mail Conference Lists) <?>**, **Directory of Scholarly Electronic Conferences, Kovacs <?>**, or **Subject Search of Listservs <?>**. You'll be able to tell by the title the item deals with the lists we've been discussing in this chapter. The **<?>** indicates the item allows you to do some searching. When you choose the item you'll be prompted to enter one or more keywords. Then you'll get a menu of items that contain the keyword(s) in their descriptions. Selecting one of those items will give you the information you need to subscribe to the list (in some cases this follows the heading **SU:**). You may not find an entry allowing this type of searching on the main menu. You'll probably first choose an entry that points toward Internet Resources. For example, if you start a Gopher session with **marvel.loc.gov** (Library of Congress) and choose the item **Internet Resources**, you'll see an entry referring to Listserv and Usenet. Choose it and start searching!

Use Programs and Services Available on the World Wide Web to Search for Lists

You can access the World Wide Web using Lynx, Mosaic, or a similar World Wide Web browser (such as Netscape Navigator, covered in Appendix B; World Wide Web is covered in Chapter 11). In any case you need to follow the Web page entries until you either find one that deals with Listserv or some other form of mailing lists. Once there you'll most likely be able to search for lists. The home page for Inter Links (**http://alpha.acast.nova.edu/start.html**) has an entry titled **Internet Resources**, and that page has the entry **E-Mail Discussion Groups** (**http://alpha.acast.nova.edu/cgi-bin/lists**), which is a searchable index. Give a keyword or keyphrase, and it searches a database of list names, descriptions, and associated addresses. You'll get the information you need (list name, address for joining the list, address of the list, address of the list owner or moderator, etc.) for the appropriate lists.

Proper Etiquette or Behavior within an Interest Group

Interest groups and lists are great ways to communicate with people throughout the world or maybe even nearby. Members have discussions, post information, or ask questions. All of this is carried on within a community (the members of the list) sharing a common interest. Most communities have some rules of etiquette or behavior which may not be written down. Some things to remember about working with a list follow.

❑ Send messages going to the entire list to the *list address*. Send commands or requests to be interpreted by the software that manages the list to the *administrative address*. Send special requests or questions you can't resolve to the address of the list owner, administrator, or moderator.

❑ Spend some time getting to know the list. When you first join a list, take a little while to see the types of items discussed and the tone of the discussion. You may also find questions you have are currently being answered.

❑ Write easy-to-read messages. The material you write to the list should be grammatically correct, concise, and thoughtful. It's a lot easier to read something that is well written, and many members of the list may not have the time to deal with writing that is incorrect, long-winded, and without any real point. If the posting must go on for several screens it's a good idea to summarize it and invite others to ask you for more information.

❑ If you're writing a response to something from the list, include only the pertinent portions of the original message. Let's say someone starts a discussion in the group and writes something about 40 lines long. You want to respond, but only to one portion of it. Include only the portion that's relevant to your response in your follow-up message. Members of the group may not have the time or space to deal with long e-mail messages.

❑ When you ask a question of the members of the list, be sure to post a summary of the responses you receive. That way everyone on the list can benefit from the responses to your question. Naturally, this applies only if you get several responses and the answers to the question would be of general interest.

❑ Posting or sending a message to the group is a public act. Everything you write to the list may be distributed to all members of the list. If the list is moderated, your messages may be read first by the moderator(s) and then passed on to the list. If you're working with a list that isn't moderated (most aren't), your messages go directly to all the members of the list. Don't embarrass yourself. A friend, relative, or supervisor may also be a member of the list.

❑ The members of a list are people like yourself and need to be treated with respect and courtesy. Respond to messages as if you were talking face-to-face. A member may be from a different culture, may not be familiar with your language, and may have different views and values from yours. Don't respond too quickly to something that upsets you, and don't criticize others too hastily or without good reason. It's better to think before you write than to be sorry afterward.

❑ Avoid sarcasm and be careful with humor. You are communicating entirely by your words. You don't have the benefit of facial expression, body language, or tone of voice to let somebody know you're "only kidding" when you make a sarcastic remark. Members of the list will appreciate well-written humorous pieces or responses, but be sure your writing will be interpreted that way.

❑ Think about whether a response to a message should go to the list or to an individual. Messages to the list should be of general interest, or a request on your part for advice, or help in solving a problem. You'll know the e-mail address of the person who made the original request and you can send a response to that person if it's appropriate.

Internet Sources of Information of Interest Lists

Several groups or individuals have assembled collections of information about interest groups, discussion groups, Listserv, and mailing lists. Some of the collections of lists are very large, often too large for an individual to store. But these lists can be searched on the Internet as described above. Also, some of the collections of lists are broken into smaller groups, so it may be feasible for you to retrieve some of these lists.

Before giving sources on the Internet for these lists we'll first discuss two files you might want to retrieve. These files contain documents about using mailing lists or interest groups and about finding sources of information about mailing lists.

❑ "How to Find an Interesting Mailing List," by Arno Wouters, identifies and describes several sources of lists and other information related to interest groups and mailing lists. The document also contains some information about using Internet services to search for lists. The file containing the document is available by e-mail and anonymous FTP. The URL for anonymous FTP access is **ftp://vm1.nodak.edu/new-list/new-list.wouters**. To retrieve it by e-mail send the message:

```
GET NEW-LIST WOUTERS F=MAIL
```

to **listserv@vm1.nodak.edu**.

❑ The document "Discussion Lists: Mail Server Commands," by James Milles, contains information about working with discussion lists, interest groups, and mailing lists. The file is available by anonymous ftp and by e-mail. To retrieve it by anonymous FTP use the URL **ftp://sluaxa.slu.edu /pub/millesjg/mailser.cmd**. To retrieve the file by e-mail send the message

```
GET MAILSER CMD NETTRAIN F=MAIL
```

to **listserv@ubvm.cc.buffalo.edu**.

Here is a collection of sources for "lists of lists" on the Internet.

❑ "Directory of Scholarly E-Mail Conferences," prepared by Diane Kovacs (Kent State University Libraries) and a team of researchers, announced its ninth edition in 1995. This group has prepared information on several thousand interest groups whose topics would be interesting to scholars. This is an extensive list, often used as the list searched at Gopher sites. The list is arranged as a collection of files, and it's available in text form as well as in a HyperCard version (**ACADSTAC.HQX**). All the files are available by anonymous FTP at **ksuvxa.kent.edu** in the directory library, available through Gopher at **gopher.usask.ca**, and by sending e-mail to **listserv@kentvm.kent.edu**. Before you go after all the files it would be best to get a copy of the file **ACADLIST.README** because it contains all the explanatory information you'll need to retrieve and use the directory. To retrieve that file by e-mail send the message:

```
GET ACADLIST README F=MAIL
```

to **listserv@kentvm.kent.edu**.

❑ The global list of Listserv lists. Send e-mail to any Listserv site, for example, **LISTSERV@KENTVM.KENT.EDU**, with the message:

```
LISTS GLOBAL
```

to retrieve a list of Listserv groups and a short description of each.

❑ "Publicly Available Mailing Lists," containing names, addresses, and information about lists available through the Internet, is contained in a list of fourteen or more files. Use anonymous FTP to **rtfm.mit.edu** and change directory to **/pub/usenet-by-group/news.answers/mail/mailing-lists** to retrieve the files. They're named **part1**, **part2**, and so on. The list is periodically updated and also available through the Usenet newsgroup **news.answers**. The lists could also be retrieved through e-mail by sending the message:

```
send usenet/news.answers/mail/mailing-lists/*
```

to **mail-server@rtfm.mit.edu**.

❑ The file **interest-groups**, currently maintained by Vivian Neou, is one of the oldest lists of lists on the Internet. It's large—almost 1 megabyte—and very complete. Not every user needs her own copy, but it may be suitable to have one copy available at an easily accessible site. It's available by anonymous FTP from **sri.com**. The URL for the file is **ftp://sri.com/netinfo/interest-groups**. It can also be retrieved by sending the e-mail message:

```
send interest-groups
```

to **mail-server@sri.com**.

❑ The file **INTERNET.LISTS** is another list of lists. This one is maintained by David Avery at Dartmouth College. It lists and classifies several thousand groups. The site also has software available for a variety of computer systems so users may work with the list. To get started, retrieve the file **read.me**. You can do this by anonymous FTP. The URL for the file is **ftp://dartcms1.dartmouth.edu/siglists/read.me**. You can also use e-mail to ask for the file by sending the message:

```
get read.me f=mail
```

to **listserv@dartcms1.dartmouth.edu**.

Summary

Several thousand interest groups are available and active on the Internet. Some are called mailing lists, discussion groups, Listserv lists, or interest groups. Regardless of the name, each consists of a group of members anywhere on the Internet, and all communication is carried on by e-mail. Messages sent to the list are generally broadcast to all members of the group. This way communities or collections of people can discuss items related to a common topic, find information about the topic, make announcements to the group, or ask questions and get help from other members of the group. The large number of lists guarantees a wide range of topics. Being a member of an interest group means you'll have access to others sharing some of your interests or your experiences. The groups are particularly useful to people who want to discuss issues with a large or diverse group. The groups extend your resources beyond a local site.

You send messages to the list by using the *list address*. Commands and requests for service are usually sent to another address called the *administrative address*. For example, the list PHOTO-L, which deals with a variety of topics related to photography, has **PHOTO-L@csuohio.edu** as the list address and **listproc@csuohio.edu** as the administrative address. Some commands and services available include joining a list, leaving or unsubscribing from a list, getting archived files from the lists, and getting a list of the members of the list. Be sure you use the correct address when you communicate with the group or list. Most lists also have a person designated as the *list owner*, *list administrator*, or *moderator*. That person is in charge of the list and you send him e-mail if you have problems using the list or regarding operation of the list. In many cases you can also address some questions about using the lists to the list address as well. Some lists are moderated. Messages sent to the list are first viewed by the moderator who decides whether to pass the messages on to all members of the list.

Most day-to-day operations of the list and responding to commands or requests are managed by software. Different types of software perform this function, and the exact form of the commands may be different. You can usually tell the type of software by the administrative address. For example, PHOTO-L has **listproc@csuohio.edu** as its administrative address and it is managed by Listproc software. Commands sent to the administrative address need to be in a precise form since the commands are being interpreted by computer programs, not humans.

The lists can be thought of as communities of people sharing common interests. There are generally accepted rules of behavior or etiquette for list members. These generally deal with providing appropriate, thoughtful, and concise messages to the list, providing a summary of the responses you've received to a question you posed, and treating other members of the list (through your communications to the list) in a civil and respectful manner.

Several "lists of lists" and other documents related to using interest groups are available on the Internet. Some of the lists can be searched using Listserv services, Gopher, or through the World Wide Web. The lists and documents are also available by anonymous FTP or by e-mail through commands sent to the administrative address of a list.

You go through these steps in working with a list or group:

1. Identify or choose a group. You'll find out about lists by reading things on the Internet, getting recommendations from friends or searching a collection of lists.
2. Find the address used to join a group. This is usually the administrative address. For example, the address used to join the list PHOTO-L, mentioned above, is **listproc@csuohio.edu**. You'll send e-mail to this address with the body of the message having the form *subscribe list-name your-name*. (Check the section in this chapter that gives the proper form for the type of list or group you're working with.)
3. Find the address used to contribute to a group. You send e-mail to the group address, not to the administrative address, to communicate with the members of the group. The group address for PHOTO-L is **PHOTO-L@csuohio.edu**. So if you want to post a question, make a statement, or help someone out, you send e-mail to **PHOTO-L@csuohio.edu**.
4. Use services available from the list. The services available and the ways to access these services will most likely be contained in the reply you get from the administrative

address when you join the list. Save that reply since you may need it later. Services include a list of members, access to archives of previous discussions, etc.

5. Unsubscribe or leave a group. Send e-mail to the administrative address, not to the group. In most cases the body of the e-mail message is *signoff list-name your-name*. (Check the section in this chapter that gives the proper form to use for the type of list or group you're working with.)

Exercises

Here is a list of ten interest groups or lists. You'll be asked to choose some of these for working the exercises.

When you've completed the exercises, be sure to sign off or unsubscribe from the lists if you don't want to get any more e-mail from them.

List Name:	SF-LIST
Administrative Address:	**listproc@unicorn.acs.ttu.edu**
List Address:	**SF-list@unicorn.acs.ttu.edu**
List Name:	DINOSAUR
Administrative Address:	**listproc@lepomis.psych.upenn.edu**
List Address:	**Dinosaur@lepomis.psych.upenn.edu**
List Name:	HELP-NET
Administrative Address:	**listserv@vm.temple.edu**
List Address:	**Help-Net@vm.temple.edu**
List Name:	WISENET
Administrative Address:	**listserv@uicvm.uic.edu**
List Address:	**Wisenet@uicvm.uic.edu**
List Name:	ENVIROETHICS
Administrative Address:	**mailbase@mailbase.ac.uk**
List Address:	**Enviroethics@mailbase.ac.uk**
List Name:	COMPUTERS-AND-PSYCHOLOGY
Administrative Address:	**mailbase@mailbase.ac.uk**
List Address:	**Computers-and-Psychology@mailbase.ac.uk**
List Name:	GASLIGHT
Administrative Address:	**mailserv@MtRoyal.AB.CA**
List Address:	**Gaslight@MTROYAL.AB.CA**
List Name:	POPCULT
Administrative Address:	**mailserv@camosun.bc.ca**
List Address:	**Popcult@camosun.bc.ca**
List Name:	HEMING-L
Administrative Address:	**majordomo@mtu.edu**
List Address:	**Heming-l@mtu.edu**
List Name:	Rocks-and-Fossils
Administrative Address:	**majordomo@world.std.com**
List Address:	**Rocks-and-Fossils@world.std.com**

1. Subscribe to three lists from the group above.
    a. Make sure each list is managed by a different type of software.
    b. Compare the e-mail you get welcoming you to each list. Which was the most helpful? Why?

2. Subscribe to three lists, different from the ones you chose in Exercise 1.
    a. Send the command to the administrative address to get a list of members.
    b. Send the command to the administrative address to get a list of archives or files.

3. Get the list of files or archives for the list HELP-NET.
    a. Find the names of files that deal with either e-mail or etiquette.
    b. Retrieve one of those files.

4. In the text we showed how to find names of lists available at Listserv and other sites.
    a. Find the names of the lists available through Majordomo at **world.std.com**.
    b. Subscribe to one of those lists.

5. Using techniques described in the chapter search the list of all lists available through Listserv for the names of lists dealing with travel. Subscribe to one of those lists.

6. Retrieve and read the file **ACADLIST.README** using a method described in the text.
    a. What are the up-to-date instructions for accessing the directory through the World Wide Web (WWW)?
    b. Section four lists the names of the files that make up the directory. Name three of them that you think you might find useful.

7. Use Gopher, as described in the chapter, to search for the list WISENET mentioned above. What is the purpose or description of WISENET? (If you can't find a Gopher menu to use for searching, point your Gopher to **gopher.mwc.edu**, choose the item titled **The Internet**, and then choose the item **Listserv, Usenet, and Other Network Discussion Groups**.)

8. Again using Gopher or by accessing the World Wide Web, find the names of the list owners or moderators for five of the lists in the table above.

9. For about a week, keep track of the e-mail from two of the groups you've joined.
    a. Write a couple of sentences describing the type of mail that came to each list.
    b. Is the mail from these groups the type of mail you expected? Explain.

10. Send or post a question to one of the lists you've joined. Think about the question before you post it and check your spelling and typing before you send it.
    a. What responses did you receive by the end of one week?
    b. Summarize the responses and post the summary to the list.

Usenet
Reading and Writing the News

The interest groups or mailing lists we talked about in the last chapter are great ways to participate in discussions, read what others are discussing, distribute information, get questions answered, or help others with questions. All of this takes place through e-mail; you join a list and all the messages for the list are sent to your personal mailbox. Another popular means of exchanging information in this way is *Usenet*; sometimes it's called *Netnews* and sometimes you'll see it written as *USENET*. You use Usenet for the same reasons you use an interest group: to exchange or read information dealing with specific topics. Some ways that Usenet differs from interest groups are:

❏ With Usenet you have access to lots of groups. Some sites carry hundreds or thousands of groups; others carry fewer groups or different ones depending on the policies and procedures of that site.

❏ Messages to a group aren't exchanged between individuals using e-mail; instead, messages are passed from one computer system to another.

❏ You use software called a *newsreader* to read and deal with the news (articles) available through Usenet, instead of using your e-mail program or sending commands to a remote site.

Usenet is similar to a bulletin board system (bbs), except that most bulletin boards have one manager and one computer supporting the bbs. There is no single person, group, or computer system in charge of Usenet. All the computers and people that are part of Usenet support it and manage it. Usenet is a community with its own generally agreed upon code of etiquette. Once you get comfortable using it, you'll find it to be a valuable resource to find answers to different types of questions, to give you help on a large variety of topics, and to help you keep up with what's happening on the Internet. Furthermore, it's a great place to have discussions and work with a worldwide community.

Chapter Overview

This chapter concentrates on accessing and using Usenet. The topics we'll cover include:

- ❑   Introduction to Usenet
- ❑   How Usenet Articles Are Organized
- ❑   Working with Usenet News
- ❑   Reading Articles
- ❑   Saving, Mailing, and Printing Articles
- ❑   Writing to the Author of an Article
- ❑   Posting a Follow-up to an Article
- ❑   Posting an Article
- ❑   Proper Usenet Etiquette
- ❑   Signatures, FAQs, and Finding Newsgroups
- ❑   Recommended Newsgroups and Articles

Introduction to Usenet

Usenet began in 1979 through the efforts of two people who wanted to have their computers call each other over telephone lines and exchange files. Since then it has grown to encompass thousands of computers, millions of people, and several megabytes of traffic each day. The traffic is in the form of articles passed from one system to another. There is no central control, but the news has a worldwide distribution.

It's not easy to define Usenet because it's so diverse. Instead, we'll try to describe how it works and (most importantly) how to work with it. Usenet is made up of computers and people that agree to exchange or pass on collections of files. Each file is called an *article* and belongs to one or more *newsgroups*. You can tell what types of articles you're likely to find by the name of the newsgroup. People at each site can read the articles, ignore the articles, save or print the articles, respond to an article's author through e-mail, or *post* their own articles. Posting means distributing either an original article or a response to someone else's article and then passing it on to Usenet. There are thousands of computers involved and estimates of the number of people who read Usenet news range between 5 and 30 million. So Usenet is a great way to reach a large audience, but remember that posting articles is a public act.

There are newsgroups on all sorts of topics: Some are specialized or technical groups such as **comp.protocols.tcp-ip.domains** (topics related to Internet domain style names), some deal with recreational activities such as **rec.outdoors.fishing.saltwater** (topics dealing with saltwater fishing), and one, **news.newusers.questions**, is dedicated to questions from new Usenet users. That last one is a good one to start with. You'll also want to participate in that group, to get answers to your questions and to help others with questions. You've probably realized by now that Usenet news isn't necessarily news in the sense of what's printed in a newspaper or on a news broadcast.

You may find the typical discussions in some groups offensive. But you don't have to read the articles in those groups. Remember, there is no overall control over Usenet. What offends you may not offend others, and it may be important to others to be able to read and discuss topics that bother you. Some of the vitality and vigor of Usenet comes from the fact that a wide range of topics and opinions can be expressed through the news. You have the option of subscribing to or naming the groups that will be on your usual list of groups to read. Also, you have the option of talking with your news administrator about the appropriateness of carrying a certain group.

A Quick View of How Usenet Works

Someone posts an article to a newsgroup; using an editor on his system, he creates a file and passes it on to a newsgroup. The article is passed from that person's site to another site on Usenet, possibly with other articles, at some regularly scheduled time. At that other site it is distributed to other sites, and so on. People at other Usenet sites will read the article on their systems. Someone decides she would like to respond to the original article. She either sends e-mail to the original author or posts a follow-up article. The follow-up article is distributed around Usenet with the same subject heading as the original article. Sometimes, several folks at different places on Usenet respond with follow-up articles. Discussions start this way. Sometimes they stay on the same topic, but sometimes not. It's informative, it's creative, it's dynamic, its exciting! Just a few words of warning: Using Usenet can be so appealing that you spend much more time doing it than you ought. Remember, you have a life outside of Usenet and you ought to pay attention to it! Get your other work done, take a walk, and spend some time with other human beings.

Usenet Control Is at the Local Level

Someone at each Usenet site decides which newsgroups the site will receive or carry, which newsgroups it passes on to another site, which sites it receives news from, and which sites it will send news to. The person making the decisions about these issues is in charge of either the entire computer system or the news on its own. That person, sometimes called the news administrator, also decides whether users at that site can read and post articles or just read articles. Almost all control is at the local level.

How the News Is Passed Around and Stored

Each computer system that is part of Usenet runs software to receive, manage, and forward articles. The news administrator, using the software, maintains a list of newsgroups the site will carry or make available to its users, a list of Usenet sites from which the computer system will receive articles, and a list of sites to articles will be sent.

The software is set up to receive articles. Each article contains information about the newsgroup(s) it belongs to. Once an article is received, the software decides whether to accept or reject the article. It's accepted if it belongs to one of the newsgroups the site carries; otherwise it's rejected.

Each article is kept in a file and is put into a directory that corresponds with or represents the newsgroup. On a Unix system, for example, an article belonging to **rec.food.cooking** may be stored in a directory named **/usr/local/news/rec/food/cooking**.

The administrator decides how long an article will be carried on a system and thus available to the users. At the end of a certain time—usually two weeks—the article *expires*. In other words, the article is removed or deleted from the system by the software managing the news.

At certain times of the day articles from one site are passed on to another site. Only new articles are passed on. If two sites A and B agree to exchange articles and Site A sent article *great-one* to Site B, then *great-one* isn't sent back to Site A. But any new articles either created at Site B or received by B from some other site are dispatched. This way articles created at one site are passed around to other systems on Usenet.

How Usenet Articles Are Organized

All articles belong to one or more newsgroups. An article is either a follow-up to another article, or it's posted on a different topic. The term for posting an article to more than one newsgroup is *cross-posting*.

Threads

Within a newsgroup, there may be several articles on the same topic. A *thread* is a collection of articles all on the same subject. They need to be posted as follow-up articles to some original posting. Some newsreaders automatically group articles into threads; in that case we say the newsreader *threads* the articles. Newsreaders that do this automatically are called *threaded* newsreaders. You *follow a thread* by reading the articles in a thread one after the other. Threaded newsreaders such as *tin* or *trn* make this easy. It's also possible to do this with other newsreaders such as *rn* or *nn* if you give the right commands.

Newsgroup Categories

Each newsgroup has a name indicating the topic or topics of the articles posted in the group. The groups are arranged or named according to a hierarchy. When you look at the name of a newsgroup you'll see it usually consists of several words or names separated by periods. The first part of the newsgroup name is the name of the top level of the hierarchy. Moving to the right, the names get more specific. Here is a nice long name:

```
rec.music.makers.guitar.acoustic
```

Starting on the left, **rec** is the name of a top-level group that includes groups that deal with artistic activities, hobbies, or recreational activities. The next name, **music**, indicates the group deals with topics related to music. The next, **makers**, tells you this group is about performing or playing music rather than another activity such as reviewing music or collecting recordings. The last two names, **guitar** and **acoustic**, pretty much nail this down as dealing with discussions or other matters related to playing or performing acoustic guitar. Here are a few other groups in the **rec.music** hierarchy to give you a feeling for this naming scheme: **rec.music.makers.piano**, **rec.music.makers.percussion**, **rec.music.marketplace**, **rec.music.reggae**, **rec.music.reviews**.

There are thousands of newsgroups and several major, top-level categories. Some of the top-level categories are given in the Table 6.1.

Name	Description
alt	**alt** stands for alternative. This includes newsgroups presenting alternative views of the world, groups dealing with bizarre topics, groups discussing unusual subjects, and other newsgroups that don't go through established channels. Two examples are **alt.aliens.visitors** and **alt.cinchilla**. (Newsgroups in this hierarchy may not be available outside the U.S.)
bionet	The groups in this category deal with topics in biology, e.g., **bionet.molbio.molluscs**.
bit	The **bit** hierarchy carries groups dealing with the network BITNET. The category **bit.listserv** has newsgroups for many of the Listserv discussion groups, e.g., **bit.listserv.film-l**.
biz	The newsgroups in this hierarchy deal with discussions related to business. This is where to post and find announcements of new products or books, and also an acceptable place to market those items. An example of a newsgroup in this category is **biz.books.technical**.
comp	This hierarchy consists of hundreds of groups dealing with topics related to computers, computer systems and peripherals, computer science, and other topics related to computing. For example, the newsgroup **comp.answers** carries regular postings of FAQs (Frequently Asked Questions—and answers) on a wide variety of topics in computing.
k12	Newsgroups dealing with issues related to teachers and students in grades kindergarten through 12, e.g., **k12.ed.math**.
misc	Miscellaneous topics; things that may not fit into other categories, e.g., **misc.health.diabetes**.
news	This category includes newsgroups dedicated to the use and discussion of Usenet. Two important ones you'll want to read are **news.answers**, a list of regular postings of FAQs (Frequently Asked Questions—and answers) on a variety of topics in all areas, and **news.newusers.questions**, a newsgroup where beginning or novice Usenet users can ask questions and get some help.
rec	This includes newsgroups that deal with artistic activities, hobbies, or recreational activities. An example is **rec.video.production**.
sci	This hierarchy has groups that deal with scientific topics. Two such groups are **sci.med.aids** and **sci.virtual-worlds.apps**.
soc	The newsgroups in this hierarchy deal with social issues and various cultures, e.g., **soc.culture.latin-america**.
talk	This hierarchy houses newsgroups dedicated to talking or discussing. One example is **talk.politics.medicine**.

Table 6.1   Some Top-Level Newsgroup Categories

There are a number of other categories, and we can't list them all. Some categories have to do with topics of regional interest such as **ba** for the San Francisco Bay Area, **dc** for the Washington, D.C. area, and **aus** for Australia. These are useful if you live, work, or will be traveling to an area that has some newsgroups. For example, to find out about places to eat in and around Washington, D.C., read some news in the group **dc.dining**.

Working with Usenet News

This section will cover a number of topics you'll want to know about so you'll be able to work with the news. The software that manages the news sends articles from one computer system to another. You may not be involved with managing the news, but you will be involved with software called a *newsreader* that enables you to read the articles that make up the news and write articles to be sent to other sites. We'll concentrate on working with a newsreader in this section. We'll also include some examples of using a newsreader to work with Usenet.

What Is a Newsreader?

You use software called a *newsreader* to work with Usenet. The newsreader is the interface between a user and the news itself. It allows you to go through the newsgroups one at a time, and once you've chosen a newsgroup it allows you to deal with the articles it contains. Several different newsreaders are available. Some make it easier to select newsgroups and read articles than others. Some give you a menu to work with, some have a character-based or text-only interface, and some have a graphical interface. You'll have to find out which ones are available to read the news on your system, and then, if there is an option, choose the one you'll use.

Keeping Track of Groups and Articles—.newsrc. In addition to letting you work with the groups and articles in Usenet, a newsreader will create and maintain a file named **.newsrc**. This important file contains the list of the newsgroups you usually read and a numeric list of the articles you've read in each newsgroup. When you give a command to use a newsreader, the newsreader program first checks to see if you have a file named **.newsrc**. If you don't, the program creates a new copy of **.newsrc**. A new version could contain the names of all the newsgroups available at your site or a selected list of newsgroups. If the file **.newsrc** already exists (meaning it has already been set up for you or that you've used a newsreader before), the newsreader program checks to see if any newsgroups have been added to or deleted from the list of all the groups your Usenet site carries. The newsreader will prompt you to add any new groups to your personal list or delete ones that have been removed. Newsgroups on your personal list that aren't carried by your site are called *bogus*. The newsreader program changes the file **.newsrc** when you add or delete newsgroups. Here's an example of an entry in **.newsrc**:

```
soc.culture.african.american:  1-3106,3108,3111,3114-3115,3117-3120
```

This is for the newsgroup **soc.culture.african.american**. The numbers after the name of the group represent articles in the group that have been read. Each article is numbered.

Subscribe or Unsubscribe? When you start a newsreader, it checks the file **.newsrc** to see which newsgroups you'd like to read. We'll call this list of newsgroups the *subscription* list. The newsreader checks this list to see if your site has any articles belonging to these groups which you haven't read. The groups containing unread articles are either listed in a menu or you go through them one at a time, depending on which type of newsreader you're using. You can add groups to the subscription list by *subscribing* to a group. The newsreader also automatically creates a subscription list the first time you use one. The file **.newsrc**, at first, is your subscription list. As you read the news you may want to *unsubscribe* from some groups. Perhaps you don't read the group regularly and you want to pay attention to other groups; the group or articles aren't interesting to you, or the topic or articles are offensive. It's easy to unsubscribe; press **u** at the name of a group. After you unsubscribe the name of the group and the numbers representing the articles you've read remain in **.newsrc**. That way, if or when you decide to subscribe again you'll only see the articles you haven't read. There is a colon after the name of each group on your subscription list and an exclamation point after the names of the groups from which you've unsubscribed. Here are two entries from somebody's **.newsrc**. Whoever owns this **.newsrc** is subscribed to **biz.books.technical** and is unsubscribed from **rec.arts.animation**.

```
biz.books.technical: 1-240
rec.arts.animation! 1-7730,7732,7735-7736,7738-7739
```

Selecting Newsgroups and Articles. Once you've started the newsreader program you'll have to go through two steps to read articles. First, you have to choose a newsgroup. Once you've chosen a newsgroup you'll be ready to select articles to read. With some newsreaders you go through the newsgroups and articles consecutively, one after the other. Other newsreaders allow you to select a newsgroup from a menu of the groups you'd like to read or browse, and then to select articles. Regardless of which method is used, you're at *article selection level* when you can select an article. So in these terms, a newsreader starts in *group selection level*, and you have to move to *article selection level* to read the articles themselves.

The Newsreader tin

There are several popular newsreaders; some are rn, nn, trn, and tin. You'll find those programs or something like them on almost any system that supports Usenet. Each one lets you read the news, post articles or a follow-up to an article, and do other things we'll describe later in this chapter. We'll demonstrate working with Usenet by using tin, a text-based newsreader. You type in commands to work with the news; there aren't any buttons to click with a mouse or boxes to fill in. Tin lets you work with newsgroups and articles in a full-screen mode. You'll be selecting newsgroups and articles from a menu. It also arranges articles into threads. Having articles arranged in threads brings everyone's comments on an article to one place. You'll see it's easier to keep track of a discussion that way.

Starting a Usenet News Session

You type **tin** and press Enter. That's easy!

What To Expect When a Session Starts. The first time you use tin several things happen. Tin displays one or two screens giving you an overview of how to use the program, and then tin checks some files dealing with newsgroups on your system. What you don't see is tin setting up your working environment by creating the directories and files it needs to let you read and manage the news. Tin will create the file **.newsrc** and also a directory named **.tin**. If you haven't used a newsreader before, tin will automatically subscribe you to several newsgroups by placing their names in **.newsrc**. Remember that .newsrc holds the list of your current newsgroups. As you use tin, it makes modifications to **.newsrc**, so you don't see the same article more than once, and it updates the list of newsgroups to which you've subscribed or unsubscribed. The directory **.tin** contains some files that keep track of your working environment so tin can work in full-screen mode, save articles in the right places, attach a signature to your replies or postings, and arrange for articles in a thread to be listed together. (There are several technical details here that you don't have to worry about the first time you're working with Usenet. They really belong in a complete or advanced users' guide to tin. You can pick up these details later or ask a local expert when you need some advanced help.) You'll eventually see a full-screen display of the newsgroups you can choose from; you'll be at the group selection level.

If You've Already Used a Newsreader on This System. If you've already used a newsreader on this system, the file **.newsrc** was already created and contains the list of newsgroups to which you are subscribed. Tin checks the list in **.newsrc** with the list of all newsgroups available on your system. This master list of all newsgroups on the system is kept in a file named **active** in the directory used to set up and manage Usenet for your system.

If there are new newsgroups listed in **active**, but not in your list (**.newsrc**), you'll be asked if you want to subscribe to them. You can type

❑ **y** to subscribe to a group

❑ **n** to not subscribe to the group

❑ **q** to stop tin from asking you about other groups

If there are newsgroups listed in your file **.newsrc** that aren't in the file with the names of all newsgroups available on your system, those newsgroups are deleted. Figure 6.1 shows an example.

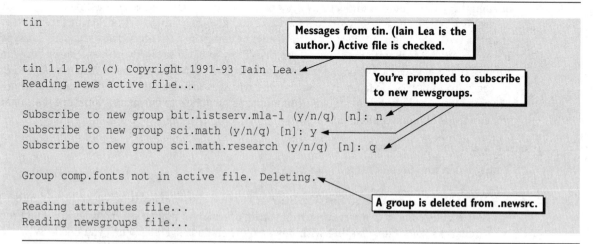

```
tin


tin 1.1 PL9 (c) Copyright 1991-93 Iain Lea.
Reading news active file...


Subscribe to new group bit.listserv.mla-l (y/n/q) [n]: n
Subscribe to new group sci.math (y/n/q) [n]: y
Subscribe to new group sci.math.research (y/n/q) [n]: q


Group comp.fonts not in active file. Deleting.


Reading attributes file...
Reading newsgroups file...
```

Messages from tin. (Iain Lea is the author.) Active file is checked.

You're prompted to subscribe to new newsgroups.

A group is deleted from .newsrc.

Figure 6.1   Starting tin

The last two lines in the figure tell you tin is checking the files it uses to set up your working environment and keep track of the newsgroups you're using.

After the initial few lines or screens you'll get a menu of newsgroups. You are at the group selection level. This is the place to select a newsgroup. Each line in the menu has a number you can use to select the newsgroup, the number of unread articles in the newsgroup, the title of the newsgroup, and a brief description. You can press **h** for help anywhere. The help is a list and brief explanation of the commands you can use. Near the bottom of the screen you'll see the keystrokes to use for some commands you're likely to use. Figure 6.2 shows a sample screen.

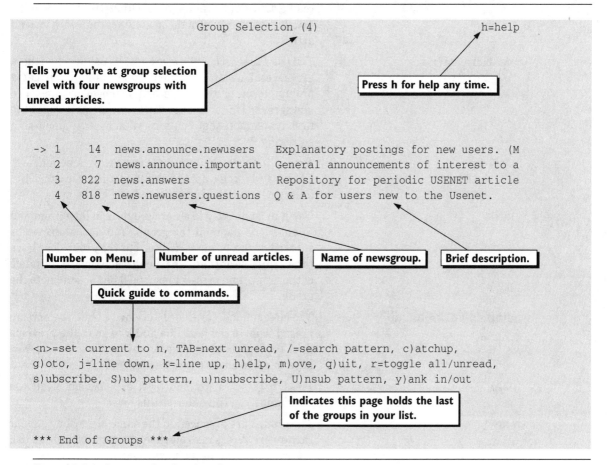

Figure 6.2   Group selection Level

The current group is marked with → or is highlighted. Pressing Enter takes you to the articles in the newsgroup, the article selection level.

Table 6.2 explains the commands given on the screen.

<n>=set current to n

n stands for a number. Type the number of a menu item and press Enter to move to the item on the menu. For example entering **3** will move → to **news.answers**.

TAB=next unread

Press the Tab key and you'll go to the article selection level of the current newsgroup, provided there are unread articles in the newsgroup. Otherwise you go to the article selection level of the next newsgroup with unread articles.

/=search pattern

You use / to search for newsgroups. Its useful when there are several pages of groups. Type / and you'll get a prompt to enter the name or portion of a name of a newsgroup. Tin then takes you to the menu item for the first newsgroup that contains what you've typed as a substring.

c)atchup

Type **c** to mark the current newsgroup as being read. That way it won't appear the next time you start tin, unless new articles have arrived.

g)oto

Use **g** to go directly to a newsgroup. You'll be prompted to enter the name of the group. You don't have to be subscribed to a group to do this, but the group does have to be available at your site. Type **g**, then type in the name of the group, and press Enter. You'll be subscribed to the group.

j=line down, k=line up

These commands are used to move about the screen; press **j** to go to the next line and **k** to go to the previous line. You'll probably be able to use the up and down arrow keys to move about the screen as well.

h)elp

Press **h** to see a list and brief explanation of all the commands you can enter at this level.

m)ove

The groups are arranged in the same order they appear in **.newsrc**. Press **m** to move the current newsgroup to a different position in the menu.

q)uit

Pressing **q** quits tin. In general, pressing **q** takes you to the previous level. Since the group selection level is the top level, pressing **q** here takes you out of the program.

r=toggle all/unread

The groups listed on the menu are usually the ones that contain unread articles. To list all the groups on your subscription list press **r**. It's a toggle. Press **r** again and you'll get a menu of unread articles.

s)ubscribe S)ub pattern

Each of these lets you subscribe to a group. The name of the group has to be on the menu. Typing **s** subscribes to the current group, the one marked with → or highlighted. Typing **S** subscribes you to a several groups whose

	names match a pattern you type. Use * as a "wild card" character. For example, to subscribe to all the **rec.music groups** enter **rec.music.***.
u)nsubscribe U)nsub pattern	Press **u** to unsubscribe from the current group. Press **U** to unsubscribe from a collection of groups.
y)ank in/out	Pressing **y** puts all the newsgroups carried at your site on the menu. This is useful to see what's available to you, and to subscribe to the groups you'd like to read regularly. Pressing **y** again will list only the groups in **.newsrc**.

Table 6.2   Commands to Use to Choose a Newsgroup

Ending a Usenet News Session

Pressing **Q** (uppercase Q) quits tin at any level. Pressing **q** (lowercase q) at the group selection level quits tin. Regardless of the level you're using, pressing **q** takes you to the previous level. You'll eventually go to the **group selection** level and then you can quit.

Selecting or Choosing a Newsgroup to Read

You select a newsgroup when you're at the group selection level. Choosing a group is really easy: move the → opposite a group name or highlight the name of a group and then press Tab or Enter. Then you'll be taken to the article selection level, and you'll be ready to read articles.

We'll call the newsgroup whose name is marked with → or highlighted the *current group*. So the way to select a newsgroup is to make it the current group and then press Tab or Enter. This, of course, works only for groups on the menu. Putting *all* the newsgroups carried by your site on the menu is called *yanking* the list. You do this by pressing **y**. You can go directly to a group, whether it's on your menu or not, by typing **g** and then typing the name of the newsgroup. Table 6.3 lists some commands for selecting a newsgroup or listing the names of newsgroups.

Command	Explanation
Select a group by name.	Press **g** and then type the name of the newsgroup to go directly to the newsgroup, whether it's on your menu or not.
	Press **/** and then type the name or part of the name of a newsgroup. The first newsgroup on the menu whose name contains what you've typed as a substring becomes the current group.
Choose a group by number on the menu.	Type the number of the group as it appears on the menu; the group with the number will be the current group.
Put all the newsgroups on the menu.	Press **y** to list all the newsgroups carried at your site.

| Move to the next or previous newsgroup. | You can move from one menu item to another by using **j** to go up one line or **k** to go down one line. You'll probably also be able to use the arrow keys to go up or down one item. |
| Move to the next or previous screen. | You go to the next screen of newsgroups, if there is one, by pressing the spacebar. You go to the previous screen by pressing **b**. |

Table 6.3   Commands for Selecting Newsgroups

Reading Articles

In order to read articles you have to be at the article selection level. You get to this level by first being at group selection level and choosing a newsgroup, or by having just read an article. What you do now depends on the newsreader you're using. Some newsreaders present the articles in a serial fashion. Other newsreaders are *threaded* so that articles on the same subject are easily accessible one right after the other. With some newsreaders the articles are listed in a menu so you can choose the one you'd like to read. In any case, when you're at article selection level you choose from among the unread articles. What does it mean that an article is unread? It means *you* haven't read the article; others may have read it. (Remember there is one copy of the article that everyone using the computer system can read.) You're always presented with unread articles. However, some newsreaders, such as tin, let you give a command so you can select from all the available articles.

Choosing an Article

To get to the article selection level you first choose a newsgroup and then press Enter. The list of unread articles in the newsgroup is displayed as a menu. You choose an article in the same way you chose a newsgroup. Either type the number of the article or move the arrow → or highlight bar to the article you want to read and press Enter or the Tab key.

In Figure 6.3 you see what we got choosing the group **news.answers**. The first line gives the name of the group and some other numbers that need explaining. The first item, **681T**, gives the number of threads, or articles on different topics, and the second, **809A**, is the total number of unread articles in the newsgroup. The next two items list the number of articles that have been removed because they're on a *kill list*, **0K**, and the number, **0H**, on a *hot list* of special articles. So there aren't any articles on the kill list or hot list. The idea is to take special action with articles dealing with certain topics or from certain authors. We can set up our environment by using tin to build a kill list for articles we don't want displayed or a hot list for articles we want to give special attention. The uppercase **R** means we're considering only the unread articles.

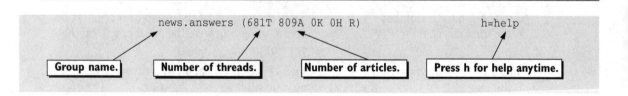

```
-> 1   +        misc.invest FAQ on general investment topics   Christopher Lott
   2   +        misc.invest FAQ on general investment topics   Christopher Lott
   3   +        misc.invest FAQ on general investment topics   Christopher Lott
   4   +        misc.invest FAQ on general investment topics   Christopher Lott
   5   +        FAQ: comp.lang.tcl Tcl Language Usage Questio   Joe Moss
   6   +        rec.food.veg FREQUENTLY ASKED QUESTIONS LIST   Michael Traub
   7   + 3      rec.audio.car FAQ (part 1/3)                   Jeffrey S. Curtis
   8   +        comp.os.msdos.mail-news FAQ (02/02) software   commafaq@alpha3.er
   9   +        comp.os.msdos.mail-news FAQ (01/02) intro          commafaq@alpha3.er
  10   + 11     Rec.skate Frequently-Asked Questions: General  Tony Chen
  11   + 3      alt.folklore.urban  Frequently Asked Question  Terry Chan
  12   +        Standards FAQ                                  Markus Kuhn
  13   +        comp.protocols.iso FAQ                         Markus Kuhn
  14   +        Shamanism-General Overview-Frequently Asked Q  Dean Edwards
  15   +        soc.religion.shamanism-Frequently Asked Quest  Dean Edwards
  16   +        Waffle Frequently Asked Questions (FAQ)        Comp.Bbs.Waffle FA

<n>=set current to n, TAB=next unread, /=search pattern, ^K)ill/select,
a)uthor search, c)atchup, j=line down, k=line up, K=mark read, l)ist thread,
|=pipe, m)ail, o=print, q)uit, r=toggle all/unread, s)ave, t)ag, w=post
```

Figure 6.3   Article Selection Level

Each article listing on the menu starts with the menu number. If a plus sign, **+**, appears by the article name it means the article hasn't been read. Either the name comes next or a numeral telling how many articles are in the thread. The author's name is the last entry on the line. See Figure 6.4.

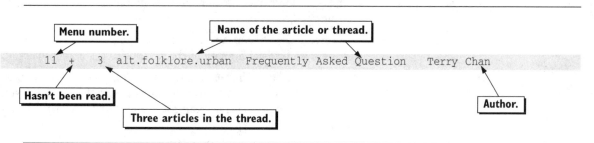

Figure 6.4   Parts of an Article Listing

This listing at the bottom of the screen gives the keystrokes to use for several commands. These commands deal with selecting, marking, or listing articles, as well as printing, posting, mailing or saving articles or threads. Table 6.4 explains those commands.

Command	Explanation
\<n>=set current to n	**n** stands for a number. If you type 6, menu item 6 becomes the current article. Press Tab or Enter to read the article.
TAB=next unread	Press Tab to make the next unread article the current article.
/=search pattern	Search for an article by title. Press / and enter one or more keywords to search. **Tin** makes the first article whose name contains the keyword(s) a substring of the current one.
^K)ill/select	**^K** represents Ctrl-K, meaning hold down the Ctrl key, press the K key, and release them both. This will give you a screen you can use to set up a kill list or hot list. You enter keyword(s) for the title or an author's name, and whether articles matching these are to be suppressed (kill list) or marked as special (hot list). This is a way to ignore or pay attention to certain types of articles.
a)uthor search	Pressing **a** (lowercase a) lets you search for an article based on the name of an author.
c)atchup	Pressing **c** (lowercase c) marks all articles as being read, so the next time you read Usenet there may be no articles to read in this group.
j=line down, k=line up	These keys let you move around the menu; **j** to go to the next article or thread and **k** to go to the previous one. You will probably also be able to use the up or down arrow keys to move about the screen.
K=mark read	Press **K** (uppercase K) to mark the current article or thread as being read.
l)ist thread	A thread is a list of articles on the same topic. You press **l** (lowercase l) to get a menu of the articles in the current thread.
l =pipe	The vertical bar **l** character is used as a "pipe" in Unix computer systems. The current article or thread is sent to the command you type after you press **l** . For example, if you wanted to download an article you might type **l kermit -s -**.
m)ail	To send an article or a thread by e-mail to someone press **m** (lowercase m). You'll be prompted for the Internet address of the receiver.
o=print	Press **o** (lowercase o) to print the current article or thread. Where it's printed depends on your local configuration.
q)uit	Press **q** (lowercase q) to quit the current level and move to the previous one. This will take you back to newsgroup selection level.
r=toggle all/unread	When you move to article selection level, only the unread articles are on the menu. To get a menu of all the articles in the newsgroup press **r** (lower-case r). This is a toggle. Press **r** again to go back to a menu of only the unread articles.

s)ave	Pressing **s** (lowercase **s**) saves the current article or thread in a file.
t)ag	If you press **t** (lowercase **t**), you'll **tag** the current article or thread. This way you can group a collection of possibly unrelated articles for printing, mailing, saving, etc.
w=post	Press **w** (lowercase **w**) to post an article.

Table 6.4   Commands for Choosing an Article

Reading an Article

After selecting an article or thread, you can read it. Press Enter or Tab to read the selected article, or the first article in the thread if you've selected a thread. The article is displayed one screen at a time. There are many options at this level, the *article reading level*, but we won't go through all of them. For a complete list, press **h** for **help**. You need to know only a few commands to do most of your reading. In fact, you can go from screen to screen and article to article by pressing the spacebar. But there are commands you can give to stop reading one article and move on to the next. You don't have to finish reading an article to have it marked as read. Table 6.5 is a short list of commands.

Command	Explanation
Go to the next page of the current article.	Press the spacebar. This also takes you to the next article if you're at the end of an article.
Go to the next article.	Press **n** (lowercase n) to go to the next article. Press **N** (uppercase N) or Tab to go to the next *unread* article. Either of these keeps you in a thread. The article you were reading is marked as read.
Go to the previous article.	Press **p** (lowercase p) to go to the previous article. Press **P** to go to the previous *unread* article.
Go to the next thread.	Press Enter. Remember, it takes you to the next thread. The article or thread you were reading is marked as read.
See a list of all commands.	Press **h**.

Table 6.5   Commands for Working with an Article

Once you do select an article to read you'll see something like the example in Figure 6.5. In addition to seeing the article or posting you're able to tell when it was posted, how many responses have come in to the article, who posted it, and that person's e-mail address. The article contains some other pieces of information as well. As you can see, you can tell a lot about the article in addition to the main reason it was posted—to be read!

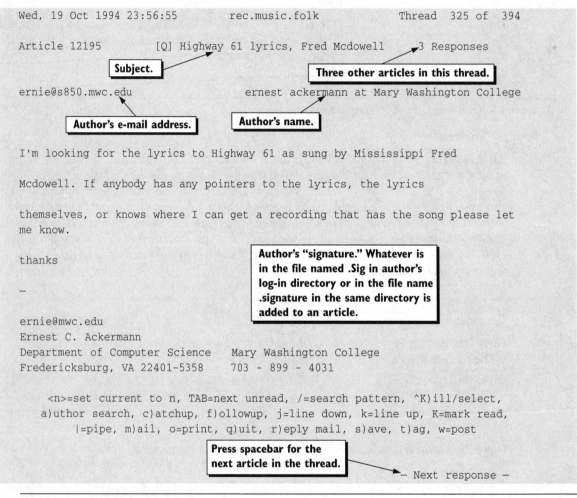

```
Wed, 19 Oct 1994 23:56:55      rec.music.folk          Thread  325 of  394

Article 12195        [Q] Highway 61 lyrics, Fred Mcdowell    3 Responses
```

Subject.

Three other articles in this thread.

```
ernie@s850.mwc.edu                  ernest ackermann at Mary Washington College
```

Author's e-mail address.

Author's name.

```
I'm looking for the lyrics to Highway 61 as sung by Mississippi Fred

Mcdowell. If anybody has any pointers to the lyrics, the lyrics

themselves, or knows where I can get a recording that has the song please let
me know.

thanks
```

Author's "signature." Whatever is in the file named .Sig in author's log-in directory or in the file name .signature in the same directory is added to an article.

```
—

ernie@mwc.edu
Ernest C. Ackermann
Department of Computer Science   Mary Washington College
Fredericksburg, VA 22401-5358    703 - 899 - 4031

    <n>=set current to n, TAB=next unread, /=search pattern, ^K)ill/select,
  a)uthor search, c)atchup, f)ollowup, j=line down, k=line up, K=mark read,
       |=pipe, m)ail, o=print, q)uit, r)eply mail, s)ave, t)ag, w=post
```

Press spacebar for the next article in the thread.

```
                                                          — Next response —
```

Figure 6.5   A Usenet Article

Marking an Article as Unread (tin)

When you read an article it's marked so you won't have to read it again. Sometimes you *do* want to see the article again, so after you've read it you have to mark it as being **unread**. You do this at the article selection level. Make the article the current article by entering its number or moving → or the highlight bar to the group and pressing **Z** (uppercase Z).

Saving, Mailing, and Printing Articles

There are going to be articles you will want to save. Many newsgroups have a list of frequently asked questions (FAQ) and answers for the topics they deal with, and there are lots of articles containing important information about Usenet and the Internet.

When you find something you like you can save it to a file, send it by e-mail to any Internet address, or print the file. All of this, as always, depends how you're accessing Usenet and the Internet. If your personal system isn't directly connected to the Internet and you have to use a modem to call another computer system to access Usenet, you may not be able to print an article. If your file space is very limited you may not be able to save a file. If you can do these things, here's how.

Saving an Article to a File

You can save an article into a file when you're reading an article or when you're at the article selection level. You press **s** and press Enter. Once you do that you'll see the prompt

```
Save a)rticle, t)hread, h)ot, p)attern, T)agged articles, q)uit: t
```

With tin you can save an article or a thread. (You can also save a group of articles marked by other means—hot list, pattern matching, or tagging. We won't discuss here saving groups of messages these ways.) You press the first letter of the word describing what you're going to save. Pressing **a** saves the article and pressing **t** saves the thread to a file. You'll then be prompted to enter the name of the file that will hold the article or thread. Type a name in and press Enter. Then you'll get this prompt:

```
Process n)one, s)har, u)ud, l)ist zoo, e)xt zoo, L)ist zip, E)xt zip, q)uit: n
```

All of the options here deal with whether the file should be processed—have some program do something with the file—before being saved. If you can read the article, it's probably in text format and no processing is necessary. Press **n**. The file will be saved just as it is. The other options have to do with processing certain types of files that could contain a group or archive of files, or files that have been compressed or processed in some way. You probably won't need to deal with any of these at first. When you do need help working with these types—shar, uuencoded, zoo files, or zip files—ask a local expert, check the postings in **news.answers** or **news.announce.newusers**, or post a question to **news.newusers.questions**.

The file will be saved on the computer you use to work with Usenet. If there already is a file with the same name you've chosen, tin gives you the choice of appending the article or thread to the file. If you choose not to append the article to an existing file, tin forces you to choose another name. Once you get any naming conflicts straightened out the article is saved in a file. The file may be in your current directory or in the directory named *News* which is a subdirectory of your log-in directory. Where it goes depends on how tin has been configured or set up.

To summarize the usual actions for *saving* a file:

1.   Press **s** (lowercase s) to save a file.
2.   Type in the name of a file and press Enter.
3.   Press **n** for no processing to save the file just as it is.
4.   If a file exists with the same name you've chosen, you can either append the article to the file or choose another name
5.   Each time you have a prompt you can press **q** (lowercase q) to quit going through the steps for saving a file.

Mailing an Article

To *mail* an article or thread to someone via e-mail, press **m** when you're reading the article or when you've selected it on the menu at the article selection level. You'll see the same prompt you see when you want to save an article.

```
Mail a)rticle, t)hread, h)ot, p)attern, T)agged articles, q)uit: t
```

Press **a** to send an article and **t** to send the thread. Note that you can press **q** to quit the process. If you do continue you'll be prompted for the Internet address.

```
Mail article(s) to [myfriend@great.place.edu]>
```

You type the address after the **>** and press Enter. The address in the square brackets is the address you used the last time you mailed an article, thread, or some other collection of articles to someone. Then you'll see a prompt like this:

```
q)uit, e)dit, i)spell, s)end [Re: Marvel (Billy Gates' new tool) is coming]: s
```

You have the choice of quitting—press **q**; editing the article—press **e**; checking the spelling—press **i** (*ispell* is the name of the preferred spelling checker program on Unix systems); or sending the article—press **s**. The title of the article is what's in the square brackets. Just type in the first letter of the command and take it from there.

Printing an Article

You can print an article when you're reading it or when at the article selection level. Instead of pressing **s** to save or **m** to mail, press **o** (lowercase o) to **print** the file. (Sorry, *p* is already used to go to the previous article or thread.) Pressing **o**, you get this prompt:

```
Print a)rticle, t)hread, h)ot, p)attern, T)agged articles, q)uit: a
```

You can print the article—press **a**; print the thread—press **t**; or print a collection of articles. You can also press **q** to quit printing an article. Soon after you make your choice and press the correct key, the article(s) is printed. Where? That depends on how tin is set up. Talk with your local news administrator to see where an article is printed.

Writing to the Author of an Article

Eventually you will want to respond to a statement or a question on Usenet. Here are a couple of situations that might make you want to respond to the author of an article: Somebody asks a question, you know the answer, and you want to send it. Someone makes a statement with which you strongly agree or disagree, and you want to tell your feelings and offer your opinions.

You have the choice of either posting a follow-up article, which is passed to all other Usenet sites, or writing directly through e-mail to the author. In many cases it's best to write directly to the author, particularly when the original posting asks for specific information that isn't of general interest to everyone else reading the articles in the newsgroup. If your communication with the author is personal in any way, then you *definitely* need to send something by e-mail, not Usenet. There is a lot of traffic on Usenet; many, many bytes are passed around. This isn't meant to discourage you from posting a follow-up article; just think a little about how appropriate it is to post an article that gets wide distribution.

You can send a reply to an article only while you're reading an article. You *cannot* send a reply from the article selection level. If you're using tin,

❑ Pressing **r** sends a reply that includes the original article.

❑ Pressing **R** sends a reply *without* including the original article.

Regardless of which you choose you'll be composing an e-mail message to the author, and it will be obvious if the original article is included. The newsreader handles setting the address; it's taken from the **From:** header. Including the original article sets the context for your reply; it's preferable to include the relevant parts of the original.

Once you press **R** or **r** the newsreader takes over and sets things up to create an e-mail message to the author of the article. You may not be able to use your favorite editor or your usual e-mail program. It depends on the newsreader you're using and how things are set up on the system you use to read Usenet. If you're using a Unix computer system, you have an editor you like to use, and you're not pleased with the one available through tin, you can change the editor by changing the value of the shell variable **VISUAL**. Enter the following commands before you start tin to change the editor to pico, for example, which is relatively easy to use.

```
VISUAL=pico
export VISUAL.
```

On some Unix systems you'll have to use the editor named vi. If your not familiar with vi here are some tips for replying to a message using vi:

❑ Use the down-arrow key or the **j** key to move the cursor so there is one or more blank lines in your reply. There should be at least one blank line after the header lines.

❑ Press **i** (lowercase i, the key to press when you want to insert text) and start writing.

❑ When you're done with the article, press Esc and then enter **:wq**.

After you've entered your message you'll get a prompt asking if you want to send the message, forget it, or edit it again. If you're using tin, you'll see something like:

```
q)uit, e)dit, s)end: s
```

You need only type the first letter:

q	to abandon sending a reply
e	to edit your reply again
s	to send your reply to the author

Posting a Follow-up to an Article

When you respond to a Usenet article you can, as we discussed in the section above, send a reply via e-mail to the author or you can post a *follow-up* article. Posting a follow-up means replying to an article and sending your reply to every Usenet site that carries the newsgroup that contained the original article. Suppose an article is posted in **rec.music.bluenote.blues** discussing the impact of Muddy Waters' music on English rock bands, and you think something important was left out. You might want to post a follow-up responding to the original and sent to any site that carries **rec.music.bluenote.blues**. You ought to post a follow-up for the same reasons you send a reply via e-mail to an author, *except* your reply is interesting to enough people that it is distributed to all of Usenet.

Be sure to summarize or quote from the original article in your follow-up, and read any other follow-up articles so you don't repeat an answer or comment. Since a follow-up is distributed through Usenet, take some time to compose the follow-up; don't reply without thinking about others who will read it. Be concise, be thoughtful, be considerate, and make sure the reply is grammatically correct.

If you're using **tin**:

❑   Pressing **f** will post a follow-up that includes the original article.

❑   Pressing **F** will post a follow-up *without* including the original article.

Regardless of which you choose you'll be composing an article. The newsreader program sets up the follow-up. It fills in a number of headers so the article is recognized as a follow-up article to the correct newsgroup, etc. Here's a view of what you might see if you pressed **f** to post a follow-up to the article we mentioned before.

```
Subject: Re: [Q] Highway 61 lyrics, Fred Mcdowell
Newsgroups: rec.music.folk
References: <384pq7INN9aa@s850.mwc.edu>

ernest ackermann (ernie@s850.mwc.edu) wrote:

> I'm looking for the lyrics to Highway 61 as sung by Mississippi Fred

.. the rest of the original article appears here ...
```

You then compose your follow-up article.

If you use **rn** you'll see advice about posting a follow-up, such as in Figure 6.6.

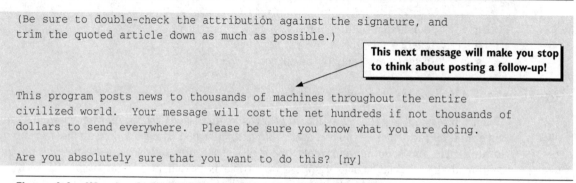

Figure 6.6   Warning from the Program about Posting a Follow-up

Including the original article sets the context for your reply; it's preferable to include at least a portion of it.

You may not be able to use your favorite editor to compose the follow-up. It depends on the newsreader you're using and how things are set up on the system you use to read Usenet.

On some Unix systems you'll have to use the editor named vi. Here are some tips for writing a follow-up using vi:

❑ Use the down-arrow key or the **j** key to move the cursor so there is at least one blank line in your follow-up. There ought to be at least one blank line between all the header information and your article.

❑ Press **i** (lowercase i, the key to press when you want to insert text) and start writing.

❑ When you're done with the article, press Esc and then enter **:wq**.

After you're done writing your follow-up and you're ready to send it off you'll get the prompt:

```
q)uit, e)dit, i)spell, p)ost: p
```

You have the choice of abandoning the follow-up—press **q**; editing the article—press **e**; checking the spelling—press **i** (ispell is the name of the preferred spelling checker program on Unix systems); or posting the article—press **p**. Once you press **p** the follow-up is distributed to other sites on Usenet.

Posting an Article

Posting an article means composing an article—a message, a question, a great discourse on some deep philosophical or extremely important political topic—and distributing it to a newsgroup. To post an article you first choose the newsgroup. Usenet is a fairly wide-open forum. There is no central control and there are thousands of newsgroups on all sorts of topics. But some topics are not appropriate for some newsgroups. Before you post anything, read "A Primer on How to Work with the Usenet Community." You'll find it posted in **news.announce.newusers**. (If you can't find it there, send e-mail to **ernie@mwc.edu** to get a copy.)

Now to the *how* of posting an article. When you're using tin:

1. Select a group, or if you're reading or selecting articles your post will go to the group you're reading.
2. Give the command to post an article to that group; press **w** (lowercase **w**).
3. You'll be prompted for the subject of your article. Choose a subject that isn't too long and clearly states the purpose of your article. Get readers' attention with a clear and succinct subject. Read several articles in the group to see the form that others use.
4. Compose your article. How you do that depends on the editor or software you use to compose messages with tin. In any case, the heading **Subject:** will be filled in by tin as will the heading for the newsgroup. Be sure to leave at least one blank line after the heading **Keywords:**.
5. You'll get the prompt:

```
q)uit, e)dit, i)spell, p)ost: p
```

6. Press **q** to forget about or abandon posting the article, press **e** to edit or modify the article, press **i** to spell-check the article (ispell is the name of the preferred spelling checker on many systems using tin), or press **p** to post the article.

Example 6.1   Posting an Article Using Tin

In this example we'll post an article to a newsgroup using tin. The article is going to ask about newsgroups or FAQs dealing with allergies in humans. It's a typical question to pose to the newsgroup **news.newusers.questions**. You don't have to be a new user to post a question to that group, and not only new users read that newsgroup.

The steps we'll go through are

1. Start **tin**.
2. Select the newsgroup **news.newusers.questions**.
3. Press **w** to post an article.
4. Enter the subject.
5. Compose the article.
6. Post it!

Except for the choice of a newsgroup, you follow the same steps for any newsgroup.

Start tin

☞ **Type** `tin` **and press** Enter.

The way you'll start tin or any newsreader depends on the type of system you're using. On a Unix system you type tin and press Enter.

```
$ tin
```

Select the Newsgroup news.newusers.questions

☞ **Use the down arrow key to highlight the newsgroup**
`news.newusers.questions` **and press** Enter.

Once tin starts, you'll get a screen with newsgroups listed in your file **.newsrc** arranged in a menu. To select a group use the down arrow key or press the **j** key to move the highlight bar or the → to the group **news.newusers.questions**. Since the newsgroup is number **3** on this menu you could also select it by pressing **3**. See Figure 6.7.

```
Group Selection (13 R)                    h=help

      1     14  news.announce.newusers  Explanatory postings for new users. (
      2    863  news.answers            Repository for periodic USENET articl
  ->  3    950  news.newusers.questions  Q & A for users new to the Usenet.
      4    120  rec.arts.animation      Discussion of various kinds of animat
      5    166  rec.arts.fine           Fine arts & artists.
      6   1444  rec.arts.books          Books of all genres, and the publishi
```

Example 6.1 — Posting an Article Using Tin 163

```
 7  3294   rec.arts.movies         Discussions of movies and movie makin
 8     5   rec.arts.poem
 9   391   rec.arts.dance          Any aspects of dance not covered in a
10  1898   rec.food.cooking        Food, cooking, cookbooks, and recipes
11  1039   rec.gardens             Gardening, methods and results.
12    87   rec.music.bluenote.blues The Blues in all forms and all aspect
13   820   rec.music.folk          Folks discussing folk music of variou

<n>=set current to n, TAB=next unread, /=search pattern, c)atchup,
g)oto, j=line down, k=line up, h)elp, m)ove, q)uit, r=toggle all/unread,
s)ubscribe, S)ub pattern, u)nsubscribe, U)nsub pattern, y)ank in/out


            *** End of Groups ***
```

Figure 6.7   Selecting the Newsgroup news.newusers.questions

Press w to Post an Article

☞ **Type** w **and press** Enter.

When you press **w** you'll see:

```
    Post subject []>
```

at the bottom of the screen.

Type in the Subject

☞ **Type** Which Newsgroups or FAQs discuss allergies? **and press** Enter.

You type the subject and press Enter. (The subject is the first thing most readers see about the post, so make it good.) You can see below what is entered for the subject in this case:

```
    Post subject []> Which Newsgroups or FAQs discuss allergies?
```

Compose the Article

After you press Enter, you compose the article. Tin will supply the Subject: and Newsgroups: headings. You supply the rest. Figure 6.8 shows what it would look like when complete.

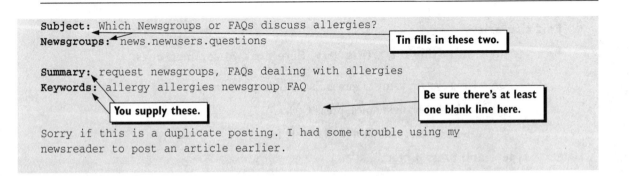

```
Subject: Which Newsgroups or FAQs discuss allergies?
Newsgroups: news.newusers.questions          [Tin fills in these two.]

Summary: request newsgroups, FAQs dealing with allergies
Keywords: allergy allergies newsgroup FAQ
         [You supply these.]                 [Be sure there's at least
                                              one blank line here.]

Sorry if this is a duplicate posting. I had some trouble using my
newsreader to post an article earlier.
```

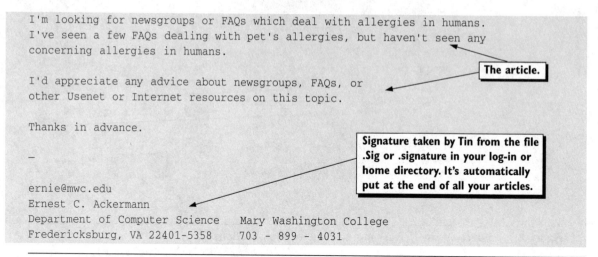

I'm looking for newsgroups or FAQs which deal with allergies in humans.
I've seen a few FAQs dealing with pet's allergies, but haven't seen any
concerning allergies in humans.

> **The article.**

I'd appreciate any advice about newsgroups, FAQs, or
other Usenet or Internet resources on this topic.

Thanks in advance.

—

> **Signature taken by Tin from the file
> .Sig or .signature in your log-in or
> home directory. It's automatically
> put at the end of all your articles.**

ernie@mwc.edu
Ernest C. Ackermann
Department of Computer Science   Mary Washington College
Fredericksburg, VA 22401-5358   703 - 899 - 4031

Figure 6.8   An Article Ready for Posting

☞ **Type the article in the following manner. (Press Enter only when you see it on the example below; otherwise let the words wrap on the screen. The words Summary: and Keywords: will be supplied by tin; you type in the rest):**

Summary: request newsgroups, FAQs dealing with allergies [Enter]
Keywords: allergy allergies newsgroup FAQ [Enter]
[Enter]
[Enter]
I'm looking for newsgroups or FAQs which deal with allergies in humans.
I've seen a few FAQs dealing with pet's allergies, but haven't seen any
concerning allergies in humans. [Enter]
[Enter]
I'd appreciate any advice about newsgroups, FAQs, or
other Usenet or Internet resources on this topic. [Enter]
[Enter]
Thanks in advance. [Enter]
[Enter]

Post the Article

☞ **Methods of posting the article vary. Here are two common ones:**

On a Unix system using vi, press Esc and then type **:wq**.

On a Unix system using pico, press Ctrl-X.

For other systems, contact a local expert for advice.

☞ **Type p and press Enter.**

Now you have to stop using the editor to compose the article and send it. The way you stop using the editor depends on which you were using. Two common ones on Unix systems are vi and pico.

Example 6.2 — Using Pnews to Post an Article ─────────────────── 165

If you were using vi press Esc and then **:wq**. If you were using pico then press **^X** (Ctrl-X). If you were using something else, ask a local expert or read up on how to work with it. In any case you'll get the prompt:

```
q)uit, e)dit, i)spell, p)ost: p
```

Press **p** to post the article.

You'll want to check the newsgroup regularly to see what response your article brings. You may also get some replies by e-mail.

Example 6.2   Using Pnews to Post an Article

You can use the program *Pnews* to post an article. If Pnews isn't available, you may not have permission to post an article or you'll have to post through the newsreader program. Type the command **Pnews** and press Enter. You'll have to give the newsgroup to which the article will be posted, the *distribution*, and the subject or title of the article. The distribution is used to limit where the article will be sent. Choosing **world**, the default, sends the article to all the sites on Usenet carrying the newsgroup. You can limit distribution to your organization or to other categories such as **can** for Canada, **uk** for United Kingdom, and **usa** for United States. Choosing a good title or subject for the article is important; it's usually the first thing someone sees. After you've responded to the preliminary prompts and other questions you'll be able to compose your message.

This example shows how to use the program Pnews to post an article to the newsgroup **alt.test**. It's a good newsgroup to choose for a first try; **alt.test** exists for testing. There are other newsgroups for posting test articles; they all have test as part of their name. You should post all test articles to these test newsgroups; it's a waste of time and space to post to other newsgroups. Besides, if your post was successful, you'll get e-mail back from around the world telling you your post succeeded. That e-mail is usually generated automatically, so you won't be bothering anyone.

Here are the steps to follow:

1. Start the Pnews session.

☞ **Type** pnews **and press** Enter.

2. Type in the name of the newsgroup and select the area of distribution.

☞ **Type** alt.test **and press** Enter.

3. Enter the title or subject.

☞ **Type** Just a test: Can I post?? **and press** Enter.

4. Post your entry and enter file to include.

☞ **Type** y **and press** Enter.

☞ **You have no file to include, so press** Enter.

5. Enter your article.

☞ **Type the following**

`Testing.` [Enter].

`Don't mean to bother anyone.` [Enter].

`Thanks.` [Enter].

6. Post the article.

☞ **Type** s **and press** [Enter].

As you work through this example, your screen will look similar to the screens that follow.

You start by entering the command (type **Pnews** and press Enter).

```
Pnews
```

The program prompts you for the name of the newsgroup and the distribution. If you press Enter after the distribution prompt, you post to all sites on Usenet that carry **alt.test**. See Figure 6.9.

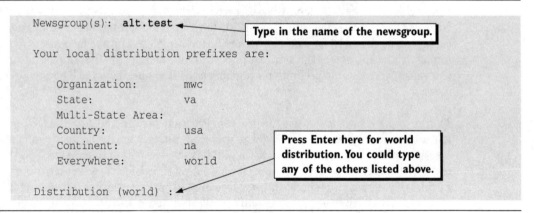

Figure 6.9   Setting a Distribution When Using Pnews

Next you're prompted for the title or subject of the article. This is the first thing users see when viewing lists of articles, but it's not too important in this case since we're testing. See Figure 6.10.

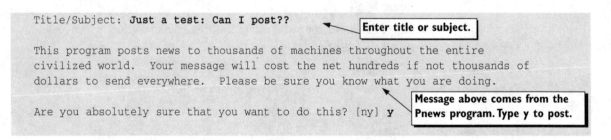

Figure 6.10 Warning from Pnews

Example 6.2 — Using Pnews to Post an Article   167

Pnews then asks for the name of a file you've made up beforehand to put in the article. If you have one, type its name here. We have none so we press Enter; we'll write the article while using Pnews. See Figure 6.11.

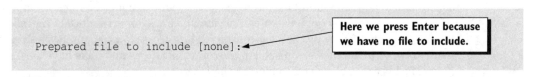

```
Prepared file to include [none]:
```
> Here we press Enter because we have no file to include.

Figure 6.11 Pnews Prompt for Including a Prepared File

Pnews then starts an editor session so you can compose your article. You'll see a screen with the headers **Newsgroups:**, **Subject:**, **Distribution:**, and **Organization:** filled in by Pnews. You can complete or change any of the headers. You do need to leave one blank line after the header **Keywords:**. If you're on a Unix system and have to use the editor vi, move the cursor to two lines below **Keywords:**, press **i** (for insert), type your article, and when the article is complete press Esc and then :**wq**. See Figure 6.12.

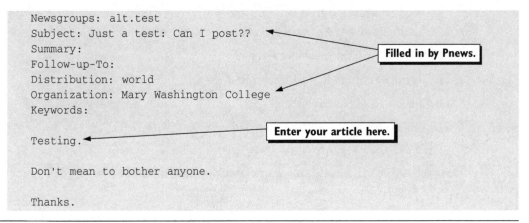

```
Newsgroups: alt.test
Subject: Just a test: Can I post??
Summary:
Follow-up-To:
Distribution: world
Organization: Mary Washington College
Keywords:

Testing.

Don't mean to bother anyone.

Thanks.
```
> Filled in by Pnews.

> Enter your article here.

Figure 6.12 A Test Article

After you enter the article you'll be prompted to either send (post) the article, abort (throw away) the article, edit the article, or list it. See Figure 6.13.

```
Send, abort, edit, or list ? s
```
> Type s to post the article, then press Enter.

Figure 6.13 Options for Posting

End of Example 6.2

Proper Usenet Etiquette

From 5 to 30 million people throughout the world read the news through Usenet. That is a lot of people! And they're not all only reading; a lot of them post articles or respond to articles in some way. It's reasonable to think about the people who use Usenet as a community of users. With such a large and diverse community some rules of behavior or etiquette are necessary. Many of the sites that are part of Usenet have rules, policies, and procedures that need to be followed as well. In some cases, not following the rules means you lose access to a computer system. Additionally, there are several laws governing electronic communications and folks have been sued for libel or arrested because of remarks made on the Internet.

There isn't any central control for Usenet, and there is no one except local news or system administrators to enforce rules (not laws) of behavior on Usenet. This absence of central control gives Usenet some of its vitality. It's essential that the users follow some guidelines to make using Usenet as effective, efficient, and pleasant as possible.

Over the years several documents have been developed about proper Usenet etiquette. These are regularly posted in **news.announce.newusers**, **news.answers**, or **news.newusers.questions**. Here is a list of some of them you ought to read:

❑ "A Primer on How to Work With the Usenet Community"

❑ "Emily Postnews Answers Your Questions on Netiquette"

❑ "Hints on Writing Style for Usenet"

❑ "How to Find the Right Place to Post (FAQ)"

❑ "Please Read before Posting"

❑ "Rules for Posting to Usenet"

❑ "A Weekly FAQ on Test Postings"

As you look over the rules and examples of proper behavior on Usenet you'll see they break into two categories:

1. **Rules for Using Usenet in an Effective and Efficient Manner.** These rules are based on the observation that there are many, many Usenet sites and participants, and most of the participants are busy folks. So before you post an article, post a long article or follow-up, or post a test message, think about the effect it will have on Usenet. Think about how many sites and networks will be dealing with your material. Make your postings concise and appropriate. Avoid duplication and repetition; do your own research before asking a question. Use a response by e-mail rather than a follow-up whenever you can. Use descriptive and accurate headings, since the readers can tell at a glance if they would like to read your posting. By all means attach a "signature" to your articles, but don't make it too large or difficult to understand. There are several newsgroups where you can advertise or announce products, but there are many newsgroups where this isn't appropriate. The readers will rise up against advertisements, demand an apology from the person posting an advertisement, or demand the author of the article be banned from Usenet.

2. **Rules for Working with Other Usenet Users.** These rules are based on a desire to treat others with courtesy and respect. As you read articles and think about writing your own remember that the folks writing and reading these things are humans. They make mistakes in judgment sometimes, so don't get crazy over a remark that someone has made, since they may have just made a mistake. The term *flame* refers to a message or a posting that's meant to insult someone or provoke controversy. Take the time to think before you post a flame or respond to one hastily. Also remember that other Usenet users have feelings like yours and sometimes they're easily hurt. Don't try to be sarcastic or use subtle humor—it's really hard to do effectively in writing. The folks who read your writing won't have the benefit of seeing your face, hearing a change in your voice, or seeing your body language. Realize that your writing gets worldwide distribution, and you never know who will read it. It can be read by people whose cultural background is very different from yours. Also consider the possibility that your postings will be read by your friends, supervisors, teachers, or parents. Be considerate, careful, and conscientious.

Signatures, FAQs, and Finding Newsgroups

Signatures

As you read articles in Usenet you'll see a few lines at the end of most messages with the author's name, e-mail address, and sometimes a phone number, a graphic image, or a clever saying. That's called a *signature*. (You've probably guessed they don't type an elaborate signature each time they send e-mail or post an article on Usenet.) Most newsreaders and e-mail systems will append whatever is in a file named **.signature** to articles you post and all your e-mail. Tin does just that. To have a signature attached to all your posts and replies through tin, put the items you want to display in the file **.Sig** or **.signature**. Tin first checks for **.Sig**, and if that doesn't exist then the file **.signature**.

You probably can make a fancy or long signature, but think twice about it. Every character in your signature is another byte. If you post a message and it goes to thousands of sites, each byte is multiplied by thousands. Each character is passed between lots of systems and stored on lots of disks. Everybody on Usenet knows you are a creative and clever person. You don't need to prove it to them through your signature. Keep the file **.signature** simple. It's enough to put your name, e-mail address, phone number, and some mention of your company, school, or agency.

FAQs

FAQ stands for Frequently Asked Questions, a collection of common questions with answers, or a single Frequently Asked Question. Many newsgroups have volunteers who put together and maintain a collection of questions and answers. Most newsgroups have a FAQ and they're very informative and useful. You can find them posted either in the newsgroup the FAQ was created for, or posted to **news.answers**. Several newsgroups hold these FAQs; you'll see them referred to as the ***.answers** newsgroups. Some of these are **alt.answers**, **comp.answers**, and **sci.answers**. Here is a short list of FAQs to give you an idea of the variety of topics.

rec.games.netrek FAQ List	Comp.Object FAQ
MINIX Frequently Asked Questions	rec.sport.hockey FAQ
HOLOCAUST FAQ: The "Leuchter Report"	FAQ: Sci.Polymers
Tolkien: Frequently Asked Questions	FAQ: rec.music.dylan
rec.martial-arts FAQ	comp.graphics.animation FAQ

This is just a small sample of the articles from **news.answers**.

Be sure to consult the FAQ for information *before* you post a question to a newsgroup. A newsgroup's FAQ was created to be consulted. It may be embarrassing for you if you post a question to a newsgroup and you get several replies (or follow-ups) letting you (and everyone else reading the newsgroup) know that you should read the FAQ before asking other questions. It also could be annoying to other members of the group to see questions that could be answered by a little research beforehand. The FAQ for a group will be posted regularly to the group and also posted to one of the *.answers groups, such as **news.answers**. If you can't find the FAQ you're looking for there, try anonymous FTP to **rtfm.mit.edu** and look in the directory **/pub/ usenet-by-group** or **/pub/usenet-by-hierarchy**. Many groups have a directory there that contains the FAQ for the group. For example, to find the FAQ for **rec.food.cooking**, look in either of these directories:

```
/pub/usenet-by-group/rec.food.cooking
/pub/usenet-by-hierarchy/rec/food/cooking
```

Also, the directory **/pub/usenet-by-group/news.answers** contains all the FAQs. You'll also find FAQs available through several Gopher sites, for example, **gopher.physics.utoronto.ca**.

Finding Newsgroups

There are thousands of newsgroups. How can you find out which to read or even which ones exist?

To find the groups that your site carries you can ask your local Usenet administrator for a list of groups. Or, when you're using tin, press **y** at the group selection level to "yank in" the list of all the available newsgroups.

There are several lists of newsgroups available through Usenet. Keep your eye on the newsgroups **news.answers**, **news.lists**, or **news.groups** so you can read or save these listings when they appear (usually monthly). Also, there are several anonymous FTP sites you can access to get the lists. (See Chapter 4 for details about using FTP.) Use anonymous FTP to **ftp.uwasa.fi**, and retrieve the file **newsgrps.zip** from the directory **pc/doc-net** to get a file which, when you uncompress it, will give you several lists of newsgroups on Usenet. The URL for that file is:

```
ftp://ftp.uwasa.fi/pc/doc-net/newsgrps.zip.
```

Two URL specifications for other anonymous FTP sites and directories that contain these lists of newsgroups are:

```
ftp://ftp.uu.net usenet/news.lists/
ftp://rtfm.mit.edu/pub/usenet-by-group/news.lists/
```

Recommended Newsgroups and Articles

There are several newsgroups that a beginning or infrequent user should browse. These newsgroups include information about Usenet, lists of FAQs for Usenet and several newsgroups, and articles that will help you use Usenet. The newsgroups are:

news.announce.newgroups   Articles dealing with forming and announcing new newsgroups. A place to get the lists of all newsgroups.

news.announce.newusers   Explanatory and important articles for new or infrequent Usenet users.

news.answers   This is where periodic Usenet postings are put. The periodic postings are primarily FAQs. This is often the first place you should look when you have a question.

news.newusers.questions   This newsgroup is dedicated to questions from new Usenet users. There is no such thing as a "dumb question" here. You ought to browse this group to see if others have asked the same question that's been bothering you. Once you get some expertise in using Usenet, you'll want to check this group to see if you can help someone.

The articles you will want to read are posted in **news.announce.newusers**. Here's a list:

❑   "A Primer on How to Work with the Usenet Community"

❑   "Answers to Frequently Asked Questions about Usenet"

❑   "Emily Postnews Answers Your Questions on Netiquette"

❑   "Hints on Writing Style for Usenet"

❑   "How to Find the Right Place to Post (FAQ)"

❑   "Rules for Posting to Usenet"

❑   "Usenet Software: History and Sources"

❑   "Welcome to news.newusers.questions"

❑   "What is Usenet?"

Summary

Usenet news was started to share information among users of Unix computer systems. The news is a collection of messages called articles where each one is designated as belonging to one or more newsgroups. These articles are passed from one computer system to another. An administrator at one site determines which newsgroups his site will receive and send on to another site.

Users at a site can usually select any of the groups that are available and often have the capability to reply to, follow-up, or post an article. Some estimates put the number of participants at over 30 million worldwide.

There isn't any central control over Usenet. A local administrator can decide which groups to receive and whether to allow articles to be passed along. There usually isn't a means to screen articles from a group or screen articles that go out. It's close to anarchy, but the independent participation gives it vibrancy and strength.

Usenet is a community of users helping each other and exchanging opinions. A code of behavior has developed. The rules can be divided into two categories: making efficient use of Usenet and treating other Usenet users with respect. The rules are, of course, voluntary, but users are expected to get a copy of some of the articles dealing with working with Usenet and to follow the rules. Several newsgroups carry regular postings of articles meant to inform the Usenet community. These are often found in the groups **news.announce.newgroups**, **news.announce.newusers**, and **news.answers**.

There are several thousand newsgroups, arranged into categories. Some of the major categories are:

alt	Anything goes
bit	Groups also available through Listserv on BITNET
comp	Groups dealing with computing and computer science
rec	Groups that are recreational
sci	Groups dealing with topics in the sciences
soc	Groups dealing with social issues and various cultures

The articles that make up the news are read by software called *newsreaders*. There are several different types of newsreaders. Which one you use will depends on your preferences and what's available on the system you use to access Usenet. Some of the more popular newsreaders are rn, nn, trn, and tin. The last two collect articles in a group into *threads*—collections of articles all dealing with a single posting. Having the newsreader keep track of threads makes it easier to follow a discussion. In this chapter we concentrated on using tin.

Tin is software that supports a convenient way to manage your dealings with Usenet; it's a newsreader. The articles are arranged into threads, so tin is called a threaded newsreader. You use tin to select which newsgroups you would like to read by subscribing or unsubscribing from the groups available where you access Usenet. Once a group is chosen you can deal with individual articles by reading them, saving them in a file, printing them, mailing articles to any e-mail address, or responding to them by either posting a response to be read by anyone who reads Usenet or mailing a response to the author. You can also post an article to a newsgroup.

To start tin, type **tin** and press Enter. You'll see a list of newsgroups and an opening screen. You are at the *group selection level* of tin. You will see a numbered listing of the newsgroups you currently subscribe to. The numeral after the group number indicates how many articles are available in that group. Near the bottom of the screen is a list of several commands available at this level. To read articles you have to go to the *article selection level* of tin. You do that by selecting a group and pressing Enter. Here's a brief list of instructions for using tin:

Getting Help. Press **h** (lowercase) for a list of commands available at the current level.

Quitting Tin. Type **q** (lowercase) to go to previous level and eventually quit. Press **Q** (uppercase) to quit **tin** any time.

Mailing an Article. Press **m** to mail an article to an e-mail address. Press **a** to mail the article, or press **t** to mail the thread. You will be prompted for an address. Enter an e-mail address, then press **s** to send it. Before sending it you have the option to **q**)uit, **e**)dit, or **i**)spell—this checks the spelling.

Replying to the Author by E-Mail. Press **r** to mail a response which includes the original article or press **R** to mail a response that does not. You will then be editing a file with your editor to formulate your response.

Posting a Follow-up. Press **f** to include the original article in the response or press **F** to write a follow-up that doesn't include the article. You will then be editing a file with your editor to formulate your response.

Posting an Article. Press **w** (lowercase) to post an article. Enter a subject when prompted. You will then see a screen with the headings **Subject:**, **Newsgroups:**, **Summary:**, and **Keywords:**. Use your editor (vi) to complete the article. The cursor should be two lines below the line that begins with **Keywords:**. If you're on a Unix system and have to use vi as the editor, start writing on that line by pressing **i** to insert text. When you're done, press Esc and then enter **:wq**. Follow the instructions to post the article. Remember, posting an article to a newsgroup is a public act; your e-mail address is attached to the posted article. Whatever you write and post will be read by all readers of that newsgroup and many of the newsgroups have worldwide distribution.

Finding Newsgroups. At the **Group Selection Menu** press **y** to yank in the list of all groups available at your site. You'll be at the group selection level so you can browse the groups if you wish: **j** to move down, **k** to move up, or spacebar to go to next page. A **u** in front of a group name means that you haven't subscribed to it.

Subscribing. Choose a group and press **s**. Another way is to type **g** followed by the name of the group (then press Enter). You will be asked for the position it should have in your group menu. From then on, until you unsubscribe, that group will appear in the **Group Selection Menu**.

Unsubscribing. Choose a group and press **u**. From then on, until you subscribe to the group again, it won't appear on your group selection menu.

You'll probably find Usenet a valuable resource for information on a wide array of topics. You'll probably also enjoy reading and participating in the discussions on Usenet. Just remember, get your other work done and live your life outside the Internet.

Exercises

1. Find out a few things about the system you use to read the Usenet news.
   a. How many newsgroups are available at your site?
   b. Whom do you contact, by e-mail or phone, if you have questions about adding or removing newsgroups?
   c. Which newsreaders are available on your system?

2. Use your newsreader to look at the articles listed in **news.announce.newusers**.
   a. Which articles are listed? (You don't have to list more than 10.)
   b. Read one of the articles that would give some guidance to a new user.
   c. Send by e-mail a copy of the file to a friend who would benefit from reading it.

3. Browse the newsgroups in the hierarchy **rec.music** (use your local newsreader). Find one you think is interesting.
   a. What is its name?
   b. If there is a FAQ for the newsgroup, read or retrieve a copy of it. If you can't find one, post a request to **news.newusers.questions** or the newsgroup itself, asking if there is a FAQ for the newsgroup.
   c. Give a brief description of the types of articles you've found in the group.

4. Browse the articles in **news.newusers.questions**. If you find an article that poses a question you think you could answer, send the author the answer by replying to the article. If you can't find any you can answer, find one that's interesting and send e-mail to the author asking for a copy of the answer.

5. This chapter deals with Usenet. The previous chapter dealt with interest groups or mailing lists.
   a. Which one do you prefer working with? Explain.
   b. Are there some sorts of discussions or groups for which using Usenet would be preferable to using an interest group? Explain.
   c. What situations are more suited to working with interest groups rather than Usenet? Explain.

6. Suppose you could read articles from only five newsgroups. Which would they be? Why?

Hytelnet
Working on the Internet
Using Telnet

Telnet, covered in Chapter 3, is the service you'll likely use to log in to other computer systems on the Internet. The examples and exercises in Chapter 3 show the variety of services and resources you can take advantage of and the things you can do using Telnet. There are literally thousands of Telnet sites. Having all those opportunities sometimes makes it hard to keep track of what is available, hard to find a source for some information or service when you need it, and awfully hard to remember the domain name or IP address of all the sites you'd like to contact. It's a common situation on the Internet: There are so many interesting resources available that you need guides to help find what you want.

Hytelnet is a tool for working with Telnet. It was created by Peter Scott and others at University of Saskatchewan. Hytelnet makes it relatively easy to look through and use an organized list of Telnet sites. You browse the collection using a hypertext interface; that's why it's called Hytelnet. The sites are arranged in categories by the type of service, such as library catalog, database, bulletin board, electronic book, or network information. Hytelnet also comes with a glossary of network terms and other information about Telnet, Hytelnet itself, and software used on various library systems. It's great to be able to access or get information about all sorts of services and resources from one program. Hytelnet is available by anonymous FTP (for PC, Mac, Unix, or VMS systems) or you can try it out through Gopher. Fortunately, it's common for someone on the Internet to put together something useful and share it with others.

When you use Hytelnet you move from one item to another through a hypertext interface. Hytelnet runs locally on your system and, if your system allows, it's possible to make Telnet connections from your site while you're using it. You need to select a library, database, bulletin board, or some other type of resource. The program gives you information about contacting the site through Telnet and information about using the services at the remote site. The Unix and VMS versions allow you to invoke Telnet to connect to any sites listed. In this way Hytelnet is a tool and a guide. If it's not available on your system, you can try accessing it in one of the following ways:

❑ Hytelnet is available on the World Wide Web by using the URL **http://www.usask.ca/cgi-bin/hytelnet**. Chapter 11 discusses how to use the World Wide Web browsers Lynx and Mosaic. Appendix B covers the browser Netscape Navigator.

❑ Hytelnet is also available through Gopher. Start a Gopher session with **liberty.uc.wlu.edu**, choose the item **Explore Internet Resources**, and then choose **Telnet Login to Sites (Hytelnet)**. Using Gopher is covered in Chapter 9.

Chapter Overview

In this chapter the topics we'll cover include:

❑ Starting Hytelnet

❑ Using Hytelnet

❑ Using Hypertext

❑ Hytelnet Keystroke Commands

❑ Hytelnet Menus

❑ Using Hytelnet to Search a Library Catalog

Starting Hytelnet

Let's take a look at what you might see when you start Hytelnet on your system or get to it through Telnet. Figure 7.1 shows the main menu for Hytelnet on a Unix system; the display on other systems is similar.

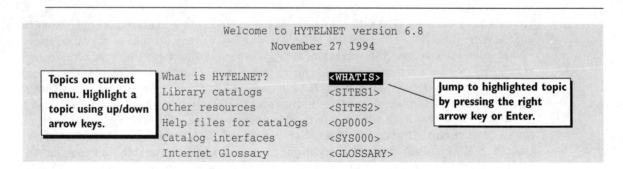

```
                    Welcome to HYTELNET version 6.8
                         November 27 1994
```

Topics on current menu. Highlight a topic using up/down arrow keys.		
What is HYTELNET?	`<WHATIS>`	Jump to highlighted topic by pressing the right arrow key or Enter.
Library catalogs	`<SITES1>`	
Other resources	`<SITES2>`	
Help files for catalogs	`<OP000>`	
Catalog interfaces	`<SYS000>`	
Internet Glossary	`<GLOSSARY>`	

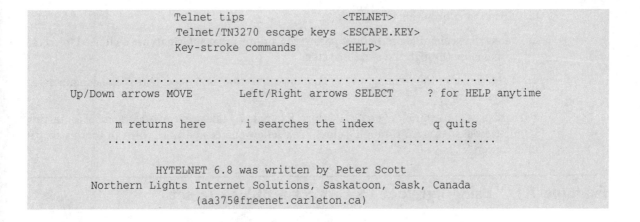

```
        Telnet tips               <TELNET>
        Telnet/TN3270 escape keys <ESCAPE.KEY>
        Key-stroke commands       <HELP>


.........................................................
Up/Down arrows MOVE      Left/Right arrows SELECT    ? for HELP anytime


   m returns here     i searches the index       q quits
.........................................................


      HYTELNET 6.8 was written by Peter Scott
Northern Lights Internet Solutions, Saskatoon, Sask, Canada
          (aa375@freenet.carleton.ca)
```

Figure 7.1   Hytelnet Main Menu

The topics you can select are on the screen, with the selected topic highlighted. If you press Enter or the right arrow you'll select the item that's highlighted. Hytelnet is a hypertext browser, which means that you move from one highlighted region of the screen to another using up/down arrows, jump to another topic by using the right arrow key (→), and return to the previous topic using the left arrow key (←). You can see the help screen by pressing **?** at any time. Whenever you press **m** you're brought back to the main menu. To quit Hytelnet, press **q**. The Unix version also has an option **i** to search the list of names of sites based on a keyword. We'll explain each of the items and commands in the following sections of this chapter.

Once you get to a screen that has instructions for reaching a specific site you can start a Telnet session. If you're using Hytelnet on a Unix system you then press the right arrow or Enter to start Telnet.

The categories and lists of Telnet sites were compiled by Peter Scott (**aa375@freenet.carleton.ca**). He also maintains the lists with regular updates. The Unix and VMS software was written by Earl Fogel (**fogel@herald.usask.edu**), and the Macintosh software by Charles Burchill (**burchil@ccu.umanitoba.ca**). Hytelnet is shareware; see the section labeled **READ.ME** in the section **What is HYTELNET?** of the main screen for information about paying your fair share. You can retrieve the software by using anonymous FTP to **ftp.usask.ca** and looking in the directory **/pub/hytelnet** (**ftp://ftp.usask.ca/pub/hytelnet/**).

Using Hytelnet

In this section we'll look at some of the commands and methods you'll use working with Hytelnet. You begin using Hytelnet by starting the program on your system or going to another system through Telnet. Then you select topics and jump to them using the arrow keys.

When you come to a screen with information about a specific site you'll see the domain name and IP address to connect to the site. You'll also see instructions about what to do once connected; things such as user name, password, or menu choices to make to get to the service. Be sure to:

❏ Read the information on the screen.

❏ Make notes about log-in names, passwords, or any other information you'll need to access or navigate through the remote system.

❏ Press Enter or the right arrow to make the connection, or make a note of the domain name or address.

To start, here's an example of using Hytelnet. Example 7.1 takes you up to the point of contacting a bulletin board system through Telnet. You follow the comparable steps to contact or get information for any site.

Example 7.1   Using Hytelnet to Contact a BBS by Telnet

In this first example we're going to start Hytelnet and go through a couple of menus until we get to the list of bulletin board systems (BBS) you can reach through Hytelnet. Then you'll see the information Hytelnet gives about contacting a specific BBS named "Classroom Earth!" The steps we'll go through are the same you would use to contact any BBS listed in Hytelnet; you use similar steps to contact any site. For this example, we're assuming Hytelnet is being used on a Unix computer system. The steps are similar for any system.

1. Start Hytelnet and select the topic **Other Resources <SITES2>**.
2. Use the arrow keys to select the topic **<BBS000> General Bulletin Boards**.
3. Use the arrow keys to select any site; here it's **<BBS071> Classroom Earth!**
4. Take note of important information. Then make the Telnet connection or copy down the address.

Start Hytelnet and Select the Topic Other Resources <SITES2>

☞ **Type** `hytelnet` **and press** Enter. **Press** ⬇ **twice to highlight** <SITES2>.

At Hytelnet's main menu, use the down arrow key to highlight **<SITES2>**. See Figure 7.2.

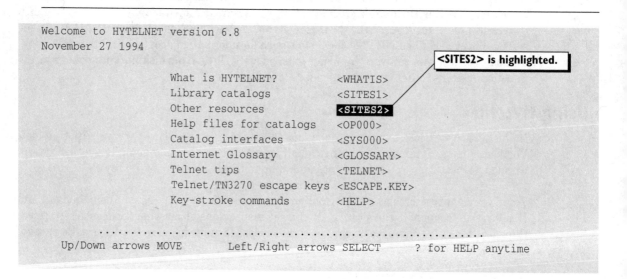

```
Welcome to HYTELNET version 6.8
November 27 1994
                                                    ┌─────────────────────────┐
                                                    │ <SITES2> is highlighted. │
                                                    └─────────────────────────┘
              What is HYTELNET?          <WHATIS>
              Library catalogs           <SITES1>
              Other resources           ▌<SITES2>▐
              Help files for catalogs    <OP000>
              Catalog interfaces         <SYS000>
              Internet Glossary          <GLOSSARY>
              Telnet tips                <TELNET>
              Telnet/TN3270 escape keys  <ESCAPE.KEY>
              Key-stroke commands        <HELP>


 . . . . . . . . . . . . . . . . . . . . . . . . . . . . . . . . . . . . . . .
 Up/Down arrows MOVE      Left/Right arrows SELECT     ? for HELP anytime
```

Example 7.1 — Using Hytelnet to Contact a BBS by Telnet——————179

```
    m returns here      i searches the index        q quits
..........................................................

            HYTELNET 6.8 was written by Peter Scott
Northern Lights Internet Solutions, Saskatoon, Sask, Canada
                (aa375@freenet.carleton.ca)
```

Figure 7.2   Selecting <SITES2> on the Main Menu

☞ **Press →** or **Enter** **to jump to the topic** Other resources.

Use the Arrow Keys to Select the Topic <BBS000> General Bulletin Boards

☞ **Press ↓ until** <BBS000> **is highlighted.**

You'll see the screen in Figure 7.3.

```
Other Telnet-accessible resources

<ARC000>    Archie: Archive Server Listing Service
<FUL000>    Databases and bibliographies
<DIS000>    Distributed File Servers (Gopher/WAIS/WWW)
<BOOKS>     Electronic books
<FEE000>    Fee-Based Services
<FRE000>    FREE-NETs & Community Computing Systems
<BBS000>    General Bulletin Boards
<NAS000>    NASA databases
<NET000>    Network Information Services
<DIR000>    Whois/White Pages/Directory Services
<OTH000>    Miscellaneous resources
```

<BBS000> is highlighted.

**Figure 7.3   Selecting <BBS000> General Bulletin Boards from the
Other Telnet—accessible Resources Menu**

☞ **Press →** or **Enter** **to jump to the following screen,** General Bulletin
Boards.

You see the screen in Figure 7.4.

```
General Bulletin Boards

<BBS001> Advanced Technology Information Network (Calif Ag Tech Institute)
<BBS039> AfterFive BBS
<BBS089> Automated Library Information Xchange (ALIX)
<BBS043> Badboy's Better Bulletin Board System (BBBBS)
<BBS002> Bergen By Byte A/S - Bergen - Norway
<BBS051> Bulletin Board of the ProMAX Users Group
<BBS052> CAPPnet: California Academic Partnership Program
```

```
<BBS071> Classroom Earth!  ◄─────────────
<BBS005> Cosy at Victoria, British Columbia, Canada
<BBS007> Delft University Bulletin Board System (Netherlands)
<BBS038> Edinburgh University Computing Service - EUCS
<BBS074> Electric Ideas Clearinghouse bulletin board system (EICBBS)
<BBS058> European Southern Observatory Bulletin Board
<BBS087> Federal Bulletin Board U.S. Government Printing Office (GPO)
<BBS090> Federal Highway Administration Electronic Bulletin Board System
<BBS068> FedWorld: National Technical Information Service
<BBS008> Florida Atlantic University (CYBERNET)
<BBS093> Galacticomm Major BBS Demo System
<BBS086> Global Integrated Pest Management Information System
<BBS041> Grants Bulletin Board (CALSTATE)
<BBS084> GREX: Cyberspace Communications
- press space for more -
```

> Select <BBS071>
> Classroom Earth!
> Jump to high-
> lighted topic by
> pressing the right
> arrow key or Enter.

Figure 7.4   First Screen of General Bulletin Boards Menu

Use the arrow keys to select topic <BBS071> Classroom Earth!

☞   **Highlight** <BBS071>**, then press ➡ or** Enter**.**

You will see the screen in Figure 7.5

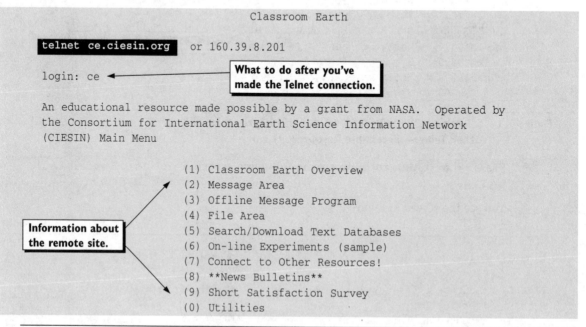

```
                              Classroom Earth

   telnet ce.ciesin.org    or 160.39.8.201

   login: ce  ◄──────────
                            What to do after you've
                            made the Telnet connection.

   An educational resource made possible by a grant from NASA.  Operated by
   the Consortium for International Earth Science Information Network
   (CIESIN) Main Menu

                          (1) Classroom Earth Overview
                          (2) Message Area
                          (3) Offline Message Program
                          (4) File Area
   Information about      (5) Search/Download Text Databases
   the remote site.       (6) On-line Experiments (sample)
                          (7) Connect to Other Resources!
                          (8) **News Bulletins**
                          (9) Short Satisfaction Survey
                          (0) Utilities
```

Figure 7.5   Hytelnet Screen for Classroom Earth!

☞   **With** telnet ce.ciesin.org **highlighted, press** Enter **or** ➡ **to connect to Telnet.**

Example 7.2 — Using Hypertext————————————181

When you connect to Telnet you'll be asked if you want to make the connection. Before you actually start Telnet, be sure to take note of any information on this screen about how to log in, any usernames or passwords you might need, and how to log out or disconnect. In this case, you'll have to give the log-in name **ce** once you're connected.

————————————End of Example 7.1————————————

Using Hypertext

Hytelnet is a hypertext browsing tool for finding the information you'll need to contact a site through Telnet. You use the arrow keys to go from topic to topic. Each screen you'll see is kept in a file. The items in brackets < >, for example **<SITES1>**, are called *links*. When a link is highlighted and you press the right arrow or Enter key, you move or jump to the screen the link represents. The links in this case are the names of files. So as you move from topic to topic or link to link you're looking at files. Hytelnet keeps track of where you are so you can go forward or backward, and also finds the files represented by the links. You use the right arrow key to go from one topic to another, and the left arrow key to return to a previous topic. You follow the paths you've created one link at a time.

Getting to Main Menu, Help, and Quitting

Some keys allow for larger jumps. You can always get to the main menu by pressing **m**, get help by pressing **?**, and quit the program by pressing **q**.

Working with More Than One Screen

Some of the files you'll look at fill more than one screen. In that case the message:

```
- press space for more -
```

will be at the bottom of the screen. Once you go on to another screen you press **-** or **u** to go to a previous screen.

Searching the Index

Some versions of Hytelnet, e.g., Unix and VMS, include a feature that allows you to search an index of sites. The index is the list of the names of all the sites as they appear in the menus. You perform a keyword search after pressing the **i** key or the **/** key.

Example 7.2   Using Hypertext, Working with More Than One Screen, Searching the Hytelnet Index, Quitting Hytelnet

This example demonstrates using hypertext, working with more than one screen, and searching the Hytelnet index. We'll start Hytelnet and press **i** to start a search of the index using the keyword *environment*. Press the right arrow or Enter key and we'll see a list of sites whose titles contain the word *environment*. They can be selected in hypertext fashion. You can pick one, take a look, go back to the list, select another, and so on. In order to conserve space we won't list everything you'll see on the screen. Here are the steps:

1. Start Hytelnet and press **i**.
2. Enter the keyword **environment** and press the Enter key.
3. Choose an item and jump to the selected item.
4. Go back to the list by pressing the left arrow key, then choose another, and so on.
5. Press **q** to quit Hytelnet.

Start Hytelnet and Press i, then Enter the Keyword environment

☞ **At the system prompt, type** `hytelnet` **and press** ⌗Enter⌗.

You will see the screen in Figure 7.1.

☞ **Type** i.

The phrase Search Index: will appear on the bottom of the screen as shown in Figure 7.6. This is a prompt for you to enter a keyword.

☞ **Type** environment **and press** ➡ **or** ⌗Enter⌗.

Figure 7.6 shows the main menu after you type **i** and the keyword environment. When you press Enter, Hytelnet uses the keyword to search its entire list of items. When it's done searching, a list of items containing the keyword is displayed on the screen. Figure 7.6 shows the list of items found with the keyword *environment*.

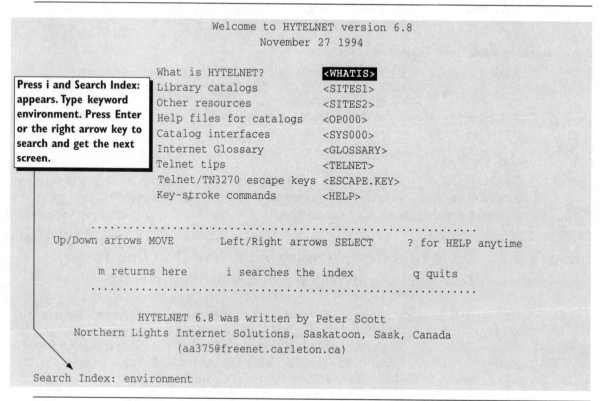

```
                  Welcome to HYTELNET version 6.8
                         November 27 1994

                  What is HYTELNET?        <WHATIS>
                  Library catalogs         <SITES1>
                  Other resources          <SITES2>
                  Help files for catalogs  <OP000>
                  Catalog interfaces       <SYS000>
                  Internet Glossary        <GLOSSARY>
                  Telnet tips              <TELNET>
                  Telnet/TN3270 escape keys <ESCAPE.KEY>
                  Key-stroke commands      <HELP>


   ............................................................
   Up/Down arrows MOVE      Left/Right arrows SELECT    ? for HELP anytime

       m returns here      i searches the index       q quits
   ............................................................

          HYTELNET 6.8 was written by Peter Scott
   Northern Lights Internet Solutions, Saskatoon, Sask, Canada
              (aa375@freenet.carleton.ca)


Search Index: environment
```

> Press i and Search Index: appears. Type keyword environment. Press Enter or the right arrow key to search and get the next screen.

Figure 7.6 Hytelnet Main Menu With Search Index: and Keyword

Example 7.2 — Using Hypertext 183

Choose an Item and Jump to the Selected Item

☞ **Press ⬇ twice to select** `<ful015>`.

Figure 7.7 shows the list of items resulting from Hytelnet using the keyword environment to search its collection of items. This list is just like any other Hytelnet menu. To select the item **Meeman Archive of environmental journalism**, press the down arrow (or **j**) twice so that **<ful015>** is highlighted as shown in Figure 7.7.

```
<bbs056>  University of Illinois Division of Environmental Health and Safety BBS
<ful008>  Environmental Education database
<ful015>  Meeman Archive of environmental journalism
<nas006>  ENVIROnet (The Space Environment Information Service)
<oth140>  EE-Link: The Environmental Education Gopher Server
<oth026>  NOAA-Space Environment Services Center
<us192>   U.S. Environmental Protection Agency, EPA National Online Library System
<us179>   Syracuse University and, SUNY College of Environmental Science & Forestry
```

> **Press down arrow or j to select this topic. Then press the right arrow key or Enter to jump to this topic.**

Figure 7.7   Results of Keyword Search with <ful015> Selected

☞ **Press ➡ or** Enter **to jump to the selected item.**

Being able to jump from any screen to another or from any topic to another is what hypertext is all about. You easily move from one topic to another.

Figures 7.8 and 7.9 show the screens connected with **<ful015>**.

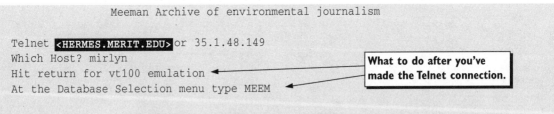

```
              Meeman Archive of environmental journalism

Telnet <HERMES.MERIT.EDU> or 35.1.48.149
Which Host? mirlyn
Hit return for vt100 emulation
At the Database Selection menu type MEEM
```

> **What to do after you've made the Telnet connection.**

```
                  INTRODUCTION TO THE MEEMAN ARCHIVE

The Meeman Archive is a database covering environmental journalism. The
Archive has over 1,000 entries and grows yearly. Established by the
Scripps-Howard News Service in 1982, MEEM contains articles from 1980 to
the present.  In addition to the articles indexed in MEEM, the Meeman
Archive contains clippings from the Ann Arbor News, several
environmental periodicals, and the National Park Service's publication,
"Feedback".
```

```
The Meeman Archive is located in UM's School of Natural Resources, 2036
Dana Building. All articles are located there and can be copied for five
cents per page. Please allow 24 hours for copying. Archive staff can be
contacted by calling (313) 763-5327 or by visiting the archive. Please
bring the item call number, which is found on the first line of each
item record.
- press space for more -
```

Press spacebar for next screen.

Figure 7.8   First Screen for Meeman Archive of Environmental Journalism

☞ **Press the spacebar to see the next screen.**

This entry, like many in Hytelnet, goes on for more than one screen. Press the spacebar to get to the next screen, shown in Figure 7.9.

```
               To search by:    TITLE:            t=
                                AUTHOR:           a=
                                SUBJECT:          s=
                                KEYWORD:          k=
               Enter NEWS [return] for more information on searching MEEM
```

Figure 7.9   Second Screen for Meeman Archive of Environmental Journalism

Go Back to the List and Choose Another Item

☞ **Press ← or u.**

Pressing the left arrow key or **u** takes you back to the list as shown in Figure 7.10. Once again you're using the features of hypertext to jump from one item to another. Use the arrow keys to select another item. In Figure 7.10 the first one on the list is selected.

```
<bbs056>   University of Illinois Division of Environmental Health and Safety BBS
<ful008>   Environmental Education database
<ful015>   Meeman Archive of environmental journalism
<nas006>   ENVIROnet (The Space Environment Information Service)
<oth140>   EE-Link: The Environmental Education Gopher Server
<oth026>   NOAA-Space Environment Services Center
<us192>    U.S. Environmental Protection Agency, EPA National Online Library System
<us179>    Syracuse University and, SUNY College of Environmental Science & Forestry
```

Figure 7.10   Results of Keyword Search with <oth140> Selected

☞ **Press → or Enter.**

Pressing the right arrow key or Enter takes us to the first screen for the **The Environmental Education Gopher Server**. It's shown in Figure 7.11.

```
EE-Link: The Environmental Education Gopher Server
TELNET NCEET.SNRE.UMICH.EDU  or 141.211.152.61
login: eelink
                    NCEET's EELink
    1. Using EE-Link, the Environmental Education Gopher/
    2. NCEET, The National Consortium for Environmental Education.../
    3. NCEET's Environmental Education Toolbox/
    4. Classroom Resources for Environmental Education/
    5. Literature, Articles & Newsletters on EE/
    6. Grants/Awards/Employment/
    7. Networking: LISTSERVs/Newsgroups/
    8. Conferences/Meetings/Courses/
    9. Organizations/People/Projects/
   10. .
   11. ===========================================.
   12. Education Resources on the Internet/
   13. Environmental Resources on the Internet/
   14. Environmental Facts and Data/
   15. .
   16. ===========================================.
 - press space for more -
```

Figure 7.11 First Screen for The Environmental Education Gopher Server

You could spend some time looking through the services and resources offered by selecting this item. Exit Hytelnet when you're ready.

Press q to quit Hytelnet

☞ **Type** q **and press** Enter.

You end a Hytelnet session by pressing **q**.

—————————————————End of Example 7.2—————————

Hytelnet Keystroke Commands

You use the keys and arrows on your keyboard to move through Hytelnet. You can always see the keystroke screen by pressing **?**. There's some variation on how the keys behave from one version of Hytelnet to another, but the following keystrokes are common to all.

Moving from Topic to Topic

Select the next topic	↓	or **j**
Select the previous topic	↑	or **k**
Jump to the highlighted topic or item	→	or Enter
Jump back to the previous topic	←	or **u**

Moving within a Topic Screen

Go to next page   +   or   Space Bar
Go to previous page   −   or   **b**

Other Commands

Get help   **?**
Jump to main menu   **m**
Quit Hytelnet   **q**

Hytelnet Menus

You move from menu to menu when you're using Hytelnet. Eventually you reach a screen that has information about a specific site. Two of the menus, the **Main Menu** and the **Other Resources Menu**, lead you to several other categories. We'll give a brief explanation of each heading on those menus. This will be useful if you're not familiar with Hytelnet. The other menus are either shorter or contain lists of sites.

The Main Menu

The main menu gives top-level access to the other topics:

        What is HYTELNET?   <WHATIS>

A very brief explanation of Hytelnet. It has links to more information about Hytelnet, instructions on customizing an entry, library catalogs, and other resources.

        Library catalogs   <SITES1>

The first of several screens used to access library catalogs. In the first few screens the libraries are arranged geographically, first by continent, then country. You follow those links to the catalogs.

        Other resources   <SITES2>

Telnet sites that aren't library catalogs. Some are campuswide information systems, databases and bibliographies, Gopher/WAIS/WWW, general bulletin boards, and miscellaneous resources.

        Help files for catalogs   <OP000>

A collection of instructions for using the different library catalog systems you'll find using Hytelnet. Not all libraries use the same type of electronic catalog, so the commands used for searching vary.

        Catalog interfaces   <SYS000>

This takes you to collections of libraries that use specific types of catalog systems. This is where you go to find all the libraries that use a specific type of catalog interface.

        Internet Glossary   <GLOSSARY>

A glossary of Internet terms; included topics cover a range from "anonymous FTP" to "Z39.50 protocol."

```
   Telnet tips                    <TELNET>
```

Tips on how to use Telnet on different types of computer systems.

```
   Telnet/TN3270 escape keys<ESCAPE.KEY>
```

A list of Telnet escape keys for different types of systems. You use the escape character to send commands such as quit to the Telnet program that's running on your system. See Chapter 3 for a discussion of using the escape keys or escape character with Telnet.

```
   Key-stroke commands            <HELP>
```

A one-screen explanation of the keystrokes you can use with Hytelnet. You get to this screen any time by pressing **?**.

Other Resources <SITES2>

This is your jumping-off point to all sorts of things on the Internet other than those listed under the section Library Catalogs. Take some time to browse these sites for interesting items.

```
   <ARC000> Archie: Archive Server Listing Service
```

A list of sites you can contact to use Archie to search for files available by anonymous FTP. Archie is a service that searches several databases for the names of files. You give Archie the name or a part of the name of a file you'd like to find; Archie gives you a list of anonymous FTP sites that contain files whose names match your query. See Chapter 8, "Archie: Locating Files to Retrieve by Anonymous FTP" for a complete discussion about using Archie.

```
   <FUL000> Databases and bibliographies
```

Several screens of listings from around the world. These two listings give you an idea of the range of topics: **ABSEES: American Bibliography of Slavic & East European Studies**, and **World Paleomagnetic Database**.

```
   <DIS000> Distributed File Servers (Gopher/WAIS/WWW)
```

This is where you can connect to other types of services for working on the Internet. You'll find lists of sites that permit Telnet access to Gopher, Wide Area Information Servers (WAIS) and the World Wide Web (WWW) project. These services are described in detail in Chapter 9, "Gopher: Burrowing through the Internet," Chapter 10, "WAIS: Searching Databases on the Internet," and Chapter 11, "WWW: World Wide Web."

```
   <BOOKS> Electronic books
```

A list of books that are available on-line in electronic form. The list goes on for a few screens. Two Telnet sites are listed to access the books. Take the time to browse the list.

```
   <FEE000> Fee-Based Services
```

A list of services, Internet service providers, and other networks. This is a place to look, for example, if you're thinking of changing how you connect to the Internet. Most of the services allow for guest or trial access, but you'll have to pay to use the service regularly.

```
   <FRE000> FREE-NETs & Community Computing Systems
```

A list of publicly accessible systems with connections to the Internet. In most cases anyone can become a registered member of a free-net. The free-nets are run entirely through user and corporate donations, they depend heavily on volunteers, and they're often created to serve a geographical region. Like public television or public radio stations, they are the forerunners of a robust National Public Telecommunications Network (NPTN).

<BBS000> General Bulletin Boards

A list of bulletin board systems that covers a diverse set of topics. All are accessible through Telnet; some can also be reached on a dial-up basis with a modem. Most allow on-line registration, so you can become a member immediately.

<NAS000> NASA databases

NASA has a number of databases available to Internet users. Jump to this list, then pick the ones you want to use.

<NET000> Network Information Services

This list contains information centers for major networks throughout the world.

<DIR000> Whois/White Pages/Directory Services

These are the services you'll want to use when you're searching for an e-mail address or other information about someone who uses the Internet.

<OTH000> Miscellaneous resources

This is an eclectic and interesting collection. Some items listed are American Philosophical Association, Compact Disc Connection, Federal Job Opportunity Board, Language Bank in Sweden, National Space Development Agency of Japan (NASDA), and Subway Navigator.

Using Hytelnet to Search a Library Catalog

Hytelnet has an extensive list of several hundred library catalogs; the list covers libraries throughout the world. You use the same methods and techniques to reach any library:

1. Use the up/down arrow keys to select Library Catalogs from the Main Menu.
2. Press the right arrow or Enter key to jump to the next screen.
3. Select the region of the world for the library and jump to that page.
4. If it's in the U.S., select the topic for specific type of library: Consortia, Other Libraries, Law Libraries, Medical Libraries, Public Libraries, Community College Libraries, or K-12 Libraries.
5. Make a selection based on the name of the library, and then press the right arrow or Enter key to jump to the screen for the library you've selected.

Now you're at the point of having a screen in front of you with the name, domain name, IP address, instructions about logging in and leaving the system, and the type of library catalog. In some cases instructions for using the catalog are on the screen and in other cases you'll see a link to a file that describes how to use the catalog system. Figure 7.12 is an example.

Boise State University

TELNET CATALYST.IDBSU.EDU or 132.178.18.2

```
Login: catalyst
Press RETURN
Select 5 for VT100 emulation

OPAC = GEAC ADVANCE <OP007>

To exit:
Type E until you get back to the main menu
Select Log Off (option 4)
```

Figure 7.12 Hytelnet Screen for Boise State University Library

Before you connect remember to

❑ Read the information on the screen.

❑ Make notes about log-in names, passwords, or any other information you'll need to access or navigate through the remote system.

You'll be using Telnet to reach the library catalog. Make sure you know the escape character so you can get out of an undesirable situation should one arise at the remote site.

Summary

Hytelnet is a tool and a guide for using Telnet. You use a hypertext browser to work with a systematic collection of sites, which you can reach through Telnet. The sites are organized primarily according to whether they are a library catalog or some other resource on the Internet. The other resources are classified as Archie servers, databases and bibliographies, electronic books, fee-based services, free-nets, bulletin boards, NASA databases, network information services, Whois/White Pages/Directory Services, and miscellaneous resources.

Once you start Hytelnet you can go from screen to screen by first selecting a topic and then going to the screen the topic represents. You use the up/down arrows to select a topic (the selected topic is highlighted), press the right arrow or Enter key to jump to the topic, and press the left arrow to return (jump back) to the previous topic. You can get help with the keyboard commands by pressing **?** any time. You quit the program by pressing **q**, and jump to the main menu by pressing **m**.

When you get to a screen that represents a site you'll see the name of the site, the domain name, the IP address, and instructions about connecting and working at the Telnet site. On some versions, you can actually make the Telnet connection as you're viewing a page. Hytelnet is available for Macintosh, PC, Unix, and VMS computer systems. By using this one program, you can select and reach a wide variety of Telnet sites.

Exercises

When you do these exercises use either the version of Hytelnet on your system or one of the methods to access Hytelnet given in the chapter. These exercises are designed to give you some experience using Hytelnet. As you go through them you'll probably come across some interesting sites you can reach through Telnet. Feel free to explore!

Learning about Hytelnet

1. Jump to the screen "What is Hytelnet?" Use what you find there to answer these questions.
   a. What version of Hytelnet are you using?
   b. What links are on that screen? In other words, what other screens or topics can you access from that screen?

2. Jump to the screen "What is Hytelnet?" and then go to the screens associated with the link "READ.ME."
   a. Who holds the copyright to Hytelnet?
   b. What does the author expect as payment for using Hytelnet as shareware?
   c. What is the author's postal address?

3. Look at the Internet Glossary that comes with Hytelnet and answer the following questions.
   a. What is TN3270?
   b. What does OPAC stand for?
   c. What's IP and what is an IP address?

Searching Library Catalogs

4. Go to the main menu. Select "Library Catalogs" and jump to that screen.
   a. Follow the menus until you get to a law library catalog in the United States. Find at least three references to books that deal with the subject "contract."
   b. Follow menus to search a library catalog in the country in which you were born. Find at least three references to books by an author whose name is the same as yours.

5. Go to the main menu. Select "Library Catalogs" and jump to that screen. Then select "Europe/Scandinavia" and jump to that screen. You'll see the names of several countries listed. Some of the library catalogs have menus only in the language of the country; others provide an interface in more than one language (English is a common alternative).
   a. List at least three libraries that have search menus in a language you understand.
   b. Search one or more of those library catalogs and come up with a list of three items that have something to do with the topic "money."

6. Find and write down the different ways of searching for entries in library catalogs that use the following.
   a. DRA
   b. GEAC
   c. OCLC
   d. VTLS
   Hint: Jump to the topic "Help files for catalogs."

7. For each of the following library catalog systems, list three library catalogs, preferably each in a different country, that use the system.
   a. DRA
   b. GEAC
   c. OCLC
   d. VTLS
   Hint: Jump to the topic "Catalog Interfaces."

Browsing for Sites on the Internet

8. Free-Nets are community based organizations that provide free or low-cost access to the Internet. Look at the ones listed under **<FRE000> FREE-NETs & Community Computing Systems** in the section **Other resources <SITES2>**. Find one located in or near where you live. Use Telnet to connect to that free-net. Describe the services and resources available.

9. The section **<BOOKS> Electronic books** gives directions for using Telnet to browse some on-line electronic versions of several books. Follow the directions given in Hytelnet to connect to the site hosting the books and to get to the section of its Gopher menu for the books. Figure out how to read Chapter 3 of *Peter Pan* or *The War of the Worlds*. Write down these instructions so they could be followed by a 12-year old.

10. Supreme Court decisions are available on the Internet. Use Hytelnet to find out where they're located. Connect to that site and write down a list of opinions or decisions on three different cases.

11. The **Miscellaneous resources** section of **Other resources** lists several screens' worth of sites. Using the items listed there, select some appropriate sites so you could create a separate topic titled **Entertainment**.

12. This exercise involves using the Search Index feature of Hytelnet. If it's not available, skip this exercise.
    a. Give the domain names of at least three sites whose Hytelnet entry contains the word *space*.
    b. Jump to the page of one of those sites and use what you find there to Telnet to the site. Write a few sentences about what was available at that site and whether you recommend it to others.

Archie
Locating Files to Retrieve by Anonymous FTP

There are millions of files available to anyone on the Internet by using the service anonymous FTP. (Anonymous FTP is explained in Chapter 4.) With all those files available, you need a tool or service to find their locations so you can retrieve them. Archie is an information service that helps you locate a file to be retrieved by FTP. You use it by giving the name of a file or a portion of the name to one of several specific computers (called Archie servers) on the Internet. The Archie server looks through a database or archive of file names and returns the Internet location of the file. The location is the domain name of an anonymous FTP site and the directory that holds the file. Then you can use anonymous FTP to retrieve the file. Because there is so much available by anonymous FTP you really need Archie to find the files you need. An Archie server also will tell you about directories whose names correspond to the name you send it.

Chapter Overview

In this chapter we'll cover these topics:

❑ About Archie

❑ Using Archie

❑ Archie Servers

❑ Using E-Mail to Work with Archie

❑   Using Telnet to Work with Archie

❑   Using an Archie Client

About Archie

The term *Archie* is just a shortened form of the word archive. Archie was designed to effectively deliver information about items available in FTP archives. (It wasn't named after the comic book character.) Archie was conceived and implemented by Alan Emtage, Peter Deutsch, and Bill Heelan of McGill University, Quebec, Canada. The development and dissemination of Archie has made working on the Internet more productive. Many users on the Internet owe them and others who have developed tools for searching the Internet a great deal of gratitude for their work. The following figure shows what Archie does.

SUPPOSE YOU WANT TO FIND A FILE

BECAUSE THERE IS SO MUCH AVAILABLE, YOU NEED ARCHIE TO FIND FILES YOU NEED

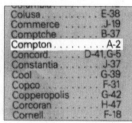

ARCHIE SEARCHES THROUGH THE ARCHIVE OF FILE NAMES...

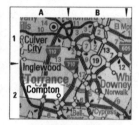

...AND RETURNS THE INTERNET LOCATION OF THE FILE

This is how Archie works. You give a file name to an Archie server and it tells you where to find the file. This is the simplest way of using Archie. You can also give some commands to tailor your search. The commands allow you to ask for an exact match, use the name you give as a substring of names of files and directories so you don't have to know the exact name of what you'd like to retrieve, and request that the results be sorted in any one of several ways. You can always give a command to see the current list of Archie servers and the list of all commands (with explanations). An Archie server will accept your request by any of three ways:

1.   Send the server an e-mail message containing commands. Your results will be sent back to you through e-mail.
2.   Reach the server through Telnet. (See Chapter 3 for details about using Telnet.) After logging in, give commands as if you were directly connected to the Archie server. Your results will appear on your screen or you can have them sent to you by e-mail.
3.   Contact the server through a client on your system. The results are shown on the screen, or you can put them in a file. This is best, since it puts the least load on the Archie server.

Archie servers are generally very busy. It may take several hours or day to get a response to a request sent by e-mail; Archie servers generally limit the number of Telnet connections. Using a client program makes the least demand on a server, and often gives the quickest results.

Here is an example of one part of what you might expect from an Archie search. The search here was done giving the server the string *medicine*.

```
Host ftp.cco.caltech.edu      (131.215.48.151)
Location: /pub/aquaria/admin/bin/resources
    FILE    -rw-r—r—    2299 bytes  21:09  3 Oct 1993  medicine
```

From those three lines you get:

❑ The name of the anonymous FTP host, **ftp.cco.caltech.edu**, and its IP address. That's shown in the line that begins with **Host**.

❑ The name of the directory that holds the file, **/pub/aquaria/admin/bin/resources**. That's shown in the line that begins with **Location:**.

❑ Information about the file or directory including its size, the date it was created or last modified, and its name. In this case the item we matched was a file, its size is 2299 bytes, it was last modified October 3, 1993, and its name is **medicine**.

You retrieve this file by starting an anonymous FTP session with **ftp.cco.caltech.edu**, changing to the directory **/pub/aquaria/admin/bin/resources**, and then getting the file named **medicine**. Another way of saying this is the URL for the file is as follows:

ftp://ftp.cco.caltech.edu/pub/aquaria/admin/bin/resources/medicine.

See Chapter 4 for more details about using FTP and URLs.

Using Archie

You use Archie to locate files to retrieve and directories to browse through anonymous FTP. The steps in this process are:

1. You contact an Archie server by e-mail, Telnet, or through an Archie client on your system.
2. You give a word (a string of characters) to the server. Optionally you can give the server some commands that control the type of match, exact or substring, and the order in which the items will be displayed.
3. The server searches a database to find the names of files and directories that match— either exactly or partially—the string you gave it.
4. The server either displays the list of the items found or sends the list to you through e-mail. That list contains the name of an anonymous FTP site, the location of the file or directory you're searching for, and the name of a file or directory that matches the string you sent. The order of the list either matches the order in which the items were found or is arranged according to your commands.

That's it! Archie tells you where things are and you can retrieve them using anonymous FTP.

There are several commands you can give to a server. The next sections cover the major ones.

Getting Help from Archie

You can get extensive help and information about the commands to use with Archie. If you're using e-mail or Telnet to access Archie ask for the help information to be sent to you by e-mail. If you're using an Archie client on a Unix system you can get information on Archie by entering the command **man archie**.

Different Types of Searches

When you contact an Archie server you give it a string of characters that represents the name or part of the name of a file or directory. The server searches its database using that string and returns the locations of anonymous FTP sites that have a file or directory whose name exactly or partially matches that string. The commands you send can specify the type of search. You can ask for the following types of matches:

Exact match. The server returns information on files and directories whose names exactly match the string you gave it. This is the fastest search.

Subcase match. The server returns information on files and directories whose names contain the string you gave as a substring. It pays attention to the case of the letters. For example, if you ask for a subcase match with the string *music,* Archie will match the string with *musical* or *music,* but won't match with *Music.*

Substring match. This is the most general of the three. It's like a subcase match, except that Archie doesn't differentiate between upper- and lowercase letters. Archie treats all letters the same. So an Archie search with a substring match with the string *music* will match with *musical, music,* or *Music.*

Here are some concrete examples. The string or name we give to the server is *medicine.*

❑ **Exact match**. You ask Archie to search for files or directories with the name *medicine.*

```
Host ftp.utas.edu.au
Location: /departments
    DIRECTORY drwxr-xr-x        512  Apr 26 04:04  medicine
```

❑ **Subcase match**. You ask Archie to search for the names of files and directories whose names contain the string *medicine.* You'll get a list containing items from the exact match and others such as:

```
Host ds.internic.net
Location: /pub/conf.announce
    FILE -rw-r--r--     9692  Dec 10 1993      medicine.healthcare
    FILE -rw-r--r--     2377  Jul 14 08:11     vr-medicine.94
```

❑ **Substring match**. You ask Archie to search, disregarding the case of the letters, for files and directories whose names contain the string *medicine.* The list Archie produces will include items from the previous two types of searches along with other items such as:

```
Host ftp.diku.dk
Location: /pub/music/guitar/b/Band
   FILE -r-r-r-      2031  Aug  4 1992  WSWalcottMedicineShow.crd
```

Either the substring or subcase match can be useful for browsing for sources. For example, if you do a subcase search and use the string *medic,* you can turn up information that would match *medic, medicinal, medicine, medical,* and so on.

Sorting the Results

Searches using Archie sometimes produce many lines of results. These can be sorted by

Filename:	List items according to lexical or alphabetic order.
Hostname:	List items according to the name of the anonymous FTP host holding the files or directories.
None:	List items in no specified order.
Size:	List items according to the size, in bytes, of the files or directories; the largest ones appear first.
Time:	List items according to the date the files or directories were created or last changed; the most recent ones appear first.

Archie Servers

Archie servers are distributed around the world. Proper etiquette dictates that you contact one geographically near to you. Sometimes, though, it makes sense to contact one in a different time zone. For example, at 2 P.M. in New York you can be fairly sure that the servers in North America are busy. At that same time the servers in Europe and Asia may not be very busy, so it may make sense to contact one of those servers. You will find the results you get may depend on which server you use. If you want Archie to search a database that includes anonymous FTP sites in a certain region, you'll want to select a host from that region. To be sure of searching a good sampling of sites in Asia, for example, you may want to use a server from that continent. However, you ought to first try to contact a local server and then go elsewhere if it's necessary. Figure 8.1 shows a list of servers. Notice the first part of their names is archie.

archie.au	139.130.4.6	Australia
archie.edvz.uni-linz.ac.at	140.78.3.8	Austria
archie.univie.ac.at	131.130.1.23	Austria
archie.uqam.ca	132.208.250.10	Canada
archie.funet.fi	128.214.6.100	Finland
archie.th-darmstadt.de	130.83.22.60	Germany
archie.ac.il	132.65.6.15	Israel
archie.unipi.it	131.114.21.10	Italy
archie.wide.ad.jp	133.4.3.6	Japan
archie.kr	128.134.1.1	Korea
archie.sogang.ac.kr	163.239.1.11	Korea
archie.rediris.es	130.206.1.2	Spain
archie.luth.se	130.240.18.4	Sweden
archie.switch.ch	130.59.1.40	Switzerland
archie.ncu.edu.tw	140.115.19.24	Taiwan

archie.doc.ic.ac.uk	146.169.11.3	United Kingdom
archie.unl.edu	129.93.1.14	USA (NE)
archie.internic.net	198.48.45.10	USA (NJ)
archie.rutgers.edu	128.6.18.15	USA (NJ)
archie.ans.net	147.225.1.10	USA (NY)
archie.sura.net	128.167.254.179	USA (MD)

Figure 8.1   Archie Servers

Using E-Mail to Work with Archie

You send e-mail to a user named *archie* at an Archie server, for example, **archie@archie.unl.edu**. You're not communicating with a human at the server; all the mail that comes in addressed to archie is handled by the Archie server program. Every line in your message, including the subject, is treated as a command and commands are assumed to begin in column 1. Any lines not in proper form are ignored. The commands are interpreted, executed, and the results are sent back to you via e-mail. The optional commands to set the type of search and the sorting of the results should come first, before the command to search the database. If they're listed after that command, they'll be ignored.

We'll go over some commands and tasks here. You'll see that you use the same commands by e-mail that you do by Telnet. You don't need to set any options. You can do a straightforward Archie search by sending only a one-line message to an Archie server.

```
find topic
```

Here **topic** is the string you want to use for the search. It's the **find** command that starts the search.

Finding Files and Directories

You use the command **find** followed by a string. For example, **find medicine**.

Setting the Type of Search (Optional)

You use the command **set search** followed by the type of search you'd like to have done. You use **set search exact** for an exact match; **set search subcase** for a subcase match; or **set search sub** for a substring match.

Setting the Form of Output (Optional)

You give commands to see the output in verbose or terse format. You use the command **set sortby** to control the order of the results of the search:

set sortby none	No sorting; this is the default condition—how items are displayed if no set sortby command is given.
set sortby filename	Sorting in alphabetic or lexical order by the name of the file or directory.
set sortby hostname	Sorting in alphabetic or lexical order by the name of the anonymous FTP site.

set sortby size	Ordering the names of the files or directories according to their size in bytes; largest are listed first.
set sortby time	Ordering the names of the files or directories according to the time they were last changed; the ones most recently changed are listed first.

Quitting or Ending the Session

When you use Archie through e-mail you're not involved in any sort of interactive work. It may not make too much sense to talk about quitting or ending the session, but you use the command **quit** to tell the Archie e-mail server to ignore any following lines in the e-mail message. You might use this if your e-mail program automatically includes a signature file with your mail.

Getting Help

Include the command **help** in your message. You'll get back a complete guide to all the commands you can send to an Archie server. The guide includes the commands we've discussed here as well as some others.

Example 8.1   Using E-Mail for an Archie Search

To perform an Archie search via e-mail you send a list of your commands to an Archie server. In this case we'll send e-mail to **archie@archie.internic.net** and include the commands to:

1. Request a substring match.

☞ **Type** set search sub **and press** Enter.

2. Request the results be sorted by time so the most recent ones appear first.

☞ **Type** set sortby time **and press** Enter.

3. Search for files or directories whose names match **medicine**.

☞ **Type** find medicine **and press** Enter.

4. Quit the session, so Archie ignores any other lines in the message.

☞ **Type** quit **and press** Enter.

The message, then, will consist of

```
set search sub
set sortby time
find medicine
quit
```

You'll get mail back in a few minutes or a few hours. When you get a response it will contain items such as those in Figure 8.2. Most of the list was cut to conserve space.

```
Return-Path: <archie-errors@ds.internic.net>
To: ernest ackermann <ernie@s850.mwc.edu>
From: (Archie Server) archie-errors@ds.internic.net
```

> **This is part of the e-mail message you receive from the Archie server.**

```
>> set search sub
>> set sortby time
>> find medicine

# Search type: sub.
```

These are the commands the server received. The find command starts the search

```
Host ds.internic.net     (198.49.45.10)
Location: /pub/conf.announce
    FILE     -rw-r-r—    2377 bytes  08:11 14 Jul 1994  vr-medicine.94


Host anubis.ac.hmc.edu    (134.173.32.18)
Location: /pub/science/sci.answers
     DIRECTORY    drwxr-xr-x     512 bytes  02:29 25 Feb 1994  medicine
```

Lots of items deleted here to conserve space.

```
Host ftp.uu.net    (192.48.96.9)
Location: /usenet/rec.food.recipes/meat
    FILE     -rw-r-r—    1542 bytes  01:00  2 Jan 1992  chinese-medicine-meal.Z

>> quit
```

This was the last command sent to the server.

Figure 8.2   An Archie Server's Response to an Archie Search by E-Mail

The server we used for this example sent back lots of names of files, directories, and hosts. If you send this request to another server you may receive a different list.

The items in the list are either files or directories. You can reach each host by anonymous FTP to retrieve the files or browse the directories. (See Chapter 4 for more details on using anonymous FTP.) For example, to retrieve the first file listed above enter the commands shown in bold in the following:

```
ftp ds.internic.net
Name: anonymous
Password: your e-mail address
cd  /pub/conf.announce
get vr-medicine.94
quit
```

—————————————End of Example 8.1———————————————

Using Telnet to Work with Archie

You can also use Telnet to contact an Archie server. You start a Telnet session and connect with a server. Regardless of the server you contact, use the log-in name archie when you get the prompt **login:** or **username:**. We'll go over this in Example 8.2. After you've logged in you enter each command on a separate line. The search starts when you enter the command **find**. The results are listed on the screen, but there may be so many that it's better to have them sent to you by e-mail. If you enter a command that isn't in proper form the server will respond with a message like **Unrecognized Command**. You can do several searches in one session; a new search is started each time you enter the command **find**. The results of each search appear on the screen and you can have each sent to you by e-mail. Finally, you end the Telnet session with the command **quit.**

We'll go over some commands and tasks here. You'll see that you use many of the same commands with Telnet that you do with e-mail. You don't have to set any options. You can do a simple, direct Archie search by using Telnet to reach an Archie server and then using the command **find** (followed by a string) to search the database.

Finding Files and Directories

You use the command **find** followed by a string. For example, **find medicine**.

Setting the Type of Search

You use the command **set search** followed by the type of search you'd like to have done. You use **set search exact** for an exact match; **set search subcase** for a subcase match; or **set search sub** for a substring match.

Setting the Form of Output

You give commands to see the output in verbose or terse format. You use the command **set sortby** to control the order of the results of the search:

set sortby none	No sorting; this is the default condition—this is how items are displayed if no set sortby command is given.
set sortby filename	Sorting in alphabetic or lexical order by the name of the file or directory.
set sortby hostname	For sorting in alphabetic or lexical order by the name of the anonymous FTP site.
set sortby size	Ordering the names of the files or directories according to their size in bytes; largest are listed first.
set sortby time	Ordering the names of the files or directories according to the time they were last changed; the ones most recently changed are listed first.

Having Results Sent to You by E-Mail

You use the command **mail** followed by your e-mail address. You can set a variable named **mailto** with your e-mail address so that when you give the command **mail** you won't have to give your e-mail address. Here is how to use the commands:

Example 8.2 — Using Telnet for an Archie Search — 201

Example Command	Explanation
set mailto ernie@mwc.edu	Set the variable mailto to an e-mail address
mail	You can use this *only* if you've set a value for mailto
mail ernie@mwc.edu	E-mail the results of the search

Quitting or Ending the Session

When you use Archie through Telnet you're working in an interactive session. You use the command **quit** to log off the Archie Telnet server. This usually terminates your Telnet session as well.

Getting Help

Give the command **help**. You'll see a complete guide to all the commands you can send to an Archie server. The guide includes the commands we discussed here as well as some others. You may want to have it sent to you by e-mail. To do that enter the **mail** command discussed above.

Example 8.2   Using Telnet for an Archie Search

Suppose you wanted to see what was available by anonymous FTP on the topic of computer viruses. Maybe you've heard there are programs available on the Internet that will scan your computer for viruses and eliminate them. It's true! Now you need to find some. An Archie search will find anonymous FTP sites that have information about viruses or programs to use to protect your system from a virus, or eradicate the virus. Let's hope there isn't a virus on the computer you're using!

The steps to follow to do this Archie search are:

1.   Use Telnet to contact and log in to an Archie server.
2.   Give a command so that the most recent entries appear first. That way you'll be most up-to-date.
3.   Set the variable **mailto** so it will be easy to send the results of the search to you by e-mail.
4.   Give the command **find virus** to start the search.
5.   Mail the results to yourself.
6.   Quit the Archie search.

In this case we'll use the server at **archie.internic.net**. Some of the responses from that server are shown in Figure 8.3; most have been deleted to conserve space. The lines that begin with **#** are messages from the remote Archie server. They give information about how the system is set up. The lines beginning with **archie>** are prompts to you from the remote system; you enter commands.

Use Telnet to Contact and Log In to an Archie Server.

☞ **At the prompt type** `telnet archie.internic.net` **and press** [Enter].

Once the Telnet connection is made and the server responds you'll see the prompt **login:** as in Figure 8.3. Use the log-in name **archie**.

☞ **Type** `archie` **and press** Enter.

After you log in, you'll see some information about the remote system and then get the prompt **archie>** as shown in Figure 8.3.

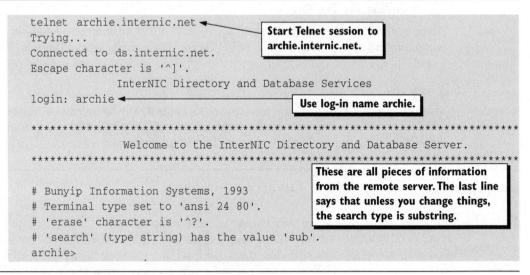

```
telnet archie.internic.net ◄──── [Start Telnet session to archie.internic.net.]
Trying...
Connected to ds.internic.net.
Escape character is '^]'.
                InterNIC Directory and Database Services
login: archie ◄──── [Use log-in name archie.]

*************************************************************************
            Welcome to the InterNIC Directory and Database Server.
*************************************************************************
                                    [These are all pieces of information
                                     from the remote server. The last line
                                     says that unless you change things,
# Bunyip Information Systems, 1993    the search type is substring.]
# Terminal type set to 'ansi 24 80'.
# 'erase' character is '^?'.
# 'search' (type string) has the value 'sub'.
archie>
```

Figure 8.3   Starting an Archie Session with Telnet

Give a Command So That the Most Recent Entries Appear First

☞ **At the** `archie>` **prompt type** `set sortby time` **and press** Enter.

Using **set sortby time** sets things so the most recent entries, probably the most up-to-date, virus programs are listed first. After you press Enter you'll see another prompt **archie>** as shown in Figure 8.4.

Set the Variable mailto

☞ **At the** `archie>` **prompt type** `set mailto` **your e-mail address and press** Enter.

You type your Internet e-mail address in place of *your-e-mail-address*. This makes it possible for you to have the results of the Archie search sent to you by e-mail. In Figure 8.4 we've typed in a fictitious address **me@great.place.edu**.

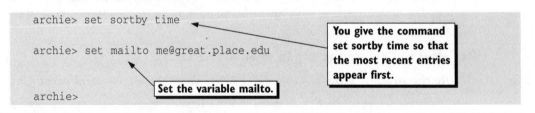

```
archie> set sortby time ◄────          [You give the command
                                        set sortby time so that
archie> set mailto me@great.place.edu   the most recent entries
                                        appear first.]

                    [Set the variable mailto.]
archie>
```

Figure 8.4   Setting sortby and mailto Variables during an Archie Telnet Session

Example 8.2 — Using Telnet for an Archie Search 203

Give the Command find virus to Start the Search

☞ **At the** archie> **prompt type** find virus **and press** Enter.

☞ **Press** Enter **to see the results.**

Use the Archie command find to start the search. You'll see a few responses from the Archie server and eventually things will be ready so the results can be displayed on the screen. This is shown in Figure 8.5.

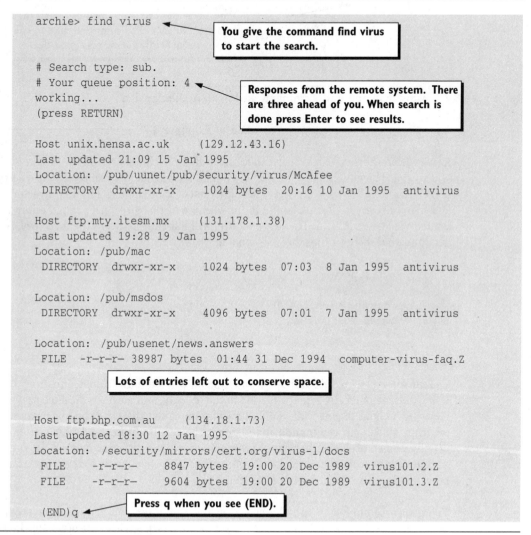

```
archie> find virus                    You give the command find virus
                                      to start the search.

# Search type: sub.
# Your queue position: 4              Responses from the remote system. There
working...                            are three ahead of you. When search is
(press RETURN)                        done press Enter to see results.

Host unix.hensa.ac.uk      (129.12.43.16)
Last updated 21:09 15 Jan 1995
Location: /pub/uunet/pub/security/virus/McAfee
  DIRECTORY  drwxr-xr-x    1024 bytes  20:16 10 Jan 1995  antivirus

Host ftp.mty.itesm.mx      (131.178.1.38)
Last updated 19:28 19 Jan 1995
Location: /pub/mac
  DIRECTORY  drwxr-xr-x    1024 bytes  07:03  8 Jan 1995  antivirus

Location: /pub/msdos
  DIRECTORY  drwxr-xr-x    4096 bytes  07:01  7 Jan 1995  antivirus

Location: /pub/usenet/news.answers
  FILE  -r-r-r- 38987 bytes  01:44 31 Dec 1994  computer-virus-faq.Z

              Lots of entries left out to conserve space.

Host ftp.bhp.com.au      (134.18.1.73)
Last updated 18:30 12 Jan 1995
Location: /security/mirrors/cert.org/virus-l/docs
  FILE   -r-r-r-    8847 bytes  19:00 20 Dec 1989  virus101.2.Z
  FILE   -r-r-r-    9604 bytes  19:00 20 Dec 1989  virus101.3.Z

(END)q          Press q when you see (END).
```

Figure 8.5   Results of an Archie Search

Mail the Results to Yourself

☞ **At the** archie> **prompt type** mail **and press** Enter.

The command **mail** sends the results of the search to the Internet address that was set with the command **set mailto** we used before. Figure 8.6 shows using the **mail** command.

Quit the Archie Search

☞ **At the** `archie>` **prompt type** `quit` **and press** [Enter].

After you press Enter the Archie server responds with **Bye** and ends the Telnet session.

```
archie> mail
archie> quit
# Bye.

Connection closed by foreign host.
```

You enter the command mail to e-mail the results. You enter the command quit to end the session. Archie server says good-bye.

Figure 8.7   Using mail and quit Command during an Archie Session

―――――――――――――――――――――――End of Example 8.2―――――――――――――――――――――――

As we've done here, you can look at the results of the Archie search on the screen *and* have them sent to you. The advantage of having the e-mail list is that you can refer to it when you need to in the future. Either way you'll have a lengthy list of anonymous FTP sites, directories to browse, and files to retrieve. For example, to browse one of the directories listed enter the following commands shown in bold. The last one, **dir**, will list the entries in the directory. At that point, it's up to you; retrieve files, browse some more, or quit.

```
ftp ra.nrl.navy.mil
Name:    anonymous
Paaword: your e-mail address
cd   /MacSciTech/virus
dir
```

Using an Archie Client

You can query an Archie database in a number of ways: e-mail, Telnet, or using an Archie client. Using a client generally gets the results to you quickly, and most Archie sites prefer that you use it. Using a client means that you run a program called the *client* on your computer and that program sends your commands and displays the results from the Archie server. The client is usually named *archie*. Other client programs may have different names, but they are used in essentially the same manner. Check your software or check with your system administrator to see if you have an Archie client available.

You give a command to run the client on the computer you are using or accessing that is connected to the Internet. If you want to set any options, such as the order in which the results are displayed, give those as part of the command. Here are two examples:

Example 8.2 — Using Telnet for an Archie Search —————— 205

Command	Explanation
archie compression	The client contacts a server. The server searches its Archie database for the names of all files/directories that exactly match the string, and returns a list of those items along with their locations on the Internet. The client displays the results.
archie -t compression	This is the same as the previous command except that the results are displayed so that the most recently modified files/directories are displayed first.

When you use the client you give the name of a file along with any options to the client. The client passes it along to the server, and the server returns the information to the client. Archie is an information service; it finds things for you. You use anonymous FTP to actually retrieve the files.

We'll go over some commands and tasks here. When you use a client you give the options and the search string on one line, so it's all done at once. You can do a simple, direct Archie search using an Archie client by just typing archie and a file name or string. For example, the command

```
archie medicine
```

will search for names of files or directories that exactly match the string *medicine*.

Specifying Files and Directories

You include the string you want to use for searching. Issuing the command **archie medicine**, for example, results in having Archie return the list of files and directories whose names match the string *medicine*.

Specifying the Type of Search

There are three types of searches: exact, subcase, and substring. The exact search is the fastest. The Archie client requests an exact search if you don't specify anything else. That's called the default case. You specify the type of search by using an option, a dash (-) followed by a letter, to the Archie command. The options are listed here.

Option	Type of Match	Example
-e	Exact match	archie -e medicine
-c	Subcase match	archie -c medicine
-s	Substring match	archie -s medicine

Specifying the Form of Output

There is only one option you can specify here. You can request that the results appear so that the most recently modified files or directories are displayed first. (This is the same as the **set sortby time** option for an e-mail or Telnet Archie session.) To do that use **-t** as an option on the command line, for example, **archie -t medicine**.

Getting Help

Here are three ways to get help or information about Archie:

1. If you've got the option of using an Archie client on a Unix system type **man archie**. You'll get several screens of information with a prompt to continue at the bottom of each screen.

2. Enter the command **archie** (type **archie** and press Enter). The Archie client displays a list of all options and a brief note about how to use each one.

3. Send e-mail to any Archie server with the word **manpage** as the only thing in the message. You'll get e-mail back from the server with some information about using Archie through e-mail, Telnet, and with a client.

Dealing with the Output

Your Archie search may produce several screens of information. You can use the option **-o** to have the output sent to a file that you can look through one screen at time. The command

```
archie -o wmed medicine
```

saves the results of using Archie to search for files and directories whose names exactly match the string *medicine* in the file named **wmed**.

Choosing a Server

Your Archie client always contacts a specific Archie server. If you don't explicitly specify a server, the server that's contacted is called the **default server**. To list the servers that were known when the client was created enter **archie -L**. That will also list your default server. You can get a list of all the servers by sending e-mail to any Archie server with your message having the word **servers** on a line by itself. You contact other Archie servers by using the option **-h**. The command

```
archie -h archie.internic.net health
```

will have your client contact the Archie server at **archie.internic.net**. The server will search for files and directories whose names exactly match *health*, and the results will be displayed on the screen.

Getting an Archie Client

If you don't have a client on your system, you can get one by anonymous FTP from FTP archive sites at some of the Archie servers. For example, versions of the Archie client software are available by anonymous FTP from **ftp.sura.net** in the directory **/pub/archie/clients**. The software is written to run on Unix or compatible systems.

Summary of Options

Here is a summary of the options that were discussed above.

Option	Explanation
-e	Exact string match. (This is the default.)
-c	Search substrings paying attention to upper- and lowercase.
-s	Search substrings ignoring the case of the letters.
-t	Sort the results so the most recent entries are first.
-o *filename*	Place the results of the search in a file; *filename* is the name of that file.
-L	List all known (to the client) Archie servers, as well as default server.
-h	Specify an Archie server to contact for the search.

Example 8.3 — Using an Archie Client 207

For example, the command

```
archie -h archie.ans.net -ct -o medic.lst medic
```

❏ uses the Archie server **archie.ans.net** (**-h**),

❏ searches for the names of files and directories that have the given string as part of their name and to match letters of the same case (**-c**),

❏ arranges the output so the most recent entries are first (**-t**),

❏ puts the results of the search in the file **medic.lst** (**-o medic.lst**),

❏ searches using the string *medic*

Example 8.3   Using an Archie Client

Suppose you wanted to find out what was available by anonymous FTP on the topic *ethics*. This is going to be a general search, you're looking for all occurrences of the term *ethics*, so you'll use the **-s** option. That way the search will turn up matches as a substring and without differentiating between upper- and lowercase letters. The search will likely produce many items, so you ought to direct the output to a file so you can more easily look at the results when the search is finished. To direct the results to a file you use the **-o** option, and in this case we'll put the results in a file name **ethics.lst**. The command that's used for the search is shown in Figure 8.8.

☞ **Type the command** `archie -o ethics.lst -s ethics` **and press** Enter.

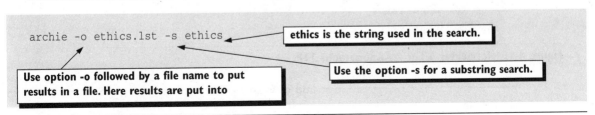

Figure 8.8   Using the Command Archie

Figure 8.9 shows an excerpt from what you might see in the file **ethics.lst**.

```
Host ditmela.mel.dit.csiro.au
Location: /pub/SAGE-AU
  DIRECTORY drwxr-xr-x          512  Sep 18 15:08   Ethics
Location: /pub/SAGE-AU/Ethics
  FILE -rw-r—r—       87138  Jul  8 15:18   ethics.self-assessment
Location: /pub/USENIX/winter89
  FILE -rw-r-r-       29428  Feb  4 1993   ethics-of-breakins.ps.Z

Host ftp.cis.ohio-state.edu
Location: /internic/resources/science
```

```
 FILE -r—r—r—        1235  Aug 23 19:31  bioethics.b.Z

Host sunsite.unc.edu
Location:  /pub/academic/medicine/brazil-mirror/documents
 FILE -r—r—r—        3015  Mar 21 1993  ethics.txt
Location:  /pub/docs/books/gutenberg/ippe/preprints
 DIRECTORY drwxr-xr-x   512  Jun 13 05:05  Ethics
Location:  /pub/docs/books/gutenberg/ippe/preprints/Ethics
 DIRECTORY drwxr-xr-x 512  Feb 19 06:09  Austen.Bradley_and_Feminist_Ethics


Host nic.nordu.net
Location:  /networking/security/virus-1/docs
 FILE -r—r—r—        13986  Aug 19 1993  ferguson.ethics
```

Figure 8.9   Results of an Archie Search

There will be several files and directories listed as the result of this Archie search. Depending on when you do the search and the server you use, you may find different results. You retrieve the files or browse the directories using anonymous FTP. (See Chapter 4 for more details on using anonymous FTP.) For example, to retrieve the last item in Figure 8.9, type each bold item in Figure 8.10 and press Enter.

```
ftp   nic.nordu.net
Name:  anonymous
Password: your e-mail address
cd /networking/security/virus-1/docs
get ferguson.ethics
quit
```

Figure 8.10 Retrieving a File by Anonymous FTP

————————————————————————End of Example 8.3————————————————————————

Summary

Archie is an Internet service you use for finding the location of files and directories available by anonymous FTP. You send a file name to an Archie server (a specific computer on the Internet) and the server sends back a list of anonymous FTP sites that hold matching files and directories. Archie tells you where to find things; then you use anonymous FTP to retrieve the files or browse directories.

You can use Archie by e-mail, Telnet, or an Archie client. In any case you contact a specific computer on the Internet designated as an Archie server. The servers are distributed throughout the world. What is returned depends on what you're searching for. The results will contain the domain name of an anonymous FTP site (Host), the name of the directory that holds the items (Location), and the names of the items themselves. These two listings show a file and a directory found through an Archie search:

```
Host nctuccca.edu.tw
Location:  /Macintosh/info-mac/game
           FILE -r-r-r-     457237  Dec 12 1993  planet-minus-hc.hqx


Host cs.dal.ca
Location:  /comp.archives
       DIRECTORY drwxrwxr-x         512  Jan 17 00:00  sci.astro.planetarium
```

When you use Archie you send a string of characters (often a complete or partial file name) to an Archie server. The server uses the string you give to search a database of anonymous FTP sites. It will return the names of files and directories that match your strings exactly or partially. You can specify the type of match as well as the way the output is displayed.

You'll use many of the same commands when you use e-mail or Telnet to contact an Archie server. You first give the options you want to use and then give the command **find** to begin the search. When you use e-mail to send commands to an Archie server the results are sent back to you by e-mail. When you use Telnet, the results appear on the screen or you can have them sent to you by e-mail. When you use an Archie client, you give the options and the search string all at once. You can specify that the results be put into a file or have them displayed on the screen. Having the results sent to you by e-mail or having the client put them in a file is convenient when the search produces lots of results and you want to keep a record of what you've found.

Exercises

Browsing the Internet With Archie

1. Can you find money on the Internet? Use Archie to search for files whose name is *money*. What did you find?

2. Do an exact match search using the word *sports* to see what Internet resources Archie can find on this topic. What turns up?

3. Suppose you have a strong desire for a cake that has chocolate in it. You want to find a recipe for something exotic, and you are willing to make the cake. Use Archie to find recipes and anonymous FTP to retrieve one of those recipes. (*Hint:* Try a subcase search using the word *chocolate*.) Then make the cake and send the recipe along with your opinion of the cake to a friend.

4. In other chapters we've mentioned how useful it is to have a copy of Scott Yanoff's "Special Internet Connections." It's an up-to-date list of resources on the Internet. At some anonymous FTP sites the file is stored under the name **inet.services.txt**. Use Archie to locate a recent copy of that file. Then retrieve it using anonymous FTP.

5. It's time to plan a meal again!
   a. Use Archie to find location(s) on the Internet that hold recipes.
   b. Use anonymous FTP to browse and retrieve enough recipes for dinner from a site you found in part a.

6. In this exercise you'll use Archie to help search for information about museums.
   a. Do an Archie search using the word *museum*, and be sure you request an exact match. If the server reports that there were no matches, use another server. What did you find?
   b. Now do an Archie search using the word *museums*. Again, be sure you're asking for an exact match and if there are no matches, use another server. What did you find this time?
   c. Now do an Archie search, with a subcase match using the word *museum*. The results of this search should include the results of the searches you did in part a and part b. What did you find that's different?
   d. Finally do an Archie search, with a substring match, using the word *museums*. How do the results in this case compare with the ones you got in part c?

7. Some of the files at anonymous FTP sites are stored in some sort of compressed or archived format. Pointers on working with compressed files are in Chapter 4. There's more information on the Internet about working with compressed files, as well as some of the compression programs themselves. Some of the programs are written for specific types of computer systems. Use Archie to find the location(s) of compression programs or utilities that are suitable for your computer system.

Practice Using Archie

8. Using e-mail, get a list of the current Archie servers.

9. Using e-mail
   a. Request an Archie server to do a subcase search of its database using the string *dinos*, and sort the results according to the hostname.
   b. Request an Archie server to do a substring search of its database using the string *dinos*, and sort the results according to the time the entries were last modified.

10. Using Telnet, ask an Archie server to search its database for files and directories whose names exactly match the string *astronomy*. Have the results sorted by size and sent to you by e-mail.

11. Using any of the ways to access an Archie server, do the following: Contact three servers, each on a different continent, and request an Archie search with an exact match using the string *planet*.
    a. Which server gave the most results?
    b. Which server gave the results that would be most useful to you?

12. Contact an Archie server and search its database, with an exact match and results sorted by time, using the string *environment* through *each* of the three methods: e-mail, Telnet, and client.
    a. How did the results from the three methods differ?
    b. Which of the three returned results the most quickly?
    c. Which of the three returned results in the most convenient form?

Gopher
Burrowing through the Internet

Gopher is an effective and popular tool for maneuvering through the Internet. It's also relatively easy to use. You work with one or more menus, choosing items that are documents (files), directories, links to other Internet sites, tools to help you find information, or other Internet services. You don't have to know many techniques to use Gopher; most of the time you only need to be able to choose items from a menu. If the information is a document, you can view it on the screen one page at a time, save it to a file, print it, download it, or send it to someone (yourself included) by e-mail. A list of all the commands you can use is available by pressing the **?** key. Gopher allows you to build your own menu of favorite or useful items through the use of bookmarks. When you use Gopher you concentrate on the information you want, not necessarily knowing its Internet address or how to retrieve it.

Chapter Overview

This chapter treats Gopher as a tool to be used in searching for and retrieving information on the Internet. The topics covered include:

❑   About Gopher

❑   Understanding How to Use Gopher

❑   Working with Gopher Menus—Basic Gopher Commands

- ❏ Displaying, Saving, Printing, Mailing, Downloading

- ❏ Items on a Gopher Menu—Files, Directories, Telnet Services, and Search Services

- ❏ Setting Up and Using Gopher Bookmarks

- ❏ Searching Gopher Systems Using Veronica

- ❏ Finding Gopher Sites

- ❏ Internet Sources of Information About Gopher

About Gopher

The software for Gopher was created and developed at the University of Minnesota to allow users to browse and retrieve documents in a campus environment. It is software that is designed to work on any computer system that can be connected to the Internet: microcomputers, workstations, mainframes. Because it's easy to install, easy to manage, and easy to use there are thousands of sites that provide Gopher services. If you have access to Gopher you can contact many of these sites through a list maintained at the University of Minnesota. You'll also find specialized lists or collections of sites throughout the Internet. The term *gopherspace* refers to the collection of Gopher sites and the information you can access through those sites. The gopher is the mascot of the University of Minnesota; that may be connected to how the software got its name. You can also think of the software working, tunneling, or burrowing its way through the Internet, in the same way a gopher tunnels through the earth.

You begin a Gopher session by either starting the program on your computer or using Telnet to contact a Gopher site. The Gopher program you use to retrieve information from local or remote sources is called a *Gopher client*. The client then contacts a *Gopher server* somewhere on the Internet. There is usually a default server, one that your client contacts automatically. You start the client by either clicking on an icon for Gopher or typing the command gopher and pressing Enter.

If you don't have a working Gopher client on your system you can use Telnet to access one of several Internet sites that make Gopher available to the public—one site is **consultant.micro.umn.edu** (that's the home of the first Gopher at the University of Minnesota)—and use **gopher** as a log-in name. You can find a listing of other sites by using Hytelnet, going to **<SITES2> Other Resources** and then to **<DIS000> Distributed File Servers (Gopher/WAIS/WWW)**. For more details on using Telnet see Chapter 3, and see Chapter 7 for more details about using Hytelnet.

The Gopher server sends a menu to your client. The client then displays the menu and waits for you to choose an item. There are other commands you can give in addition to choosing a menu item. These include moving a pointer to select an item, getting help, moving to a previous menu, and quitting. The items on the menu can be documents or links to other directories or Internet sites. To retrieve a document or go to another Internet site on a menu you only have to choose the item. Choosing means typing the number of the item on the menu and pressing Enter, moving → to the item and pressing Enter, or using a mouse to click on an icon near the name of the item. The menus and documents can reside anywhere on the Internet. Furthermore, the documents can be one of a variety of types: file, directory, CSO phone book, BinHexed Macintosh file, DOS binary archive, uuencoded file, Telnet session, some sort of image file, or index-search server. You choose an item on the menu, then the client and server work together to either deliver a document or go to another location on the Internet.

| MAKE YOUR SELECTION FROM A HIERARCHICAL MENU | GOPHER WILL DO ITS BEST TO RETRIEVE IT | WHILE YOU CAN REMAIN OBLIVIOUS AS TO HOW GOPHER GOT IT |

It is possible to retrieve the software for Gopher by anonymous FTP. One possible source is **ftp://boombox.micro.umn.edu/pub/gopher/**. The software can be used by educational and nonprofit organizations without paying any fees to the University of Minnesota. Commercial users are required to obtain a license for use and pay an appropriate fee.

Understanding How to Use Gopher

Starting Gopher

If a Gopher client program is on your system, you start gopher by typing the command **gopher** or clicking on an icon. Otherwise, you can use Telnet to contact a publicly available Gopher client at one of the sites mentioned above or some other site near you, and (in most cases) log in as **gopher**. In either case, you're starting a Gopher client.

What to Expect

Once Gopher is started it will most likely connect to a prearranged (default) Gopher server on the Internet. When the connection is made, the server sends a menu that appears on your screen. The items on the menu can represent one of several things: the names of files on the server, the names of directories on the server, or items that represent links to other Internet services or locations. If you choose an item that is a directory or an item that's a link to another location or service on the Internet, another menu is retrieved and displayed. If the item you choose is a file or document it will be displayed, one page at a time, on the screen. In either case the current menu is replaced with another screen of information. You can always go back to a previous menu by pressing **u**, and you can quit a Gopher session by pressing **q**.

Connecting to Gopher Servers

You can direct Gopher to contact any Gopher server on the Internet. This is sometimes called *pointing* your gopher to a server. Precisely how you do that depends on the type of client you're using. If you're using Gopher on a Unix system you can point your client to a server by typing the command **gopher** followed by the Internet address or domain name of the server. To point your gopher to the "home" Gopher server, the first one, at University of Minnesota, for example, enter:

```
gopher gopher.tc.umn.edu
```

If you're using a client with a graphical interface you specify the location of the server to contact in a dialog box. In any event, you start the client as usual but give the domain name of a server somewhere on the Internet.

Gopher servers, like other Internet resources, are set to communicate with the outside world through specified logical channels or *ports*. The port isn't a physical location, but rather a communication channel. We don't need to get too technical here; the port number of an Internet service is similar to the station number of a radio station. The standard port for a Gopher server is *port 70* and a Gopher server is usually set up to communicate through port 70. When you give a command such as

```
gopher gopher.mwc.edu
```

the client communicates with the system at **gopher.mwc.edu** through port 70. You could also use

```
gopher gopher.mwc.edu 70
```

If, instead, a server is set up to communicate through a nonstandard port, then you have to give the port number when you want to contact the server. Suppose there is a server at **base.great.place.com** and it's set to communicate through port 1234. To contact that server you would use the command

```
gopher base.great.place.com 1234
```

You'll sometimes see references to specific Gopher sites in the form of a Uniform Resource Locator (URL); for example, **gopher://gopher.tc.umn.edu**. Sometimes these references will include the port number, such as in **gopher://base.great.place.com:1234**. A URL for Gopher can get complicated, as in the URL: **gopher://riceinfo.rice.edu:70/11/Subject/Networks**, which is a reference to a Gopher menu at **riceinfo.rice.edu**, two menus down from the main menu. The **11** indicates the reference is to a directory on the path **1/Subject/Networks**. You usually won't need to get this complicated. The beauty of Gopher is that it handles these details without your knowing about it.

Gopher Commands

Gopher contains a set of commands for working with menus, getting help, searching for listings on a menu, and setting bookmarks. The Gopher commands for dealing with menus include choosing an item, returning to the previous menu, and jumping back to the main menu. You get a list of commands and some information about them by pressing **h**. Gopher also has a feature that allows you to save a *bookmark*, a reference to a menu item somewhere in gopherspace. That way you can collect a personal list of items or places you would like to reference quickly.

Once you retrieve a document or file it can be displayed, saved to a local file, printed, mailed to anyone with an Internet address, or downloaded to your computer system if, for example, you're using a modem to contact another system that has an Internet connection. You can use Gopher to locate, read, or retrieve information. The information can be in one of several formats including text, images, programs, or compressed files.

Types of Items on a Menu

Items on a menu can represent one of several different types of items. Each item will either be the name of a document, the name of a directory or link to an Internet site, or the name of another Internet service. The term *document* is general; it can represent a plain text file, an archive (possibly in compressed form), or an image or some other sort of binary file. If you're using a graphical interface it will be plain whether the menu item refers to a file. When using a text-based interface, menu items that correspond to directories or other Internet sites end with the character / ; choosing one of those takes you to another menu. Some Internet services have a special designation on a menu. If a menu choice will initiate a Telnet session, for example, then you'll see **<TEL>** as part of the menu entry. Other services include searching documents or menus at a site for a keyword or phrase. You'll see **<?>** marking those items. In any case you choose the menu item and let Gopher take the steps necessary to retrieve an item or make a connection.

Canceling a Request and Dealing with Errors

Occasionally you'll select an item that's no longer active or you'll request something from Gopher that it just can't do. In that case a window may pop up informing you of the problem. If you're using a text-based interface you may see something that includes the text

```
[Cancel: ^G] [OK: Enter]
```

The symbol **^G** represents the Ctrl-G keystroke; hold down the key labeled Ctrl, press the key labeled G, and then release them both. That will cancel the current request. Pressing Enter means to continue. It may also be the case that Gopher is trying to contact a site or in the process of retrieving an item and is taking a long time. It seems as if nothing is happening; nothing is changing on the screen. If you're working on a Unix system you can press **^C** (Ctrl-C) to interrupt Gopher. When you do that you'll see:

```
Really quit (y/n)?
```

at the bottom of the screen. Pressing **y** or Enter now will terminate the Gopher session. Pressing **n** brings back the current menu.

Working with Gopher Menus—Basic Gopher Commands

Figure 9.1 is a Gopher menu taken from the Virtual Reference Desk, offered on the Internet by University of California, Irvine. It contains a list of different types of items: documents, directories, links to other sites on the Internet, and access to other services. This is the view you'd get if your client has a text-based (not graphical) interface on a Unix system. If your client gives you a graphical interface, some things will be different: the items won't be numbered and you move from item to item by using a mouse. However, the concepts we cover are the same for either type of interface. Here are some things to note about this menu:

❑ At the top of the screen you see the *version number* of the client. It tells you the version of the software you're using. That's not too important when you start using Gopher, but may be important to note if you have to report any problems with the software.

❑ The next item is the name of the menu supplied by the server.

❑ The items in the menu are numbered and you can select an item by typing the number.

❑ The item marked with the → is the one that will be selected if you press the Enter key.

❑ The line of text at the bottom gives some commands you're likely to use and a page number; sometimes Gopher menus go on for several pages.

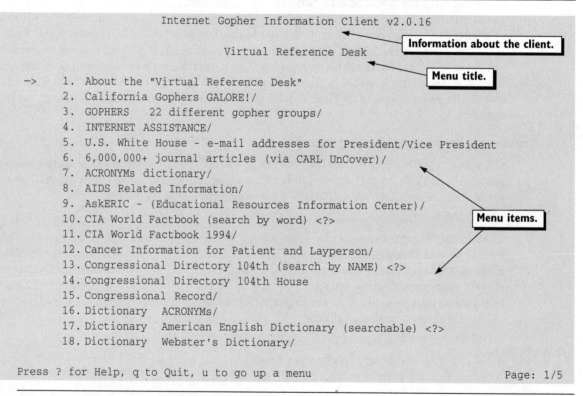

```
              Internet Gopher Information Client v2.0.16        ┌─────────────────────────────┐
                                                                │ Information about the client. │
                          Virtual Reference Desk                └─────────────────────────────┘
                                                                ┌──────────────┐
   ->    1.  About the "Virtual Reference Desk"                 │ Menu title.  │
         2.  California Gophers GALORE!/                         └──────────────┘
         3.  GOPHERS    22 different gopher groups/
         4.  INTERNET ASSISTANCE/
         5.  U.S. White House - e-mail addresses for President/Vice President
         6.  6,000,000+ journal articles (via CARL UnCover)/
         7.  ACRONYMs dictionary/
         8.  AIDS Related Information/
         9.  AskERIC - (Educational Resources Information Center)/
        10.  CIA World Factbook (search by word) <?>          ┌──────────────┐
        11.  CIA World Factbook 1994/                          │ Menu items.  │
        12.  Cancer Information for Patient and Layperson/     └──────────────┘
        13.  Congressional Directory 104th (search by NAME) <?>
        14.  Congressional Directory 104th House
        15.  Congressional Record/
        16.  Dictionary   ACRONYMs/
        17.  Dictionary   American English Dictionary (searchable) <?>
        18.  Dictionary   Webster's Dictionary/

Press ? for Help, q to Quit, u to go up a menu                      Page: 1/5
```

Figure 9.1   Gopher Menu at Virtual Reference Desk

The last line shown in Figure 9.1 gives three keystrokes you're likely to use. Press **?** to see a list of commands, press **q** to quit Gopher, and press **u** to go to the previous menu. At the right of the last line you see **Page: 1/5**. This indicates this is the first of five pages for this menu.

In order to select an item you either move the → to that item and press Enter, type the item number and press Enter, or (if you have a graphical interface) use your mouse or pointing device to select an item and click on it.

There may be times when you select an item, press Enter or click on the item, and get the message "nothing available" or a message about not being able to connect to the host. That may mean that either the directory is empty or the link to another Internet site is no longer valid. Gopher menus often represent information that someone thought was useful or interesting. Over the course of time, the server supplying the information for an item may no longer be in service, may be temporarily out of service, or the items are no longer available. The reference to the item exists but the item isn't around anymore. Most of the items are provided as a service to the Internet community, and the items aren't guaranteed to always be there. If you can't connect to any host, there may be a problem with your connection to the Internet.

Table 9.1 lists and explains the basic Gopher commands you would use at this point. They're all done by a single keystroke and are for users who are using a character-based interface to Gopher. If you're using a graphical interface to Gopher, pull down a menu or click on the appropriate item to get help and list commands.

Action	Keystroke	Explanation
Display an item	Enter	Press Enter to display item marked by →.
	Item number	Type item number and press Enter.
Get help	?	Pressing ? displays a list of all the commands you can use at this point.
Quit	q	Press q to quit. Gopher will ask if you're sure. Type y to really quit and n to continue the session.
Go to previous menu	u	Press u to return to or go up to the previous menu.
Move up a line	↑, k	Pressing either the up arrow key or k moves → up a line.
Move down a line	↓, j	Pressing either the down arrow key or j moves → down a line.
Go to the main menu	m	Pressing m will take you to your client's main menu; the one you saw when you started Gopher.
Search the menu	/	To search for an item in the current menu press /. You'll be prompted to enter a string to use in searching.
Go to next page	Space Bar, +, >	Press the spacebar, the plus key, or > to view the next page on this menu.
Go to previous page	b, −, <	Press b, -, or < to see the previous page of this menu.

Table 9.1   Basic Gopher Commands

Example 9.1   Accessing Virtual Reference Desk through Gopher

This example introduces you to Gopher. Calvin Boyner at the University of California, Irvine maintains a service called the Virtual Reference Desk. We'll use it to demonstrate what you're likely to see during a Gopher session and to show how to use some of the commands. This example was generated using a text-based Gopher client on a Unix system. The concepts for using Gopher to find information about a topic, the types of commands to use, and the types of results you're likely to get are the same regardless of the type of Gopher client you'll use.

Suppose you want to find information about gardening, specifically raising figs. To get that information you might go to a library and ask the reference librarian for some references to general information about gardening and some references to specific information about raising figs. Here we'll use Gopher to access the Virtual Reference Desk in the same way you might work with a reference librarian. The steps we'll go through are:

1. Use Gopher to reach the Virtual Reference Desk.
2. Search the menu for an entry containing the word *garden*.
3. Chose the entry dealing with gardening.
4. Get to the menu dealing with figs.
5. Display one document about figs.
6. Quit Gopher.

You'd probably want to view more than one document. In some instances we'll leave items out of the menus to conserve space.

Use Gopher to Reach the Virtual Reference Desk

First we'll start a Gopher session by pointing the Gopher client to the home Gopher server at the University of California, Irvine. You enter the domain name or Internet address of the Gopher server to contact.

☞ **Type** gopher peg.cwis.uci.edu **and press** Enter.

Once the client gets the information from UCI you'll see a screen such as the one in Figure 9.2. The Virtual Reference Desk isn't listed on the main menu. We need to go through a couple of other menus, just like walking through a building.

```
              Internet Gopher Information Client v2.0.16
                 Home Gopher server: peg.cwis.uci.edu


         1.              University of California, Irvine Gopher
         2.      -------------------------------------------------------
         3.  UCI's New Gopher!
         4.  UCI: Information, Facts, and Calendars/
```

Example 9.1 — Accessing Virtual Reference Desk through Gopher ⸺ 219

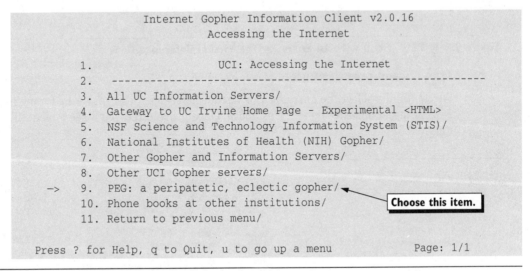

```
      5.  Academic Programs and Research/
      6.  Administrative Offices and Services/
      7.  Computing Services/
      8.  Entertainment, Events, Food, and Shopping/
      9.  Especially for Students/
      10. Help Desk/
      11. Library/
      12. Newsstand/
  ->  13. Accessing the Internet/              Choose this item.
      14. ******** UCI's old Gopher Menu is below **************
      15. Gateway to UC Irvine Home Page - Experimental <HTML>
      16. Search UCI's Institutional Menus <?>
  Press ? for Help, q to Quit                      Page: 1/2
```

Figure 9.2   Main Menu at University of California, Irvine

Select the item "Accessing the Internet" (number 13) from this menu

☞ **Type** 13 **and press** Enter .

You could also press **j** or the down arrow key to move the pointer → opposite the item to choose. (If the menu has changed since our last visit we would pick the same topic, but it may have a different number.) The menu in Figure 9.3 shows on the screen; we have to select one more item from this menu to get to the Virtual Reference Desk. These are a few steps to follow, but it's easy to work through the menus. Next we'll select an the item **PEG: a peripatetic, eclectic gopher/** from the menu.

```
               Internet Gopher Information Client v2.0.16
                          Accessing the Internet

      1.                UCI: Accessing the Internet
      2.  -------------------------------------------------------------
      3.  All UC Information Servers/
      4.  Gateway to UC Irvine Home Page - Experimental <HTML>
      5.  NSF Science and Technology Information System (STIS)/
      6.  National Institutes of Health (NIH) Gopher/
      7.  Other Gopher and Information Servers/
      8.  Other UCI Gopher servers/
  ->  9.  PEG: a peripatetic, eclectic gopher/
      10. Phone books at other institutions/       Choose this item.
      11. Return to previous menu/

  Press ? for Help, q to Quit, u to go up a menu     Page: 1/1
```

Figure 9.3   "Accessing the Internet" Menu at the University of California, Irvine

☞ **Type** 9 **and press** Enter .

The item we want to select is number **9** in Figure 9.3; we can choose it either by typing its number or by moving the → to it with the **j** key or down arrow key. When we press Enter the menu for PEG appears, as shown in Figure 9.4, and it has an entry for the Virtual Reference Desk.

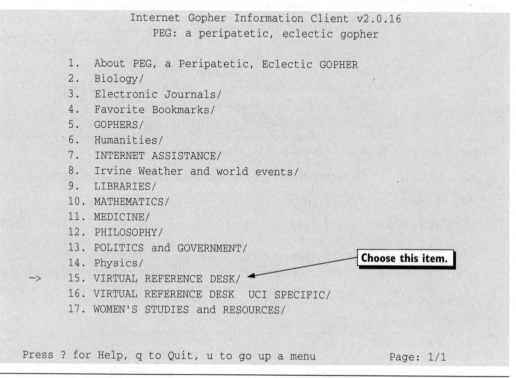

```
                Internet Gopher Information Client v2.0.16
                    PEG: a peripatetic, eclectic gopher


           1.  About PEG, a Peripatetic, Eclectic GOPHER
           2.  Biology/
           3.  Electronic Journals/
           4.  Favorite Bookmarks/
           5.  GOPHERS/
           6.  Humanities/
           7.  INTERNET ASSISTANCE/
           8.  Irvine Weather and world events/
           9.  LIBRARIES/
           10. MATHEMATICS/
           11. MEDICINE/
           12. PHILOSOPHY/
           13. POLITICS and GOVERNMENT/
           14. Physics/                              ┌─────────────────┐
                                                     │ Choose this item.│
      ->   15. VIRTUAL REFERENCE DESK/ ◄─────────────└─────────────────┘
           16. VIRTUAL REFERENCE DESK  UCI SPECIFIC/
           17. WOMEN'S STUDIES and RESOURCES/



      Press ? for Help, q to Quit, u to go up a menu        Page: 1/1
```

Figure 9.4   "PEG" Menu with an Entry for the Virtual Reference Desk

☞ **Type** 15 **and press** Enter .

We can finally select the entry for the Virtual Reference Desk, either by typing its number or moving the → opposite its entry as above. Once it's selected you'll see a menu like the one in Figure 9.5.

```
                Internet Gopher Information Client v2.0.16
                        VIRTUAL REFERENCE DESK


    -> 1.  About the "Virtual Reference Desk"
       2.  Internet (SHOPPING) Mall (tm) by Taylor/
       3.  GOPHERS    22 different gopher groups/
       4.  INTERNET ASSISTANCE/
       5.  U.S. White House - e-mail addresses for President/Vice President
       6.  6,000,000+ journal articles (via CARL UnCover)/
       7.  ACRONYMs dictionary/
       8.  AIDS Related Information/
```

Example 9.1 — Accessing Virtual Reference Desk through Gopher   221

```
  9.   AskERIC - (Educational Resources Information Center)/
 10.   CIA World Factbook (search by word) <?>
 11.   CIA World Factbook 1994/
 12.   Cancer Information for Patient and Layperson/
 13.   Congressional Directory 104th (search by NAME) <?>
 14.   Congressional Directory 104th House
 15.   Congressional Record/
 16.   Dictionary   ACRONYMs/
 17.   Dictionary   American English Dictionary (searchable) <?>
 18.   Dictionary   Webster.'s Dictionary/


Press ? for Help, q to Quit, u to go up a menu          Page: 1/5
```

Figure 9.5   Menu for the Virtual Reference Desk

The last line on the screen gives instructions about how to get help (press **?**), quit (press **q**), and return to the previous menu (press **u**). The notation **Page: 1/5** means there are five pages or screens in this menu and this is page 1.

Search the Menu for an Entry Containing the Word garden

☞ **Press /**

☞ **Type** garden **and press** ⏎Enter⏎**.**

To search the current menu for an entry containing the word garden, press /. You'll see a window pop up, similar to the one shown below, which covers part of the menu. Type the word **garden** on the blank line and press Enter. Before pressing Enter you could press **^G** (Ctrl-G) to cancel the search or **^-** (Ctrl-Minus) to get help. The screen in Figure 9.6 includes the word **garden** typed in the window.

```
Internet Gopher Information Client v2.0.16
VIRTUAL REFERENCE DESK


 ->    1.  About the "Virtual Reference Desk"
       2.  Internet (SHOPPING) Mall (tm) by Taylor/
       3.  GOPHERS   22 different gopher groups/
       4.  INTERNET ASSISTANCE/
+----------------------------VIRTUAL REFERENCE DESK----------------------------+
|                                                                              |
| Search directory titles for:                                                 |
|                                                                              |
| garden                                                                       |
|                                                                              |
| [Help: ^-]   [Cancel: ^G]                                                    |
+------------------------------------------------------------------------------+
       13.  Congressional Directory 104th (search by NAME) <?>
       14.  Congressional Directory 104th House
       15.  Congressional Record/
```

```
16. Dictionary   ACRONYMs/
17. Dictionary   American English Dictionary (searchable) <?>
18. Dictionary   Webster's Dictionary/


Press ? for Help, q to Quit, u to go up a menu              Page: 1/5
```

Figure 9.6   Searching Directory Titles

Choose the Entry Dealing With Gardening

The menu in Figure 9.7 appears. As the result of the search the → will be opposite the entry **Gardening**. Press Enter to follow that link. You can infer from the menu that your client will make a link from UCI to Texas A&M.

```
                  Internet Gopher Information Client v2.0.16
                             VIRTUAL REFERENCE DESK

     19. Directory of Electronic Journals and Newsletters Strangelove (2nd ..
     20. Disability Information/
     21. E-MAIL ADDRESSES:   Internet-wide searches/
     22. E-MAIL ADDRESSES:   X.500 Gateway/
     23. ELECTRONIC FORUMS (listservs): Educator's Guide to E-Mail Lists
     24. ELECTRONIC FORUMS (listservs): Search - Educator's Guide to E-M. <?>
```

Some entries deleted to conserve space.

```
     30. FOOD and DRINK/
     31. FedWorld (NTIS) - 100+ electronic government bulletin boards/
     32. Foreign Currency Exchange Rates (current only)
     33. GOPHERS   22 different gopher groups/
->   34. Gardening (via Texas A&M U)/
     35. Geographic Name Server (Info U.S. cities, towns, villages)/
     36. Gopher JEWELS/
```

Press Enter to select this item.

```
Press ? for Help, q to Quit, u to go up a menu              Page: 2/5
```

Figure 9.7   Result of Searching Virtual Reference Desk Menu for garden

Get to the Menu Dealing with Figs

You'll see the Gardening menu (Figure 9.7) from Texas A&M, but it doesn't contain the word figs! Is everything lost? Was our search in vain? Choose Item **3**, **Fruits and Nuts**, to see if there is an entry for figs.

☞ **Type** 3 **and press** Enter.

```
                  Internet Gopher Information Client v2.0.16
                        Gardening (via Texas A&M U)
```

Example 9.1 — Accessing Virtual Reference Desk through Gopher — 223

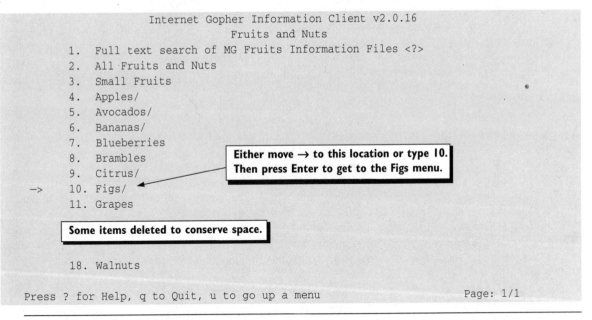

```
            1.   Full text search of Master Gardener Menus <?>
            2.   Introduction to Master Gardener files
    ->      3.   Fruits and Nuts/
            4.   Flowering Plants, Annual and Perennial/
            5.   Ornamental Trees and Shrubs/
            6.   Turf Grasses/
            7.   Vegetables/


Press ? for Help, q to Quit, u to go up a menu            Page: 1/1
```

Either move → to this location or type 3.
Then press Enter to get to the next menu.

Figure 9.8   Gardening from Texas A&M

The next menu (Figure 9.9) appears, and it contains an entry for figs! Now to go to the menu dealing with figs.

☞ **Type** 10 **and press** Enter.

The menu on figs appears as shown in Figure 9.10.

```
                Internet Gopher Information Client v2.0.16
                            Fruits and Nuts
            1.   Full text search of MG Fruits Information Files <?>
            2.   All Fruits and Nuts
            3.   Small Fruits
            4.   Apples/
            5.   Avocados/
            6.   Bananas/
            7.   Blueberries
            8.   Brambles
            9.   Citrus/
    ->      10.  Figs/
            11.  Grapes



            18.  Walnuts

Press ? for Help, q to Quit, u to go up a menu            Page: 1/1
```

Either move → to this location or type 10.
Then press Enter to get to the Figs menu.

Some items deleted to conserve space.

Figure 9.9   Fruits and Nuts Menu

Display One Document About Figs

At this point we can display the entire article about figs or go on to the next menu, which has the article available in several pieces (Figure 9.10). To display the entire article, one screen at a time, choose item **1** and press Enter.

So this example doesn't go on much longer we'll leave it to you to choose the item marked **browseable**.

```
                Internet Gopher Information Client v2.0.16

                                    Figs

-->    1.   B-1591 Home Fruit Production - Figs article (entire)
       2.   B-1591 Home Fruit Production - Figs Introduction (browseable)/
```

Figure 9.10 Figs Menu

☞ **Type** 1 **and press** Enter.

Choosing item **1**, **B-1591 Home Fruit Production—Figs article (entire)** from Figure 9.10 starts displaying the article on your screen as shown in Figure 9.11. The line at the top tells you the name of the item, how large it is in bytes, and that you've seen 4% of it. The line at the bottom gives options: **?** for help, **u** to quit, and **z** to see the next screen.

```
B-1591 Home Fruit Production - Figs article (entire) (15k)              4%
+--------------------------------------------------------------------------+
INTRODUCTION
                               B-1591
                TEXAS AGRICULTURAL EXTENSION SERVICE
                   The Texas A&M University System


                   HOME FRUIT PRODUCTION - FIGS


              Calvin G. Lyons and George Ray McEachern
                      Extension Horticulturists


Figs have been a part of Texas homesteads since the early
development of the state.  Dooryard trees can be grown in any
section of Texas.  Figs grow extremely well along the Texas GulfCoast.  However, trees
require cold protection in the far northern
and western areas and supplemental irrigation in the state's drier
areas.
+--------------------------------------------------------------------------+
[Help: ?]  [Exit: u]  [PageDown: Space]
```

Figure 9.11 First Screen of Display

If you press **u** while you're viewing a document, you'll be brought back to the menu.

☞ **Press** u.

Quit Gopher

☞ **Press** q.

Example 9.1 — Accessing Virtual Reference Desk through Gopher — 225

☞ **Press** y.

To quit Gopher or terminate this session press **q**. You'll see the following message at the bottom of the screen. You have a choice. In this case you'll press **y** to really quit!

```
Really quit (y/n)? y
```

------------------------------ **End of Example 9.1** ------------------------------

Displaying, Saving, Printing, Mailing, Downloading

Once you've selected an item by moving the → so it's pointing to the item or typing the number of the item, you press the Enter key to display the item. The term *display* can really mean several different things depending on the type of item you've selected. In general terms you're either going to see or *view* the contents of a file, display another menu, start an Internet service, or transfer a file to your system. In this section we'll concentrate on your options when the selected item is a file.

If the item is a text file, then display means to *view* the file in some reasonable way; usually one screen at a time with some means of scrolling through the file. If the item is an image file, display again means to *view* the file. In an ideal environment where you are directly connected to the Internet, all the software is in place, and the client is configured the file will be transferred to your system and an image viewing program will be started so the image appears on your screen. If the item represents a Macintosh HQX /BinHex file, an MS-DOS archived file, or some other binary file (and the client and server are configured correctly), then display means *transfer* the file from the remote site to a file on your computer. It may be that you're not working in an ideal setting and everything doesn't go as described here. If that's the case you'll want to look at the section below about saving the file.

Viewing a Text File

You've selected an item, in fact a file, on a Gopher menu and now you would like to look at its contents. All you have to do is press the Enter key or, if your Gopher client has a graphical interface, click on the name of the item. The file is copied from the Gopher server to the system that is running the client and displayed on your screen. If you're using a graphical interface, you can scroll (move forwards or backward) through the file the same way you scroll through any file. If you're using a character- or text-based client the file will be displayed through a viewing program that allows you to go forward or backward through the file and search for words within the file. In either case you'll be able to work your way through the file and on-line help is available. Which viewer you use depends on the client Gopher. We'll see an example of one below.

While you're viewing a text file you can e-mail a copy of the file to any Internet address—just press **m** and then supply the address. You can also print the file—press **p**. The printing usually takes place on a printer attached to the computer that's connected to the Internet. In both cases you'll see that you have the option to cancel your request.

Saving the Item to a File

You can have the selected file or item saved to a file on the computer that's running the Gopher client. (The item has to be a file; Gopher won't let you save other types of items in this way.) To do that press the **s** key or choose a menu item that allows you to save to a local file. You'll then be prompted to name a file to hold the file you want to save. To explain that a little, suppose you've found and selected a file named *Guide to Happiness* on a Gopher menu somewhere in gopherspace. If you press **s** or select an option to save the item in a local file, you'll be asked to give a name to the file on the local system. Most Gopher clients will suggest the local file be named the same as the remote file, so in this case it will be **Guide to Happiness** or **Guide-to-Happiness**. The actual form depends on what file names your system allows. You may need to give it a name that conforms with rules for naming files on your system. If you're saving it to an MS-DOS or MS-Windows computer system, for example, you may need to give it a name such as **guide.txt** or in a form with at most eight characters to the left of a period and three characters to the right of the period. In any event, once it's named it will be copied to the system running the client in your directory or folder.

You can use this procedure for any type of file. So if things aren't set properly for you to view images through Gopher, you can always save the image file to a local file and then copy it to another system that has the software you need to view the file.

Downloading a File

Downloading generally means copying a file from one computer system to another. It's often used when you're contacting another system through a modem and you want to copy a file from that other system down to your system. In this case suppose you're using a personal computer with a modem to log on to another computer system and *that* system is connected to the Internet. Since you're logged on to a system connected to the Internet, you're using Gopher and you've selected an item in gopherspace that you'd like to have on your personal computer. One way to get it to your personal computer is to save the item to a file, quit Gopher, and then download the file to your personal computer. Gopher allows you to download a file directly to your personal computer without having to first save it to a file on the system that's running Gopher. To download a file press **D** (be sure to use uppercase D) or, if your Gopher client has a graphical interface, select an option to download a file. Then you'll be asked to select a download protocol from a list containing Zmodem, Ymodem, Kermit, etc. Select one you've used before and do what you need to do on your personal computer to initiate the transfer. This isn't the place to go into the details about downloading files. You may want to ask someone locally about that topic, or look in gopherspace for information about downloading!

Example 9.2   Working with a Document on a Gopher Menu

In this example we'll examine some of the things you can do with a document or files you've located on a Gopher menu.

☞ **Type** gopher gopher.mwc.edu **and press** ⟨Enter⟩.

☞ **Type** 5 **and press** ⟨Enter⟩.

☞ **Type** 3 **and press** ⟨Enter⟩.

This document is listed on the menu as **Using Tin for News**. To reach it, point your Gopher to **gopher.mwc.edu**, choose item **5. The Computer Center**, choose item **3. HELP at MWC**, and then choose the file from the menu. For this example we'll assume you're at that menu, as shown in Figure 9.12. As usual, we'll abbreviate some menus or screens to conserve space.

———— Example 9.2 — Working with a Document on a Gopher Menu ———— 227

```
                 Internet Gopher Information Client v2.0.16
                              HELP at MWC
        1.   A Guide for e-mailing a WordPerfect File
        2.   Adding a Signature to Elm E-mail
        3.   Adding a Signature to Pine E-mail
        4.   Brief Guide to E-mail
        5.   How to Save e-mail to a Diskette on Your PC
        6.   Pine-user-guide
        7.   Problems-with-@-and-Backspace
        8.   Quota-explained
        9.   Quota-limits
        10.  Saving-email-messages
        11.  Using a Modem
   ->   12.  Using tin for News
        13.  Vi commands
        14.  unix.ref.card
        15.  unix_commands.doc


Press ? for Help, q to Quit, u to go up a menu              Page: 1/1
```

Figure 9.12 HELP at MWC Menu

☞ **Press Enter to view the current item.**

The first page of the document appears as shown in Figure 9.13.

```
Using tin for News (7k)                                          13%
+-------------------------------------------------------------------+
Brief Documentation for TIN. Ernest C.Ackermann, Department of Computer
Science, Mary Washington College, Fredericksburg, Va 22401.
ernie@s850.mwc.edu
                             TIN

        Tin is software that is supports a convenient or easy way to
manage your dealings with network news.  The news is arranged into
newsgroups.  Newsgroups are collections of articles, and articles on the
same topic are assembled into "threads".  You can also use tin to select
which newsgroups you would like to read by subscribing or unsubscribing
from all the groups that the College receives.  Once a group is chosen
you can deal with individual articles by reading them, saving them in a
file, printing them, respond to them by either "posting" a response for
everyone to read or mailing a response to the author, mailing articles
to any email address, etc.  You can also post an article to a newsgroup.
+-------------------------------------------------------------------+
[Help: ?]   [Exit: u]   [PageDown: Space]
```

Figure 9.13 First page of "Using tin for News"

☞ **Press ⎡Space Bar⎤ to see the next screen.**

See Figure 9.14 to view the next screen.

```
Using tin for News (7k)                                            26%
+----------------------------------------------------------------------+
                      Group Selection (4)                   h=help

     1  239  news.answers              Repository for periodic USENET
articles
     2  111  news.newusers.questions  Q & A for users new to the Usenet.
     3  294  alt.internet.services    Information about services available

     <n>=set current to n, TAB=next unread, /=search pattern, c)atchup,
   g)oto, j=line down, k=line up, h)elp, m)ove, q)uit, r=toggle all/unread,
    s)ubscribe, S)ub pattern, u)nsubscribe, U)nsub pattern, y)ank in/out

You are at the Group Selection level of tin.  You will see a numbered
listing of the newsgroups you currently subscribe to.  The numeral after
the group number indicates how many articles are available in that
group.  Near the bottom of the screen is a list of several commands
available at this level.
+----------------------------------------------------------------------+
[Help: ?]   [Exit: u]   [PageDown: Space]   [PageUp: b]
```

Figure 9.14 Second Page of "Using tin for News"

Press b to Return to the Previous Screen or Page

☞ **Press** b.

Some viewing options are listed at the bottom of each page or screen as shown in Figure 9.12. Pressing **b** takes you to the previous page, which is where we started (Figure 9.13).

☞ **Press** ? **for Help**

When you press **?** a help window pops up over the screen you're viewing. See Figure 9.15.

```
Using tin for News (7k)                                            13%
+----------------------------------------------------------------------+
Brief Documentation for TIN. Ernest C.Ackermann, Department of Computer
Science, Mary Washington College, Fredericksburg, Va 22401.        ┌──────────────────┐
ernie@s850.mwc.edu                                                 │ Help screen lists │
                +------------------Pager Help---------------+ ◄──── │ commands you      │
                |                                           |       │ can use here.     │
        Tin is  | u, ^G, left : Return to menu              |y way to └──────────────────┘
manage your deali | space, down : Move to the next page     |into
newsgroups.  News | b, up       : Move to the previous page |les on the
same topic are as | /           : Search for text          | to select
```

Example 9.2 — Working with a Document on a Gopher Menu 229

```
which newsgroups | m          : mail current document      |bscribing
from all the grou | s          : save current document      |s chosen
you can deal with | p          : print current document     |them in a
file, printing th | D          : download current document  |ponse for
everyone to read  |                                         |articles
to any email addr |                         [Cancel: ^G] [OK: Enter]  |newsgroup.
                  +-------------------------------------------+
+-------------------------------------------------------------------------+
[Help: ?]   [Exit: u]   [PageDown: Space]
```

Figure 9.15 Pop-up Help Window while Viewing a Document

Press m to Send the Document to an Internet Address via E-Mail

☞ **Press** m**, type the address, and press** Enter.

You press **m** to e-mail the document to any Internet e-mail address. When you press **m** a window pops up overlaying part of the screen. The window has a spot for the e-mail address. You type the address in that spot and press Enter. This is shown in Figure 9.16.

```
Using tin for News (7k)                                             13%
+---------------------------------------------------------------------+
Brief Documentation for TIN. Ernest C.Ackermann, Department of Computer
Science, Mary Washington College, Fredericksburg, Va 22401.
ernie@s850.mwc.edu
                         TIN

        Tin is software that is supports a convenient or easy way to
+----------------------------Using tin for News----------------------+
|                                                                    |
| Mail current document to:                                          |
|                                                                    |
| mybuddy@great.place.edu                                            |
|                                                                    |
| [Help: ^-]   [Cancel: ^G]                                          |
+--------------------------------------------------------------------+
to any email address, etc.  You can also post an article to a newsgroup.
+--------------------------------------------------------------------+
[Help: ?]   [Exit: u]   [PageDown: Space]
```

Figure 9.16 Sending a Document by E-Mail

Press s to Save the Document in a File

☞ **Press** s**, type the name of the file, and press** Enter.

You press **s** to save the document, not only what is on the screen, to a file. You'll see a window pop up overlaying a portion of the screen. It contains a spot for the name of the file. The name that appears will be the name of the document as it appeared on the menu. You can give it any name you'd like; just backspace over the name that is there and type whatever will be valid on your system. The screen in Figure 9.17 shows the window and the file name.

If you're using a modem from your PC to access the Internet through another computer the file may be saved on that other computer, not on your PC.

```
Using tin for News (7k)                                                   13%
+--------------------------------------------------------------------------+
Brief Documentation for TIN. Ernest C.Ackermann, Department of Computer
Science, Mary Washington College, Fredericksburg, Va 22401.
ernie@s850.mwc.edu
                              TIN

        Tin is software that is supports a convenient or easy way to
+--------------------------Using tin for News--------------------------+
|                                                                      |
| Save in file:                                                        |
|                                                                      |
| Using-tin-for-News                                                   |
|                                                                      |
| [Help: ^-]   [Cancel: ^G]                                            |
+----------------------------------------------------------------------+
to any email address, etc.  You can also post an article to a newsgroup.
+--------------------------------------------------------------------------+
[Help: ?]   [Exit: u]   [PageDown: Space]
```

Figure 9.17 Saving to a File

Press p to Print the File

☞ **Press** p **and press** Enter.

Press **p** to print the file. A window pops up overlaying a portion of the screen. You can cancel the request by pressing **^G** (Ctrl-G), or you start the printing by pressing Enter. See Figure 9.18.

If you're using a modem from your PC to access the Internet through another computer the file may be printed on that other computer, not the printer connected to your PC.

```
Using tin for News (7k)                                                   13%
+--------------------------------------------------------------------------+
Brief Documentation for TIN. Ernest C.Ackermann, Department of Computer
Science, Mary Washington College, Fredericksburg, Va 22401.
ernie@s850.mwc.edu
                              TIN
```

Example 9.2 — Working with a Document on a Gopher Menu ⎯⎯⎯⎯⎯ 231

```
        Tin is software that is supports a convenient or easy to
manage your dealings wit +---Print current document---+ranged into
newsgroups.  Newsgroups  |                             |d articles on the
same topic are assembled |    The filename is:         |use tin to select
which newsgroups you wou  |    /tmp/gopheBAAa09483     |or unsubscribing
from all the groups that  |                            |group is chosen
you can deal with indivi  | [Cancel: ^G] [OK: Enter]  |saving them in a
file, printing them, res +----------------------------+" a response for
everyone to read or mailing a response to the author, mailing articles
to any email address, etc.  You can also post an article to a newsgroup.


+----------------------------------------------------------------------+
[Help: ?]   [Exit: u]   [PageDown: Space]
```

Figure 9.18 Printing a Document

Press D to Download the File

☞ **Press** D.

Press **D** to download the file. A window pops up overlaying a portion of the screen (see Figure 9.19). You type in a number corresponding to a protocol you'd like to use for the transfer from the computer accessing the Internet to your computer. If you're using a modem from your PC to access the Internet through another computer, the file will download to your PC. If your computer is directly connected to the Internet you press **s** to *save* the file rather than download the file.

```
Using tin for News (7k)                                           13%
+----------------------------------------------------------------------+
Brief Documentation for TIN. Ernest C.Ackermann, Department of Computer
Science, Mary Washington College, Fredericksburg, Va 22401.
ernie@s850.mwc.edu
                            TIN
               +-------------Using tin for News-------- +
        Tin is so  |                                    |asy way to
manage your dealing  | ->  1. Zmodem                   |d into
newsgroups.  Newsgr  |     2. Ymodem                   |icles on the
same topic are asse  |     3. Xmodem-1K                |in to select
which newsgroups yo  |     4. Xmodem-CRC               |subscribing
from all the groups  |     5. Kermit                   | is chosen
you can deal with i  |     6. Text                     |g them in a
file, printing them  |                                 |esponse for
everyone to read or  | Choose a download method (1-6): |g articles
to any email addres  | [Help: ?]  [Cancel: ^G]         |a newsgroup.
               +------------------------------------- +
+----------------------------------------------------------------------+
[Help: ?]   [Exit: u]   [PageDown: Space]
```

Figure 9.19 Downloading a Document

End the Session

☞ **Press** u, **then press** q **to quit.**

We'll leave this example here. Press **u** to get back to the menu and then press **q** to quit.

—————————————————————————End of Example 9.2—————————————————————————

Files, Directories, Telnet, and Search Services on a Gopher Menu

Several types of items can appear on Gopher menus. You can often tell the item type by the way it's presented on the menu. Figure 9.20 is a menu that's meant to show some of the different types of entries you may see. (This menu is really pieces taken from others; it doesn't exist anywhere on the Internet.)

```
           Internet Gopher Information Client v2.0.16
                   Special Gopher Connections

    -> 1.  About this menu
       2.  California Gophers GALORE!/
       3.  INTERNET ASSISTANCE/
       4.  CNI Copyright Archives/
       5.  Coffee House <TEL>
       6.  Copyright Law and the Doctoral Dissertation
       7.  Eagle's Nest <TEL>
       8.  lview31.zip <PC BIN>
       9.  5,000,000+ journal articles (via CARL UnCover)/
      10.  AIDS Related Information/
      11.  CIA World Factbook (Searchable) <?>
      12.  DISABILITY INFORMATION/
      13.  Dictionary  Webster's Dictionary <?>
      14.  E-MAIL ADDRESSES:  Internet-wide searches/
      15.  TIGERS.gif <PICTURE>
      16.  gswin.zip <PC BIN>
      17.  United States Copyright Office; Form TX (Copyright Registration)
      18.  Virtus WalkDemo (350k) <HQX>



Press ? for Help, q to Quit, u to go up a menu            Page: 1/4
```

Figure 9.20 Gopher Menu with Several Different Types of Items

❑ The items that don't end with / or other special symbols usually represent plain text files or documents. You can view them by choosing the item and pressing Enter. These are items **1**, **6**, and **17** on the menu.

❑ The items that end with / are either directories or links to other Internet sites. Those are items **2**, **3**, **4**, **9**, **10**, **12**, and **14** on this menu. Choosing one of these brings up another menu.

❑ The items ending with **<TEL>**, when selected, start a Telnet session. On this menu they are items **5** and **7**. You choose one of those items, press Enter, and you'll see a notice stating you're about to start a Telnet session. If you need to use a specific log-in name or password, you'll be told about it then.

❑ The items that end with **<?>** (items **11** and **13**) are searchable indexes. Select the item and then you'll be prompted to supply a word or phrase and press Enter. The index is searched and you'll get a menu of the items that contain the word(s) you've asked for.

❑ The items that end with **<PC BIN>** and **<HQX>** are compressed files. In the first case they're files or archives that have been compressed using PKZIP. The symbol **<HQX>** indicates files in BinHex format to be uncompressed on a Macintosh system. If your client is set up correctly, the files will be transferred to the system running the Gopher client when these are selected. You can uncompress them there or download them to a personal computer.

❑ Items such as item **15** whose name ends with **.gif** or **<PICTURE>** are images, graphic files. If your client is set up properly your system will start or spawn a program to view the file when you select the item. You'll also be able to identify graphic files as those whose name ends with **.pict** or **.jpg**.

Gopher is designed so it's easy for you to retrieve, view, or move to the items on a menu. If you encounter difficulty retrieving an item and you know it's available you may need to check the documentation that came with your client or talk with a local expert. It could be your client is not set up correctly or the programs you need to view certain files such as graphic files aren't present on your system.

Setting Up and Using Gopher Bookmarks

As you use Gopher to maneuver or navigate through the Internet you'll probably find lots of interesting and useful material. You are likely to find entries on Gopher menus you'd like to go back to again or check frequently. You might also like to construct your personal menu of items from a variety of Gopher menus. Gopher has a useful feature called a *bookmark list*. The list is a collection of entries from Gopher menus. You can easily add entries, delete entries, or view the list. The bookmark list is the same as any Gopher menu; each entry represents an item that Gopher will retrieve for you.

To *view* the bookmark list means to make it the current menu. At any Gopher menu, anywhere, you can add the selected item to the bookmark list or add the entire menu to the bookmark list. It's easy to view the bookmark list, add either the current item or directory, or delete items from the bookmark list. If your Gopher client has a graphical interface you click on an item labeled **Bookmark** and choose the appropriate action. If you're using a text-based interface you work with the bookmark through single keystrokes. The rest of this section explains the actions and gives the keystrokes to use.

Adding an Item to the Bookmark List

Press **a** (lowercase a). The item that's marked with → or currently highlighted will be added to the bookmark list with its current name. You can give it a different name if you'd like. You'll want to use this when you've found a single menu entry to save in the list.

Adding the Current Directory to the Bookmark List

Press **A** (uppercase A). The current directory, which is to say the current menu, is saved in the bookmark list. It's not that all the entries in the current menu are put into the bookmark list, but rather the name of the menu page is saved in the bookmark list. You might want to press **A** when you find a menu that has several entries you'd like to keep in your bookmark list.

Viewing the Bookmark List

Press **v** (lowercase v). Your bookmark list will be brought up on the screen. You can work with this as you would with any Gopher menu. Select an item and Gopher will handle bringing the information it represents to you. If you don't have any items on a bookmark list yet, you'll receive a message about that. You need to view the bookmark list *before* you can delete any items from the list.

Deleting an Item from the Bookmark List

Press **d** (lowercase d). This deletes the entry with the → pointing to it (or highlighted if your client interface allows you to use a mouse). You do this while you are viewing the bookmark list *after* you've pressed **v**. As you've added items to the bookmark list you may want to trim its size by deleting items that aren't useful to you or that are no longer active.

Example 9.3 demonstrates working with a bookmark list.

Example 9.3   Working with Bookmarks

In this example we'll look at setting up bookmarks and adding items to the bookmark list. (Deleting an item from the bookmark list isn't shown to conserve space.) As you move through gopherspace you'll find items you'll want to return to or use often. You can save those items in a bookmark list, call up the bookmark list any time you're using Gopher, and go directly to the items you've saved *without* having to go through the menus you worked through to get there in the first place. Also, the bookmark list stays with you whenever you use Gopher; not just for a single Gopher session.

In the example you'll see several different menus without a clear connection of how you get from one to the other. That's intentional. We want to concentrate on setting and using bookmarks. The screens that appear here could have come from one session or several sessions.

To start, suppose you've discovered or worked your way to this menu (Figure 9.21), which lists sources of information relating to news and weather. You want to put the selected item, **4. National Weather Service Forecasts**, in your bookmark list. (When this example was constructed we got to the menu in Figure 9.21 by pointing our Gopher to **gopher.mountain.net** and then choosing **News & Weather** from the main menu.)

```
                  Internet Gopher Information Client v2.0.16
                              News & Weather
```

Example 9.3 — Working with Bookmarks   235

```
        1.   Daily News - Free Internet Sources/
        2.   NASA News
        3.   NOAA Environmental Information Gopher/
        4.   National Science Foundation (atm.geo.nsf.gov) [atm.geo.nsf.gov]/
   ->   5.   National Weather Service Forecasts/
        6.   News and Weather/
        7.   News, Periodicals, and Journals/
        8.   Notiziari Televideo RAI/
        9.   Publications and News/
       10.   Selected Usenet News Groups <HTML>
       11.   Television News Archive (Vanderbilt University)/
       12.   The Electronic Newsstand (magazines, periodicals, journals)/
       13.   The UofI Weather Machine/
       14.   USENET News (NNTP News Read)/
       15.   USENET News (from Michigan State)/
       16.   USENET News Available from MountainNetWORKS   [28Nov94, 1kb]
       17.   Weather Information (Ohio State University)/


Press ? for Help, q to Quit, u to go up a menu                  Page: 1/1
```

Figure 9.21 News and Weather Menu

☞ **Press** a **(lowercase) to add the selected item to the bookmark list.**

A screen will pop up showing the name the bookmark will have once it's saved. You can use that name or give it another. See Figure 9.22.

```
Internet Gopher Information Client v2.0.16
News & Weather


        1.   Daily News - Free Internet Sources/
        2.   NASA News
        3.   NOAA Environmental Information Gopher/
        4.   National Science Foundation (atm.geo.nsf.gov) [atm.geo.nsf.gov]/
+---------------------National Weather Service Forecasts---------------- +
|                                               |
| Name for this bookmark:          The window surrounding this box pops up. The name
|                                  of the bookmark is taken from the menu (you can
| National Weather Service Forecasts   type any name you'd like). Press Enter to add it to
|                                  the bookmark list or press ^G (Ctrl-G) to cancel.
| [Help: ^-]  [Cancel: ^G]
+---------------------------------------------------------------------- +
       13.   The UofI Weather Machine/
       14.   USENET News (NNTP News Read)/
       15.   USENET News (from Michigan State)/
```

```
     16. USENET News Available from MountainNetWORKS   [28Nov94, 1kb]
     17. Weather Information (Ohio State University)/


Press ? for Help, q to Quit, u to go up a menu                Page: 1/1
```

Figure 9.22 Adding a Menu Item to the Bookmark List

Add a Menu to the Bookmark List

☞ **Press** A **(uppercase).**

Figure 9.23 shows another menu related to consumer information. You've found it in gopherspace and you'd like to add the entire menu to your bookmark list. Press **A** (uppercase) to add the menu to the bookmark list (see Figure 9.24).

```
              Internet Gopher Information Client v2.0.16
                              Consumer
     1.  Consumer Guide (RiceInfo)/
 ->  2.  Consumer Information (UIUC)/
     3.  Consumer News Service (Cornell)/
     4.  Consumer Product Safety Commission (U.S.)/


Press ? for Help, q to Quit, u to go up a menu                Page: 1/1
```

Figure 9.23 A Gopher Menu on Consumer Information

```
              Internet Gopher Information Client v2.0.16
                              Consumer

     1.  Consumer Guide (RiceInfo)/
 ->  2.  Consumer Information (UIUC)/
     3.  Consumer News Service (Cornell)/
     4.  Consumer Product Safety Commission (U.S.)/
+------------------------------Consumer------------------------------------+
|                                                                          |
| Name for this bookmark:      ┌──────────────────────────────────────┐   |
|                              │ The window surrounding this box pops up. The name │
| Consumer                     │ of the bookmark is taken from the menu (you can │
|                              │ type any name you'd like). Press Enter to add it to │
| [Help: ^-]  [Cancel: ^G]     │ the bookmark list or press ^G (Ctrl-G) to cancel. │
+------------------------------└──────────────────────────────────────┘----+


Press ? for Help, q to Quit, u to go up a menu                Page: 1/1
```

Figure 9.24 Adding a Menu to the Bookmark List

Example 9.3 — Working with Bookmarks   237

☞ **Press** v **to view your bookmark list.**

If you press **v** your bookmark list appears (Figure 9.24). This list is really a Gopher menu with two entries in this case. You work with it just as you work with any Gopher menu.

```
            Internet Gopher Information Client v2.0.16
                              Bookmarks


  ->    1.  National Weather Service Forecasts/
        2.  Consumer /


Press ? for Help, q to Quit, u to go up a menu          Page: 1/1
```

Figure 9.25 Bookmark List

Add Another Item to the Bookmark List

☞ **Press** a **(lowercase).**

Here we'll add another item, **3. Eff.org gopher server** (Electronic Frontier Foundation), to the bookmark list. Press **a** to add it. See Figures 9.26 and 9.27.

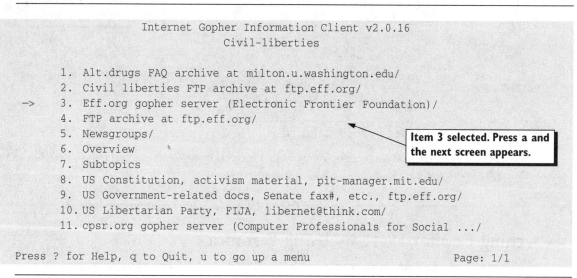

```
            Internet Gopher Information Client v2.0.16
                            Civil-liberties


      1.  Alt.drugs FAQ archive at milton.u.washington.edu/
      2.  Civil liberties FTP archive at ftp.eff.org/
  ->  3.  Eff.org gopher server (Electronic Frontier Foundation)/
      4.  FTP archive at ftp.eff.org/
      5.  Newsgroups/
      6.  Overview
      7.  Subtopics
      8.  US Constitution, activism material, pit-manager.mit.edu/
      9.  US Government-related docs, Senate fax#, etc., ftp.eff.org/
     10. US Libertarian Party, FIJA, libernet@think.com/
     11. cpsr.org gopher server (Computer Professionals for Social .../


Press ? for Help, q to Quit, u to go up a menu          Page: 1/1
```

Item 3 selected. Press a and the next screen appears.

Figure 9.26 Civil-liberties Menu

```
            Internet Gopher Information Client v2.0.16
                            Civil-liberties


      1.  Alt.drugs FAQ archive at milton.u.washington.edu/
      2.  Civil liberties FTP archive at ftp.eff.org/
```

```
-> 3.  Eff.org gopher server (Electronic Frontier Foundation)/
    4.  FTP archive at ftp.eff.org/
+--------------Eff.org gopher server (Electronic Frontier Foundation)--------+
|                                                                            |
| Name for this bookmark:
|
| Eff.org gopher server (Electronic Frontier Foundation)
|
| [Help: ^-]  [Cancel: ^G]                                                   |
+----------------------------------------------------------------------------+


Press ? for Help, q to Quit, u to go up a menu              Page: 1/1
```

> **This pops up with the default name of the bookmark item. Press Enter to accept it.**

Figure 9.27 Saving the Gopher Server for Electronic Frontier Foundation (gopher.eff.org) as a Bookmark

☞ **Press v to view the bookmark list.**

The latest item is added to the end of the list. See Figure 9.28.

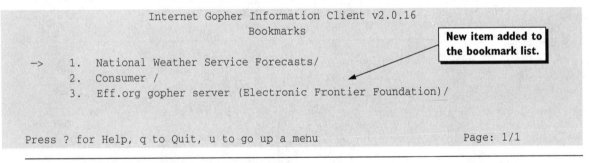

```
                Internet Gopher Information Client v2.0.16
                             Bookmarks

   ->    1.  National Weather Service Forecasts/
         2.  Consumer /
         3.  Eff.org gopher server (Electronic Frontier Foundation)/


Press ? for Help, q to Quit, u to go up a menu              Page: 1/1
```

> **New item added to the bookmark list.**

Figure 9.28 New Item Added to Bookmark List

This is the end of the example. Remember that you have this bookmark list available to you whenever you use Gopher.

————————————————————————————————— **End of Example 9.3** —————————————————————————————————

Searching Gopher Systems Using Veronica

Gopher has become such a popular means for distributing information on the Internet that there are thousands of Gopher servers throughout the world. That gives us lots of opportunities for finding the information we want, but the sheer number of Gopher servers means it's necessary to have a tool to search Gopher directories and titles. An effective and popular tool to do just that is *Veronica*. Performing a *veronica search* means that you supply a word or string of words to the Veronica service and it returns a Gopher-style menu of items containing the word(s) you provided. It's said that Veronica is an acronym formed from Very Easy Rodent-Oriented Net-wide Index to Computerized Archives. But it's hard to miss the connection with Archie, the tool you use to find files available by anonymous FTP (see Chapter 8). Veronica, a tool to search and

Example 9.4 — Searching Gopherspace with Veronica 239

find things in gopherspace, is similar to Archie. Furthermore, who is Archie's girl friend in the comics? Veronica, of course! After Veronica completes a search you get a menu of items that is in fact a Gopher menu.

You initiate a Veronica search by choosing Veronica on a Gopher menu, and then selecting one of several sites providing the Veronica service. The remote site then prompts you to supply a keyword or keywords for Veronica to use in the search. Gopher servers are searched and you receive a menu of topics that contain your keyword. The menu contains a collection of Gopher menu entries from throughout gopherspace. It's a "live menu"; you use it as you would use any Gopher menu. The menu will generally consist of any of the types of entries found on Gopher menus, but in some cases you can have the Veronica service return only directory names. You'll see how it works in Example 9.4.

There are several Veronica servers, just as there are several Archie servers, throughout the world. At times they may be too busy to satisfy your request for a search. You'll get a message if the server is too busy. Either try the same server later or try another. To try another, get back to the menu with the list of Veronica sites by pressing **u** enough times, and make another choice. You may need to be persistent to find a Veronica site that will meet your needs. As an alternative, plan your search for some time of the day outside of normal working hours. You'll probably have a choice of servers throughout the world, so there is always somewhere where the local time is not peak working time.

You give Veronica either a single word or a series of words, called the search string, to use in the search. When you use more than one word as the search string you can enclose the words in quotes to ensure that entries returned will contain the words in the same order. Using "commercial use," for example, will return entries that have both words in the order specified such as:

```
Conservation and commercial use of trees in Costa Rica.
```

Not including the words in quotes will return entries that have the words in any order or just one or a few of the words. An example of an item found using the string commercial use is:

```
Monitoring Energy Use in Commercial buildings.
```

Several Gopher sites list entries that can give you complete information about using Veronica. Look for entries similar to "FAQ: Frequently Asked Questions About Veronica" and "How to Compose Veronica Queries—READ ME." These are also available by anonymous FTP. The section below titled "Internet Sources of Information About Gopher" lists some sources for these files.

Example 9.4   Searching Gopherspace with Veronica

You use Veronica to either search gopherspace or search for Gopher directory (menu) titles. The search of gopherspace is more general; you'll retrieve entries that are both directories and files. To start a Veronica search you need to select a Veronica server. That's a site (on a Gopher menu) that will perform the search once you supply it with the word(s) to use. In this case we'll select a site by first pointing our gopher at the Gopher server at the Library of Congress. This example shows using Veronica to search Gopher directories.

In what follows you'll see a mention of a Jughead server. Jughead is like Veronica except Veronica searches Gopher sites throughout the Internet while Jughead is usually set up to search Gopher menus at a single site. (It's no coincidence that Jughead is also a character in the Archie comics.)

This example shows what you're likely to see if you use a Gopher client on a Unix system. The client you use may differ, but the principles are the same. Here are the steps to follow:

1. Start a Gopher session with the Gopher server at the Library of Congress.
2. Choose the item **Internet Resources** and then choose the item **Veronica and Jughead Servers (search gopherspace)/**.
3. Choose the item that allows a Veronica search of directories using the server at the University of Cologne.
4. Search for directories (menus) whose titles contain the word *biodiversity*.

After that the rest is up to you. You may want to explore some entries. If they look useful you may want to add them to your bookmark list.

Start a Gopher Session with the Gopher Server at the Library of Congress

☞ **Point your gopher at** `marvel.loc.gov.`

```
gopher marvel.loc.gov
```

You'll see the screen in Figure 9.29.

```
                Internet Gopher Information Client v2.0.16
                       Library of Congress - Marvel


          1.   About LC MARVEL/
          2.   Events, Facilities, Programs, and Services/
          3.   Research and Reference (Public Services)/
          4.   Libraries and Publishers (Technical Services)/
          5.   Copyright/
          6.   Library of Congress Online Systems/
          7.   Employee Information/
          8.   U.S. Congress/
          9.   Government Information/
          10.  Global Electronic Library (by Subject)/
      ->  11.  Internet Resources/
          12.  What's New on LC MARVEL/
          13.  Search LC MARVEL Menus/


     Press ? for Help, q to Quit, u to go up a menu          Page: 1/1
```

Figure 9.29 Main Menu Library of Congress Gopher

Example 9.4 — Searching Gopherspace with Veronica ————————— 241

Choose "Internet Resources"

☞ **Move the → to item 11, or type** 11, **and then press** Enter .

You'll see the screen in Figure 9.30.

Choose "Veronica and Jughead Servers (search gopherspace)/"

☞ **Move the → to item 13, or type** 13, **and then press** Enter .

```
                 Internet Gopher Information Client v2.0.16
                             Internet Resources


      1.   Archie and FTP/
      2.   Bulletin Boards - Telnet-Accessible (via Texas A&M)/
      3.   Campus Wide Information Systems/
      4.   Commercial Network Services (accounts required)/
      5.   Directories: Finding People and Organizations/
      6.   Frequent Systems/
      7.   Gophers/
      8.   HYTELNET - Connect to Library Catalogs & Other Systems/
      9.   Internet Guides, Policies, and Information Services/
      10.  Library Catalogs and Databases/
      11.  Listservs, Usenet, and Other Network Discussion Groups/
      12.  Sales, Catalogs, and Commercial Services/
 -->  13.  Veronica and Jughead Servers (search gopherspace)/
      14.  Wide Area Information Servers (WAIS)/
      15.  World Wide Web (WWW)/
      16.  Shortcut to Global Electronic Library/ Reference/

 Press ? for Help, q to Quit, u to go up a menu              Page: 1/1
```

Figure 9.30 Internet Resources Menu at Library of Congress Gopher

Choose the Item That Allows a Veronica Search of Directory Titles Using the Server at the University of Cologne

☞ **Move → to Item 6 or type** 6 **and press** Enter .

This item ends with **<?>** which means it's "searchable." You'll be asked to supply a word to use for searching. See Figure 9.31.

```
                 Internet Gopher Information Client v2.0.16
                 Veronica and Jughead Servers (search gopherspace)


      1.   Veronica FAQ (Frequently Asked Questions about Veronica)
      2.   How to Compose Veronica Queries
      3.   Jughead — Readme
      4.   Search Gopher Directory Titles Using Veronica at America Online <?>
```

```
        5.   Search Gopher Directory Titles Using Veronica at PSINet <?>
   ->  6.   Search Gopher Directory Titles at University of Cologne <?>
        7.   Search Gopherspace Using Veronica at America Online <?>
        8.   Search Gopherspace Using Veronica at NYSERNet <?>
        9.   Search Gopherspace Using Veronica at PSINet <?>
       10.  Search High-level Gopher Menus Using Jughead at Wash. & Lee U. <?>
       11.  Search gopherspace at University of Cologne <?>
       12.  The Australian Veronica Server <?>
       13.  Veronica Directory at University of Nevada, Reno/
       14.  Veronica Directory via MINITEX (UMN)/
       15.  Veronica via UTexas, Dallas (feedback to billy@utdallas.edu)/
       16.  Washington and Lee U. — Finding Gopher Resources/


Press ? for Help, q to Quit, u to go up a menu                    Page: 1/1
```

Figure 9.31 Veronica and Jughead Servers Menu

Search for Directory (Menus) Titles Containing the Word "biodiversity"

A window will pop up overlaying a portion of the screen. There will be a spot in the window for you to supply the word(s) to use in searching.

☞ **Type** biodiversity **and press** Enter.

Gopher will contact the site and Veronica will perform the search. See Figure 9.32.

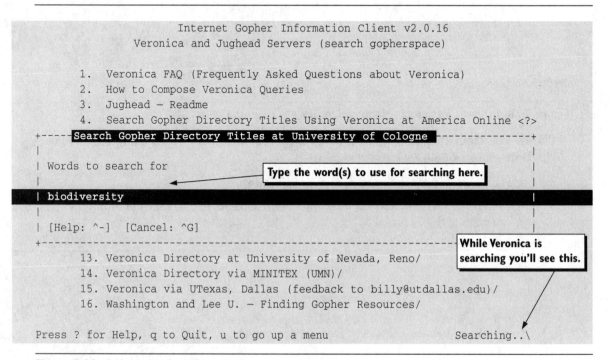

Figure 9.32 A Veronica Search

Note: You may encounter a couple of problems here. Veronica servers, as you might imagine, are often very busy. If the server or site you've selected for the Veronica search is too busy you'll be notified before the search begins. In that case you'll have to choose another server. Also, sometimes a search takes a very long time. In that case you may want to abort the search. To do that press Ctrl-C. You'll be asked if you want to quit the Gopher session.

When Veronica completes the search you'll get a menu of items whose titles contain the word(s) you supplied for the search. Figure 9.33 shows what was returned in this case. You can see, by looking at **Page 1/7** in the lower right, that seven pages of directory titles were found.

```
                Internet Gopher Information Client v2.0.16

     Search Gopher Directory Titles at University of Cologne: biodiversity

   -> 1.  Harvard Biodiversity and Biological Collections Gopher/
      2.  Plant Biodiversity and Conservation /
      3.  Biodiversity-Conservation/
      4.  BIODIVERSITY DATA/
      5.  Other Biodiversity and Environmental Resources/
      6.  Biodiversity Information Resources/
      7.  biodiversity/
      8.  Other Biodiversity Gophers/
      9.  biodiversity-tltp-images/
      10. Biodiversity and Biological Collections Gopher/
      11. . . . . . . . . . Ftp to life.anu.edu.au... Natnl. Univ., biodiversity/
      12. All Taxa Biodiversity Inventory (ATBI)/
      13. More General Biodiversity Information/
      14. Biodiversity Journals and Newsletters/
      15. biodiversity.books/
      16. Biodiversity/
      17. Biodiversity/
      18. Biodiversity-ecology-and-evolution/

Press ? for Help, q to Quit, u to go up a menu               Page: 1/7
```

Figure 9.33 Results of Veronica Search

The rest is up to you. You can retrieve information, explore the menus, and add items to your bookmark list.

──────────────**End of Example 9.4**──────────────

Finding Gopher Sites

The Gopher server at the University of Minnesota and a variety of other Gopher servers contain entries for many of the Gopher servers in the world. You need to look for a menu entry there or on other servers with a title similar to "Other Gopher and Information Servers." The entry for a specific site can be found by going through several menus. The first menu gives at least three methods for finding Gopher servers. You can retrieve a list of all the registered servers (this is a very long list), search for a specific server by supplying a search string consisting of some terms that describe the site or location you'd like to find, or choose an entry that allows you to search according to a specific continent or region of the world.

For example, to find the Gopher server at the World Data Center on Microorganisms in Riken, Japan, you could choose to search using the words microorganisms, riken, or japan. To take an alternate approach, to find the Gopher servers in Montana you might choose the item titled North America, choose USA from the next menu, and then choose Montana.

To contact the Gopher server at the University of Minnesota point your gopher at **gopher.tc.umn.edu** or use Telnet to **consultant.micro.umn.edu** and log in as gopher.

Internet Sources of Information About Gopher

There are several Internet sources of information about Gopher and its companion tools Veronica and Jughead. Much of the information is accessible by using Gopher itself. Additionally, you'll also find materials that can be retrieved using anonymous FTP and a Usenet newsgroup for discussions about Gopher use and administration. Many sites carry information about using Gopher; only a few will be listed here.

One important Gopher site is at the University of Minnesota, the home of the original Gopher system. You can reach that site by pointing your gopher to **gopher.tc.umn.edu** or using the URL **gopher://gopher.tc.umn.edu:70/1**. Once you get to the main menu there choose the topic **Information About Gopher**. A source of information in Europe is the Gopher server at EARN (European Academic and Research Network), which contains the on-line "Guide to Network Resource Tools." This is accessible by pointing your gopher at **gopher.earn.net**, choosing **User Services Documentation**, then choosing **Guide to Network Resource Tools by Chapters**, and finally choosing the chapter on Gopher. You can also use the URL **gopher:// gopher.earn.net:70/11/doc/gnrt-by-chapters/Gopher**. You'll also find information about Veronica and Jughead at these sites. Take some time to explore these resources.

Here is a list of some files with information about Gopher, Veronica, and Jughead available by anonymous FTP:

❑ "Internet Gopher User's Guide," edited by Paul Linder. It's available in PostScript formats. **ftp://boombox.micro.umn.edu/pub/gopher/docs/**

❑ "Gopher FAQ: Frequently Asked Questions about Gopher." Updated regularly.

  ftp://rtfm.mit.edu/pub/usenet/news.answers/gopher-faq

❑ "Veronica FAQ: Frequently asked questions about Veronica."

  ftp://ftp.mwc.edu/internet-info/gopher/veronica.faq

❏ "How to Compose Veronica Queries."

ftp://ftp.mwc.edu/internet.info/gopher/veronica-queries.txt

❏ "Description of Jughead."

**ftp://boombox.micro.umn.edu/pub/gopher/Unix/GopherTools/jughead/
jughead.ReadMe**

The Usenet newsgroup that deals with issues related to Gopher is **comp.infosystems.gopher**.

Summary

Gopher is a popular and relatively easy-to-use tool for maneuvering through the Internet. It was developed at the University of Minnesota and is available on a wide variety of computer systems.

The Gopher system was designed to deliver documents in an academic environment. You work with a menu system to retrieve information. The Gopher program operates according to a client/ server model. You start a client on your local system and the client communicates with a server. The server returns either a menu (directory list) or a document.

The menus and documents can reside anywhere on the Internet. Furthermore, the documents can be one of a variety of types: file, directory, CSO phone book, BinHexed Macintosh file, DOS binary archive, uuencoded file, Telnet session, image file, or index-search server. In each case you select an item from a menu and the document or file is delivered to your system, Gopher links you to another site on the Internet, or a program is run to retrieve a file, search an index, or start another Internet service.

The commands or methods you use to start a Gopher session depend on the type of computer system and client program you're using. On some systems you type the command gopher and press Enter; on others you use a mouse to click on a phrase or icon that represents the Gopher client software. You'll be connected to a Gopher server. Usually there is a specific server, called the *default server*, your client contacts. The server then displays a starting or main menu. You'll have the option of starting your Gopher session with any Gopher server on the Internet. This is called pointing your gopher at a server. The command **gopher gopher.tc.umn.edu**, for example, points a Gopher (connects to the server) to the original or home Gopher server at the University of Minnesota. The command **gopher cycling.com** points your Gopher at the Gopher server for the Global Cycling Network.

Once you locate a file or document through a Gopher menu you can display the file on your screen, save it to a local file, print it, send the file by e-mail to any Internet e-mail address, or download it to your computer.

Gopher also allows you to set *bookmarks*, which are pointers to items you've found on Gopher menus. When you find an item you'd like to save for future use you add it to the bookmark list. You can view your bookmarks any time during a Gopher session, and the list persists from session to session. Also, you can delete items for a bookmark list. In effect, you build and maintain your personal Gopher menu. The bookmark list can be used the same way you use any other Gopher menu.

You can search Gopher sites for file or directory entries by using Veronica. There are thousands of Gopher sites throughout the world, and Veronica helps you find files or directories by searching the menu entries on these servers. To use Veronica you choose a Veronica server, a computer system that will do the searching for you, from a Gopher menu. You'll be prompted to enter a word or sequence of words, called search string, which Veronica will use for the search. After you enter the search string, Veronica will search Gopher servers and return a menu of items that contain the search string. You work with this menu in the same way you'd work with any Gopher menu.

Gopher is relatively easy to use. It gives you the capability to find and retrieve information by working with a series of menus. All you need to do is to be able to select an item from a menu and you can search directories, retrieve files, use several different types of Internet services, and connect to sites throughout the Internet. These capabilities, along with the large number and diversity of Gopher servers, make Gopher an effective and popular tool for working on the Internet. When you use Gopher you can concentrate on *what* you need to do without having to learn a variety of specialized techniques or skills.

Exercises

Practice Using Gopher

1. Start a Gopher session. You'll be connected to a default server. (If for some reason a default server isn't available, set your client to connect to **gopher.mwc.edu**.)
    a. What is the name or Internet address of the default server?
    b. How many items are on the main menu?
    c. What are the items on the main menu?
    d. Select the first item on the menu. If it's a file, view it, otherwise choose that item and continue until you can view a file. What's the file's name and what does it hold?

2. Point your Gopher to the server at the University of Minnesota. In other words, start a Gopher session with **gopher.tc.umn.edu**.
    a. Choose the item **Fun & Games** from the main menu. What's on the next menu you see?
    b. Go back to the main menu. What's in the directory titled **News**?
    c. Go back to the main menu. Choose the item that gives information about Gopher and answer these questions: What is the University of Minnesota Gopher licensing policy? How do you send comments to the Gopher Development Team?

3. Go through the steps in Example 9.1, "Connecting to the Virtual Reference Desk." Find the section on the main menu titled **POLITICS AND GOVERNMENT**. (*Hint:* The subjects are arranged alphabetically.)
    a. What is in the section **POLITICS AND GOVERNMENT**?
    b. Which item on the **POLITICS AND GOVERNMENT** menu gives information about the current program schedules for the C-SPAN network?
    c. Find the item titled **U.S. House of Representatives Gopher** on the **POLITICS AND GOVERNMENT** menu. Describe what you find in that section.

4. Point your Gopher to **nmnhgoph.si.edu**, the Gopher server for the Smithsonian Institution's Natural History Gopher. Choose the item titled **About the Smithsonian Institution's Natural History Gopher**.
   a. View the contents of the document.
   b. Press **?** to get help while you're viewing the file. What options are available to you?
   c. Send the file to yourself through e-mail.
   d. Send the file to a friend through e-mail.
   e. Either save the file on your system or download the file to your personal computer if you're using one to access another system connected to the Internet.

Exploring the Internet and Working With Bookmarks

5. Connect to the Smithsonian Institution's Natural History Gopher (point your Gopher **nmnhgoph.si.edu** to choose the item titled **Related Gopher and Information Servers**, then choose **Other Biological Information Servers**.
   a. Choose a server that's located in Japan from the menu. What is the name of that server and what is on its main menu? Add it to your bookmark list.
   b. Choose a server that's located in the United Kingdom from the menu. What is the name of that server and what is on its main menu? Add it to your bookmark list.

6. Because there are so many Gopher servers throughout the world, some folks have arranged or classified servers according to subject headings. One place to look for such a subject classification is the Gopher server at the Library of Congress (**marvel.loc.gov**). Point your gopher to the Library of Congress Gopher and select the menu item titled **Global Electronic Library (by Subject)**. For each of the following subject areas, choose the subject area and add three items from that subject area to your bookmark list.
   a. The Arts
   b. Natural Sciences
   c. Sports and Recreation

7. Point your gopher at the server at the University of Minnesota to find a gopher server in each of the these three regions of the world: South America, Africa, and Asia. For each server you've found:
   a. Add it to your bookmark list.
   b. Describe what is available through that Gopher.

8. Delete five entries from your bookmark list.

Searching Gopher Menus and Using Veronica

9.   Some servers provide a service that lets you search the titles on their menus. Point your Gopher at any one of these three sites:

UC Santa Cruz Infoslug	**gopher.ucsc.edu**
North Carolina State University Library Gopher	**dewey.lib.ncsu.edu**
University of Durham (UK)	**delphi.dur.ac.uk**

Choose an item on the menu that indicates you can search the list of titles at that site (such items usually end with **<?>**) and search for items on each of the following topics. Describe what you find in each case.
a.   biochemistry
b.   dream
c.   recreation

10. Point to a Gopher server that permits Veronica searches of gopherspace. Perform a Veronica search using each of the following as a search string: *museum*; *art museum*; *art museums*.
a.   Save at least three items from each search in your bookmark list.
b.   Write a few sentences describing the differing results obtained when you use *art museum* and *art museums* as the search strings.
c.   On any of the Veronica searches you'll see files that are images or pictures. If you can't find any at the first menu that appears, look through the menus until you find one. Choose an image file or a picture and display it on your system. (If you get error messages, your client may not be configured correctly. Get some help from a local expert, or download the file and display it on your system.)
d.   Choose a different Veronica server and perform a Veronica search using *art museum* as the search string. You might want to pick a Veronica server in a country different from the first. Do you get the same results? Why do think that is the case?

Browsing the Internet with Gopher

11. Once again, use the Virtual Reference Desk to:
a.   Use the CIA World Fact Book to find the land area of Costa Rica and a description of its climate.
b.   Use a dictionary available on the menu to find some meanings for the word *gopher*.
c.   Describe the information that's available about cancer.
d.   Find the area code(s) for San Francisco, California, Fort Worth, Texas, and Washington, D.C.

12. "Gopher Jewels" is a collection of links to some of the best Gopher sites throughout the world. The emphasis is on information by subject. One way to access Gopher Jewels is through the Virtual Reference Desk. When you access Gopher Jewels you'll see a menu of different subject areas. Pick one and spend some time exploring. As you find interesting links to sites, save them in your bookmark file. Write a short report telling about some interesting sites you visited in one of the items from the main menu of Gopher Jewels.

WAIS
Searching Databases
on the Internet

WAIS (pronounced *ways*), or Wide Area Information Server, is a system for searching and retrieving items from databases. The databases can be anywhere on the Internet. The search is based on one or more keywords. In some cases, depending on the software you're using, you search a single database or have the capability to search several simultaneously.

When you use WAIS you don't explicitly connect to the sites that hold the databases; WAIS takes care of that. You start a WAIS client, then you choose one or several sources or databases, and then supply the keyword(s). WAIS handles your request and sees to it that the databases you've requested are searched. The result is a list of articles arranged in a list according to how closely they match the keyword(s). You can select any of the articles from the list to view on the screen, save to a file, or send to an Internet address via e-mail.

You access WAIS either through a client on your system, or through Telnet, Gopher, or other Internet services. When you access WAIS through Telnet you may not be able to save an article to a file or send it by e-mail. Several hundred text databases are available through WAIS, although not all of these may be accessible from every site. In any case the topics available cover a wide range including social sciences, natural sciences, computing, Asian studies, literature, technical material, humanities, and the arts.

Chapter Overview

This chapter focuses on using WAIS to search for and retrieve information from the Internet. The topics covered include:

❏ Introduction to and Overview of WAIS

❏ Starting a WAIS Session

❏ Selecting Databases to Search

❏ Using Keywords for a Search

❏ Performing a Search

❏ Working with the Results of a Search

❏ Finding and Connecting to WAIS Systems

❏ Sources of Information about WAIS

Introduction to and Overview of WAIS

WAIS lets you search a collection of databases from one location. The databases themselves may be organized in a variety of ways. You don't have to learn the specific query language or techniques of each database. WAIS handles the searching. You choose one or more WAIS sources—the databases—and specify keywords to use in the searching. WAIS performs the search and returns a list of items or articles ranked according to the number of times the keyword(s) appeared in the article. The database was indexed to allow for full-text search and retrieval. Every word in the database is accounted for and can be found.

The WAIS client software is available for several types of computer systems and operating environments. The specific steps necessary to use WAIS and the way WAIS is presented to a user may be different in these different environments. Regardless of those differences the user, working with the software, goes through these steps:

❏ Start a WAIS client program.

❏ Select one or more sources (databases) to search.

❏ Give one or more keywords to use for the search.

The WAIS system then contacts the sources and performs the search. The user gets a list of items, called articles, arranged by a score that WAIS gives to each item. The score is roughly determined by the number of times each keyword appears in an article. Then the user can view the article and display it one screen at a time. If the user accessed WAIS through Telnet that may be all she can do. If she is using a WAIS client on her local computer system she can also:

❏ Save the article to a file.

❏ Mail the article to an Internet e-mail address.

WAIS searching can also be done through Gopher. The result of the search is a list of items or entries on a Gopher menu. With the usual Gopher commands the articles can be sent to any Internet address via e-mail or saved to a file.

The user always has the option of going back and adding more keywords for another search or changing the sources used for the search. However, WAIS doesn't allow for a Boolean search. That means if the words *water quality* are used for the search, then WAIS may return articles that contain the word *water*, the word *quality*, or both. There isn't any way to specify that you'd like only articles that contain both words. It's conceivable that articles with both words would get a higher score, but it's just as possible that an article containing the word *water* many times would get a higher score than an article containing the string *water quality* only a few times. Therefore, some recommend that you use a collection of keywords that are likely to appear together in a paragraph.

WAIS allows you to concentrate on what you'd like to find rather than having to deal with a variety of different techniques for finding it. In that respect it's similar to Gopher, but Gopher is a more general purpose tool, since Gopher items can be documents, connections to other Internet sites, access to WAIS-type searches, and access to other Internet services.

If you don't have direct access to a WAIS server or have a WAIS client program on your system you may be able to access WAIS through Telnet. Several servers are available through Hytelnet (choose **SITES2**, then **Distributed File Servers**, and finally **Wide Area Information Servers**). A WAIS client is started automatically when you use Telnet to connect to one of those sites. Using Telnet, the WAIS client that starts up is known as SWAIS—Screen WAIS. It gives you a full-screen, text-based interface.

Another way to use WAIS is to point your gopher to a site that has a menu entry for WAIS searching. Many Gopher sites provide this service. Look for a menu entry with a title that indicates that Internet services or resources might be available. Some examples of these menu items are **Internet Resources** at **marvel.loc.gov** (Library of Congress), **The Internet** at **gopher.mwc.edu** (Mary Washington College), and **Other Sources (explore the Internet!)** at **info.asu.edu** (Arizona State University). Some Gopher servers include WAIS services on the main menu. Two sites are **gopher-gw.micro.umn.edu** (University of Minnesota) and **munin.ub2.lu.se** (Lund University Electronic Library Service).

WAIS was developed at Thinking Machines Corporation as a joint effort of Thinking Machines, Apple Computer, and Dow Jones. The client and server software is available for several types of computer systems and working environments. A good place to find information on the Internet about WAIS and the software is **wais.com**. Point your gopher to **gopher.wais.com** if you want to browse through the information. To retrieve items you can use Gopher or anonymous FTP to **ftp.wais.com**.

Starting a WAIS Session

There are several ways to start a WAIS session. The method you use may depend on the way you access the Internet and how you'd like to use WAIS. You start a WAIS session by using a WAIS client program on your system, using Telnet to connect to a site that automatically starts a WAIS client when you log in, or using Gopher to connect to a site that includes access to WAIS searches on one of its menus. You'll see an example of starting a WAIS session in Example 10.1 below. When you use Telnet to access WAIS, you'll be using *SWAIS*. SWAIS is a full-screen, text-based program. In this case you work with WAIS by typing single character keystroke commands, and you'll be able to search one or more WAIS databases simultaneously. With Gopher you'll find the user interface may be easier to use, but you'll be able to search only one database at a time. Example 10.2 in this chapter shows how to use Gopher for WAIS. In this section we demonstrate using SWAIS or Gopher.

SWAIS Client Locally or through Telnet

Two sites that allow Telnet access are **quake.think.com** and **wais.com**. In each case you start a Telnet session to the site and use WAIS as the log-in name. You'll probably be asked to supply your e-mail address and identify your terminal type. The standard terminal type is VT100, a common type of terminal. Most communication programs for personal computers provide the capabilities of emulating or mimicking a VT100 terminal. If you use Telnet to **wais.com**, a SWAIS client is started automatically and you'll see a screen similar to the one in Figure 10.1. You'll be at the **Source Selection** menu. The term SWAIS indicates you're using the character-based Telnet interface to WAIS. Here you can see there are 521 sources available through WAIS. Each source is numbered and the domain name, name of the database, and the cost for accessing the database are listed. Notice there isn't any cost for accessing any of the databases. The last line lists some commands you can give with a single keystroke.

```
SWAIS                     Source Selection                  Sources: 521
   #          Server                 Source                    Cost
 001:   [          archie.au]   aarnet-resource-guide       Free
 002:   [ndadsb.gsfc.nasa.gov]  AAS_jobs                    Free
 003:   [ndadsb.gsfc.nasa.gov]  AAS_meeting                 Free
 004:   [      munin.ub2.lu.se]  academic_email_conf         Free
 005:   [        sv3.cnusc.fr]  acubase                     Free
 006:   [    archive.orst.edu]  aeronautics                 Free
 007:   [         wolfnet.com]  afrophile                   Free
 008:   [bruno.cs.colorado.ed]  aftp-cs-colorado-edu        Free
 009:   [nostromo.oes.orst.ed]  agricultural-market-news    Free
 010:   [     wais.oit.unc.edu]  alt.gopher                  Free
 011:   [     wais.oit.unc.edu]  alt.wais                    Free
 012:   [      munin.ub2.lu.se]  amiga_fish_contents         Free
 013:   [   coombs.anu.edu.au]  ANU-Aboriginal-EconPolicies $0.00/minute
 014:   [   coombs.anu.edu.au]  ANU-Aboriginal-Studies      $0.00/minute
 015:   [        150.203.76.2]  ANU-ACT-Stat-L              $0.00/minute
 016:   [   coombs.anu.edu.au]  ANU-Ancient-DNA-L           $0.00/minute
 017:   [        150.203.76.2]  ANU-Ancient-DNA-Studies     $0.00/minute
 018:   [        150.203.76.2]  ANU-Asia-Pacific-Security-L $0.00/minute

Keywords:

<space> selects, w for keywords, arrows move, <return> searches, q quits, or ?
```

Figure 10.1   Source Selection Menu

Gopher

For Gopher access choose an item on a menu whose name indicates that you'll be able to access WAIS. For example, when you point your gopher to **marvel.loc.gov** and choose the item **Internet Resources** from the main menu you'll see an item titled **Wide Area Information Servers (WAIS)**. Choose that item to begin a WAIS session.

Selecting Databases to Search

Before you give the keywords for the search you need to specify which database to search. It's generally up to you to know which database(s) to choose. That's one of the difficulties of using WAIS: You may make a selection with little information about what the database contains. You can pick one by name, have one recommended to you, or experiment with a few that seem promising. Each of the sources listed does have a description associated with it so you're not working entirely in the dark; press **v** to *view* the description of a highlighted source. Some WAIS servers give you the option of searching these descriptions to come up with a list of databases appropriate to your search. The discussion on selecting databases to search will be broken into two major categories: Telnet and Gopher. Searching the collection of databases will be covered as well.

SWAIS Client Locally or through Telnet

If you have a SWAIS client on your computer systems, you'll be able to start a session by typing swais and pressing Enter. Otherwise, you use SWAIS by starting a Telnet session to another computer system. One site that allows anyone on the Internet to use SWAIS is **quake.think.com**. Start a Telnet session with **quake.think.com**, use **wais** as a log-in name, give your e-mail address, and select a terminal type. The instructions for searching for a database appear on the screen. (This may sound like a lot to do, but you'll get used to it if you do it a few times.) You'll see a listing on your screen similar to the one in Figure 10.1.

> **Choosing one or more databases from a menu.** Here we're assuming there is a menu or listing of databases on the screen. You have to *select* the ones you'll use for the search. Selecting means choosing the item by either typing the number of the item or (if the items are highlighted) moving to the appropriate item and then pressing the spacebar. A database source won't be used in a search unless it's selected. When an item is selected you'll see an asterisk (*) near its number. You can *deselect* a source by choosing it and pressing the spacebar.

There are several commands you may find useful here:

❏ Press **?** or **h** to see a list of commands.

❏ Press **j** to move down one item.

❏ Press **k** to move up one item.

❏ Press **J** to move to the next screen of items.

❏ Press **K** to move to the previous screen of items.

❑ Type / followed by a string of characters and press Enter to search for a source whose name begins with those characters. For example, **/scien** will move to the first item whose name begins with the characters *scien* (such as **Science-Fiction-Series-Guide**).

❑ Type **v** to see a description of the database.

Once you've selected the databases or sources you'll use in the search you're ready to specify one or more keywords for searching.

Gopher

Searching for a Database. Many Gopher servers that list WAIS on their menus also provide facilities for searching the descriptions of the sources or databases. Being able to search the descriptions will help you select from the long list of all the servers. You'll see a menu item similar to:

```
Search WAIS database descriptions <?>
```

Choose that item in the same way you would choose any item on a Gopher menu. A window will pop up asking you to enter one or more keywords to use in the search. Type in the keyword(s) and press Enter. The list of servers will be searched and you'll see a menu of servers or databases whose descriptions contain the keyword(s). Be as specific as you can with the keywords to get an appropriate listing of databases, but not so restrictive that some important ones are missed.

Some Gopher servers group the list of servers by letter so you can select the one you'd like more easily if you know its name. A list of servers arranged by subjects is available by pointing your Gopher to **gopher.slu.se**. That can help you select a server appropriate to your search.

In any event you should now have a menu of sources or databases from which you can choose.

Choosing One or More Databases from a Menu. You select a database or source in the same way you select any item from a Gopher menu—either click on the item with the mouse, move → until it points to the item you want to choose, or type the number of the item. Once the database is selected a window will pop open with a space for you to enter one or more keywords to use to search the database.

Using Keywords for a Search

You'll be entering one or more keywords for WAIS to use in the search of the selected database(s). You can enter as many keywords as you'd like. After the database(s) are searched you'll get a list of articles. These are ranked according to how well they match the list of keywords. A good rule of thumb is that the ranking depends on how many times one or more of the keywords appear in the article. The order of the keywords doesn't matter, and the ranking doesn't depend on whether two or more words appear in the same article. The keywords *rain forest* may turn up articles that contain one of the words but not the other, or both words. Be careful choosing keywords so the search returns appropriate articles. Be specific but not too specific so as to exclude some articles.

SWAIS Client Locally or through Telnet

Press **w** to specify the keywords for the search. The cursor will move to the section of the screen labeled **Keywords:**. Now you type the keyword(s) that will be used for the search, separating them with spaces. You can use the delete or backspace keys to make corrections. Type as many words as you'd like and choose them appropriately. Most WAIS clients available through Telnet return at most 40 articles. After you've specified the keyword(s) press Enter. Then WAIS starts contacting and searching the databases. If you've already searched some databases in this WAIS session you can press **w** again to add or delete keywords.

Gopher

A window pops up containing the title of the database and a place for you to enter the keywords to use in the search. Now you type the keyword(s), separating them with spaces, and press Enter. You can use backspace or delete to make corrections. Once you press Enter the search will begin. If you've already done a WAIS search in this Gopher session you'll be able to modify the list of keywords each time you do a search.

Performing a Search

After you've selected the databases or sources and given the keywords, you're ready to let WAIS search the databases for the keywords. You press Enter and WAIS does the searching. After WAIS handles connecting to the source(s) on the Internet and does the searching, you'll see a menu or list of the results.

Sometimes the servers you'll want to contact are busy, already handling several other requests, or the systems that hold the database may not be in operation. In these cases you'll get a message such as **Can't make connection**, **Too busy try later**, or **Nothing available**. There isn't much you can do at this point except to try other sources or use WAIS at some other time.

SWAIS Client Locally or through Telnet

Once you start the search (after you've selected sources and given keywords) WAIS connects to the sources and searches them. You'll see messages on the screen that WAIS is contacting a source and then searching it. For example, you've selected *biology-journal-contents* as a source or database to search. When the search begins you'll see messages such as **Initializing connection ..** and **Searching biology-journal-contents.src**. If the system that holds the database can't be contacted you'll get a message about that here. The system that holds the database (not the WAIS system) could be busy and there could be a delay in searching.

Gopher

Once you start the search (after you've selected a source and given keywords) WAIS attempts to connect to the source and perform the search. You'll see terms such as **Connecting** and **Searching** on the screen, as progress is being made. Here is where you may get a message that it's not possible to contact the system holding the source or database, a message about the system being too busy, or **Nothing available**.

Working with the Results of a Search

Once WAIS does the search you'll get a menu of search results. This is a numbered list of articles selected from the database(s). They'll be ranked according to how closely they match the keywords. For each article you have the option of viewing it, saving it in a file, or sending it by e-mail to an Internet address. If you're using Gopher for WAIS or using a local WAIS client then you ought to be able to exercise those options for any document. If you're using Telnet to access a WAIS client you may find you're only able to view a file, or you're able to view it and send it by e-mail. In any case, you can move through the menu working with individual articles. After you're done you can press **q** to quit the WAIS session. The specific commands you use to work with the articles are different if you're accessing WAIS through Telnet or using Gopher.

SWAIS Client Locally or through Telnet

WAIS performs the search and gives you a list of articles or items that contain the keyword(s); they're displayed on a screen titled **Search Results**. The menu tells you how many items were found (they may not all fit on one screen), gives a numbered list ranked by a "score" assigned by WAIS, gives the title of each item, where (the source or database) it was chosen from, and the number of lines in the item. The ranking or score depends on things such as how often one or more of the keywords appear in an item and whether the keyword is in the title of the item. Figure 10.2 is an abbreviated example. The keyword was *cyberspace* and several databases were searched.

```
SWAIS                         Search Results                     Items: 23
   #     Score      Source                 Title                     Lines
 001:   [1000] (            cpsr)  s285kxsemxxtranscript              4374
 002:   [1000] (Science-Fiction)  WILLIAM GIBSON    Sprawl; "Neuromance  65
 003:   [1000] (         eff-talk) max@gac.ed Re: Shoulds, Oughts & Expecta  32
 004:   [1000] (          educom)  01.94-Disinformocracy    /user/ftp/pub/ed 248
 005:   [1000] (            cacm)  Coming into the Country. (cyberspace, th 216
 006:   [ 961] (Science-Fiction)  samd@goofy Re: Summary of *Best Virtual   82
 007:   [ 875] (         eff-talk) Stanton Mc Re: ONLINE OUTPOSTS — Cybers 1089
        ┌─────────────────────────────────────┐
        │ Items deleted to conserve space.    │
        └─────────────────────────────────────┘
 018:   [ 548] (            cpsr)  virtcomm                           2364

<space> selects, arrows move, w for keywords, s for sources, ? for help
```

Figure 10.2   SWAIS Search Results

The last line on the screen gives some of the keystroke commands you can use at this point. To get a complete list press **?** or **h**. Pressing **w** takes you back to the Source Selection menu and you can modify the list of keywords for a new search. Pressing **s** also takes you back to the **Source Selection** menu so you can modify the sources you search. We'll return to dealing with this option a little later. First we'll take a look at working with an item on the menu.

The current item will be highlighted. In order to view an item or do anything else with it you first have to choose it by one of the following actions:

Example 10.1 — WAIS Searching Several Databases with SWAIS using Telnet 257

- ❑ Type the number of the item and press Enter.
- ❑ Move the highlight bar to the item by pressing the arrow keys.
- ❑ Move the highlight bar down by pressing **j**.
- ❑ Move the highlight bar up by pressing **k**.

Once the item is chosen you can:

- ❑ View the item by pressing the spacebar or Enter. The item is retrieved from the source or database and displayed one screen at a time. To get to the next screen you press the spacebar. Press **q** to quit viewing the item and return to the menu.

- ❑ Save the item to a file by pressing **S** (uppercase). You'll be prompted for a file name—the name of a file on the system you're using that's connected to the Internet. The file is retrieved from the source and saved in a file. (*Note:* If you're not directly connected to the Internet, but using a personal computer and a modem to contact a system that is connected to the Internet, the file won't automatically be saved on your personal computer. Also, you can't save an article in a file in the cases where you're using Telnet only to access WAIS.)

- ❑ Mail the item via e-mail by pressing **m**. You'll be prompted for an Internet e-mail address. The item will be retrieved from the source and sent to the address you give. (*Note:* This isn't available at all sites that allow Telnet access to WAIS.)

You'll be able to work with all the items on the menu. Whenever you have the Search Results menu you can return to the Source Selection menu by pressing **s**. You'll want to do this to include other sources or exclude some sources from the search. Including another source means selecting the source and excluding sources means *deselecting* the source. When the search is done again you may get different results.

Gopher

WAIS performs the search and gives you a Gopher menu of the articles or items that contain the keyword(s). The menu is just like any other Gopher menu, except the items are ranked according to a score assigned by WAIS. (Chapter 9 contains all the details for working with items on a Gopher menu.) To perform a search with different keywords or with a different database, press **u** to get to the menu that contains the list of sources and select another database or choose different keywords.

Example 10.1 WAIS Searching Several Databases with SWAIS using Telnet

This example demonstrates accessing WAIS through a Telnet session. After log-in the SWAIS— a full-screen text-based client program—will automatically start. We'll take up the task of finding references or items containing the word *cyberspace*. The items are going to come from either science fiction databases or databases that deal with computing. The selected databases and a brief description of each follows.

cacm	Communications of the Association for Computing Machinery, selected articles.
cpsr	Computer Professionals for Social Responsibility, selected files also available by anonymous FTP from **ftp.cpsr.org**.
educom	EDUCOM documents, review articles, reports, etc.
eff-talk	Electronic Frontier Foundation, archives of newsgroup **comp.org.eff.talk**.
Science-Fiction-Series-Guide	A guide to science fiction literature.

We'll start the Telnet session with **wais.com**, and go through these steps:

1. Start a Telnet session with wais.com and log in as **wais**.
2. Select sources.
3. Specify the keyword.
4. Perform the search and see results.
5. Work with the items.
6. Quit the session.

Before we start there are a few things to note. This example uses one keyword, but in your work you can always specify more keywords. There isn't room here to show all the screens, but we'll include examples of each type of screen. In some cases we'll show abbreviated versions of the screen listings to conserve space.

Start a Telnet Session with wais.com and Log In as wais

☞ **Type** `telnet wais.com` **and press** Enter.

☞ **Type** `wais` **and press** Enter.

☞ **Press** Enter **to accept the vt100 terminal type, or key in your terminal type and press** Enter.

```
telnet wais.com
Trying...
Connected to wais.com.
Escape character is '^]'.


SunOS UNIX (wais)

login: wais    ◄──── Type wais here.
Last login: Wed Feb 15 17:22:17 from isum1.iastate.ed
SunOS Release 4.1.3 (X25-BIG-IPC) #4: Mon Dec 12 17:49:35 PST 1994
Welcome to swais, the text-terminal telnet client to WAIS.
Please type user identifier (optional, i.e user@host):testing@great.place.net
```

Messages from WAIS.COM.
Enter your e-mail address here.

———————Example 10.1 — WAIS Searching Several Databases with SWAIS using Telnet——————— 259

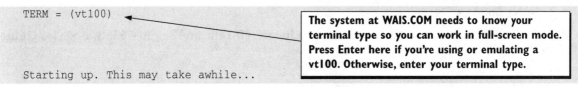

```
TERM = (vt100)
```

The system at WAIS.COM needs to know your terminal type so you can work in full-screen mode. Press Enter here if you're using or emulating a vt100. Otherwise, enter your terminal type.

```
Starting up. This may take awhile...
```

Figure 10.3   Starting a Telnet SWAIS Session with wais.com

Now you're connected. After a short wait you'll see a screen similar to the one in Figure 10.4. It is the first of several screens listing the databases available through **wais.com** for WAIS searching. You see there are 549 databases! The second line has the headings # (this is column holds the number of the database; each is numbered), **Server** (the Internet name of the system that hosts the database), **Source** (the name of the database), and **Cost** (you'll see they're all free). The screen is titled **Source Selection**. This is where you'll select sources, specify the keyword, and start the search.

```
SWAIS                           Source Selection              Sources: 549

001:    [ wais.access.gpo.gov]   103_cong_bills                     Free
001:    [ wais.access.gpo.gov]   103_cong_bills                     Free
002:    [ wais.access.gpo.gov]   104_cong_bills                     Free
004:    [ wais.access.gpo.gov]   1993_cri                           Free
005:    [ wais.access.gpo.gov]   1994_cri                           Free
006:    [ wais.access.gpo.gov]   1994_hob                           Free
007:    [ wais.access.gpo.gov]   1994_record                        Free
008:    [ wais.access.gpo.gov]   1994_register                      Free
009:    [ wais.access.gpo.gov]   1994_unified_agenda                Free
010:    [ wais.access.gpo.gov]   1995_cri                           Free
011:    [ wais.access.gpo.gov]   1995_hob                           Free
012:    [ wais.access.gpo.gov]   1995_record                        Free
013:    [ wais.access.gpo.gov]   1995_register                      Free
014:    [ wais.access.gpo.gov]   1995_unified_agenda                Free
015:    [            archie.au]   aarnet-resource-guide             Free
016:    [ndadsb.gsfc.nasa.gov]   AAS_jobs                           Free
017:    [ndadsb.gsfc.nasa.gov]   AAS_meeting                        Free
018:    [      munin.ub2.lu.se]   academic_email_conf               Free

Keywords:
<space> selects, w for keywords, arrows move, <return> searches, q quits, or ?
```

Figure 10.4   Sources Selection Menu

The last line on the screen lists the keystrokes to use for common commands. If you press the spacebar you select the current database for searching. Press **w** to give the keywords of the search. Use the arrow keys to move up or down the list. Press **q** to quit the search and press **?** to get a complete list of keystroke commands.

Select Sources

The sources to select are **cacm**, **cpsr**, **educom**, **eff-talk**, and **Science-Fiction-Series-Guide**.

☞ **Press /.**

You'll see

```
Source-Name:
```

pop up in place of

```
Keywords:
```

The screen will be as it is above except for the last few lines as shown below:

```
018:    [    munin.ub2.lu.se]  academic_email_conf                         Free

Source-Name:

<space> selects, w for keywords, arrows move, <return> searches, q quits, or ?
```

☞ **Type** cacm **and press** Enter.

You'll get the screen containing the entry for **cacm**; it will be highlighted. Press the spacebar to select that source or database. Then the screen will be similar to Figure 10.5.

```
SWAIS                         Source Selection                    Sources: 566

   127:   [    wais.ece.uiuc.edu]  bit-listserv-novell                      Free
   128:   [    munin.ub2.lu.se]    bit.listserv.cdromlan                    Free
   129:   [    munin.ub2.lu.se]    bit.listserv.pacs-l                      Free
   130:   [    wais.oit.unc.edu]   Book_of_Mormon                           Free
  131:    [orion.lib.virginia.e]   bryn-mawr-classical-review               Free
   132:   [orion.lib.virginia.e]   bryn-mawr-medieval-review                Free
   133:   [    SunSite.unc.edu]    bush-speeches                            Free
   134: * [    quake.think.com]    cacm                                     Free
   135:   [weeds.mgh.harvard.ed]   Caenorhabditis_elegans_Genome            Free
   136:   [    biomed.nus.sg]      cancernet                                Free
   137:   [    borg.lib.vt.edu]    catalyst                                 Free
   138:   [ transcap.capcon.net]   Cato_Institute_Reports                   Free
   139:   [fragrans.riken.go.jp]   CCINFO                                   Free
   140:   [         cs.uwp.edu]    cdbase                                   Free
   141:   [ istge.ist.unige.it]    Cell_Lines                               Free
   142:   [ wais.wu-wien.ac.at]    cerro-1                                  Free
   143:   [    wais.concert.net]   cert-advisories                          Free
   144:   [    wais.concert.net]   cert-clippings                           Free

<space> selects, w for keywords, arrows move, <return> searches, q quits, or ?
```

Figure 10.5   Selecting the Source cacm

Example 10.1 — WAIS Searching Several Databases with SWAIS using Telnet 261

Now repeat the previous step to select the other sources:

☞ **Type** /cpsr **and press** Enter. **Press** SpaceBar.

☞ **Type** /educom **and press** Enter. **Press** SpaceBar.

☞ **Type** /eff-talk **and press** Enter. **Press** SpaceBar.

☞ **Type** /science-fiction-series-guide **and press** Enter. **Press** SpaceBar.

If you do them in the order given above you'll end up with this screen.

```
SWAIS                         Source Selection                  Sources: 566

451:   [RANGERSMITH.SDSC.EDU]  Salk_Genome_Center                    Free
452:   [      quake.think.com]  sample-pictures                      Free
453:   [ wais.access.gpo.gov]  sample_104_cong_bills                 Free
454:   [ wais.access.gpo.gov]  sample_1994_record                    Free
455:   [ wais.access.gpo.gov]  sample_1994_register                  Free
456:   [ wais.access.gpo.gov]  sample_1995_record                    Free
457:   [ wais.access.gpo.gov]  sample_1995_register                  Free
458:   [       scholastic.com]  scholastic-all-lib                   Free
459:   [       scholastic.com]  scholastic-ep-lib                    Free
460:   [       scholastic.com]  scholastic-it-lib                    Free
461:   [       scholastic.com]  scholastic-ms-lib                    Free
462:   [       scholastic.com]  scholastic-rl-lib                    Free
463:   [       scholastic.com]  scholastic-seas-lib                  Free
464:   [       scholastic.com]  scholastic-sik-lib                   Free
465:   [       scholastic.com]  scholastic-store                     Free
466:   [    wfpc3.la.asu.edu]  sci.astro.hubble                      Free
467:   [     wais.oit.unc.edu]  sci                                  Free
468: * [  coral.cs.jcu.edu.au]  Science-Fiction-Series-Guide         Free


<space> selects, w for keywords, arrows move, <return> searches, q quits, or ?
```

Figure 10.6   Selecting Source Science-Fiction-Series-Guide

Specify the Keyword

Now you're ready to specify the keyword *cyberspace* for this search.

☞ **Press** w.

When you press **w** the word **Keyword** will appear after the last entry (**468:**) and the line that lists the keystroke commands.

☞ **Type the keyword** cyberspace.

You should see the following near the bottom of the screen:

```
467:   [    wais.oit.unc.edu]  sci                                Free
468: * [ coral.cs.jcu.edu.au]  Science-Fiction-Series-Guide       Free


Keywords: cyberspace


Enter keywords with spaces between them; <return> to search; ^C to cancel
```

Perform the Search and View the Results

☞ **Press Enter.**

Press Enter to start the WAIS search. You'll see messages on the bottom of the screen as WAIS connects to each database and searches it:

```
Initializing connection ...
Searching cacm.src
```

When all the databases are searched, the Search Results menu or list will appear on the screen. Figure 10.7 shows what appeared when this example was created. You see there are 25 items found; some are on another screen. Each item is numbered and ranked according to the score WAIS assigned to it. Items with a higher score generally contain more instances of the keyword. There was one keyword and WAIS returned at most 40 items, so these are all the items in the selected databases containing the keyword.

```
SWAIS                        Search Results                     Items: 25
  #    Score     Source              Title                       Lines
001:  [1000] (           cpsr)  s285kxsemxxtranscript            4374
002:  [1000] (       eff-talk)  max@gac.ed Re: Shoulds, Oughts & Expect  32
003:  [1000] (         educom)  01.94-Disinformocracy   /user/ftp/pub/ed  248
004:  [1000] (Science-Fiction)  WILLIAM GIBSON      Sprawl;    "Neuromance  65
005:  [1000] (           cacm)  Coming into the Country. (cyberspace, th  216
006:  [ 961] (Science-Fiction)  samd@goofy Re: Summary of *Best Virtual  82
007:  [ 875] (       eff-talk)  Stanton Mc Re: ONLINE OUTPOSTS — Cybers  1089
008:  [ 778] (         educom)  01.94-SciFi   /user/ftp/pub/educom.revie  308
009:  [ 778] (         educom)  edupage-01.18.94   /user/ftp/pub/edupage  160
010:  [ 667] (         educom)  markoff_article   /user/ftp/pub/educom.r  128
011:  [ 667] (         educom)  mason_article   /user/ftp/pub/educom.rev  203
012:  [ 667] (         educom)  edupage-03.10.94   /user/ftp/pub/edupage  156
013:  [ 637] (           cacm)  Consensual realities in cyberspace. (col  195
014:  [ 637] (           cacm)  Private life in cyberspace. (Electronic  261
015:  [ 625] (       eff-talk)  mech@eff.o Re: Online Activism Resource  1067
016:  [ 578] (Science-Fiction)  hvaisane@c Re: List of sf/fantasy/horror  134
017:  [ 548] (           cpsr)  virtcomm                         1867
018:  [ 548] (           cpsr)  virtcomm                         2364


<space> selects, arrows move, w for keywords, s for sources, ? for help
```

Figure 10.7   SWAIS Search Results

Example 10.1 — WAIS Searching Several Databases with SWAIS using Telnet 263

The last line shows keystroke commands you are likely to use. For a complete list press **?** or **h**.

Work with the Items

Now you're ready to view any of the items. You can also return to the list of sources, if you want to extend or restrict the list of databases to search, by pressing **s** (lowercase). You can change the keyword(s) by pressing **w**, making any additions or deletions or corrections, and then pressing Enter. After you press **s** or **w** another search will take place. To see a list of all the commands available to you press **?** or **h**.

To view an item type the number of the item and press the spacebar or Enter. WAIS will handle connecting to the database and retrieving the article. It will be displayed one screen at a time. You can press **q** any time to quit.

Note: If the client allows it you can also save an item to a file, or send an item by e-mail. This client doesn't presently allow for articles to be saved to a file or sent by e-mail. However, these operations are included here for completeness. Perhaps by the time you read this those capabilities will be available.

To save an item in a file press **S** (uppercase). The last few lines on the screen will be replaced with:

```
018:    [ 548] (           cpsr)  virtcomm                           2364

FILE:

Enter the file name into which to save this item; ^C to cancel
```

^C means to press Ctrl-C (hold down the key labeled Ctrl, press the C key, and release them both). You use that to cancel a request. Type a file name here and press Enter. To send the item via e-mail to an Internet address, press **m** (lowercase). The last few lines of the screen will be replaced by:

```
018:    [ 548] (           cpsr)  virtcomm                           2364

Address:

Enter your e-mail address; ^C to cancel
```

Again **^C** means to press Ctrl-C to cancel the request. Otherwise enter your (or any) e-mail address and press Enter. WAIS will handle connecting to the database, retrieving the item, and sending it by e-mail to the address you've given. Most of the time you'll probably want to mail it to yourself unless you're doing a favor for someone else.

Quit the Session

☞ **Type** q **and press** Enter **to quit the session.**

———————————————————————**End of Example 10.1**———————————————————————

Example 10.2 Using Gopher to Access WAIS

This example demonstrates using Gopher to access WAIS. Since we're using Gopher we can search only one database. We'll look up information dealing with the topic *cooperative learning* (briefly put, cooperative learning is a technique used by educators to get students involved in learning by working in groups that allow for cooperative interaction). First we'll find an item on a Gopher menu that allows access to WAIS; then we'll request a search of the directory of WAIS servers using the keyword *education*. We'll then select the database ERIC-digest. ERIC is an acronym for the Educational Resources Information Center.

When we access the appropriate Gopher menu you'll see that, instead of searching for a database, we could choose a menu of databases based on the first letter of the name of the database. It may seem artificial for us to search the directory of sources when we already know the database we want to search. However, we want to demonstrate using the ability to search for sources.

In this example we'll access WAIS by using the Gopher server at Arizona State University, **info.asu.edu**. The steps to follow are:

1. Start a Gopher session and locate a menu item that allows for a WAIS search.
2. Search the directory of WAIS servers using the keyword **education**.
3. Select ERIC-digest as the database to use for the search.
4. Perform a search using the keywords **cooperative learning**.
5. Work with the items on the menu—**view**, **save in a file**, **mail via e-mail**.
6. Quit the session.

In some cases we'll show abbreviated versions of the screen listings to conserve space. Also, we won't go through the details of working with a Gopher menu. See Chapter 9 for details about that.

Start a Gopher Session and Find a Menu Item That Allows for a WAIS Search

☞ **Start a Gopher session with** info.asu.edu.

```
gopher info.asu.edu
```

You'll see a screen similar to Figure 10.8:

```
            Internet Gopher Information Client v2.0.16
                 Home Gopher server: info.asu.edu


 -> 1.   About the Arizona State University Gopher
    2.   ASU On-Line Consulting System/
    3.   ASU Electronic Directory (Accessible by ASU Campus Only) <?>
    4.   Telnet to ASU Systems (Terminal Sessions)/
    5.   ASU FTP File Transfer Server (On-line Software)/
    6.   Other Sources  (explore the Internet!)/
```

Example 10.2 — Using Gopher to Access WAIS 265

```
      7.  ASU Campus-Wide Information/
      8.  ASU Campus Services and Facilities/
      9.  Arizona State-Wide Information/
     10.  ASU Network Information Center/
     11.  Internet Phone Books/
     12.  News/
     13.  Local Time in Tempe, Arizona, USA (Mountain Standard Time)


 Press ? for Help, q to Quit                              Page: 1/1
```

Figure 10.8   Main Gopher Menu at info.asu.edu

☞ **Choose item 6 and press `Enter` to get the next menu.**

The item we want is titled **WAIS Sources (Wide Area Information System)**. It's shown in Figure 10.9.

```
                Internet Gopher Information Client v2.0.16
                    Other Sources   (explore the Internet!)


      1.  Items of Interest  (new items & items needing a home)/
      2.  VERONICA (search menu items in most of GopherSpace)/
      3.  Other Gopher and Information Servers/
  ->  4.  WAIS Sources (Wide Area Information System)/
      5.  Discipline Specific Internet Resources/
      6.  Information about Gopher/
      7.  Internet File Server (FTP) Sites/
      8.  Free-Nets (Community Based Networks)/
      9.  Libraries/

          ┌──────────────────────────────────┐
          │ Items deleted to conserve space.  │
          └──────────────────────────────────┘

     15.  Hytelnet (Telnet Login to Various Sites)/
     16.  Miscellaneous and Experimental Goodies.../


 Press ? for Help, q to Quit, u to go up a menu          Page: 1/1
```

Figure 10.9   Select WAIS Sources from Gopher Menu

☞ **Choose item 4 and press `Enter` to go to the WAIS source menu.**

You'll see a screen similar to the one in Figure 10.10. We'll want the first item, although we could see all sources or select an item that gives a list of sources based on the first letter in the name of the source.

```
                Internet Gopher Information Client v2.0.16
                WAIS Sources (Wide Area Information System)

  ->  1.  Directory of WAIS Servers (Search Database Descriptions) <?>
      2.  All WAIS Sources (over 485 items!)/
      3.  A-D WAIS Sources/
      4.  E-H WAIS Sources/
      5.  I-L WAIS Sources/
      6.  M-P WAIS Sources/
      7.  Q-T WAIS Sources/
      8.  U-Z WAIS Sources/
      9.  ASU WAIS Sources/
     10.  Sample WAIS Sources/


Press ? for Help, q to Quit, u to go up a menu          Page: 1/1
```

Choose this item to search descriptions of WAIS databases.

Figure 10.10   WAIS Sources Menu

Search the Directory of WAIS Servers Using the Keyword education

☞ **Press** Enter . **Type** education **and press** Enter .

A window will pop up in which you'll have a space to type the word(s) to use in the search. In this case type the word *education*. After that you'll see something like Figure 10.11.

```
                Internet Gopher Information Client v2.0.16
                WAIS Sources (Wide Area Information System)

  -> 1.  Directory of WAIS Servers (Search Database Descriptions) <?>
     2.  All WAIS Sources (over 485 items!)/
     3.  A-D WAIS Sources/
     4.  E-H WAIS Sources/
+------------Directory of WAIS Servers (Search Database Descriptions)---------+
| Words to search for                                                         |
|                                                                             |
| education                                                                   |
|                                                                             |
| [Help: ^-]  [Cancel: ^G]                                                    |
+-----------------------------------------------------------------------------+

Press ? for Help, q to Quit, u to go up a menu          Page: 1/1
```

Figure 10.11   Searching for Sources

Select Eric-Digests as the Database to Use for the Search

After you press Enter, the directory of servers is searched and you'll get a Gopher menu similar to the one in Figure 10.12.

Example 10.2 — Using Gopher to Access WAIS   267

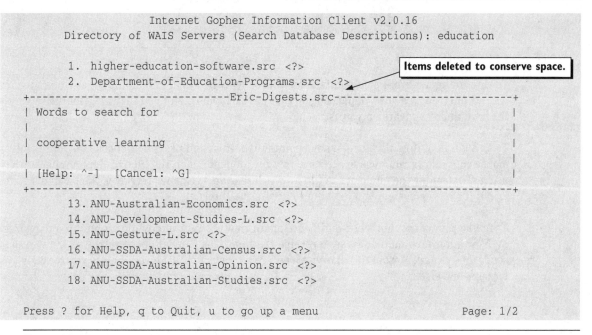

```
              Internet Gopher Information Client v2.0.16
      Directory of WAIS Servers (Search Database Descriptions): education


       1.   higher-education-software.src <?>
       2.   Department-of-Education-Programs.src <?>
       9.   ANU-Vietnam-SocSci.src <?>                  ┌─────────────────────────────────┐
                                                        │ Items deleted to conserve space.│
   -> 10.   Eric-Digests.src <?>                        └─────────────────────────────────┘
      11.   IAT-Documents.src <?>         ┌──────────────────────────────────────┐
      12.   eric-digests.src <?>          │ Choose this item to search Eric-Digests.│
      18.   ANU-SSDA-Australian-Studies.src <?>         └─────────────────────────────────┘
                                          ┌─────────────────────────────────┐
                                          │ Items deleted to conserve space.│
                                          └─────────────────────────────────┘
Press ? for Help, q to Quit, u to go up a menu                    Page: 1/2
```

Figure 10.12   Select Eric-Digests.Src

☞ **Choose the item titled** `Eric-Digests.src` **and press** Enter .

If there are problems using that database you could try again using the item **eric-digests.src**.

Perform a Search Using the Keywords Cooperative Learning

☞ **Press** Enter , **type** `cooperative learning`, **and press** Enter .

Press Enter to pop up a window into which you type the keywords **cooperative learning**. Press Enter and WAIS connects to the database and searches for keyword items. See Figure 10.13.

```
              Internet Gopher Information Client v2.0.16
      Directory of WAIS Servers (Search Database Descriptions): education

                                                   ┌─────────────────────────────────┐
       1.   higher-education-software.src <?>       │ Items deleted to conserve space.│
       2.   Department-of-Education-Programs.src <?>└─────────────────────────────────┘
+------------------------------Eric-Digests.src----------------------------+
| Words to search for                                                      |
|                                                                          |
| cooperative learning                                                     |
|                                                                          |
| [Help: ^-]   [Cancel: ^G]                                                |
+--------------------------------------------------------------------------+
      13. ANU-Australian-Economics.src <?>
      14. ANU-Development-Studies-L.src <?>
      15. ANU-Gesture-L.src <?>
      16. ANU-SSDA-Australian-Census.src <?>
      17. ANU-SSDA-Australian-Opinion.src <?>
      18. ANU-SSDA-Australian-Studies.src <?>

Press ? for Help, q to Quit, u to go up a menu                    Page: 1/2
```

Figure 10.13   Keyword Search of Source

Work with the Items on the Menu—View, Save in a File, Mail via e-mail.

WAIS connects to the database and returns a menu of items such as those in Figure 10.14. Now you use familiar Gopher commands to work with the items.

```
                  Internet Gopher Information Client v2.0.16
                     ERIC-digests.src: cooperative learning

   -> 1.   ED347871  Feb 92  Cooperative Learning: Increasing College..
      2.   ED317087  Dec 89  The Role of Styles and Strategies in Lang..
      3.   ED264162  Sep 85  Cooperative Learning in Social Studies Educati..
      4.   ED296121  88  Learning Management. ERIC Digest No. 73.
      5.   ED312457  89  Supporting and Facilitating Self-Directed Learn ..
      6.   ED306003  88  Cooperative Learning Strategies and Children. ..
      7.   ED341890  31 Dec 91  Learning Styles Counseling. ERIC Digest.
      8.   ED338295  Aug 91  Learning Centers for the 1990's. ERIC Digest.
      9.   ED334469  91  Collaborative Learning in Adult Education. ERIC ..
     10.   ED335175  May 91  American Indian.. Research and Practice. ERIC ..
     11.   ED301143  88  Learning Styles. ERIC Digest.
     12.   ED340272  Sep 91  Active Learning: Creating Excitement in theClas..
     13.   ED314917  89  College Planning for Students with Learning Disabil..
     14.   ED253468  Sep 84  Active Learning. ERIC Digest No. 17
     15.   ED287684  87  Cognitive Learning in the Environment: Elementary S..
     16.   ED312455  89  Cooperative Education: Characteristics and Effectiv..
     17.   ED291204  86  Learning Disabilities. ERIC Digest #407. Revised.
     18.   ED310881  89  Cooperative Problem-Solving in the Classroom.

Press ? for Help, q to Quit, u to go up a menu                Page: 1/3
```

Figure 10.14   Search Results

To view an item move → so it points to an item or type the item number and press Enter, or click on the item using a mouse, depending on the type of Gopher client you're using. Gopher retrieves the item and it appears on your screen.

To save an item in a file move → so it points to an item and press **s** or choose an option with a mouse that allows you to save the item in a file, depending on the type of Gopher client you're using. Then enter the name of the file in which to save it. Gopher retrieves the item and saves it in a file on the system you're using to access the Internet.

To mail a copy of the item via e-mail, once again view the item and while it's on the screen press **m**. Now enter an e-mail address to receive the item. The Gopher client retrieves the item and sends it by e-mail. Most of the time you'll enter your own e-mail address unless you're retrieving for someone else.

Quit the Session

☞ **Click on the appropriate box with the mouse or type** q **and press** Enter.

─────────────────────────End of Example 10.2─────────────────────────

Finding and Connecting to WAIS Systems

Two ways to connect to systems that provide the capabilities for WAIS searching are through Telnet and Gopher.

Use Hytelnet to find WAIS systems you can access through Telnet. Start Hytelnet, then choose **SITES2**, then **DISTRIBUTED FILE SERVERS**, and finally **WIDE AREA INFORMATION SERVERS**. See Chapter 7 for the details on using Hytelnet.

To find WAIS on Gopher menus you usually first have to look for a heading that deals with Internet resources or Internet services. Some Gopher sites provide direct access to WAIS. Two such sites are **gopher-gw.micro.umn.edu** (University of Minnesota) and **munin.ub2.lund.se** (Lund University Electronic Library Service).

Sources of Information about WAIS

There are several sources of information about WAIS on the Internet. They're worth exploring if you'd like to find out more about using WAIS, how it works, and current developments in WAIS applications. Some of these sources also include the software necessary to set up the client software on different types of computer systems. Additionally, there is an e-mail discussion group and a Usenet newsgroup that concentrate on WAIS. You might want to start by retrieving the file named getting-started by using anonymous FTP. Some sources for that file are:

❑ **ftp://rtfm.mit.edu/pub/usenet-by-group/news.answers/wais-faq/getting-started**

❑ **ftp://ftp.mwc.edu/internet.info/wais/getting-started**

The file is also regularly posted to the Usenet newsgroup **news.answers**.

Here is a list of other Internet resources about WAIS.

By FTP: **ftp://ftp.wais.com/pub/**
                   ftp://quake.think.com/pub/wais/
                   ftp://fly.bio.indiana.edu/util/wais/
                   ftp://ftp.cnidr.org/pub/NIDR.tools/
                   Look for files dealing with WAIS or freeWAIS.

By Gopher: **gopher://gopher.wais.com**
                   (Point your gopher to **gopher.wais.com**.)

Discussion Group: **wais-discussion**

A moderated list dealing with WAIS.
To subscribe send e-mail to: **wais-discussion-request@wais.com**.
The message you send should be **sub wais-discussion** *your_full_name*.
Put your name in place of *your_full_name*

Usenet Group: **comp.infosystems.wais**

Summary

WAIS (Wide Area Information Service) is an Internet service that allows you to search one or more databases. The databases can be on various computer systems on the Internet, but you can access them all through one program called a WAIS client. Once you access WAIS you choose the source or database to search, give one or more keywords to use in the search, and WAIS handles the details of contacting the database, performing the search, and returning a list of items in the database that contain your keyword(s). The items in the list are ranked by WAIS so the items are arranged by how closely they match the keywords. Searching for keywords doesn't depend on the order of the keywords. In fact, you can't ask for a search that returns items containing all the keywords. Often an item that contains one of the words many times may have a higher ranking than one that contains more than one of the keywords. For each item on the list you have the option of viewing it, saving it to a file, or mailing it to an Internet address via e-mail.

You can access WAIS either through a WAIS client program, through Gopher, or some other Internet services. If WAIS isn't on your local system you can use a WAIS client by starting a Telnet session with one of several sites on the Internet. These are available through Hytelnet and are listed in the chapter. In this case the WAIS client is often SWAIS or Screen WAIS. This gives you a full-screen character-based interface. These clients may not allow you to save an item in a file or send it by e-mail. When you use WAIS through Gopher you first have to find an entry on a Gopher menu, which takes you to a menu dedicated to WAIS searching. You choose a source or database and supply the keyword(s). The results are returned to your gopher as a Gopher menu. You work with these items in the same way you would work with any other Gopher menu. In this case you can view an item, save it to a file, and send it to an Internet address by e-mail.

Finding appropriate databases to search can sometimes be a problem. Some WAIS clients allow you to search the directory of WAIS sources. This directory has a description of each database. Likewise, when you access WAIS through Gopher you can often search the directory of servers. This search is handled in the same way as other WAIS searches. You supply one or more keywords and start the search. Once you have a list of databases you can select the one(s) to use for the search so that you get a list of items based on the keyword(s) you supply.

WAIS allows you to search databases for material based on keywords you supply. It handles the details of working with the individual databases. You can concentrate on *what* you want to retrieve rather than the details of working with different types of databases.

Exercises

Practice Using WAIS

1. Use Telnet to start a SWAIS session. (Two sites that allow Telnet access to SWAIS are **wais.com** and **quake.think.com**.)
   a. Select one source from the first screen and search them using the keyword *money*. How many items were found? What were the names of the first three? (Keep selecting sources until you get at least three items found.)
   b. Go back to the sources and select a few more and search again using the same keyword. How many items were found this time? What were the names of three that weren't on the first list?

2. Use Telnet to start a SWAIS session. Select the sources *afrophile* and *the-scientist*. Search the sources using the keywords *health nutrition*.
   a. How many items were found from each source?
   b. Read one item from each source. What were the items you read about?

3. Use Gopher to use WAIS. (Several Gopher sites offering a gateway to WAIS are mentioned in this chapter.) Choose one source from the list of sources whose name begin with *A*. Search the database or source using the keyword *health*. How many items were found? What are the names of first three?

4. Use Gopher to use WAIS.
   a. Search the source *afrophile* using the keywords *health money*. How many items did you find?
   b. Choose what looks like will be an interesting article, and send it to yourself by e-mail.

Practice Searching Databases with WAIS

5. You are getting ready to take a trip to a foreign country. The database **US-State-Department-Travel-Advisories** is generally available through WAIS. Find at least one travel advisory for a country you'd like to visit.

6. The database **Poetry**, sometimes listed as **poetry.src**, contains the full text of many poems.
   a. Search the database for poems using the keywords *love*, *youth*, and *strength*. Retrieve at least one poem and list the names of five others you found.
   b. Using the name of a poet as the keyword, search the database poetry to see which of the poet's poems are in the database. How many did you find?

7. There are several databases of the Occupational Safety and Health Administration (OSHA) of the U.S. Government available through WAIS.
   a. Search the OSHA Standards database for items dealing with the topic of asbestos. Retrieve at least one and prepare a list of at least three items.
   b. Search all the OSHA databases for a list of five different items dealing with asbestos.

8. Two databases that deal with music are **rec.music.early** and **Sheet_Music_Index**. Find and retrieve at least three items dealing with the topic of *solo music for the lute*.

9. The database **USDACRIS** holds the Current Research Information System (CRIS) of the United States Department of Agriculture (USDA). Search the database for items relating to nutrition and youth. Retrieve at least two articles and a list of at least four articles.

10. The database **biosci** has information relating to a number of different topics in biology. See what you can find out on the topic *immune systems*.

11. a. Octavia Butler has written a number of fine pieces of science fiction. What articles can you find dealing with her or her work? (*Hint:* Consider using the databases **Science-Fiction-Series-Guide** or **sf-reviews**.)
    b. Search the same database(s) for information about two other science fiction authors. Which ones did you choose and what did you find?

12. You are writing a research paper and you'd like to use some quotations from e-mail messages. What's the proper form for making citations from e-mail messages? Search the database **cool-net** for information about the proper way to make citations from e-mail messages.

13. This exercise is for folks with more than one way to access WAIS. In addition to the ways of accessing WAIS discussed in this chapter you can also access WAIS through the World Wide Web by using the URL **http://server.wais.com/company.html**. The WWW is discussed in detail in Chapter 11. Do any of the previous exercises using two different ways of accessing WAIS (for example, using Gopher and SWAIS). Write a short paper—at most two pages—giving the advantages and disadvantages of each method.

World Wide Web, Lynx, and Mosaic

The World Wide Web (WWW) project is a hypertext networked information system started at CERN, the European Laboratory for Particle Physics in Geneva, Switzerland. One of the goals of the project is to give a uniform means of accessing all the different types of information on the Internet. Needing to know only one way to get information, you concentrate on *what* you want, not how to get it. Instead of having to contact and know the addresses of many different Internet sites, and having to know all the details of using different Internet services such as Telnet, FTP, WAIS, or Gopher, you start a program that lets you access a WWW site. From there you can go to other locations on the Internet to search for, browse, and retrieve information in a variety of forms. You'll be able to select items by pressing Enter, pressing an arrow key, or clicking with a mouse. The items you choose from are images, icons, or text. The text is either underlined, in bold, or highlighted. The information you retrieve or view can be text, graphics, digitized video or sound, or in some other form. WWW is very easy to use and removes many of the difficulties presented by other services and resources on the Internet.

When you use WWW you work in a *hypertext* or *hypermedia* environment. That means you move from item to item and back again without having to follow a predefined path. You follow leads, or *links* as they're called, according to your needs. Sometimes the items you select are part of other sentences or paragraphs. These links to other Internet resources are presented in context, rather than as a list or menu. Gopher also hides many of the details of making connections to different Internet sites and using Internet services. However, when you use Gopher you're always dealing with menus, so you have to work according to the ways the menus are defined. The entries on menus can't be very long, which means they may not be descriptive; you sometimes end up choosing a menu item that doesn't represent the type of information you wanted. These problems can be avoided with WWW, provided the information is presented in a helpful way. You'll still see menus and lists but you'll also see sentences or phrases describing the information.

| WWW MAKES EVERYTHING EASY | POINT AT WHAT YOU WANT, AND YOU GET IT | YOU JUST HAVE TO BE PATIENT |

A program that lets you contact a WWW site is called a *WWW browser* or *Web browser*. WWW doesn't require that you always use the same browser. We'll look at two popular Web browsers in this chapter, *Lynx* and *Mosaic*. Appendix B covers *Netscape Navigator*, another popular browser. Lynx is entirely text-based so you can use it regardless of the type of Internet connection you have. Mosaic works through a graphical user interface (GUI). It lets you work with the Internet in a multimedia setting, but you need a full Internet connection to use it. Both browsers are easy to use. As you use a WWW browser you'll be able to save the locations of information or sites you find interesting, so that you'll be able to return to them any time you use Lynx or Mosaic, the same idea as a list of bookmarks in Gopher. Also, you'll be able to go to places not mentioned on the screen through the use of a notation called a *Uniform Resource Locator* or *URL*. When you save a link or the way to get to a resource on the Internet it's saved as a URL. We've talked about a URL before and we'll go over it again in this chapter.

Chapter Overview

In this chapter you'll get an exposure to using WWW so you can take advantage of what it has to offer. We'll cover the following topics with examples to demonstrate using a Web browser.

❑ How the WWW Works

❑ What Are Hypertext and Hypermedia?

❑ Explaining URL—Uniform Resource Locator

❑ Using Lynx to Access the WWW

Example 11.1 — A First Look at Lynx and the World Wide Web — 275

❑ Using Mosaic to Access the WWW

❑ Searching the World Wide Web

How the WWW Works

The World Wide Web project was started to give a single means of access to the wealth of services and resources on the Internet. You access WWW by using a program called a Web browser. There are several browsers available; two we'll work with in this chapter are Lynx and Mosaic (Netscape Navigator is covered in Appendix B). Lynx operates in text-only mode. It gives you a full-screen display called a page. You can go from page to page and move to other items on the Internet through items called links (notice the play on words!), by either typing commands or pressing the arrow keys. You can access it by either running a copy of Lynx on the computer you use which is connected to the Internet or by using Telnet to the University of Kansas. Mosaic gives you a full-screen graphical interface and you work your way through the Web by using a mouse to click on icons or items. You need to have a direct Internet connection to use it. It may not be possible to use it if you use a modem to contact a computer for your Internet connection. In that case, you need a SLIP connection for your modem to have the type of Internet access that allows you to use Mosaic. These two browsers are fundamentally the same. They give hypertext access to the Internet so you don't have to know any other techniques except how to select a title, phrase, word, or icon.

Both Lynx and Mosaic are examples of programs called *client software*. While they are running they communicate with a computer known as a *server* communicating your commands and receiving information. You work with the client and it communicates with the server. You don't have to know the details of how the communication is accomplished.

To put talking about WWW in context, we'll start with an example of what you'll see when you use Lynx to access the WWW.

Example 11.1 A First Look at Lynx and the World Wide Web

Lynx was developed through Academic Computing Services at the University of Kansas. If the computer you use to access the services on the Internet has a copy of Lynx, you start the program by typing **lynx** and pressing Enter. Otherwise, you can use Telnet to the University of Kansas. We'll use Telnet to access Lynx here, using the address or domain name below. You also can get to Lynx through Hytelnet (Chapter 7).

```
Telnet  lynx.cc.ukans.edu or  129.237.17.47
login: www
```

Figure 11.1 Information for Accessing Lynx at University of Kansas by Telnet

In this example we'll follow these steps:

1. Start a Telnet session with the University of Kansas.
2. Log in as **www** so you can use Lynx.
3. Explain the items on the screen.
4. Follow one link to the World Wide Web Subject Catalog.
5. Leave Lynx.

This will give us a chance to look at using Lynx, explain some of the commands, and set a context for other topics in this chapter. Let's get started!

Start a Telnet Session with University of Kansas

We'll assume you're logged in to the computer you use to access the Internet.

☞ **Type** `telnet lynx.cc.ukans.edu` **and press** Enter.

Once Telnet starts up you'll see something like the following:

```
Connected to eagle.cc.ukans.edu.
Escape character is '^]'.


               Welcome to The University of Kansas

Login as 'lynx' for access to the World Wide Web using Lynx.
        'www' for access to the World Wide Web using Lynx.
        'linemode' for access to the World Wide Web using Line Mode.

For assistance call 864-0110 or to report network problems call 864-0200.

Linux 1.2.0 (eagle.cc.ukans.edu) (ttyp3)

eagle login:
```

At this point you're connected, through Telnet, to a computer system at University of Kansas. You know from Figure 11.1 you should log in as **www**.

Log in as www So You Can Use Lynx

☞ **Type** www **and press** Enter.

☞ **Press** Enter **or type in your terminal type and press** Enter.

The cursor will be right after the colon in **login:**.

```
eagle login:www
```

You'll get a message asking about your terminal type. In order for things to work well, you need to use a terminal that either is or emulates a type of terminal known as VT100. Most systems have this capability. Press Enter after the screen prompts you to **Enter a terminal type:** or key in the type of terminal you're using.

```
Your Terminal type is unknown!

Enter a terminal type: [vt100]
```

Example 11.1 — A First Look at Lynx and the World Wide Web 277

Now you'll be taken to the first screen of Lynx access to WWW.

Explaining the Items on the Screen

You'll see a screen similar to the one in Figure 11.2. The document here is called the *home page* for this WWW site. In the upper right-hand corner you'll see a note telling you which of the one or more screens you're viewing. The links are in bold, and they represent links to other information on the Internet. The information could be at a different site from the one whose page you're reading or it could be local. It could be a link to another WWW item or take you to a Gopher menu or an anonymous FTP site. The links here are meant to represent *what* you want to see, rather than how to get to it. This screen also shows how information can be represented in context. If these links were represented in Gopher, you'd be choosing items from a menu.

You follow a highlighted link by pressing Enter or a right arrow. You move from link to link by pressing the down or up-arrow keys. The highlighted line near the bottom of the screen tells you how to move to another screen, get help, or quit. Below that line you'll see more helpful information about using Lynx.

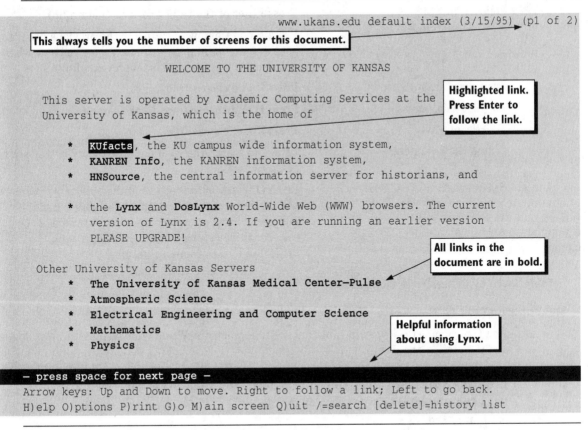

Figure 11.2 Home Page for Lynx at University of Kansas

There's a distinction made between *following* a link and *moving* to a link. Following a link means going to another portion of the Internet or Web. You can follow only the link that's highlighted. This link can take you to another site or different type of service on the Internet. Moving from one link to another means highlighting a link.

Table 11.1 explains the items in the lower portion of the screen.

How to	What to do
Go to the next screen or page	Press spacebar.
Move to the next link	Press up or down arrow keys. Down arrow takes you to a link below the current one on a page or to the next page, and up arrow takes you to one above.
Get help	Press **H** or **?** to see a list of helpful topics. Choose one in the same way you select any link.
Quit	Press **Q** or **q**.
Follow a link	Press Enter or the right arrow to follow a link.
Go back to previous document	Press the left arrow to return to the previous link. If you're at the main page—the first page you saw when you started Lynx—there is no previous link.
Print document	Press **P** and choose from a list.
Download document	Press **D** and choose from a list.
Mail document	Press **P** and choose from a list.
Search the document	Press **/** to search the document for a word or any string of characters.
Select options	Press **O** to set options. Some of the options you can set are the name of your bookmark file, your e-mail address, and whether you want your searches to be case sensitive or case insensitive (upper- and lowercase letters treated the same).

Table 11.1   Lynx Keystroke Commands

Follow a Link to the World Wide Web Subject Catalogue

Now you're going to move to the link that will take you to the World Wide Web Subject Catalogue, and then follow the link.

☞ **Press the spacebar to get to the next page and then press the down arrow (⬇)** **until the phrase** by Subject **in the line** * WWW Information By Subject **is highlighted.**

It should look like Figure 11.3.

Example 11.1 — A First Look at Lynx and the World Wide Web   279

```
INFORMATION SOURCES ABOUT AND FOR WWW
      + For a description of WWW choose Web Overview          ┌──────────────────────┐
      + About the WWW Information Sharing project             │ Link to WWW information│
      + WWW Information By Subject ◄────────────────────────  │ arranged by subject.   │
      + WWW Information By Type                                └──────────────────────┘
```

Figure 11.3 Selecting the Link to WWW Information Arranged by Subject

☞ **Press ➜ or Enter.**

You may see some messages on the screen telling you Lynx is contacting another site, getting a file, and that a certain quantity of bytes are being transferred. Eventually, you'll see the first screen of the World Wide Web Virtual Library Subject Catalogue (a good place to start searching for material in a specific subject area). When this example was constructed there were 14 screens of information in the subject catalog covering topics from **Aboriginal Studies** to **Unidentified Flying Objects**. See Figure 11.4.

```
The World-Wide Web Virtual Library: Subject Catalogue (p1 of 14)

                VIRTUAL LIBRARY THE WWW VIRTUAL LIBRARY

   This is a distributed subject catalogue. See Category Subtree, Library
   of Congress Classification (Experimental), Top Ten most popular
   Fields (Experimental), Statistics (Experimental), and Index. See also
   arrangement by service type ., and other subject catalogues of network
   information .

   Mail to maintainers of the specified subject or
   www-request@mail.w3.org to add pointers to this list, or if you would
   like to contribute to administration of a subject area.

   See also how to put your data on the web. All items starting with !
   are NEW! (or newly maintained). New this month: [IMAGE] Electronic
   Journals [IMAGE] Finance [IMAGE] Human Rights [IMAGE] Medieval
   Studies [IMAGE]


   Aboriginal Studies
           This document keeps track of leading information facilities in
 — press space for next page —
   Arrow keys: Up and Down to move. Right to follow a link; Left to go back.
  H)elp O)ptions P)rint G)o M)ain screen Q)uit /=search [delete]=history list
```

Figure 11.4 Home Page for the World Wide Web Virtual Library: Subject Catalogue

At this point you could:

❑ Go back to the previous document, the Lynx home page at the University of Kansas, by pressing the left-arrow key (⬅).

❑ Go on to another page of this document by pressing the spacebar.

❑ Follow a link by selecting an item that already is in bold and pressing the right arrow key (➡) or Enter.

You ought to try all the possibilities mentioned above to become comfortable using the WWW and Lynx.

Leaving Lynx

☞ **Press** q, **press** Enter, **then press** y **at the prompt asking if you really want to quit.**

Eventually you'll have to leave Lynx. Press **Q** to leave Lynx unconditionally. If you press **q** you'll be asked if you really want to quit.

─────────────────**End of Example 11.1**─────────────────

Now that you've seen an example of accessing and using the World Wide Web, you probably have some inkling of how it works. The links on the screen can represent anything that's in digital form and on the Internet: documents, files, sounds, images, and motion video. You'll have to use Mosaic or Netscape Navigator to view any of the images or videos since Lynx deals only with text. The information can be accessible by any of the usual Internet services—Telnet, FTP, Gopher, or WAIS; the links can let you read Usenet news or files on the local computer system. Remember that Gopher also allows for this same sort of exchange of information. The thing that WWW does better is to allow for more than just a menu to be passed from a server to a client. As you navigate or travel about the Internet using Lynx or Mosaic you're able to see whole screens of text with the links as part of the text. With Mosaic or Netscape Navigator you can also see images in combination with text, and the links can be represented by images or icons.

The documents or screens are passed from a server to a client according to a specific protocol (a formality for exchanging the information). This really isn't new for you. The other services on the Internet operate according to a protocol—Gopher clients get menus from Gopher servers, FTP clients get directories and files from anonymous FTP servers. The WWW protocol is named *http*, which stands for *Hypertext Transfer Protocol*, because the documents, pages, or screens passed from servers to clients are in hypertext form. The rules for creating or writing a Web page are all specified as *html—Hypertext Mark-up Language*. This language gives the formal rules for marking text so it's in boldface or italics and for marking something as an image or sound file. The language allows for text to be displayed in different forms and for some connection to be made between what you see and what the programs need to allow access to the Internet. For example, the links you see as boldface type are represented and interpreted by an http client in another form called a *URL* or *Uniform Resource Locator*. URLs are becoming the favored way of specifying items on the Internet.

What Are Hypertext and Hypermedia?

The WWW project aims to give access to the Internet in a *hypertext* or *hypermedia* environment. When you're working with a screen or page you see items in bold or underlined. Each one represents a link to another screen, page, document, file, image, or other Internet resource. Selecting one of these links allows you to follow the link by essentially jumping to the information the link represents. Also, you can return to a previous link. So as you work with a WWW browser you can go from link to link, forward and backward, as you wish. There's a definite starting point, but the path you take after that is one you choose. You can go up, down, right, or left from any link. WWW browsers allow the links to be represented by text, images, or digitized sound. The term *hypertext* was originally coined by Ted Nelson in the mid-1960s to talk about moving through text in some nonlinear manner.

Suppose this book were written as a hypertext document and you were reading it with a WWW browser. Some lines from earlier in this chapter might be represented as

```
We'll use telnet to access lynx here, using the address or domain name
below. You also can get to Lynx through Hytelnet (Chapter 5).
```

If you were to choose one of the words in **bold** and click on it with a mouse or press Enter you'd be taken to another part of the book. For example, choosing **Hytelnet** might take you to a definition or brief explanation of Hytelnet. From there you could choose to see one of several examples. The examples might contain references to other Internet services and so you'd go on from there. You could always follow the links back to return to where you started. The information in the book wouldn't change, but the way you access it and the order in which you access it would.

Many of the sources, sites, and services you access as part of the World Wide Web are accessible by other means. WWW allows you to browse and select those resources by letting you choose your own path within the context of Web pages and links on those pages or screens. Since the links in a WWW browser can be represented by different media (images, sounds, etc.) we use the term *hypermedia*.

Explaining URL—Uniform Resource Locator

Each of the links in hypertext or hypermedia documents used on the World Wide Web represent a *Uniform Resource Locator* or *URL*. The URL is used by a WWW browser (and Gopher clients as well) to give the location and the means to get to a resource on the Internet. You need to know about URLs if you want to access something that isn't on the Web page you're working with. Also, you'll often see a URL mentioned when someone writes about a Web page or service. Suppose you're interested in subscribing to some interest groups (Chapter 5) and you read about a Web page that allows you to search for interest groups with the URL **http://alpha.acast.nova.edu/ listserv.html**. You can enter that URL when using Lynx or Mosaic and go to that Web page.

You'll find it helpful to think of a URL as having the form

```
how-to-get-there://where-to-go/what-to-get
```

Its general form is

```
service://domain-name-of-site-supplying-service/full-path-name-of-item
```

Essentially this is like a sign pointing to something on the Internet. Starting at the far left, the portion of the URL up to the colon (:) tells what type of Internet service to use. The Internet domain name or address of the site supplying the information comes just after the characters ://. After the first single slash you have the full path name of the item.

In the chapter on anonymous FTP (Chapter 4) we used URLs to specify the location of a file or directory that was accessible by anonymous FTP. For example, the URL

```
ftp://ftp.cni.org/CNI/documents/tech.schol.human/summary.txt
```

is interpreted as stating that the file **summary.txt** in the directory **/CNI/documents/ tech.schol.human**, available by anonymous FTP from the Internet site **ftp.cni.org**.

Some other URLs with the same form for other Internet services follow:

```
file://myplace/goodfile.txt
```

The **file** URL is used to specify a file on your local system. This one references the file named **goodfile.txt** in the directory **myplace**.

```
ftp://sluaxa.slu.edu/pub/millesjg/mailser.cmd
```

FTP stands for *file transfer protocol*. It's used to exchange files on the Internet. The ftp URLs mean that the file can be retrieved by anonymous FTP (Chapter 4). This is the URL for "Discussion Lists: Mail Server Commands," by James Milles, mentioned in Chapter 6. This could also be specified by **file://sluaxa.slu.edu/pub/millesjg/mailser.cmd**.

```
gopher://ashpool.micro.umn.edu/11/Weather
```

It's probably no surprise that this URL says to use Gopher to contact the gopher server at **ashpool.micro.umn.edu**. The **11** is a code interpreted to mean to choose **Weather** from the main menu.

```
http://www.uwm.edu/Mirror/inet.services.html
```

http stands for *hypertext transport protocol*. WWW clients and servers use it to exchange documents. This is one for "Special Internet Connections" by Scott Yanoff. It was mentioned in the chapter on Telnet (Chapter 3).

Here are some URLs of a slightly different form.

```
telnet://www@UKANAIX.CC.UKANS.EDU
```

This starts a Telnet session with the address following the @. The log-in name you need to use comes before the @. So this starts a Telnet session with **ukanaix.cc.ukans.edu**. You need to type **www** after you get a **login:** prompt. (At some sites you'll see the prompt **username:**.) Telnet is discussed in Chapter 3. If there's to be a port number with the Telnet session, it's specified after the name of the Internet site. For example, to get the weather report from **madlab.sprl.umich.edu** you need to use Telnet with port number 3000. It's expressed as the URL **telnet://madlab.sprl.umich.edu:3000**. A log-in name usually isn't required with a port number.

```
mailto:mbuddy@great.place.edu
```

This is what you'd use to send e-mail. It's straightforward, the protocol name **mailto** and the e-mail address. Unlike the others it has no //.

```
news:news.answers
```

This is what's used to read Usenet news with a WWW browser. This URL specifically reads the articles in **news.answers**. You have to have Usenet news available from your system to use this. Usenet news is discussed in Chapter 6.

Using Lynx to Access the WWW

Lynx is a World Wide Web browser; it is software you run to access the World Wide Web. It was designed to work on text-based terminals, and when you use it you work in a hypertext environment. You don't need a sophisticated or an expensive connection to the Internet. However, you need to be sure your terminal is a VT100 terminal or can emulate one. You need the same type of terminal or terminal emulation for many other Internet resources, so this shouldn't be a problem. Most software packages that get you connected to the Internet include what you'll need so your PC or terminal can work with Lynx.

Example 11.1 showed how to use Lynx through Telnet. All the commands are typed in using the keyboard. You use the arrow keys to take you around a document and to follow links to other documents. The screen contains only text or characters; no images or icons. You would have to use Mosaic, Netscape, or some other graphics-based WWW browser to see images and icons. You can access the same information regardless of its form; any link can be followed and images or other types of information can be downloaded. When you use Lynx, jumping from one page to another through a link often takes less time than when you're working with a graphics-based WWW browser, because only text has to be transferred. Lynx gives you a straightforward easy way to access the World Wide Web.

When you start Lynx you begin with what is known as a *home page*. When you used Telnet you got the home page at the University of Kansas. If you start Lynx on your system, you may see a different home page. Each time you follow a link you're taken to what could be text, prose, a list of items, another home page, a Gopher menu, an anonymous FTP site, or some other type of item. Regardless of what type of item or object you get to when you follow a link or when you start Lynx, we'll call it a *document*. Giving one name to all these different types of things makes it easier to talk about using Lynx.

Starting Lynx

If the computer you use to access the Internet has Lynx software you start a session by typing:

```
lynx
```

all in lowercase and pressing Enter. Naturally, you do this after you log in and aren't in the middle of running another program. You can also start Lynx by typing the command and the name of a file on your system, or by typing the command and a URL.

To view the file **realgood.one** in the current directory using Lynx, type the following and press Enter:

```
lynx realgood.one
```

To start Lynx at the Virtual Environmental Library type the following and press Enter:

```
lynx http://envirolink.org/elib/
```

If Lynx isn't available on your computer you can use Telnet to start a session with a site that has Lynx available to the public. One site is **lynx.cc.ukans.edu** at the University of Kansas. Its IP address is **129.237.17.47**. You also need to give the log in name **www** when you Telnet there to access Lynx. We showed how to do that in Example 11.1. You can use Hytelnet to find other sites.

Leaving Lynx

You press either **q** or **Q** to quit a Lynx session. When you press **q** (lowercase) you'll get a prompt asking you if you really want to quit.

```
Are you sure you want to quit? [Y]
```

The **[Y]** after the question means y is the default answer; pressing Enter is the same as pressing **y**.

When you press **Q** (uppercase) you aren't asked if you're sure you want to quit. The session ends.

Getting On-Line Help

Press **H** or **?** for on-line help. You'll jump to a screen listing several links to documents to help you use Lynx. All the documents are written as hypertext and nicely done. Some you'll expect to see are

```
* Key-stroke commands
* About Lynx
* Lynx users guide version 2.3
* Help on version 2.3
* Help on HTML
* HTML Quick Reference Guide
* Help on URLs
```

Moving Around a Document

To move from the present screen to the next screen within a document, press **+** (plus) or the spacebar. To move to the previous screen, press **-** (minus) or **b**.

To move the highlight from one link to another use the up and down arrow keys. The down arrow moves the highlight to the next link in the document, and the up arrow takes you to the previous one.

Following Links

You follow a link, take off into the Internet or maybe just go to another portion of the same document by pressing Enter or the right-arrow key. You return from a link by pressing the left arrow.

Searching a Document

Some folks say a nice home page or document is one that fits on a screen. That way you can see everything it has to offer. *But* some long documents fill several screens. In this case you might want to search a document for a word or phrase. To do that press /. You'll get a prompt asking you to enter a search string. Once you type it in and press Enter, the document is searched for the first piece of text that matches your string. To search using the same search string press **n**. To search using a different search string press / again. If the string you're searching for isn't in the document you'll be told. If it is there, the display will change so the item that matches your search is at the top of the screen.

Downloading a Document

To download a document press **D**. You'll jump to a document containing links similar to the ones in Figure 11.5. Some Lynx sites give more or fewer choices for download protocol. This is one you'll likely see if you access Lynx through Telnet.

```
                                                    Lynx Download Options
                          DOWNLOAD OPTIONS

       You have the following download choices
       please select one:


       Save to disk disabled.
       Use kermit to download ASCII text to your local machine
       Use kermit to download a binary file to your local machine
```

Figure 11.5 Download Options for Lynx (Telnet)

In this case it's not possible to save the document to a disk on the computer that's running Lynx. (We've accessed Lynx through Telnet so saving to disk on the remote system probably wouldn't do us any good, and it would use resources on the system that's allowing us to use Lynx.) If you're using Lynx on your own computer then you'll be able to save a document in a file. You can also transfer the document to your local system by using Kermit. Kermit is the name of a protocol and a program you'd use to upload or, as in this case, download a document. If you don't know anything about downloading an ASCII text or binary file, ask a friend or local expert for help. If you do know how to use Kermit, select one of the download options in the same way you'd follow a link. You'll be prompted to start receiving the file. After the download is complete press the left arrow key to return to the document.

Printing a Document

When a document is printed by Lynx it's usually printed on a printer that's connected to the computer system running Lynx. So if you're using Telnet to access Lynx on some remote computer, it may not make sense to print the document. In fact, most sites that allow remote access don't allow you to print. With that said, let's assume you can print on the computer you're using to access Lynx.

You press **P** to print a document. When you do you'll see a screen similar to Figure 11.6. The top part tells you the number of lines to print. You have a few choices. To print the file you would move the highlight to the item **Computer Center Printer**. Then press Enter, and the document ought to be printed.

```
                                                          Lynx Printing Options
                        PRINTING OPTIONS

   There are 50 lines, or approximately 1 page, to print.
   You have the following print choices
   please select one:

   Save to a local file
   Mail the file to yourself
   Print to the screen
   Computer Center printer


 Commands: Use arrow keys to move, '?' for help, 'q' to quit, '<-' to go back
   Arrow keys: Up and Down to move. Right to follow a link; Left to go back.
 H)elp O)ptions P)rint G)o M)ain screen Q)uit /=search [delete]=history list
```

Figure 11.6 Printing Options for Lynx

Some computer systems allow users to define their own printer command or print to a printer attached to a personal computer. It's up to you to find the options you have.

Mailing a Document

You can mail (e-mail) the current document to any valid Internet address. You press **p** just as if the file were going to be printed, and you'll see a screen similar to Figure 11.6. Move the highlight bar to

```
   Mail the file to yourself
```

and press Enter. Then you'll get the prompt

```
   Please enter a valid internet mail address:
```

Type in an Internet address, press Enter, and away it goes!

Saving a Document to a File

When a document is saved to a file by Lynx, the file is saved on the computer system that's running Lynx. So if you're using Telnet to access Lynx on some remote computer, it may not make sense to save the document to a file. Most sites that allow remote access don't allow you to save a document in a file. If you do want to save it to a file, send it to yourself by e-mail and then save it on the computer where you receive your mail. Let's assume you can save the document to a file on the computer you're using to access Lynx.

To save the document to a file, press **p**. You'll see a screen similar to Figure 11.6. Move the highlight bar to

```
   Save to a local file
```

Press Enter. You'll be prompted for a name for the file. Type in a valid file name, press Enter, and it's done!

Keeping Track of Where You've Been

Lynx is easy to use and allows you to move through the Internet easily, concentrating only on *what* you're working with, not how you're doing it. You choose one topic or link that leads to another, which leads to another, and then you find something really interesting! Since you've been using hypertext you may not be sure how you arrived at this spot. Also you'll probably want to make a note of the URL for this interesting document so you can come back to it. Lynx provides two ways of handling this situation:

1. History List, a list of documents you've been through to get to the current one.
2. Lynx Bookmarks, a list of links you've saved from this and other sessions.

History List. To take a look at a list of all the documents or sites you've been through to get to where you are press the delete key or the backspace key. You'll be taken to a document that has a list of all the sites or documents you've visited to get to the current document. They're all links so you can go to any of them by moving the highlight bar to one and pressing Enter.

Lynx Bookmarks. You can save the links to interesting sites you find by making them a Lynx *bookmark*. Then you'll be able to revisit that document by choosing it as a link from your personal collection. When you select a document or a link as a bookmark, it gets added to a file that you own. Anytime you're using Lynx you can call up your bookmark file and follow any of the links.

Press **A** to **add** a document of links to your list of bookmarks. You'll get the prompt:

```
Save D)ocument or L)ink to bookmark file or C)ancel? (d,l,c):
```

Pressing **D** saves the current document as a bookmark. Pressing **L** saves the current link, not the current document, in the bookmark file. For example, suppose you find yourself on the Inter-Links home page (URL **http://alpha.acast.nova.edu/start.html**) as shown in Figure 11.7. You'd like to add this document as a bookmark so you can always get to it directly. Also, you'd like to add the link titled **Reference Shelf** to your list of bookmarks.

```
                                                                    Inter-Links
                    INTER-LINKS INTERNET ACCESS
INTRODUCTION
     * About Inter-Links
     * New Features
FEATURES
     * Internet Resources
     * Fun and Games
     * Guides and Tutorials
     * News and Weather
     * Library Resources
     * Reference Shelf
     * Miscellaneous
     * Search Inter-Links
     * Feedback
```

```
Announcement: Nova-Links is now Inter-Links.
Rob Kabacoff, Nova Southeastern University
Commands: Use arrow keys to move, '?' for help, 'q' to quit, '<-' to go back
 Arrow keys: Up and Down to move. Right to follow a link; Left to go back.
 H)elp O)ptions P)rint G)o M)ain screen Q)uit /=search [delete]=history list
```

Figure 11.7 Home Page for Inter-Links http://alpha.acast.nova.edu/start.html

Press **A** to add a bookmark. To add the document to the list press **D**. Now press **A** again and this time press **L** to add the link.

Press **V** to view your bookmarks. The bookmark list will become the current document and you can choose any link from it. Assuming you added the bookmarks from the document in Figure 11.7 and pressed **V**, you would see them as the last two in the bookmark list. See Figure 11.8.

```
                                                          Bookmark file

 This file may be edited with a standard text editor. Outdated or
 invalid links may be removed by simply deleting the line the link
 appears on in this file. Please refer to the Lynx documentation or
 help files for the HTML link syntax.

 1. Starting Points for Internet Exploration
 2. National Center for Atmospheric Research
 3. Honolulu Community College WWW Service
 4. World-Wide Web Guide
 5. Inter-Links
 6. Reference Shelf



Commands: Use arrow keys to move, '?' for help, 'q' to quit, '<-' to go back
 Arrow keys: Up and Down to move. Right to follow a link; Left to go back.
 H)elp O)ptions P)rint G)o M)ain screen Q)uit /=search [delete]=history list
```

Figure 11.8 Sample Bookmark List

The other bookmarks were added previously.

Go to a Link by Typing In a URL

While you're viewing a document you can **go** to any document by pressing **G** and typing in a URL. When you type **G** you'll be prompted to enter a URL. For example, to go to the **Asian Studies** section of the WWW Virtual Library (URL) from wherever you are, press **G**. You'll see the prompt:

```
 URL to open:
```

Type in the URL above so you have:

Example 11.2 — Using Lynx to Browse the WWW Virtual Library——————————289

```
URL to open: http://coombs.anu.edu.au/WWWVL-AsianStudies.html
```

and press Enter. If it's possible to follow the URL you've typed, you'll be taken there!

Example 11.2 Using Lynx to Browse the WWW Virtual Library

In this example we'll use a number of the features of Lynx we've mentioned in the previous section. We'll be browsing the WWW Virtual Library arranged by subject. You could spend hours, days, weeks browsing this library. We don't have the space to show too many items. For this example, we'll go to the section on **Sport**, save the link to **Water Sports** in the bookmark list, and mail a copy of the **Sport** document to a friend. You'll be able to browse any other area in much the same way. We'll assume we have Lynx on the computer system you're using. If you need to access Lynx through Telnet, see Example 11.1. Here are the steps we'll follow.

1. Start Lynx.
2. Go to the WWW Virtual Library subject catalog.
3. Search the document for information under the heading **Sport**.
4. Follow the link to the section on **Sport**.
5. Jump to the portion of the document on **Water Sports**.
6. Add items related to water sports to the bookmarks.
7. Mail the WWW Virtual Library section on **Sport** to a friend.
8. Leave Lynx.

Start Lynx

☞ **At the prompt, type** `lynx` **and press** `Enter`.

```
$ lynx
```

Go to the WWW Virtual Library Subject Catalog

Once Lynx starts you'll see a home page or document. Which one you see depends how Lynx is set up on your system. Figure 11.9 shows a home page at Mary Washington College in December, 1994. The URL is **http://www.mwc.edu**.

```
                                                         MWC Home Page   (p1 of 3)
```

There is an image here, but you can't see it with Lynx. You need Mosaic or something similar to see it.

```
                        MARY WASHINGTON COLLEGE
                        FREDERICKSBURG, VA 22401


                             HELLO WORLD!




     [IMAGE] Welcome to the home page for Mary Washington College, a public
     coed college of the liberal arts and sciences. Feel free to browse
     our gopher, Mary Washington College Gopher, for information about the
     College.
```

```
    This list is just a few starting points for accessing the Internet
    through the World-Wide Web.


    The World-Wide Web Virtual Library: Subject Catalogue


    Inter-Links
 - press space for next page -
    Arrow keys: Up and Down to move. Right to follow a link; Left to go back.
    H)elp O)ptions P)rint G)o M)ain screen Q)uit /=search [delete]=history list
```

Figure 11.9 Home Page for Mary Washington College URL: http://www.mwc.edu

☞ **The WWW Virtual Library is on this home page. Move the highlight bar to it by pressing ⬇ once. Then press Enter.**

You'll jump to the first screen for the WWW Virtual Library Subject Catalogue. See Figure 11.10.

```
The World-Wide Web Virtual Library: Subject Catalogue (p1 of 14)

                    VIRTUAL LIBRARY THE WWW VIRTUAL LIBRARY

    This is a distributed subject catalogue. See Category Subtree, Library
    of Congress Classification (Experimental), Top Ten most popular
    Fields (Experimental), Statistics (Experimental), and Index. See also
    arrangement by service type ., and other subject catalogues of network
    information .

    Mail to maintainers of the specified subject or
    www-request@mail.w3.org to add pointers to this list, or if you would
    like to contribute to administration of a subject area.

    See also how to put your data on the web. All items starting with !
    are NEW! (or newly maintained). New this month: [IMAGE] Electronic
    Journals [IMAGE] Finance [IMAGE] Human Rights [IMAGE] Medieval
    Studies [IMAGE]

    Aboriginal Studies
            This document keeps track of leading information facilities in
 - press space for next page -
    Arrow keys: Up and Down to move. Right to follow a link; Left to go back.
    H)elp O)ptions P)rint G)o M)ain screen Q)uit /=search [delete]=history list
```

Figure 11.10 Home Page for the World Wide Web Virtual Library: Subject Catalogue

Search the Document for Information under the Heading Sport

☞ **Press /.**

Example 11.2 — Using Lynx to Browse the WWW Virtual Library   291

You'll get the prompt:

```
Enter a search string:
```

☞ **Type** sport **and press** Enter.

You'll be taken within this document to the screen similar to Figure 11.11.

```
The World-Wide Web Virtual Library: Subject Catalogue (p12 of 14)
   Sport
```
Highlight bar is on sport.

```
   Standards and Standardization Bodies

   Statistics

   Sumeria
          Files on alternative science, suppressed and neglected medical
          ideas, plus areas for politics, fiction, animal issues, and
          anything else that seems like a good idea at the time.


   Telecommunications

   Tibetan Studies

   U.S. Federal Government Agencies

   US Government Information Sources

   Unidentified Flying Objects (UFOs)
 - press space for next page -
   Arrow keys: Up and Down to move. Right to follow a link; Left to go back.
  H)elp O)ptions P)rint G)o M)ain screen Q)uit /=search [delete]=history list
```

Figure 11.11 Portion of The World-Wide Web Virtual Library: Subject Catalogue containing Sport

Follow the Link to the Section on Sport

☞ **Press** Enter **and you'll jump to the document on** Sport.

Jump to the Portion of the Document on Water Sports

The next thing to do is search for the string **water sports**.

☞ **Press** / **to search, type** water sports **as shown here, and press** Enter.

```
Enter a search string: water sports
```

This takes you to the line that contains the search string **water sports**. When this example was constructed we were taken to the line

```
   Ball Sports  Wheel Sports, Water Sports, Out and About and The
```

☞ **Press** j **or** ⬇ **until** Water Sports **is highlighted.**

☞ **Press** Enter.

We'll want to follow the link to the section on Water Sports. Press j or down arrow until the phrase **Water Sports** is highlighted. Press Enter and you'll see a screen similar to Figure 11.12.

```
The World-Wide Web Virtual Library: Sport   (p8 of 16)
Water Sports


       * The America's Cup On-Line home page provides regular news updates,
         race results, information on the competitors, the event
         organizers, racing schedules, event sponsors, yacht design,
         America's Cup history, frequently asked questions about the event
         and the schedule for television coverage.
       * The BOC Challenge page.
       * The Laser Web Server.
       * The Sydney-Hobart Yacht Race, with regular reports and commentary
         on the proceedings.
       * The Boating Home Page.
       * A repository of sailing resources.
       * An 'Aladdin's Cave' of Sailing Information.
       * Rowing.
       * Details of Rowing in Stockholm.
       * Windsurfing
            + The WWW Windsurfing Home Page.
            + The North Carolina Outer Banks Windsurfing Home Page.
- press space for next page -
  Arrow keys: Up and Down to move. Right to follow a link; Left to go back.
 H)elp O)ptions P)rint G)o M)ain screen Q)uit /=search [delete]=history list
```

Figure 11.12 First Page of Document for Water Sports

Add the Link Related to Water Sports to the Bookmarks

To add the link to Water Sports to the bookmark list, you have to have the link **Water Sports** highlighted.

☞ **Press** ⬅ **to go back to the previous screen and** Water Sports **should be high-lighted. If it is not, press the** ⬆ **or** ⬇ **to make it so.**

☞ **Press** A **to add a bookmark, then press** L.

Since we want to add the link to **Water Sports** to the bookmark list we press **L** (upper or lowercase) in response to the prompt shown below.

```
   Save D)ocument or L)ink to bookmark file or C)ancel? (d,l,c):
```

It's added. You could press **V** to check.

Mail the WWW Virtual Library Section on Sport to a Friend

To send a document by e-mail you have to press **P** for print and you'll view a document similar to Figure 11.6. Choose the option for e-mail. The document you're working with is titled **Sport**. Press **P** and move the highlight bar to the link **Mail the file to yourself** and press Enter. You won't be sending this to yourself; you can send a document by e-mail to any Internet address. You'll get a prompt to enter an e-mail address. There may already be an address here. In that case you have to press Backspace to erase it. In any case you're ready to type in the e-mail address of your friend. Press Enter and it's sent off!

```
Please enter a valid internet mail address: mybuddy@great.place.edu
```

Leave Lynx

If you're ready to leave Lynx press **q** and then type **Y** or press Enter. You can leave without being asked any questions by pressing **Q**.

————————————————————End of Example 11.2————————————————————

Using Mosaic to Access the WWW

Mosaic is a WWW browser with a graphical user interface (GUI), designed to be used in a windowed environment. It was developed at the National Center for Supercomputer Applications (NCSA), and has been responsible for some of the great popularity of WWW. It's very easy to use and very attractive. You access links and commands by clicking on icons, images, or underlined text with a mouse. Once started, you work within a Mosaic window in color. The first page you see is called the *home page*. It could contain text and images, and unlike when you're using Lynx, you'll be able to see the images! It can also contain icons that represent audio files, and if your system is properly equipped, you'll be able to click on the icon and hear what the icon represents. The text can be in bold or underlined and displayed in different sized fonts. All this really brings home the idea that WWW is a way of working with the Internet in a multimedia or hypermedia environment. There's so much you can see and find with Mosaic: art exhibits, museum displays, scientific and technical simulations, animations, sound clips of musical performances, plus all the textual information that's accessible by Lynx or other Internet tools.

Figure 11.13 is an example of a starting or home page using Mosaic. It's one you might see if you're using NCSA Mosaic with Microsoft Windows.

Figure 11.13 NCSA Mosaic Home Page Using MS Windows

Versions of Mosaic are available from NCSA, free on the Internet, to operate in a variety of computing environments including Macintosh systems, Microsoft Windows for DOS-based systems, or X-Windows on UNIX systems. There's a big advantage to using something in a windows or graphical environment: You don't have to learn a lot of commands and you use the same commands or methods of the windowing system in working with Mosaic. The sundry "flavors" of Mosaic appear slightly different, but they share the same types of commands and icons. They're all used the same way:

> You use a mouse to move a hand or pointer to an icon or underlined portion of the window and click the mouse button (the left one if your mouse has more than one button.) If you've clicked on a link within the document, you follow that link and the current document is replaced or another window pops up. Clicking on text or icons in the border of the window pops up a menu bar and you choose an action from it. Clicking on an icon or a button in the border, in some cases, causes an action without your having to choose from a menu bar or dialog box.

Mosaic is an exciting change from the text-only view you get using Lynx. However, you need a full Internet connection to use it. This means you need a computer with a network card, or a SLIP connection if you're using a modem.

You'll see that Mosaic is easy to use and generally has lots of on-line help information. Once you get comfortable with it you'll probably want to spend hours using it to explore and browse the Internet. All the versions are similar so not much will be lost if we discuss a particular version when we give some examples. We'll talk about versions used with Microsoft Windows.

Starting and Leaving Mosaic

You start Mosaic by either clicking on an icon labeled Mosaic, choosing Mosaic from a pull-down menu, or typing its name as a command and pressing Enter. The method you use depends on the type of system you're using.

One way to leave Mosaic is to close its window. You'll also be able to choose Exit as an option from a pull-down menu.

The Mosaic Window: Contents, Icons, Commands

The Mosaic window has similarities to any window on the computer you're using. The same commands are used to change its size or position, or turn it into an icon, as for any window. We'll discuss the features special to Mosaic here.

First Row—Menu Commands

Across the top you'll see a row of words called menu commands, each representing a pull-down menu. In Figure 11.13 the row is

File   Edit   Options   Navigate   Annotate   Starting Points   Personal   Help

You choose any of these by moving the mouse pointer to the word and clicking on it. To look at the Help menu, for example, move the pointer by using the mouse to **Help** and click on it. A menu will pop up. (In the Microsoft Windows environment, the underlined characters give you fast access to one of these menu commands. Press Alt and one of the underlined characters to see its menu. For example, pressing Alt-H shows the Help menu.) We'll look at the choices in several of these menus in the sections below.

The Globe

Versions of Mosaic have an image of the globe in the upper right-hand corner. It spins while Mosaic is loading a document or following a hyperlink. That's kind of fun to watch, and it lets you know Mosaic is doing something. You can't give any other commands to Mosaic while the globe is spinning. If it's taking too long to make a connection or retrieve a document, you can click on the spinning globe and interrupt the connection or stop the transmission. You won't leave Mosaic. Whatever has been assembled from the interrupted transmission will be displayed.

The Icons

On some versions of Mosaic there is a series of icons below the menu commands. There are differences between the versions. We're including the ones shown in Figure 11.14 so you'll have a guide to the version you use.

Figure 11.14 Icons in an NCSA Mosaic Window

We'll discuss the icons in order from left to right. See Table 11.2.

	Icon	Explanation
	Open a URL	Click on this to type the name of a uniform resource locator. When you're done typing and press Enter, Mosaic will jump to the resource the URL represents.
	Save to a file	Saves the current document to a file.
	Print	Click here to print the current document.
	Preview	This shows a preview of how the document will look when it's printed.

	Copy and Paste	These two icons allow you to copy a portion of a document on the screen and paste it into another windows application. You can also use it to copy a URL mentioned in a document you're reading and paste it to the Current URL line.
	Back and Forward	These two buttons with directional arrows move between existing documents. One takes you to the previous document and the other takes you forward. These don't follow any hyperlinks. They're used to move between documents you've already seen.
	The loop	Used to reload the current document. If it didn't load completely or is disturbed in some way you may want to reload it.
	The house	Takes you to your home page.
	Find	Use this to find a string, a word or phrase, in the current document.
	+ Hotlist	This icon adds the current document to the *Hotlist*. The hotlist is a list of places or links you'd like to return to in this or other Mosaic sessions.
	Read news	Click here to read Usenet News.
	Send e-mail	Click on this icon to send e-mail.
	About	This gives the version of Mosaic you're using, the copyright, names of the programmers, and other information.

Table 11.2   Icons in a Mosaic Window

Current URL

You'll see the URL for the current document displayed on the screen in the bar to the left of the globe, just below the icons in Figure 11.14. This is filled in automatically by Mosaic. You can also set it: Type any URL in that portion of the Window. Clicking on the ☑ will cause Mosaic to follow the link. You can click on ☒ if you don't want to use the URL.

Document View

The majority of the screen is taken up by the view of the current document.

Scroll Bar

The scroll bar is on the far right of the window. You use it and the associated arrows to move through the document.

Moving Around a Document

You move around or through a document by using the vertical or horizontal scroll bars on the right and bottom of the window. Use the vertical scroll bar to move up and down in the document, and use the horizontal scroll bar to move right and left. Each bar has an arrowhead on each end. You can click on these to move in the direction they indicate. Clicking on the arrowhead pointing down moves the window down one line in the document. Clicking on the up arrow has a similar effect, but the movement is up. Each scroll bar also has something called a scroll box within it. If you click on and drag the scroll box you can move very quickly in the direction it is moved. Clicking on a region of the scroll bar on one side or the other of the scroll box moves you one window in that direction.

Getting On-Line Help

The different versions of Mosaic have either a button or command for on-line help. Clicking on the menu command **Help** will open a menu from which you can choose the type of help document you'll need. The items in the menu will most likely be hyperlinks to another site. In the situation when your system and your connections to the Internet are working well you'll hardly notice where these documents are located. Two choices you're likely to see are *On Line Documentation*, a complete guide to using Mosaic, and *FAQ Page*, a list of frequently asked questions and answers about Mosaic.

Following Hyperlinks

The general rule for following a link is to move the mouse pointer or hand to the item and click on it. The links are represented in all sorts of forms: underlined text, images, icons representing sound files, or portions of larger objects such as maps. The links represent URLs, or pointers to other items. The items can be in the same document, on your system, or anywhere on the Internet. When you click on an icon representing a sound file, you'll hear the sound recorded in that file. If you click on a hyperlink representing a still image, animation, or movie, you'll see it displayed. Whether these are completely successful depends on whether the computer you're using is equipped to play audio files or display images. Not all images in a document represent a hyperlink, just as not all text represents a link. You'll be able to tell when you've come across a hyperlink by watching the pointer. When it turns to a hand you know you've moved it to a hyperlink. Click and follow the link!

Saving, Printing, and Mailing a Document

Choose the **File** command menu from the top line. You'll see items to choose for saving the current document to a file on disk and printing the document. Some versions—for example, the one for X-Windows under Unix—also give you the option of e-mailing the current document. When you choose any of these a dialog box is opened and you fill in the appropriate information: to save a file, name the file the document will be saved to; to print a document, click the item that starts the printing; to e-mail the document, fill in the address to which the document will be sent. If you're using the X-Windows version of Mosaic you'll be able to choose how you want to save, print, or mail the document: either as a hypertext document with all the information about the links or as a plain file that doesn't contain any information about links. In the latter case only the text is saved, printed, or sent by e-mail. Saving it as a hypertext document allows it to be used by Mosaic in the same form it appeared on the screen.

Here's an example of a saving a document to a file: If icons aren't present, click on the command menu **File** and then, depending on the version of Mosaic you're using, choose an item such as **Save to a local file**, **Save**, or **Save As**, and fill in the name of the file in the appropriate region of the dialog box. For versions with icons, click on the one for saving the document to a file. If you're using the version of NCSA Mosaic for Microsoft Windows and you choose **Save As** or click on the icon for saving to a file you'll see a dialog box similar to Figure 11.15. We've filled in the name **goodpage.htm**. Click on the **OK** button to save the document in the file named **goodpage.htm**.

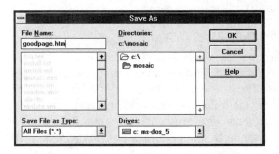

Figure 11.15 Dialog Box for Saving a File

In this case the file is saved in hypertext or hypermedia form so it can called up by Mosaic and displayed just as it appeared in the window.

Searching a Document

There will be times when you'll want to search a document for a word or phrase. The steps you go through on all systems are:

❑ Choose the correct command menu (**File** in some versions, **Edit** in others) or the correct icon (binoculars in NCSA Mosaic for Microsoft Windows).

❑ Fill in the dialog box: type the string to use for the search and press Enter.

If the string is in the document you'll be taken to the first occurrence of the string. To find the next one, repeat the process.

Keeping Track of Where You've Been

As you use NCSA Mosaic you'll be following hyperlinks to all sorts of places. You're likely to be following many links and not be keeping track of how you arrived at a document or image. You will, however, want to know how to get to some documents or images so you can return. Mosaic, like other WWW browsers, does keep track of where you've been. It has to do so to let you use the arrow icons to go backward and forward. Versions of Mosaic without icons have boxes labeled **Forward** and **Back** to let you move through the documents you've seen. To see where you've been you can look at the **History** list. This is the list of the links you've followed to get to the present document. To view it click on the menu button labeled **Navigate** and then choose the item **History**. The History list will appear on the screen and you can choose to jump to any of the items listed. If you change your mind about going to an item on the History list, click on the button labeled **Cancel**. The history list contains only items you've seen in the current session.

Keeping Track of Favorite Places

When you find a document you want to return to in the future, even in a different Mosaic session, you can save the URL to the item on a *Hotlist*, a list of important, interesting, or favorite places to refer to at any time. It's easy to add an item to a hotlist. Either click on the hotlist icon or choose the menu item **Navigate** and **Add Current to Hotlist** from the menu. The item is added to the hotlist!

You jump to an item on the hotlist by clicking on the **Navigate** menu command and then clicking on the item to view the hotlist. On some systems you'll get to use something called a "Hotlist Manager," which allows you to select hyperlinks from more than one list. Once an item from a hotlist is selected press Enter or double-click on the item so Mosaic can follow the link.

Click on the arrow right after the **URL:** box to see the list of the items written in URL form. Click on the arrow right after the box in the far right of the top row to see the titles (not URL form) of the documents in the current hotlist. Then click on one and you'll jump to that item. In this version of Mosaic you can have several hotlists, and several come with it. You can click on the arrow box right after the item labeled **Current Hotlist:** to pick the one to use.

Viewing Local Files

Mosaic can be used to browse the Internet, and it can also be used to view files, with some restrictions, on your system. First of all you have to have permission to read the file. On some types of systems, UNIX for example, not all files can be read by everyone. Also, some versions of Mosaic allow you to view only files whose names end with the suffixes **.htm** or **.html**.

Opening a URL

A URL gives Mosaic and other WWW browsers all the information they need to jump to a document or item. In fact, all the hyperlinks within a document are written as URLs; you don't necessarily see them, but they are there. There will be times you'll want to tell Mosaic to use a URL you supply, either one on a hotlist or one you've read about somewhere else, rather than follow the hyperlinks in a document. The phrase *open a URL* means just that. You type the URL into a dialog box, Mosaic interprets it, and gets the information or resource. A URL can represent any form of Internet resource.

You can open a URL by clicking on the **File** command menu and then choosing Open **URL**, or you can click on the icon used for opening a URL. In any case you'll have to type the URL into a dialog box. Once you type it in press Enter or click a button to have Mosaic follow the URL.

A Few Starting Points

All versions of Mosaic come with a list of starting points. They're interesting, nicely constructed, and usually lead to other services and resources; they really are good places to start. You just click on the command menu **Starting Points** and choose a URL from the list. In case you need it, here's the URL for the **Mosaic Starting Points Document http://www.ncsa.uiuc.edu/**

SDG/Software/Mosaic/StartingPoints/NetworkStartingPoints.html. Start here and browse the Internet. There's enough here to keep you occupied for days!

Searching the World Wide Web

The WWW, with its easy-to-use browsers, makes all of the services and resources of the Internet accessible. You've seen in the other chapters of this book how there is some tool or service to help you find information you can access with that service. Some examples are Hytelnet to help you find sites you can access through Telnet, Archie to help find files available by anonymous FTP, and Veronica to help search Gopher servers. Of all those mentioned, the WWW has been around for the shortest amount of time. Lynx, Mosaic, and browsers like them have made the WWW very popular, and the number of sites offering WWW documents and other items has grown at an astounding rate. There are a number of tools for searching the World Wide Web and the Internet. Here's a short list of the URLs for Web pages that have links to these search tools. Try opening the URL to some of these sites. They may end up on your hotlist, since they're very useful when you have to find something on the WWW or the Internet.

W3 Search Engines

URL: **http://www.utirc.utoronto.ca/Lists/W3SearchEngines.html**
Complete list of search tools for WWW (W3) and Internet.

Experimental Search Engine Meta-Index

URL: **http://www.ncsa.uiuc.edu/SDG/Software/Mosaic/Demo/metaindex.html**
A list of several search tools for the Web and the Internet.

Web Indexes

URL: **http://webcrawler.com/WebCrawler/WebIndexes.html**
Contains links to tools for specifically searching WWW.

In this section we'll give examples of using two tools, WebCrawler and a tool for searching a site called EINet Galaxy. We'll do WebCrawler with Lynx in Example 11.3 and EINet Galaxy with Mosaic in Example 11.4.

Example 11.3 Searching the WWW Using WebCrawler

WebCrawler, developed by Brian Pinkerton, is a tool to use to search items available through WWW. You supply one or more keywords and WebCrawler searches its database of items and returns a ranked list of items containing the keywords you've specified. The ranking is based on the number of times the keywords appear in the document. The list is made up of hyperlinks. Select any one and you'll follow it to the document it represents. Any one could be saved on your hotlist or as a bookmark.

Suppose you need to do some research on the regulation of public utility companies, and you're going to use Lynx to access WebCrawler. The URL for the WebCrawler home page is **http://webcrawler.cs.washington.edu/WebCrawler/WebQuery.html**. The keywords to use are *regulation public utility company*.

——————Example 11.3 — Searching the WWW Using WebCrawler—————— **301**

In this example we'll go through these steps:

1. Start Lynx.
2. Go to or open the URL for the Webcrawler search page.
3. Save it in the bookmark list.
4. Enter keywords and start search.
5. Work with the results of the search.
6. Leave Lynx.

Start Lynx

☞ **Type** `lynx` **and press** Enter.

If Lynx is on the computer system you use, start a Lynx session by typing **lynx** and pressing Enter. In a previous example we showed starting Lynx by using Telnet.

Go To or Open the URL for WebCrawler

☞ **Press** G **or** g.

☞ **Type** `http://webcrawler.com/WebCrawler/WebIndexes.html` **and press** Enter.

After you start a Lynx session, you'll see the home page or starting point for the system you're using. To go to or open the URL for WebCrawler press g or G, You'll see this prompt:

```
URL to open:
```

Type in the URL for WebCrawler so that you have

```
URL to open: http://webcrawler.com/WebCrawler/WebIndexes.html
```

☞ **Press** Enter **to let Lynx make the connections and return the next screen.**

Save the WebCrawler Search Page in the Bookmark List

☞ **Press** A **or** a, **and then press** L **to save the highlighted link.**

Lynx makes connections through the Internet to bring you the WebCrawler search page. The page you'll see will be similar to the one in Figure 11.16, except the keywords won't be typed in. You'll see links to other documents that will help you use WebCrawler more effectively.

It's a good idea to save a link to the Search Page in your bookmark list. To do that, press **A** or **a** and then **L** to save the highlighted link.

Enter Keywords and Start Search

☞ **Press** ↓ **until you get to the text-entry field, just above** `Search`.

☞ **Type the keywords** `regulation public utility company` **and press** Enter.

☞ **Press** Enter **again.**

Following the link to the search page, you'll see a screen similar to the one in Figure 11.16, except the keywords aren't typed in. This document is from the others we've talked about in this chapter. It's in *forms mode*: it has portions that can be filled in or checked off the way you fill out other types of forms. Specifically, this one has a *text entry* section where you enter the keyword(s), and a *checkbox* section where you choose whether you want to find documents that contain all the keywords. You get from each portion of the screen to another by pressing the up or down arrow. If you're at a text entry portion, type what you need to and press an up or down arrow key to move on. If it's a section of the screen where you choose one or more options, such as the (*) **AND words together** item, you press the right arrow or Enter to select an option and then the up or down arrow to move on. As you move from one boldface item to another it will be described near the bottom of your screen.

In this case, press the down arrow until you get to the portion of the screen just above the word **Search**. That's where you enter the keywords.

```
                                          WebCrawler Searching (p1 of 2)


                    SEARCHING WITH WEBCRAWLER(TM)




To search the WebCrawler database, type in your search keywords here.
Type as many relevant keywords as possible; it will help to uniquely
identify what you're looking for. Last update: June 11, 1995.

     regulation public utility company_____
     Search           (*)AND words together
     Number of results to return:  [25_]



News | Home | Searching Hints | FAQ | Top 25 Sites | Submit URLs |
Discussion | Simple Search

(Text entry field) Enter text. Use UP or DOWN arrows or tab to move off.
          Enter text into the field by typing on the keyboard
   Ctrl-U to delete all text in field, [Backspace] to delete a character
```

Figure 11.16 WebCrawler Search Page

After you type in the keywords press Enter until the link Search is highlighted. This is the link that will start WebCrawler searching its sources. Press the right arrow or Enter.

Work with the Results of the Search

Figure 11.18 shows the first page of the results. WebCrawler tells you there are three pages in this document and 35 items listed. Each item has a score attached to it. The items are listed in order of their scores. Each is a URL or hyperlink. You can select any one in the same way a link is selected in any document: Use the up or down arrow key to move the highlight to the item.

Example 11.4 — Searching the WWW Using EINet Galaxy 303

```
                                    WebCrawler Search Results (p1 of 3)
WebCrawler Search Results

The query "regulation public utility company" found 71 documents and
returned 25:

1000    TSF: Chapter 5 - Encouraging New Approaches
0720    ftp://debra.dgbt.doc.ca/pub/isc/innovative.eco/full.report.eng.txt
0677    The Center for Corporate Law
0500    ftp://ftp.eznet.net/pub/telcomlaw/Tele_Consumer.fcc
0355    Washington State Legislature Revised Code of Washington
0338    Why Multi-Pure?
0313    Autozip Home Page
0288    TSF: Chapter 2 - Industry and Environmental technology
0245    TSF: Executive Summary - Looking to the Future
0194    Environment
0186    Hill Associates Products and Services
- press space for next page -
  Arrow keys: Up and Down to move. Right to follow a link; Left to go back.
H)elp O)ptions P)rint G)o M)ain screen Q)uit /=search [delete]=history list
```

Figure 11.17 Search Results from WebCrawler, Keywords regulation public utility company

There are a number of things you can do here to work with these documents, just as with any documents or links. Here's a quick review. To select a document means to move the highlight bar to the item. You move the highlight bar by pressing the up or down arrow key.

☞ **To follow a link, select it and press Enter or the →.**

☞ **To save a document to a disk, to send a document by e-mail, or to print a document, follow the link for the document and then press** P. **You can then choose the option that best fits your needs.**

☞ **To download a document on the list, select it and then press** D. **After a time you'll be able to choose from a menu the protocol to use to download.**

☞ **To add an item to the bookmark list, select it and then press** A. **You'll want to type** L **to save the link. If you've followed a link to a document, type** D **to save the link to the document you're viewing. Regardless of which you choose you'll be able to get back to the document later by pressing** V **to view the bookmark list.**

Leave Lynx

☞ **Press** Q.

Eventually you'll have to leave. Press **Q** to leave without being given a chance to change your mind. Press **q** to leave but be asked first if that's what you really want to do.

————————————————**End of Example 11.3**————————————————

Example 11.4 Searching the WWW Using EINet Galaxy

In this example, with the help of Mosaic, we'll use a tool called *EINet Galaxy* to search the World Wide Web. EINet stands for Enterprise Integration Network. You ought to read their home page (URL: **http://www.einet.net/EINet/EINet.html**). EINet Galaxy is meant to be a directory service that makes information easy to find on the Web and the Internet. We're going to use this because it can combine keywords as *Boolean expressions*. The words can be connected with the words *and, or, not*. This makes searching more effective, as explained below.

In this example we'll search for information about **international trade laws or treaties**. Through Mosaic we'll use EINet Galaxy to search WWW and the Internet. Here are the steps we'll follow:

1. Start a Mosaic session.
2. Open the URL to EINet Galaxy—**http://galaxy.einet.net/www/www.html**.
3. Search using the Boolean expression **treaty or law and international and trade**.
4. Work with the results of the search.
5. Leave Mosaic.

Start Mosaic and Open the URL

How you start Mosaic depends on how it's used on your system. You'll type the name of the program as a command and press Enter, choose the name Mosaic from a menu, or use a mouse to click on an icon labeled Mosaic.

☞ **Select the command menu item** `File` **and then choose** `Open a URL`.

OR click on an icon to open a URL. A dialog box will open for you to enter a URL in the appropriate spot.

☞ **Type** `http://galaxy.einet.net/www/www.html` **and press** Enter .

Once Mosaic starts you'll need to open a URL to **http://galaxy.einet.net/www/www.html**. You do that by either selecting the command menu item **File** and then choosing the term **Open a URL** or clicking on an icon meant for that purpose. That will open a dialog box and you enter the URL in the appropriate spot. Once you get the URL open you'll see a screen similar to Figure 11.18.

Figure 11.18 Home Page for EINet Galaxy

Example 11.4 — Searching the WWW Using EINet Galaxy — 305

Enter Keywords and Start the Search

☞ **Point to and click the mouse in the text box at the bottom of the screen, type** `treaty or law and international and trade`**, and press** `Enter`.

When you supply the keywords for a search the programs that do the search often return a list of documents that contain one or more of the words. We mentioned this before in the chapter on Gopher. If you want to be more specific you need to do a little planning. In many cases you can perform a *Boolean* search. You include the words *and, or,* and *not* to make the search more specific. For example, using the search phrase *indoor or outdoor and recreation not sport* would return items that contained the phrases *indoor recreation* or *outdoor recreation*, but did not contain the word *sport*. Here we'll search for information on *international trade treaties* or *international trade laws*. The phrase we'll use, since it's best to put the words connected with or first, is *treaty or law and international and trade*. Type the Boolean phrase or expression in the box at the bottom of the screen as shown in Figure 11.18. Point to the box with the mouse and click on it. Then type in the phrase and press Enter. Mosaic will pass your search request to the EINet Galaxy server. The globe in the upper right will spin and when it stops the window will be replaced by one similar to the one shown in Figure 11.19.

Work with Results of the Search

Figure 11.19 shows the results of the search. Forty-two documents were found. Each has a score associated with it based on the number of times the words in the phrase were found. The documents should contain the words **treaty**, **international**, and **trade**, or the words **law**, **international**, and **trade**.

Each document found is represented by a hyperlink, in this case an underlined phrase or word. The first one here is GATT 1994, as it has the highest score. You work with these search results as you would with any hyperlinks or Mosaic window. There are a number of possibilities here. You'll probably want to browse through a few of the items listed. As you go from link to link, you might be tempted to follow links in other documents. Be sure to save items if you think they're appropriate or use the **History List** to get back to interesting places once you've left them.

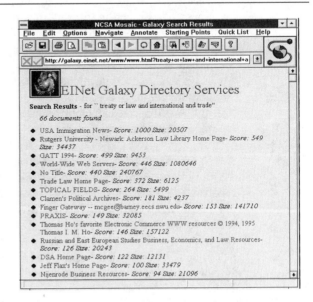

Figure 11.19 Results of Search Using the Phrase
treaty or law and international and trade

To follow any hyperlink, use the mouse to move the pointer to the link and then click on it. That way you can browse through the items selected. Once you've followed a link, you can add it to your hotlist by clicking on the Hotlist icon or clicking on the command menu item **Navigate** and adding it to the hotlist.

The current document can be saved to a file on a disk, printed, or sent by e-mail by clicking on the command menu item **File** and choosing one of these options. In this case you can also click on the disk or printer icon to save the document to a disk or print it.

Leave Mosaic

To leave Mosaic either close the window or choose the **Exit** item after clicking on the **File** menu command.

──────────**End of Example 11.4**──────────

Summary

The World Wide Web, WWW, is a networked hypertext information system. Once you start a client that accesses a WWW server you can access other sources and services on the Internet. The text you retrieve contains links to other information sources or documents. The sources are accessible by WWW, FTP, Telnet, Gopher, WAIS, etc. The information can be text, binary, still images, videos, or audio, or any combination of these. The goal is to provide one nonlinear hypertext or hypermedia interface to the Internet or Web.

You access the World Wide Web by using software called a Web browser. There are several browsers available on the Internet in versions for different computer systems. Two poplar Web browsers are **Lynx**, a full-screen hypertext browser for VT100 terminals, and **Mosaic**, a graphical interface available on X-Windows (on Unix systems), Microsoft Windows, and Macintosh systems. (Netscape Navigator, another very popular browser, is discussed in Appendix B.)**Lynx** was developed at the University of Kansas and **Mosaic** was developed at the National Center for Supercomputing Applications. Both of these browsers are relatively easy to use and install. You can obtain the source for the software from **ftp.cc.ukans.edu** and **ftp.ncsa.uiuc.edu**, respectively.

A Web browser allows you to access documents at many different WWW sites on the Internet. The documents contain links, hyperlinks, to other services and resources. The documents are constructed or written so that the links can be part of sentences or paragraphs, or part of an image. The links represented as text are either in bold or underlined so they stand out from the rest of the document. With a text-based browser such as Lynx you move from link to link by using the arrow keys. Pressing the up and down arrow keys highlights one link after another within a document. Once a link is highlighted you press the right arrow key or Enter to follow the link. In a windows-based or graphical environment you use a mouse to choose a link to follow. Following a link usually takes you to another site or document on the Internet, although it can take you to another portion of the same document or to a file on your local system.

Items, services, and resources are specified by a Uniform Resource Locator or URL. These are used by Web browsers to specify the type of Internet service or protocol to use (such as Gopher,

FTP, Telnet, etc.) and the location of the item. This URL for the list of what's new on the WWW, for example, is

```
http://www.ncsa.uiuc.edu/SDG/Software/Mosaic/Docs/whats-new.html
```

The protocol or service in this case is **http** or hypertext transfer protocol, and a Web browser using it would contact the Internet site **www.ncsa.uiuc.edu** and access a document in **/SDG/ Software/Mosaic/Docs/whats-new.html**. Other examples are in the chapter.

Once you activate a link to a document or item on the WWW, you can print the item, save it to a disk, or send it by e-mail. There are some restrictions on doing these things depending on whether you're using a Web browser on your system or using Telnet to get to another. As you move from link to link you can save interesting or important items as a part of a bookmark list (if you're using Lynx) or as part of a hotlist (if you're using Mosaic). In either case, this is a list of URLs that you can call up any time you're using the browser. The links are saved in the list with the same name as when you added them to the list. You can follow the links in the list in the same way as you would follow any links. Web browsers come with links to on-line help, so you can get help while you're using the browser. They also come with a list of starting points and other interesting links on the WWW.

The World Wide Web project has produced a number of ideas and techniques that have been very popular and have made it much easier to access the wide selection of services and resources on the Internet.

Exercises

For these exercises use Lynx or Mosaic. If Mosaic is available you'll probably like the view better with it.

Getting Some Background on Lynx, Mosaic, and WWW

1. Go to the WWW document "WWW Starting Point, University of Kansas,"
   URL **http://www.cc.ukans.edu/about_lynx/www_start.html**.
   a. Follow the link **Lynx**. Who developed Lynx?
   b. What is the current version?
   c. Go back to "WWW Starting Point, University of Kansas" and follow the link **About the WWW.** What does it say about the World Wide Web? Mail a copy of this document to yourself.

2. Go to the WWW document "NCSA Mosaic Home Page,"
   URL **http:/www.ncsa.uiuc.edu/SDG/Software/Mosaic/NCSAMosaicHome.html**.
   a. You'll read that Mosaic was developed at the National Center for Supercomputing Applications. Follow the link to that site and find a statement describing the location and purpose of NCSA.
   b. Go back to the NCSA Mosaic Home Page. What's in the section **Starting Points?**
   c. The NCSA Demo Document also contains a section titled **Exemplary Applications**. Follow the links to three of them, write them down, and save each in your hotlist or bookmark list.

Browsing and Searching the WWW

3. Access the WWW Virtual Library by Subject on WWW. The URL is **http://www.w3.org/hypertext/DataSources/bySubject/Overview.html**.
   a. What's first in the list of subjects?
   b. What's last?
   c. Follow the link to **Museums** and save it in your bookmark list or hotlist.

4. Using your bookmark list or hotlist, follow the link the **Museums** section of the WWW Virtual Library.
   a. What do you find if you follow the link **Expo Ticket Office**?
   b. Follow the link to **Art Galleries** and list the names of three galleries, each in a different country.
   c. Go to the section dealing with **virtual exhibits**. Print the list of items listed or send the list to a friend by e-mail.

5. Access the WWW Virtual Library by Subject as in Number 3. Follow the link **Astronomy and Astrophysics.** Find the section on observatories and then follow a link to the **Mt. Wilson Observatory**. You'll see a link to **tourist information**; follow the link. What are the directions for getting to the observatory? Send a copy of the directions to yourself by e-mail.

6. What sort of music do you like? Look at the **Music** section of the WWW Virtual Library. Does it have information or links to information about the type you enjoy? Add three to five links to information about your favorite type of music to your bookmark list or hotlist.

7. A well-designed WWW document is **InterLinks**, URL **http://alpha.acast.nova.edu/start.html**. There are lots of interesting things to look at here.
   a. Go to the **New Features** section. What are the five most recent additions? Follow the links to one of them and briefly describe what you've found.
   b. Return to the home page for **InterLinks**, follow the link to **Internet Resources,** and then follow the link to **Listservs**. These are the interest groups we discussed in Chapter 5. Search for interest groups dealing with archaeology. List three that you found. What, if any, are the interest groups dealing with the World Wide Web?

8. Search the WWW using WebCrawler or EINet Galaxy (see Examples 11.3 and 11.4) for information about restaurants. Follow some of the links your search turns up. Which restaurant would you like to visit for dinner? Why?

9. Search the WWW for documents dealing with indoor recreation or outdoor recreation, but not those that contain the word sport. Which ones did you find? Which were most informative about the topics?

Projects

10. Connect to Inter-Links. Its URL is **http://alpha.acast.nova.edu**. Choose the link **Guides and Tutorials** from the home page, and then follow the link **Understanding the Internet** (its URL is **http://www.screen.com/understand/explore.html**).
    a. Follow the link **An Overview** and then follow the link **Internet History**. Read one of the documents. Now print it, save it to a disk, or e-mail it to yourself. Write a paragraph describing what you learned from reading the document.
    b. Go back to the page **Understanding the Internet**, follow the link **Resource Lists and Search Tools**, and then follow the link **Yahoo — A Guide to WWW** (URL **http://www.yahoo.com**). Now select **What's Cool**. Follow the links to the first three items. What did you find at each site?
    c. Now go back to **Understanding the Internet**. Go to the area "Applications" and select **Gopher**. What does that tell you about the development of Gopher? Now select the link **World Wide Web (WWW)** and then follow **Entering the World Wide Web: A Guide to Cyberspace**. What does that say about hypertext and hypermedia?

11. Some folks prefer Gopher and some prefer a Web browser for working on the Internet. Compare the two methods for yourself. Use a Web browser to access the WWW document for the Library of Congress (URL **http://www.loc.gov**) and use Gopher to access the same site (URL **gopher://marvel.loc.gov**). Take some time to browse using both tools. Which do you prefer to use to contact this site? Why?

12. Suppose you wanted to plan a trip to anywhere in the world. Give the steps you would use and the resources you'd access to use the WWW to investigate and make plans for transportation, accommodations, and sites to see.

13. Now it is your turn to become someone who gathers links on a specific topic. Pick a topic you're interested in and put together either a bookmark list or a hotlist of five to ten links on that topic.

Issues
Ethical, Legal,
Security, and Social

It's easy to get excited about using the Internet. It's a vivacious, interesting, and important place to work, learn, do business, and enjoy yourself. The Internet always seems to have something new. You find not only new resources, but better services and programs making the Internet easier to use and more powerful. There's also a great deal of diversity; different cultures, nations, and outlooks are represented on the Internet. All these things make for an exciting environment, but as the Internet gets more popular and the number of users increases it's reasonable to expect rules, regulations, and laws governing its use. You also have to consider the effect the Internet has on our lives, our communities, and society as its use becomes more widespread. In this chapter we'll discuss a few of these issues associated with using the Internet and other networks.

Chapter Overview

The issues we'll cover include:

❑ Privacy and Civil Liberties

❑ Intellectual Property and Copyright

❑ Access: What Type, at What Cost?

❑ Internet Security

It's useful to take a brief look at the history of the Internet, which is related to some of these issues. In the late 1960s the United States Department of Defense through its Advanced Research Projects Agency (ARPA) funded research into the establishment of a decentralized computer network. Some of the researchers saw the advantages of having a network in which computer systems of differing types and operating systems could communicate. They also foresaw the development of a community among the users of this national and international network. The network, named ARPANET, linked researchers at universities and research laboratories. Throughout the 1970s ARPANET was developed further and connections were established with networks in other countries. Usenet originated in 1979, and in the early 1980s other networks in the U.S. and elsewhere were established. The number of sites or hosts on these networks was still relatively small, less than 1000. In the late 1980s the National Science Foundation (U.S.) funded the development of a network (using the Internet protocols) that would connect supercomputer centers in the United States. That network, called NSFNET, allowed colleges and universities to become connected. The number of sites or hosts increased rapidly, passing 10,000 in 1987. In 1989 there were over 100,000 hosts on NSFNET. This time period also saw the development of the Cleveland Free-Net, a community-based network, and the use of NSFNET to relay e-mail from a commercial network.

The funding for the development and operation of ARPANET, NSFNET, and several other networks throughout the world was heavily subsidized by government funds. These networks established *acceptable use policies,* which gave rules for their use, stating what type of activities were allowed on these publicly supported networks. These policies prohibited any purely commercial activities and set the tone for a developing code of network ethics or etiquette. Commercial networks were also being developed, although they could not, under the acceptable use policies, use the transmission links of the public networks. So for some time commercial activity on the major portion of the Internet in the United States was prohibited. However, in 1988 some of these commercial networks reached an agreement with NSFNET to allow e-mail from commercial networks to be carried on NSFNET. That way a user on CompuServe or MCImail could send a message to someone with an Internet address at a public institution such as a college or university. Likewise, messages could be sent from NSFNET to these private networks, but e-mail from one user on a private service couldn't be transported over NSFNET to another user on a private service.

In 1990 ARPANET ceased to exist as an administrative entity and the public network in the U.S. was turned over to NSFNET. The Internet was growing at a remarkable rate and clearly becoming bigger than the public institutions wanted to manage or support. In fact, they never did plan to support it forever. In the early 1990s commercial networks with their own Internet exchanges or gateways were allowed to conduct business on the Internet, and in 1993 the NSF created the InterNIC to provide services such as registration of domain names, directory and database services, and information about Internet services. These services are contracted to the private sector.

This explosive growth of the Internet and the inclusion of commercial networks and services has been accompanied by an astounding increase in the population of Internet users. This increase includes users who are not part of an academic or research community. Many of the new users feel that networks and computers, like a public utility, should be available anywhere, reliable, and easy to use. As the Internet becomes available to a much wider portion of the population, older modes of behavior on the Internet have changed. Commercial activity and advertising are in the process of being established at some sites and newsgroups. Businesses are in the process of determining effective and secure ways of engaging in commerce on the Internet. As the use of the Internet becomes more widespread in the areas of education, research, business, and recreation, issues of security, reliability, ownership, and liability become more important. Many local laws and international agreements are directly applicable to Internet activities. On the other hand, this is a rather new medium using technology that has come into existence *after* many applicable laws were written. New laws and agreements recognizing these changes and differences are being established.

The Internet has grown rapidly from a research project into something that involves millions of people worldwide. Much of the Internet's usefulness comes from the fact that it is shared by users, service providers, and others, in the sense that each depends on the other and needs to support the other. Hopefully, that sort of sharing and respect will continue. Your behavior, your expectations for others, and your activities will make the difference.

Privacy and Civil Liberties

What's reasonable to expect in terms of privacy and civil liberties as they relate to use of the Internet? Your initial response might be that you expect the same protection of your privacy and the same civil liberties—such as freedom of expression, safeguards against the arbitrary exercise of authority, and protection from abusive or offensive actions—on the Internet as you have in your dealings in society. Codes of behavior or rules of etiquette have developed on the Internet over the years. (Some of these are discussed in Chapters 1, 5, and 6.) In some cases laws have been adopted to provide the same level of protection of privacy and guarantees of civil liberties for working with electronic media as with any other media. An important point is that privacy and civil liberties are often defined in terms of their expression or environment. The laws in the United States dealing with privacy and expression in printed form, on paper, needed to be changed to suit electronic communications. Laws need to be modified to take into account new media and new means of transmitting information. Furthermore, the people who develop, act on, and enforce laws need to be informed of the impact of technological changes. We'll cover a few of the important issues related to privacy and civil liberties: e-mail privacy, unwarranted search and seizure, and offensive messages and libel.

E-Mail Privacy

When you send a message by e-mail, the message is broken into packets and the packets are sent out over the Internet. The number of packets depends on the size of the message. Each message has the Internet address of the sender (your address) and the address of the recipient. Packets from a single message may take different routes to the destination, or may take different routes at different times. This works well for the Internet and for you since packets are generally sent through the best path depending on the traffic load on the Internet, the path doesn't depend on certain systems being in operation, and all you have to give is the address of the destination.

The packets making up an e-mail message may pass through many different systems before reaching their destination. This means there may be several places between you and the destination where the packets could be intercepted and examined. Since all the systems have to be able to look at the address of the destination, each system could be able to examine the contents of the message. If you're using a computer system shared by others or if the system at the destination is shared by others, there is usually someone (a *system administrator*) capable of examining all the messages. So, in the absence of codes of ethics or without the protection of law, e-mail could be very public. Needless to say, you shouldn't be reading someone else's e-mail. Most system administrators adopt a code of ethics under which they will not examine e-mail unless they feel it's important to support the system(s) they administer. The truth of the matter is they are generally too busy to bother reading other people's mail.

Electronic Communications Privacy Act. One example of a law to ensure the privacy of e-mail is the Electronic Communications Privacy Act (ECPA) passed in 1986 by Congress. It prohibits anyone from intentionally intercepting, using, and/or disclosing e-mail messages without the sender's permission. The ECPA was passed to protect individuals from having their private messages accessed by government officers or others without legal permission. That bill extended the protections that existed for voice communications to nonvoice communications conveyed through wires or over the airwaves. You can, of course, give your permission for someone to access your e-mail. However, law enforcement officials or others cannot access your e-mail in stored form (on a disk or tape) without a warrant, and electronic transmission of your e-mail can't be intercepted or "tapped" without a court order. The ECPA does allow a system administrator to access users' e-mail on a computer system, if it's necessary for the operation or security of the system. The EPCA then gives the system administrator the responsibility to allow no access to e-mail passing within or through a system without a court order or warrant. She can and indeed should refuse any requests to examine e-mail unless the proper legal steps are followed.

Encryption. When you send a message by e-mail it's often transmitted in the same form you've typed it. Even though it's unethical and illegal for someone else to read it, the message is in a form that's easy to read. This is similar to sending a message written on a postcard through the postal service. One way to avoid this is to use *encryption* to put a message into an unreadable form. The characters in the message can be changed by substitution or scrambling, usually based on some secret code. The message can't be read unless the code and method of encryption are known. The code is called a *key*. Many messages are encoded by a method called *public key encryption*. If you encrypt a message and send it on to someone, that person has to know the key to decode your message. If the key is also sent by e-mail, it might be easy to intercept the key and decode the encrypted message.

With public key encryption there are two keys, one public and the other private. The public key needs to be known. To send a message to a friend, you use her or his *public key* to encrypt the message. Your friend then uses her or his *private key* to decode the message after receiving it. Suppose you want to send an encrypted message to your friend Milo. He tells you his public key; in fact, there's no harm if he tells everybody. You write the message and then encrypt it using Milo's public key. He receives the message and then uses his *private key* to decode it. It doesn't matter who sent the message to Milo as long as it was encrypted with his public key. Also, even if the message is intercepted it can't be read without knowing Milo's private key. It's up to him to keep that secret. Likewise, if he wanted to respond he would use your public key to encrypt the message. You would use your private key to decode it.

You can obtain a version of public key encryption software called PGP, Pretty Good Privacy. It's freely available to individuals, and may be purchased for commercial use. There are some licensing restrictions on the use of the commercial versions for use in the U.S. and Canada. Furthermore, U.S. State Department regulations prohibit the export of some versions of this program to other countries. In fact, current restrictions in the U.S. prohibit the export of most encryption methods, while other countries allow the export of encryption methods and algorithms. Some folks feel very strongly that these policies should be changed for the sake of sharing information and for the sake of allowing common encryption of sensitive and business messages, but others don't agree. To read a complete account of acquiring PGP get the file **getpg.asc** by anonymous FTP. The URL for the file is as follows:

        ftp://ftp.netcom.com/pup/mp/mpj/getpgp.asc

or   **ftp://ftp.mwc.edu/internet.info/encryption/getpgp.asc**.

One issue that needs to be resolved is whether it should be possible for law enforcement or other government officials to decode encrypted messages. Some argue that because of the need to detect criminal action or in the interests of national security, the means to decode any messages should be available to the appropriate authorities. Others argue that individuals have the right to privacy in their communications. In the United States, the issue has been decided in favor of government access in the case of digital telephone communications. The issue hasn't been settled yet for e-mail or other forms of electronic communications.

Unwarranted Search and Seizure

Suppose a person is suspected of having illegal items on a computer system, such as pirated software, credit card numbers, telephone access codes, stolen documents, or proprietary information, and law enforcement official obtain a court order or warrant to search or confiscate the materials. What are reasonable actions?

❑   Is it reasonable to confiscate all the disks connected to or networked to the suspect's computer system?

❑   Is it reasonable to confiscate all the suspect's computer equipment including the main computer, printers, modems, and telephones?

❑   If the items are removed from the premises for searching, how much time should pass before they are returned?

❑   If the suspect's system is part of a bulletin board or e-mail system with messages for other, presumably innocent, persons, should those messages be delivered to the innocent parties?

The answers to these and some related questions depend on the laws governing permissible searches and seizures. The actions taken in cases such as these also depend on how well the technology is understood by the courts and law enforcement officials. For example, the Fourth Amendment to the United States Constitution guards against unreasonable searches and seizures of property. In 1990, all the computer equipment and files of one company, Steve Jackson Games, were confiscated and searched by the U.S. Secret Service. The warrant application released later showed that the company was not suspected of any crime. However, the law enforcement officials, in their fervor to deal with "computer crime," appeared to disregard accepted civil liberties. Some of this was undoubtedly because they were unfamiliar with the technology at that time. A printer or modem, for example, can't store anything once the power is turned off, so there is no need to confiscate those items if one is searching for what might be illegal information. These actions and the related court cases point out the need to keep the officers of the legal system informed and educated regarding the uses and capabilities of technology.

The Electronic Frontier Foundation (EFF) was formed in 1990 to, among other things, bring issues dealing with civil liberties related to computing and telecommunications technology to the attention of the public at large, legislators, and court and law enforcement officials. As a nonprofit public interest organization, EFF maintains, at **eff.org**, collections of files and documents accessible by FTP (**ftp://ftp.eff.org**), Gopher (**gopher://gopher.eff.org**), and a World Wide Web browser such as Lynx or Mosaic (**http://www.eff.org**). EFF also produces a number of publications and other materials, many of which are available on the Internet. They have also provided legal services and opinions in cases similar to the one described above.

Offensive Messages and Libel

Virtually all codes of etiquette, ethics, and policies for acceptable use of networked computer facilities include statements that prohibit sending offensive or abusive messages by e-mail. This is, naturally, similar to the codes of behavior and laws we adhere to in everyday communications. One difference between dealing with this sort of behavior on the Internet and other forms of communication, such as the telephone or postal service, is that no one is in charge of the Internet. It is a cooperative organization. If you're having a problem with someone at your site, talk with your supervisor, their supervisor, or your system administrator about it. If the problem is coming from another site, send e-mail to the address **postmaster@the.other.site**, and talk with the system administrator at your site or your supervisor about it. (You substitute the Internet domain name of the site in question for **the.other.site**.) Individuals have been arrested and prosecuted for making threatening remarks by e-mail.

Portions of the Internet throughout the world were often started as national or military networks. Much of the startup costs were paid by the government. In that environment, advertising was generally prohibited. In the United States, it wasn't until the late 1980s that any commercial traffic was allowed on NSFNET, the primary network and portion of the Internet in the U.S. Because of a relatively recent history of little or no advertising and marketing, efforts in this direction are often met with opposition on the Internet and Usenet. One particularly offensive means of advertising is called *spamming*. When used in this way the term means sending a message to many unrelated newsgroups or interest groups. It's not too hard to do, but it almost always is met with great opposition and feelings of hatred. One way to deal with it is to send a copy of the message and a complaint to **postmaster@the.other.site** (substitute the Internet domain name of the site in question for **the.other.site**). In one case, a company that spammed virtually every Usenet newsgroup eventually lost its Internet access. It wasn't banned from the Internet, but the organization providing Internet access to the company received so many complaints they withdrew Internet services from the company. On some newsgroups it is permissible to advertise. Advertising and commerce is allowed on the Internet, but most users prefer that it be done in clearly identified newsgroups or Internet locations.

Some libel suits have been filed based on postings to Usenet or some other network. One person or company feels that another has slandered them or falsely attempted to damage their reputation. Once again, you would expect the same laws or rules for libel in the society at large to be applied to network communications. That's generally the case, but an interesting issue comes up, centering around whether the company or organization that maintains a computer telecommunication system is responsible for libelous or even illegal messages posted there. In the U.S. the courts have generally drawn an analogy between these systems and a bookstore. The owner of a bookstore is not responsible for the contents of all the books in the store, and likewise, the management of commercial networked systems on the Internet have not been held responsible for all messages on their systems. On the other hand, some commercial network systems claim to screen all messages before they're posted. In that case they may be held accountable for libelous messages. Also, consider that telephone companies aren't held responsible for the speech on their equipment since they fall into the category of a "common carrier." However, television and radio stations are responsible for the content of their broadcasts.

Intellectual Property and Copyright

You know there is a wealth of files, documents, images, and other types of items available on the Internet. They can be viewed, copied, printed, downloaded, saved in a file, or passed on to others. Just because we *can* copy or duplicate information we find on the Internet, is it legal or ethical to do so? Many, if not most, of these items don't exist in a physical form, so perhaps the issues about ownership that depend on something having a physical form don't make sense. The notion of ownership of something, whether it has a physical form, does still make sense as *intellectual property*. There are a number of laws and agreements throughout the world to protect intellectual property rights. The right to copy or duplicate materials can be granted only by the owners of the information. This is called the *copyright*. Many documents on the Internet contain a statement that asserts the document is copyrighted and give permission for distributing the document in an electronic form, provided it isn't sold or made part of some commercial venture. Even items that don't contain these statements are generally protected by the copyright laws of the U.S., the Universal Copyright Convention, or the Berne Union. Most of the copyright conventions or statutes include a provision so that individuals may make copies of portions of a document for short-term use. If information is obtainable on the Internet, and there is no charge to access the information, it often can be shared in an electronic form. That certainly doesn't mean you can copy images or documents and make them available on the Internet, or make copies and share them in a printed form with others. Quite naturally, many of the folks who create or work at providing material available on the Internet, expect to get credit and be paid for their work.

One issue that may need to be resolved is the physical nature of information on the Internet. In most cases it exists on one disk and is viewed in an electronic form. It has no tangible, physical form when it's transmitted. The copyright law in the U.S. states that copyright protection begins once the work is in "fixed form," so the original portion of these works is protected by copyright. The notion of fixed form is much easier to determine with more traditional works that exist in a physical form, such as books, poems, stories, sound recordings, or motion pictures. Naturally, it seems reasonable to say a work is in fixed form when stored on a disk, but can we say the same about material being transmitted through several networks? If the work only existed on a disk, if that was the only way to obtain the work, then it's clear when the work is being copied and who may be copying the disk. On the other hand, if the information can be accessed through the Internet, one may not know if it is being copied and stored. Current laws and conventions were written for works that exist in some definite physical form, and the nature of that form may make it difficult or time-consuming to make unauthorized copies. But information transmitted on the Internet or other networks is very easy to copy. When you copy something in digital form, you make an exact duplicate. Each copy is as good as the original. The ease with which works can be copied and distributed may require something different from current copyright statutes.

Not all cultures have the same attitudes about ownership of information. Some cultures have a long tradition of sharing information and works created by individuals. Other groups feel all information should be free, and so think it's appropriate to make works available only if there is no charge for the use of the works. The worldwide nature of the Internet and other networks requires addressing these cultural differences. When the United States deals with some countries, it may withhold a certain level of trading status if they don't abide by international copyright conventions. On the other hand, a person from a country that has copyright laws or statutes can go to a country where there are no copyright laws and establish a copyright on some works there.

Access: What Type, at What Cost?

Access to the Internet involves at least two concepts discussed in this section. One is the ability to become connected. The other is the nature of the access: one-way, only receiving information, or two-way so everyone can be an information receiver and provider. We'll also cover the topics of providing universal access, Internet connections for everyone, through Free-Nets, community-based networks, and the formation of a National Public Telecomputing Network.

Getting Connected

Getting connected to the Internet is an economic and technical issue. In order to become connected you need to find some site that is already connected and will either allow you to use its facilities or let you connect your system(s) to the Internet. If you're lucky you're part of an organization that foots the bill for the connection, but in this case there probably are expenses you're paying as part of some other general fee such as tuition or student fees, or overhead costs that could find their way to your salary.

If you aren't already connected you or your organization has to make arrangements with an Internet provider—a company that provides connection to the Internet at a cost. Many considerations go into the choice of a provider. Naturally, you're interested in the cost of the service, but the type of service needs to be specified, as it usually determines the cost. This is where technical issues come into play. Items to consider are the speed at which you access the Internet, the types of services provided, the fee structure, and associated costs for access. In some cases access at 9600 bits per second or less is appropriate; this is true if access is text-only. With this type of access you generally get a Unix shell account, which means you have a log-in name on a computer that uses the Unix operating system. If you're going to use Mosaic or some other graphical WWW browser, you'll need a full Internet connection, called an IP connection, to be able to run Internet application programs on your computer system. You'll probably want the connection to be at a higher speed, such as 56,000 per second or greater. With an IP connection the computer you use contains a network card with a cable connected to it, or your computer has SLIP (Serial Line Internet Protocol) access. These types of connections are more expensive than Unix shell accounts. They allow you to work in a graphical environment and more efficiently as well, since you can run Internet applications on your computer. Fee structures vary, and you need to choose what best fits your needs. Some providers charge a flat monthly or yearly fee, regardless of how much the connection is used, and others charge a base rate for a certain amount of hours per month, and then you pay extra if you're connected for a longer period of time. Some sites also allow a fixed amount of storage for files at the flat rate, and then charge extra if more is used. Finally, you need to consider any associated costs such as a start-up fee and communication charges—phone calls, modems, cable access fees, etc. What may turn out to be the most important item is support, someone to provide help and guidance when you or the users on your system need it.

Access: One-Way or Two-Way?

One thing that's made the Internet so lively and engaging is that it is a two-way connection. Anyone can be an information receiver or consumer, and, just as importantly, anyone can be an information provider or producer. Furthermore, there is no central control. It's more like control through cooperation. These facts have political and economic consequences; political because of the freedom it gives—freedom of expression and freedom of discussion. At the present time there is no central control of the Internet, so the topics discussed and ideas expressed range through a variety of subjects. Some of the topics are politically popular and some are not, some support actions of local governments, and others are critical of those actions. But the primary point is that the discussions go on. A network such as the Internet allows the people who use it to organize for or against national or international issues. Issues can be discussed and calls for action disseminated. If the Internet were run or designed in the same way as radio or television— essentially a one-way communication medium—it wouldn't be such a vigorous, interesting medium. The economic implications are that it allows for the startup of businesses whose services include providing information; they can gather, analyze, and provide data. Anyone can be an information provider! Because the business is accessed through the Internet, its customers can be located throughout the world. The most important aspects of the business are the services it provides and the means customers use to access the services. In physical terms, the business doesn't have to be very large. It's the virtual nature of the business that dominates. It's not too far-fetched to think of these as storefront businesses with the Internet as their Main Street.

There are, of course, down sides to this two-way access without central control. This type of access has been used to offend and abuse others, and for uncontrolled marketing. The previous section on "Offensive Messages and Libel" gives some details about this. Remember, the Internet is a cooperative venture—people sharing resources, services, and ideas. There are appropriate places for discussions on all sorts of topics and for both commercial and noncommercial activities.

Universal or Public Access

As the Internet grows in both the number of users and the physical structures needed to support it, it reaches a size sufficient to be called an *infrastructure*. An infrastructure is a basic service or facility necessary to support a community or society. If it is so important to society, then it seems reasonable that everyone should have access to it. This is the case in some parts of the world where access to the Internet is part of a national public utility. Many more nations deal with access to a voice network, the telephone network, in much the same way. As more persons learn about and use the Internet in schools and their work, it's reasonable to provide Internet access to them when they leave those environments. So it may be reasonable to view the Internet,

National Information Infrastructure (NII), or Global Information Infrastructure (GII), as a public utility, the way phone service or cable TV service is currently treated. However, the Internet has unique characteristics that contribute to its usefulness, and those, such as two-way access and little central control, need to be maintained. Viewing the Internet, NII, or GII as a public utility might help to solve some of the problems of public access. It's technologically possible to provide Internet access virtually anywhere. However, there are questions about who will pay for providing the services and how the users will be charged for access. In many countries, the government probably does not have the resources or desire to pay for the installation of equipment and other items for universal access. The Internet appears to be destined to be a private venture with government regulation. So once the decision is made to provide universal access, means of providing the access and paying for the access need to be decided and implemented.

Free-Net

One successful means of providing community access to the Internet is a Free-Net. A Free-Net allows anyone with a computer and modem to obtain a log-in account and have access to the Internet. Membership in a Free-Net is usually either free to members of the local community or within the means of members of the community. The membership fees cover some expenses, but virtually all the computer systems, modems, phone lines, and other necessary materials are supported by donations or gifts. The expertise and personnel needed for these Free-Nets are provided by volunteers or are supported by donations and membership dues. These are not-for-profit organizations, and provide access to the Internet only for community and other noncommercial purposes. They usually allow for posting of community calendars, information about health, cultural and governmental events in the community, Internet e-mail, access to some portions of Usenet, and access to other Internet sites and services. Several Free-Nets exist throughout the world. The first, the Cleveland Free-Net, was established in Cleveland, Ohio, by T. M. Grundner and others as a means to deliver community health information. Some of these Free-Nets are accessible through Telnet, Hytelnet, and by using a WWW browser.

To connect to the Cleveland Free-Net start a Telnet session with **freenet-in-a.cwru.edu** or **129.22.8.51**. Either of the following ought to work:

```
telnet freenet-in-a.cwru.edu
telnet 129.22.8.51
```

No log-in name is required at the Cleveland Free-Net. The first time you access it you enter as a visitor and have the option to become a registered user.

You can also visit this Free-Net by using a WWW browser. The URL is **http://www.nptn.org/CyberStation.Cleveland**. One way to gain access would be to enter

```
lynx http://nptn.org/CyberStation.Cleveland
```

National Public Telecomputing Network

A Free-Net is an example of a community providing its own solutions to some of the problems of Internet access for all its members. In order to address problems on a larger scale and to avoid duplication, some of the folks involved in Free-Nets have formed a National Public Telecomputing Network (NPTN). NPTN consists of a confederation of Free-Nets. The purpose of NPTN is to help establish community networks so free, open access is available to link those systems into a common network, and to supplement the services provided by the local systems with networkwide services and resources. This group can obtain resources and services and supply them to the networks that are part of NPTN. For example, the rulings of the U.S. Supreme Court are made available to the member Free-Nets by NPTN. NPTN is similar to the Corporation for Public Broadcasting and National Public Radio in the United States except that, at the present time, NPTN receives no direct support from the U.S. government.

Internet Security

When you use a computer system connected to the Internet you're able to reach a rich variety of sites and information. By the same token, any system connected to the Internet can be reached in some manner by any of the other computer systems connected to the Internet. Partaking of the material on the Internet also means that you have to be concerned about the security of your computer system and other systems. The reason for the concern about your system is obvious: You don't want unauthorized persons accessing your information or information belonging to others who share your system: you want to protect your system from malicious or unintentional actions that could destroy stored information or halt your system. You don't want others masquerading as you. You need to be concerned about the security of other systems so you can have some faith in the information you retrieve from those systems, and so you can conduct some business transactions. A lack of security results in damage, theft, and, what may be worse in some cases, a lack of confidence or trust.

Maintaining security becomes more important as we use the Internet for commercial transactions or transmitting sensitive data. There is always the chance that new services introduced to the Internet won't be completely tested for security flaws, or that security problems will be discovered. While it's exciting to be at the cutting edge, there's some virtue in not adopting the latest service or the latest version of software until it has been around for a while. This gives the Internet community a chance to discover problems. Several agencies are dedicated to finding, publicizing, and dealing with security problems. One site that does this is maintained by the National Institute of Standards and Technology (NIST), U.S. Department of Commerce. You can use Gopher to access the NIST Computer Security Gopher by pointing your Gopher to **csrc.ncsl.nist.gov**, or you can use a WWW browser to access the NIST Computer Security Resource Clearing House by using the URL **http://first.org/**.

In the section "Privacy and Civil Liberties," above, we mentioned some of the security or privacy problems associated with e-mail. Since information is passed from system to system on the Internet, not always by the same path or through designated secure systems, it can be monitored. Furthermore, you can't always be sure that the address on e-mail hasn't been forged. It appears that an important way to keep transactions secure is using encryption techniques. These are similar to the ones discussed in that same section on privacy and civil liberties.

If you access the Internet by logging into a computer system, your primary defense against intrusion is your password. You need to choose a password that will be difficult to guess. This means choosing a password that's at least six characters long. You'll also want to use a password contain upper- and lowercase letters and some nonalphabetic characters. Additionally, the password shouldn't represent a word and it shouldn't be something that's easy to identify with you such as a phone number, room number, birthdate, or license number. Some bad choices are **Skippy**, **3451234a**, **gloria4me**. Better choices might be **All452on**, **jmr!pmQ7**, or **sHo$7otg**. Naturally, you have to choose something you'll remember. Never write your password down; doing that makes it easy to find. Persons who try to gain unauthorized access to a system are called *crackers*. A cracker will, by some means, get a copy of the password file for a system. The password file contains the names of all the users on a system along with their passwords. (In some cases the permissions on a password file are set so anyone can read it. This is necessary for certain programs to run. Fortunately the passwords are encrypted.) Once a cracker gets a copy of a password file, she will run a program that attempts to guess the encrypted passwords. If a password is an encrypted version of a word, a word in reverse order, or a word with one numeral or punctuation mark, it is not too difficult for the program to decipher it. If a cracker has one password on a system she can gain access to that log-in name and from there possibly go to other portions of the system. In addition to creating a good password, you also need to change it regularly.

You don't need to be paranoid about security, but you do need to be aware of anything that seems suspicious. Report any suspicious activity or changes to your directory or files to your system administrator. The system administrator can often take actions to track down a possible break in security. Be suspicious if you're asked for your password at unusual times. You should be asked for it only when you log in. Never give your password to anyone. If a program changes its behavior in terms of requiring more information from you than it did before, it could be the original program was replaced with another by an unauthorized user. This is called a *trojan horse*, because of the similarity of the program to the classic Greek tale. What appears to be benign could hide some malicious actions or threats.

Two types of programs that cause problems for Internet users are called *worms* or *viruses*. These don't necessarily copy your data or attempt to use your system. However, they can make it difficult or impossible to use your system. A worm is a program that goes from one system to another on the Internet. At each stage it makes multiple copies of itself, each running on a system. This demands system resources and may slow down a system so that nothing else can be done. A virus is a piece of code or instructions that attaches itself to existing programs. Just like a biological virus, a computer virus can't run or exist on its own, but must be part of an executing program. When these programs are run, the added instructions are also executed. Sometimes the virus does nothing more than announce its presence; in other cases the virus erases files from your disk. A virus moves from system to system by being part of an executable program. Be careful of where you get programs. You can obtain a program that scans your system for viruses and also checks programs you load onto your system for known viruses. Use these virus scanning programs to check new programs you load on your system. Also be sure to have a backup copy of your files so they may be restored if they're inadvertently or maliciously erased. Getting documents and images from other sites on the Internet won't bring a virus to your system. It comes only from running programs on your system.

Internet security is very important to many users, as well it should be. We need to make sure that messages are private and that monetary transactions and data sources are secure. Some of these concerns are enforced by laws and acceptable codes of conduct. A good document to read about security and privacy is "Identity, Privacy, and Anonymity on the Internet," by L. Detweiler.

It's available by anonymous FTP in three parts from **rtfm.mit.edu** in the directory **/pub/ usenet/news.answers/net-privacy**. To see some papers dealing with "Electronic Payment and Privacy" use a WWW browser with the URL **http://www.research.att.com**. These are also available by anonymous FTP to **research.att.com** in the directory **/dist/anoncc**.

Summary

The Internet has had a tradition of sharing. This includes sharing data, sharing services, exchanging e-mail, having free and generally open discussions, and bringing together ideas and opinions from a diverse population. The rules for behavior, policies for acceptable use, and laws pertaining to activities on the Internet have developed over time. In some cases policies and laws have been adopted from other media, and in other cases the unique qualities of the Internet and electronic communications have been taken into account in establishing of laws and policies.

During the transmission of information on the Internet, the information or communication is divided into packets of bytes (characters) that are sent by from one system to another. The packets may pass through several different systems, may take different routes to arrive at a destination, and transmissions from one site to another may take different routes at different times. This opens the possibility for intercepting and examining e-mail or other transmissions. Be careful about what you say in e-mail, and think about using encryption techniques so the e-mail can be read only by the recipient. Laws such as the Electronic Communications Privacy Act (ECPA) have been adopted in some countries to protect and insure the privacy of electronic communications. The ECPA makes it illegal to intercept or read other people's e-mail, and requires government officials to obtain a warrant or court order before searching, seizing, or intercepting electronic communications. Laws regulating slander, libel, threats, and harassment deal with electronic communications as well. The Internet has grown very rapidly with a sharp increase in the number of users and a change in the makeup of that population. It continues to become more inclusive, representing users outside of the research and academic area. This causes some strains between some groups of users and others whose actions seem contrary to past acceptable modes of behavior. For example, in the past the Internet was almost free of commercial transactions and now commercial uses are condoned and encouraged.

In most cases the information available on the Internet is the intellectual property of someone or some organization and is protected by copyright laws. Check to see if there are any copyright notices on information. Much of it can be shared in an electronic form, provided the author is given credit and it's not modified. Problems arise because it's so easy to make copies of information available in electronic form. There are very few, if any, ways to know whether a copy has been made. This issue needs to be resolved. Some suggest using methods of encryption to protect against unauthorized copying or dissemination.

Access to the Internet or any sort of national or international network involves economic, technical, and political issues. For an individual or organization the issues are generally economic and technical. One needs to decide the type of Internet service needed (technical issue) and balance that with what is affordable (economic issue). The political issues generally arise when one thinks about giving communitywide or universal access to the Internet. Is it the government's responsibility to provide this service? Is Internet access as important as other public/private utilities? Some communities have begun Free-Nets, which give Internet and community network access to anyone with a computer and a modem. The National Public Telecomputing Network is a confederation of community networks.

Internet security is an important issue for a variety of reasons, including an individual's desire for privacy, the increased use of the Internet for commercial transactions, and the need to maintain the integrity of data. If you access the Internet by logging into a computer system, you need to take care to choose a password that will be difficult to guess. Furthermore, you should notice and report any unusual circumstances or modifications.

The Internet is an important and vivacious place to learn, work, and enjoy yourself. Some of its strengths have come from the diversity in the user population, because there is no central control, and because there is two-way access. If you can receive information, you can produce information! It's been relatively free of regulation, but not without codes of ethics, acceptable use policies, and laws to make it a reasonable and safe place for a variety of activities. As the Internet grows and changes it needs to maintain its sources of strength and vitality. Whether it will maintain its character will depend on the concerns and actions of its users. Your behavior, your expectations for others, and your activities will make the difference.

Exercises

These exercises are all small projects. They're meant to give you some focus in thinking about the issues raised in this chapter, and to involve you in accessing some Internet sites and resources appropriate to the topics in this chapter.

Acceptable Use Policies

1. a. Does your organization have a statement of policies or procedures for acceptable use of the Internet?
    b. If your answer to part a was yes, get a copy of that policy and read it. Which of the policies would you recommend be changed? Explain your answer.
    c. If your organization doesn't have a policy, then list three or more items you think ought to be in such a policy.

2. Several sites on the Internet have copies of acceptable use policies. You can browse or retrieve these policies by anonymous FTP to **nic.merit.edu** and looking in the directory **acceptable.use.policies** (URL **ftp://nic.merit.edu/acceptable.use.policies**), by using anonymous FTP to **ftp.unm.edu** and looking in the directory ethics (URL **ftp://ftp.umn.edu/ethics**), or by pointing your gopher to **gopher.internic.net** and first choosing **Internic Data and Directory Services**, then choosing **Additional Internet Resource Information**, and finally choosing **Internet Service Provider Policies and Procedures**. Retrieve or browse two of those policies.
    a. How do these policies compare with each other?
    b. What changes would you recommend making to either of the policy statements?

3. Retrieve a copy of "Ethics and the Internet," RFC 1087, URL: **ftp://ds.internic.net/rfc/rfc1087.txt**. It was written in 1989. What should be changed or added to it to make it appropriate for today's Internet?

4. Retrieve a copy of "User Guidelines and Net Etiquette," by Arlene Rinaldi. You'll see it contains guidelines for working with several types of Internet services. Pick one service you've worked with and compare the guidelines in that document with your behavior. You can retrieve the guide by anonymous FTP to **ftp.lib.berkeley.edu** and retrieving the file **netiquette.txt** from the directory **pub/net.training/FAU/**. If you prefer to use Gopher, point your gopher to **gopher.ic.mankato.mn.us**, choose the item **Information Booth**, and then choose **Netiquette Explained**, or point your gopher to **gopher.mwc.edu**, choose **The Internet**, and then choose **User Guidelines and Netiquette**. The Guide is available through the WWW with the URL **http://www.fau.edu/rinaldi/net/index.htm**.

Organizations

5. Use Gopher (**gopher gopher.eff.org**) or a WWW browser (**http://www.eff.org**) to look at the on-line resources available from the Electronic Frontier Foundation.
   a. Describe the main menu (if you used Gopher) or the home page (if you're using a WWW browser) for the EFF.
   b. The main menu for the Gopher server has an entry listing similar organizations. Write down the names of three in the United States and three elsewhere. You can reach the Gopher menu by following a link from EFF's home page if you used a WWW browser.
   c. See what you can find out about one of those organizations listed in part b. Follow a link or choose an item from the Gopher menu for a similar organization in a country different from your own. Determine the mission and aims of that organization.

6. Once again, connect to the EFF Gopher server or the EFF home page on the WWW. Pick a topic in the area of privacy, civil liberties, or legislation. Using the Internet resources available through that site write a short paper about any of those topics.

7. The EFF and Computer Professionals for Social Responsibility (CPSR) both have resources available through Gopher. To access the CPSR site point your gopher to **gopher.cpsr.org**.
   a. Retrieve or browse statements for each organization that gives its mission and aims. Write a brief summary, at most one page, comparing the two organizations and giving differences between the two.
   b. If you were to join one, which would it be? Explain.

Privacy and Security

8. Retrieve "Identity, Privacy, and Anonymity on the Internet," by L. Detweiler, from one of the sites mentioned in the text. Using the information in that document, provide answers to the following.
   a. What was the Steve Jackson Games case?
   b. List the names and give a short description of three to five Usenet newsgroups dealing with privacy.
   c. What are cypherpunks?

9. Use a WWW browser to connect to the NIST Computer Security Resource Clearing House, using the URL **http://first.org/**. Give answers to the following based on information you find there.

     a. What does FIRST stand for?

     b. What is Virus-L and what information about computer viruses is at the site?

     c. You'll see an entry that lists other computer security servers. Follow that link and list the names of the other servers you find. Which are in the United States? Which are in other countries?

10.   The text mentions some documents available at **research.att.com** dealing with electronic payment and privacy.

     a. What are the names of those documents?

     b. Retrieve one of those documents and write a brief summary.

Free-Nets and NPTN

11.   Use Hytelnet or some other method to find ways to access a Free-Net by using Telnet. (One is mentioned in this chapter.) Explore the Free-Net as a visitor. Describe the organization of the Free-Net and some of the services available to members. What is the membership fee? Describe why you would or would not pay a membership fee to join a Free-Net.

12.   The site **nptn.org** on the Internet makes information available about the National Public Telecomputing Network. You can contact it by anonymous FTP to **ntpn.org**. Using either FTP or a WWW browser with URL **ftp://nptn.org**, connect to that site and find information that gives the goals and mission of NPTN.

     a. List the name of the files or documents you think are most appropriate.

     b. Write a brief summary stating the mission and goals of NPTN.

13.   The document "Information Sources: The Internet and Computer-Mediated Communication" by John December (URL **http://www.rpi.edu/Internet/Guides/decemj/icmc**) contains a section titled "Culture" with references to information on community networking.

     a. Use what you find by working with that document to give the names of at least five Free-Nets from at least two countries.

     b. The document also lists some virtual communities. Pick one and explore it. Write a short paper describing the virtual community.

Using Unix

Guide to Using Unix

If you're using a computer with Unix as an operating system, this guide is detailed enough to get you started and keep you going. To learn more ask a local expert, get a good book about Unix, and check some of the Internet sources for information and tutorials about Unix listed at the end of this appendix.

Brief Definition of an Operating System

An operating system is the software that controls, shares, and manages the resources such as disks, memory, processors, and network connections of a computer system. It also maintains the file system so users can save information in files with security and confidence, and copy, print, and delete files. What you can do with a computer system is to a large degree determined by the operating system. The commands you use and the form of those commands depends on the operating system.

Brief Overview of Unix

Unix originated with work by Ken Thompson at Bell Labs in the late 1960s. The term "Unix" isn't an abbreviation or an acronym; it's the name of the operating system. (Just like Trigger is the name of Roy Rogers' horse.) For some time it was used mostly in academic and research settings, but now it's used in virtually every type of organization. From a technical point of view, one of

Unix's strong points is its simplicity. From a user's point of view, particularly a new user, its simplicity is a drawback. Many of the commands are cryptic and there's little on-line help on many Unix systems.

Unix is a multiuser, multitasking operating system. That means it can be used by several users at the same time, and there can be several programs running at once. The operating system has the job of making sure resources are shared among the users, an individual's files and transactions are kept relatively secure, and each user has the illusion the computer is dedicated to his tasks.

Reasons for Knowing How to Use Unix

There are several reasons for learning Unix. Many Internet services were developed on and for Unix computer systems. Some of the concepts of the organization of files and directories on Unix systems have made their way into Internet services. Most of the computers accessible on the Internet use the Unix operating system. Finally, your individual access to the Internet may be through a system that uses Unix or one of its variations as an operating system.

Form of Unix Commands

Unix interprets uppercase and lowercase letters differently. The name of a file, for example, depends on the letters and the case of the letters. The name **greatone** is different from **Greatone**, **GreatOne**, or **GREATONE**. These could be the names of four different files. Also, most Unix commands are in lowercase.

Spaces are used to separate a command from its arguments or options. The number of spaces doesn't matter, but at least one space is necessary. For example, to give the command to change to a directory named Mail you could use either of the following:

```
cd Mail
cd      Mail
```

Most commands have the form of the name of the command followed by zero or more arguments or they're in the form of the name of the command followed by options (these are preceded by a dash (-), and then zero or more arguments. For example, the command to erase or remove a file is **rm**. Giving the command

```
rm greatone
```

will delete the file (usually), no questions asked. Using the option **-i** prompts the user for approval before deleting the file, as in

```
rm -i greatone
greatone: ? (y/n)
```

Type **y** to delete it and any other character to keep it.

Logging On

A computer with the Unix operating system can support several users. To start a session you have to log on, giving your user name or log-in name and a password. Each user has a different user name and a password. This allows different users to have separate files, which only they can access and work with.

Your log-in name and initial password are assigned by a system administrator, a person in charge of seeing that the system operates properly. A log-in name is at most eight characters long. Remember that Unix differentiates between upper- and lowercase, so a user name of **jpdoe** is different from **jpDoe** or **JPDoe**.

You can log on when you see the prompt:

```
login:
```

Type your log-in name, usually all in lowercase, with no spaces between characters, and press Enter. Then you'll see the prompt:

```
Password:
```

Type your password, again making sure the case of the letters is correct, and press Enter. Your password won't show up as you type it. It's supposed to be secret!

What you see next depends how your system is set up. Some messages will probably be displayed on the screen. Take time to read them, as they usually contain some information about the system you're using.

Terminal Type

After the initial messages are displayed, again depending on your system, you'll see a prompt or message about the type of terminal you're using. Some of the commands or programs will take your input from and display results on various portions of the screen. Unix needs to know the type of terminal you're using to do that properly. You might see a prompt like

```
TERM = (vt100)
```

The type of terminal expected is a VT100. If you're using that type of terminal or using software that makes your terminal or PC emulate a VT100 terminal, press Enter. Otherwise type in the type of terminal you're using and then press Enter. If things appear normal on the screen and programs work properly, everything is OK. If you see unusual characters on the screen then you need to be sure you have the right terminal type. Check to be sure you're using the correct terminal type. If you're having problems make sure your terminal or PC is set properly or ask for help.

Many Unix systems, especially ones you contact on the Internet, expect you to be using a VT100 type terminal. You may be accessing these systems from your own computer, so you need to use software for this which emulates a VT100. By *emulate*, we mean the software has to make your terminal or PC act just as if it were a VT100.

Figure A.1 is a sample log-in session. The user name is **mozart**, the password is (we can't tell; it's a secret!), and we'll use a terminal type of vt100.

```
login: mozart
Password:

************************************************************************
    Welcome to our computer system!
```

```
>>> Special Announcement
    This system will not be available on Friday from 8:00AM to 1:00 PM.
    It's time for maintenance. Please plan accordingly.
*********************************************************************
TERM = (vt100)



You have mail.


$
```

Figure A.1   Logging In to a Unix System

In Figure A.1 the user is notified there is e-mail. The **$** at the bottom of the figure is the shell prompt. In this case it's a **$** and in some cases, depending on what shell is being used, it will be a **%**. The shell is a program run by the operating system to interpret the commands typed in. It will be discussed in a little more detail later.

If the log-in name or the password isn't typed correctly, you won't be able to log in. The prompt for the password appears even if the user name isn't typed correctly.

Logging Off

You log out or log off a Unix system to end your session. To do this type

```
exit
```

and press Enter. If you're accessing the Unix system through a modem you may also have to hang up the modem; it's the same as hanging up after you're done talking on a telephone. In many cases this means typing Alt-H; hold down the key marked Alt, press the H key, and release the keys. In other cases you choose Hang-up from a menu or dialog box.

It's important to log out. Otherwise, another person may access your information (files, directories, e-mail, etc.) if they access the Unix system through the same terminal or telephone line.

Your Password

It's important to keep your password a secret and to have a password that isn't easily guessed. If someone else knows your password, that person has access to your information, including files, directories, and e-mail. You may think you don't have anything that needs to be kept secure, but you also guard against unauthorized users accessing the Unix computer system by using the password. This is especially important if the computer system is connected to the Internet, since persons from anywhere in the world may gain access.

A good password is one that's at least six characters long, one you'll remember without having to write it down, and one that's difficult to guess. This means choosing one that isn't a common word, isn't the name of a friend or pet, and isn't your address or birthdate. While your log-in name and most commands contain all lowercase letters, the password can and should contain both upper- and lowercase characters, and some nonalphabetic characters such as numerals or punctuation symbols. (Be careful not to use @ or # in your password as these have special meanings to some Unix systems.) Some examples of good passwords are **tuM67G!** or **Fp89ow$t**.

Use the command **passwd** to change your password. It's a good idea to change it regularly. Just be sure you remember what you chose. No one, not even a system administrator, can look up your password. At a shell prompt (**$** or **%**) type:

```
passwd
```

and press Enter. You'll be prompted for your current password, and then you'll have to type in the new password twice.

Unix Shells

A *shell* is a program run by the operating system to interpret your commands. When you type a command, the shell interprets it and then starts the programs necessary to execute your command. *Interpret* means passing options and arguments (if there are any) to the program that executes the command, and could also mean expanding *wildcard* symbols so the matching file names are created. For example, the command **ls** is used to list the names of the files in your current directory. Type **ls** and press Enter (using the command without options or arguments) and you'll see a list of file names. Type **ls -t** and press Enter (using the command with the **-t** option) and the names will be listed sorted by the time they were last modified. Type **ls -t *txt** and press Enter (using the command with the **-t** option and the * "wildcard" character) and the list will contain the names of all the files whose names end with the characters **txt** sorted by the time they were last modified. File names listed might include ones like **readme.txt** or **goodtxt**. The shell creates the list by finding all the files in your directory whose names end with **txt**.

The Bourne shell, the Korn shell, and the C shell are the three most common shells. They each have their own advantages. A **$** is the shell prompt for the Bourne or Korn shell, and a **%** is the shell prompt for the C shell. Your system is ready to accept commands or start Internet services when you see the shell prompt. For the remainder of this appendix we'll use the **$** as the shell prompt.

Control Characters

In some cases you can give a command to Unix using *control characters* or *control commands*. For example, you can use Ctrl-H to backspace. This means to hold down the key labeled Ctrl, press the H key, and then release them. You'll often see a control character like Ctrl-H written as **^H**; the character **^** is shorthand for Ctrl.

Table A.1 is a list of commonly used control characters.

Purpose	Control Character	Explanation
Erase or backspace	Ctrl-H	Backspace when typing in a command or other input.
Pause display, scrolling	Ctrl-S	Pause a screen display or list that's scrolling down a screen.
Resume scrolling	Ctrl-Q	Resume the action paused with Ctrl-S

Interrupt or break	Ctrl-C	Interrupt a running program.
Kill	Ctrl-U	Ignore a command, use before pressing Enter.
End of file, logout	Ctrl-D	Designates end-of-file, or can be used to logout.

Table A.1   Commonly Used Control Characters

Ctrl-S and Ctrl-Q are useful to go through a long list or file that's being displayed on a screen. Use Ctrl-C when you need to break out of or quit a program that isn't working the way you think it should, or when you can't figure out another way to quit a program. Use Ctrl-U when you've made a mistake typing a command and you want what you've typed thrown away or ignored; it must be used before Enter is pressed. Use Ctrl-D to mark the end of a file during input. You'll use this to quit some programs or commands that display a file on the screen. It can also be used, in many cases, to log out of a Unix session.

Files

A file is a collection of information, and each file has a name. With Unix every file is a sequence of bytes (characters). The Unix commands for basic file operations are the same regardless of what the file contains—text, programs, computer instructions, images, spreadsheets, word processor documents, etc.

File Names. Any character is allowed in a file name, but it's a good idea to stick with letters, numerals, and common punctuation symbols. Since the character - (a dash or hyphen) is used to give an option to a command, *don't* use - as the first character in a file name. Also, since Unix shells use * and ? as wildcard characters, they shouldn't be used. You can create a file name with a space in it, but since the spaces are used to separate commands, options, and file names, it's best not to use a space. Most Unix systems now allow file names to be as long as 255 characters. That's too long to be practical, but you're not limited to 8 or 12 characters, as in some operating systems such as MS-DOS.

Commands

Here are some commands for working with files. The commands are typed at the shell prompt (**$** or **%**), and nothing happens until you press Enter.

Copy a file: **cp**   Example: **cp report.doc final-copy**

You get two exact copies of the file when you use **cp**. If the second name refers to a file that already exists, it will be replaced by the copy; no warning is given. The command **cp** always has to be followed by at least two names. The first is the *source*, what will be copied, and the second names the *destination*, where the copy will go. The general form of the command is

```
cp source  destination
```

Rename a file: **mv**   Example: **mv report.doc final-report**

There is only one copy of the file after **mv** is executed. As with **cp**, you aren't warned if a file with the second name already exists. The command **mv** always has to be followed by at least two names. The first is the source, the original name for the file, and the second gives the new name. The general form of the command is

```
mv old-name  new-name
```

Delete or Erase a file: **rm**   Example: **rm old_news**

Once a file is deleted, it's gone! If the file was saved on a backup disk or tape, or if the **rm** command has been modified, the file may be restored. However, it can't be brought back as easily as in some other operating systems. Also, you aren't asked whether you really mean to delete a file, so be careful. If you want to be asked whether to delete the file use the **-i** option with the commands, as in **rm -i old_news**. The general form of the command is

```
rm file-name
```

Display a file one screen at a time: **more**   Example: **more Read.me**
                                    pg   Example: **pg Read.me**

Both commands, **more** and **pg**, will display a file one screen at a time. After displaying one screen, they both pause waiting for a user to type a command. When using **more**, press the spacebar to see the next screen, Enter to see the next line, and **q** to quit. With **pg** press Enter to see the next screen, - to see the previous screen, and **q** to quit. Press **h** to see a list of all options when using either command. Many Internet services use either **pg** or **more** to show files on the screen.

Print a file: **lp**   Example: **lp Getting-connected**
              lpr   Example: **lpr Getting-connected**

Some Unix system use the command **lp** to print a file and some use **lpr**. The simplest form of this command is

```
lp file-name
lpr file-name
```

Listing the names of files: **ls**   Example: **ls**

Use the command **ls** to list the names of the files in the current directory. This command has a number of options you may find useful. **ls -l** list the names of the files, their sizes, and when they were last modified. Some files, those whose names start with a period, aren't listed by **ls**. To list the names of *all* files use **ls -a**.

Wildcard Characters

The shell will create a list of names of files to be used with a command when the characters * and **?** appear in a file name. The * is used to match any sequence of characters and **?** is used for a single character. For example, the command

```
$ lp *txt
```

will print all files in the current directory whose names end with the characters **txt**. The command

```
$ rm chapter?.notes
```

will delete all the files whose name starts with the word **chapter**, is followed by a single character, which is followed by the characters **.notes**. This includes **chapter1.notes** and **chapterA.notes**, but doesn't include **chapter10.notes**.

```
$ ls -l Internet*
```

This will list the name, size, date of last change, and other information of every file in the current directory whose name begins with the word *Internet*.

Using these characters is very helpful for dealing with groups of files. The copy command (**cp**) allows you to copy several files to a directory. (Directories are discussed in the next section.) To copy all the files with the word **notes** anywhere in their name to a directory named **my-notes**, give the command

```
$ cp *notes* my-notes
```

But, please *be careful* using * with the command **rm**. Several files can be deleted at once by typing **rm** followed by the names of the files. For example, **rm *notes*** will delete all the files copied with the previous command. If, by mistake, a space was accidentally typed so the command was **rm *notes ***, then first all the files whose names ended with **notes** are deleted and then all the files in the directory are deleted. * by itself gives a list of all the files in a directory.

Editing a Text File

A text file is a file of plain characters, ones you can type from the keyboard and see displayed on a screen. There isn't any character formatting such as underlining, boldface, or various fonts. A text editor is used to create a text file or modify an existing one.

Unix systems generally have several text editors available. Three you're likely to find are *vi*, *emacs*, and *pico*. Vi is on all Unix systems, and the other two need to be installed. Emacs is very common, and pico is the editor used with the Pine e-mail program. They all have lots of features and can't be covered here in detail. Check with your system administrator or some other users for detailed information about the text editors available to you. To create a new file, type the name of the editor—vi, emacs, or pico—and press Enter. To edit an existing file, type the name of the editor, a space, and then the name of the file. The following three lines show how to start editing a file named **README** with each of the editors:

```
$ vi README
$ emacs README
$ pico README
```

They are all full-screen editors, and emacs and pico are generally easier to use than vi.

Vi is the oldest of the three and operates in two modes—input and command mode. Characters are typed into a file when in input mode, and commands such as deleting characters, saving your work to a file, and quitting vi are done in command mode. Vi starts in command mode. Press **i** to go to input mode and then type the characters into the file. To go to command mode press Esc. To save your editing in a file press **:w**, space, type a file name, and then press Enter. To quit a vi session type **:q** or **:wq**. All these "colon" commands need to be given in command mode. Remember to press Esc to get to command mode.

The other two, emacs and pico, are always in input mode—what you type is put into the file— unless you use control characters or others to give commands. To end an emacs editing session press **^X^C** (Ctrl-X followed by Ctrl-C); you'll be asked if you want to save your work in a file. All the commands to use with pico are at the bottom of the screen during an editing session. To end a pico session press **^G** (Ctrl-G).

Directories

Unix keeps files arranged in directories. Each user has his or her own directory, called a log-in or home directory, for his or her files. One directory can hold files and other directories, each one of those directories can hold files and directories, and so on. The structure of all the directories is hierarchical or treelike. There is one directory signified by a slash, /, called the root directory. All other directories are contained in the root directory. Suppose a user's log-in name is **glautry**. Her home directory could be contained in a directory named **users**, which is contained in the directory /. Another way to say this is that the directory **glautry** is a subdirectory of the directory **users**, which is a subdirectory of the root.

Slashes are used to give the full or absolute path name of a file or directory. For example, suppose a file named **important.news** belongs to glautry and is in her home directory. The absolute path name of that file is **/users/glautry/important.news**. She could refer to the file by its relative path name (without all the slashes) as just **important.news**.

As you use the Internet you may find that some directories are created by the programs and services you use to store saved messages or files. On many Unix systems a directory named **Mail** is created by Pine (and e-mail program) as a subdirectory of your home directory. Saved Usenet articles are typically kept in a subdirectory named **News**.

Using commands to change directories, users can move from one directory to another. Unix always keeps track of your current or working directory. Because of the hierarchical or tree structure of directories each directory (except for the root directory) has another one above it, called the parent directory. Two periods or dots (**..**) is the symbolic name Unix uses for the parent directory, and one dot (**.**) can always be used to represent the current directory.

Some of the commands for working with files allow you to use a directory as an argument. Here are some examples, assuming the user **glautry** is in her log-in directory:

Copy the file **jaustin** to the subdirectory named **Mail**:

```
$ cp jaustin Mail
```

List the contents of the directory named **News**:

```
$ ls News
```

Rename or move a file named **good.offer** to the subdirectory named **Mail**:

```
$ mv good.offer Mail
```

Copy the file **getting-started** from the **News** subdirectory to the current directory:

```
$ cp News/getting-started .
```

Here are some commands to use with directories:

Show the Name of the Current Directory: **pwd**   Example: **pwd**

The command **pwd**, short for print working directory, displays the name of the current directory. Unix always keeps track of the current directory and the command is useful if you're not sure of the current directory.

Change to a Directory: **cd**   Example: **cd another-directory**

You use the command **cd** to change to another directory. Use either the absolute or relative path name for the directory. Here are some examples:

```
$ cd /users/glautry/Mail
```

Changes, from anywhere in the file system, the current directory to the subdirectory named **Mail** in the **directory /users/glautry**.

```
$ cd Mail
```

Changes the current or working directory from the current directory to a subdirectory named **Mail**. Mail *must* be a subdirectory of the current directory.

```
$ cd ..
```

Changes directories to the parent of the current directory. If the current directory were **/users/glautry/Mail** then after giving the command **cd ..** the current directory would be **/users/glautry**.

List the Names of the Files in a Directory: **ls**   Example: **ls images**

Giving the command **ls** by itself lists the names of the files in the current directory. Including the name of a directory lists the names of the files in that directory. As given above, the command **ls images** would list the names of the files in the directory named **images** (which is assumed to be a subdirectory of the current directory).

Create a Directory: **mkdir**   Example: **mkdir images**

This creates a directory named **images** as a subdirectory of the current directory. The command can also be used with path names as in **mkdir News/images**, which creates a directory named images as a subdirectory of the directory named **News**.

Delete or Remove a Directory: **rmdir**   Example: **rmdir images**
rm -r   Example: **rm -r images**

Use **rmdir** to delete a directory that's empty, has no files in it. Use **rm** with the option **-r** (**rm -r**) to remove or delete a directory that has files in it. The example above shows removing or deleting a directory named **images** for the current directory.

Getting Help

Explanations of all Unix commands are kept on-line. These explanations are called *man pages* since they are pages from the Unix manuals and since you use the command **man** to display these pages on the screen. They give a complete explanation of using a command, include all the options to use, and sometimes include examples. For example, to view the man pages for the command cp give the following command:

```
$ man cp
```

The information will be displayed one screen at a time. Press the spacebar to see the screen, Enter to see the next line, and **q** to quit.

There are a couple of drawbacks to using the man pages to learn about using Unix. The man pages are generally written for an experienced user and are meant to be used as a reference. Also, if you don't know the name of a command you can't use man directly to get information. However, you can use the man command with the **-k** option to get a list of the commands related to a topic. For example, the command

```
$ man -k print
```

will list the commands that have the word *print* in their name or in a brief, on-line description of each command.

Uploading and Downloading a File

If you access a Unix computer system by using a modem to dial a phone number, you will occasionally need to transfer files between your personal computer (the one you're using) and the Unix computer system. Moving a file from your computer to the Unix computer is known as *uploading* a file. Moving a file from the Unix system to your computer is known as *downloading* a file. The two computers need to communicate with each other to transfer files. (This is different from typing characters on your keyboard and having them appear on the screen.) The two computers communicate through the use of *protocols*, which are rules for the file transfer or communication. The protocols are set in motion by giving a command on the Unix system and by your using a similar program on your personal computer.

Two common programs (protocols) used for uploading and downloading files are *kermit* and *zmodem*. The exact commands and steps to follow depend on the software you're using on your personal computer to connect to and communicate with the Unix system, but we'll give some guidelines here.

To upload a file using kermit from your computer to the Unix computer give the command:

```
$ kermit -ir
```

on the Unix system. The option **-ir** indicates to the Unix system that it will have to run the kermit program (protocol), be ready to receive a file, and the file can be either text or another format.

To upload a file using zmodem from your computer to the Unix computer give the command:

```
$ rz
```

on the Unix system.

Now you have to give the command on your personal computer to transfer a file. That could mean pressing a special key and then typing the name of the file to upload, or choosing an action (such as transfer a file) from a command or pull-down menu. Once you've done what needs to be done on your local system, the file will be transferred (uploaded) to the Unix system. Its name on the Unix system will be the same as on your personal computer, and it will be placed in the current directory.

To download a file using kermit from the Unix computer to your personal computer give the command:

```
$ kermit -is name-of-file
```

where *name-of-file* is the name of the file you want to download. The option **-is** tells the Unix system to run the kermit program (protocol) and to send the file named **name-of-file**. Now you have to give the command on your personal computer to receive a file. That could mean pressing a special key or choosing an action (such as receive a file) from a command or pull-down menu. Once you've done what needs to be done on your local system, the file will be downloaded to your local system. The file will be placed in the directory on your local system. Which directory depends on how the communications software on the personal computer has been set up.

To download a file using zmodem from the Unix computer to your personal computer give the command:

```
$ sz name-of-file
```

where **name-of-file** is the name of the file you want to download. This will automatically start a file transfer, a download, from the Unix system to your personal computer. The file will be placed in the directory on your local system. Which directory depends on how the communications software on the personal computer has been set up.

Internet Resources for Unix

Many sites on the Internet have files and documents that deal with using the Unix operating system. There are also some Usenet newsgroups dedicated to different aspects of Unix. Here are a few Internet resources you might want to use.

Usenet Newsgroups

There are several newsgroups in the **comp.unix** hierarchy. Some are for beginners and some are for experts. Certain newsgroups deal with specific aspects of Unix, and some are dedicated to particular versions of Unix. Here's a short list:

comp.unix.admin	**comp.unix.misc**
comp.unix.aix	**comp.unix.programmer**
comp.unix.aux	**comp.unix.questions**
comp.unix.bsd	**comp.unix.shell**
comp.unix.internals	**comp.unix.wizards**

Anonymous FTP sites

ftp://ava.bcc.orst.edu/pub/BCC/UNIX_help/

A collection of documents for new and occasional users of Unix.

ftp://info.asu.edu/pub/write-ups/u/unixmisc/

A collection of information and tips on using Unix, other types of computer systems, and commands.

ftp://rtfm.mit.edu/pub/usenet/comp.answers/unix-faq

Several directories and files taken from periodic postings on Usenet. Look in the directory **faq** for the extensive Frequently Asked Questions about Unix. The file **ftp://pub/usenet/ comp.answers/unix-faq/unix/intro** has important information about working with the newsgroup **comp.unix.questions**.

ftp://ftp.mwc.edu/pub/unix

A collection of short documents about Unix, vi, emacs, and pico.

Gopher Sites

gopher.bcc.orst.edu
Choose the item **pub** from the main menu, then **BCC**, and finally **UNIX_Help**.

URL: **gopher://gopher.bcc.orst.edu:70/00/pub/BCC/ UNIX_help/Commands_and_On_Line_Help**

mercury.forest.umn.edu.

Choose **College of Natural Resources (CNR) Computer Help/** from the main menu, then choose **Documents that help (by OS)/,** and finally choose **UNIX/.**
URL: **gopher://mercury.forestry.umn.edu:70/11/CNRCH/ Documents%20that%20help%20%28by%20OS%29/UNIX**

riceinfo.rice.edu
Choose **Computer Information** from the main menu and then choose **Unix Information**.
URL: **gopher://riceinfo.rice.edu:70/11/Computer/Unix/.**

WWW Documents

Unix Help for Users, by John Smith of the University of Edinburgh, UK. A hypertext help facility for beginning and novice Unix system users. It's available at several sites. Here are three:

http://alpha.acast.nova.edu/UNIXhelp/TOP_.html
http://www.ccs.neu.edu/Cobwebs/Unixhelp/
http://www.ucs.ed.ac.uk/Unixhelp/TOP_.html

Unix Tutorial, by Scott Miller, written for the students and faculty at the University of Florida Department of Electrical Engineering. An interactive Unix tutorial in hypertext form. Available at **http://www.ece.uc.edu/hpux-tutor/.**

Netscape Navigator

Using Netscape Navigator to Access the WWW

Netscape Navigator is a WWW browser with a graphical user interface (GUI), designed to be used in a windowed environment. It was developed by Netscape Communications Corporation by some of the same people who developed Mosaic. It's easy to use and very attractive. You use a mouse to access links and commands by clicking on icons, images, or underlined text. Once started, you work in color within a Navigator window. The first page you see is called the *home page*. It could contain text and images, and unlike Lynx, the images are visible! It can also contain icons that represent audio files, and if your system is properly equipped, you'll be able to click on the icon and hear what it represents. The text can be in bold or underlined and displayed in different sized fonts. All this really brings home the idea that WWW is a way of working with the Internet in a multimedia or hypermedia environment. There's much you can see and find with Netscape: art exhibits, museum displays, scientific and technical simulations, animations, sound clips of musical performances, plus all the textual information that's accessible by Lynx or other Internet tools.

Netscape Navigator has some advantages over other WWW browsers. It appears to access and display information faster than other graphical web browsers. This is because it displays images and pages gradually, so you're able to read what's on a page while an image is being downloaded.

It also includes the option to encrypt information, making commercial or financial transactions over the Internet more secure.

Figure B.1 is an example of a starting or home page using Netscape Navigator. It's one you likely to see if you're using Netscape Navigator with Microsoft Windows.

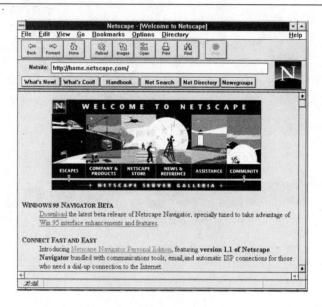

Figure B.I   Netscape Navigator Home Page Using Microsoft Windows

Netscape Navigator is a commercial product, but versions are available free on the Internet to students, faculty and staff members at educational institutions, and to employees of non-profit organizations. All others must pay a licensing fee. There are versions available to operate in a variety of computing environments including Macintosh systems, Microsoft Windows for DOS-based systems, or X-Windows on Unix systems. There's a big advantage to using something in a windows or graphical environment: You don't have to learn a lot of commands and you use the same commands or methods of the windowing system to operate Netscape Navigator. The sundry "flavors" of Netscape Navigator appear slightly different, but they share the same types of commands and icons. They're all used the same way:

> You use a mouse to move a hand or pointer to an icon or underlined portion of the window and click the mouse button (the left one if your mouse has more than one button.) If you've clicked on a link within the page, you follow that link, and the current page is replaced or another window pops up. Clicking on text or icons in the border of the window pops up a menu bar, and you choose an action from it. Clicking on an icon or a button in the border, in some cases, causes an action without your having to choose from a menu bar or dialog box.

Netscape Navigator is an exciting change from the text-only view you get using Lynx. However, you need a full Internet connection to use it. This means you need a computer with a network card to give a direct connection to the Internet, or a SLIP connection if you're using a modem.

You'll see that Netscape Navigator is easy to use and has lots of on-line help information. Once you get comfortable with it you'll probably want to spend hours using it to explore and browse the Internet. All the versions are similar so not much will be lost if we discuss a particular version when we give some examples. We'll talk about the Microsoft Windows version.

Starting and Leaving Netscape Navigator

You start Netscape Navigator by either clicking on an icon labeled **Netscape**, choosing **Netscape Navigator** from a pull-down menu, or typing **netscape** as a command and pressing Enter. The method you use depends on the type of system you're using.

One way to leave Netscape is to close its window. You can also choose **Exit** as an option from a pull-down menu.

The Netscape Window: Menu Items, Icons, Location, Directory Buttons, Contents

The Netscape Navigator window has similarities to other windows on the computer you're using. You use the same commands to change its size or position or turn it into an icon, as for any window. We'll discuss the features special to Netscape Navigator here.

First Row—Menu Items

Across the top you'll see a row of words called menu items, each representing a pull-down menu. In Figure B.1 the row is

File   Edit   View   Go   Bookmarks   Options   Directory   Help

You choose any of these by moving the mouse pointer to the word and clicking on it. To look at the Help menu, for example, move the mouse pointer to **Help** and click on it. A menu will pop up. (In the Microsoft Windows environment, the underlined characters give you fast access to one of these menu commands. Press Alt and one of the underlined characters to see its menu. For example, pressing Alt-H shows the Help menu.) In the sections below we'll look at the choices in several of these menus. Table B.1 gives a brief explanation of what you can find in each of these.

Menu Command	Description
File	The commands on this menu allow you to open another window to use with Netscape, open a location or URL so you can type in a URL to access, open a file on your computer system to view with Netscape, save the current page in a file on your computer system, mail the current page to an Internet e-mail address, print the document you're viewing, or close the current window.
Edit	Contains the usual Edit commands such as cut, copy, and paste. This allows you to copy portions of a document to other application programs. This menu also contains an item to find a string, a word, or a phrase, in the current page.
View	The items on this menu allow you to reload a copy of the current document or page (use this in case the one you see on the screen didn't load completely or is disturbed in some way), load images in case the images on a page were not loaded automatically, refresh the current page to its original state (this is useful if you've made a mistake filling out a form on the screen and want

	to start over), and view the source (html) version of the current page. This last item is useful if you want to become familiar with how to write your own pages.
Go	These items take you to different documents or pages you might have viewed during the current Netscape session. Netscape keeps a list of pages (the *history list*) you've been through to get to the current document. You can go back to the previous page, forward to a page you've just come back from, go to the Netscape home page, or take a look at the current history list. You can select any item by pointing to it with the mouse and clicking on it. There is also a command "Stop Loading" to click on to halt the connection that's attempting to bring something to the Netscape window. This is useful if it's taking too long to load something.
Bookmarks	Netscape lets you save links to places on the WWW you'd like to return to in this or other sessions. A bookmark in Netscape means the same thing as bookmark in Lynx or an item on a Mosaic hotlist. Choose this to add an item to your bookmark list, to view your bookmark list and then choose an item from the list, or to delete items from the list of bookmarks.
Options	This menu lets you specify a number of things related to the way items are displayed, the items that are displayed, and other options such as your e-mail address. You can control what's shown on the screen and how Netscape works with your network and computer system.
Directory	This contains a list of items on the WWW you might want to look at. Included are "What's New?" a list of new items available through the WWW; "What's Cool!" a list of interesting pages on the Internet; "Go to Newsgroups," to take you to newsgroups available through your Usenet news system; "Internet Directory," a directory of other Internet services available on the WWW; "Internet Search," a list of tools you can access to search the Internet; "Internet White Pages," a list of tools to use to find e-mail addresses; "About the Internet," an explanation of the Internet along with links to other items, and "Netscape Communications Corporation," which describes the company that developed Netscape Navigator. Many of these are accessible through the *directory buttons* discussed below.
Help	Choose this item to get help on using Netscape Navigator. It includes a link to frequently asked questions about Netscape and a very useful handbook, which contains a tutorial for using Netscape and an explanation of the commands you can use with Netscape Navigator.

Table B.1   Menu Commands in a Netscape Navigator Window

Icons—The Toolbar

A series of icons, called the *toolbar*, is displayed just below the menu commands on some versions of Netscape Navigator. The commands they represent are all available from the menu commands; the more frequently used commands are represented here as icons. You use them by pointing to them with your mouse and then clicking on them. There are differences between the versions. We're including the ones shown in Figure B.2; this should closely represent the version you use.

Figure B.2   Icons in a Netscape Navigator Window

We'll discuss the buttons in order from left to right. See Table B.2.

	Button	Explanation
	Back	Takes you back to the previous document, if there is one. This doesn't follow a hyperlink; it takes you to a document you've already seen.
	Forward	You can use this only if you got to where you are now by pressing **Back**. Then you'll be taken to the previous document. This doesn't follow a hyperlink, it takes you to a document you've just seen.
	Home	Takes you to your home page, the one you first saw when you started Netscape.
	Reload	This reloads the current document. If it didn't load completely or is disturbed in some way you may want to reload it.
	Images	If images are displayed automatically, this will be on the toolbar but won't be accessible to you. You use it if images aren't displayed automatically and you'd like to see the images in the current page.
	Open	Click on this to open a URL. A dialog box pops up on the screen, you type in the URL and press the button labeled **Open** to access the URL.
	Find	Click on this to find a string (one or more words) in the current page or document. A dialog box will appear, type the string to find, and then click on Find. The search goes from the current position in the document to its end, but you can specify the search to go up from the current position to the beginning.
	Stop	Clicking on the **Stop** sign stops the loading or attempt to load a URL.

Table B.2   Icons in a Netscape Navigator Window

Location:

This box, just below the icons in Figure B.1, contains the URL for the current document or page displayed on the screen.

The N

Netscape Navigator has a large N in the upper right-hand corner. As Netscape Navigator loads a document or follows a hyperlink, it appears as if asteroids or comets are streaking by the N. That animation or change in the box enclosing the N lets you know Netscape Navigator is doing something. You can't give other commands to Netscape navigator while this is going on. If it's taking too long to make a connection or retrieve a document, you can click on the N and interrupt the connection or stop the transmission. You won't leave Netscape Navigator.

The Directory Buttons

The buttons located just below the **Location:** item can be used to get quick access to some special collections of information available through the World Wide Web. All of these are also available by selecting the menu item **Directory**. They are shown in Figure B.3. See Table B.3 for a brief explanation of each.

Figure B.3   Directory Buttons in a Netscape Navigator Window

Title	Description
What's New!	A list of new services and resources available on the World Wide Web. This list is updated daily.
What's Cool!	A selected collection of interesting sites on the World Wide Web.
Handbook	A guide to help you use Netscape.
Net Search	This takes you to a page with a list of tools you can use to search for items on the World Wide Web. Examples of using the tools are also provided.
Net Directory	A directory of Internet services and resources available on the World Wide Web.
Newsgroups	An interface to Usenet News.

Table B.3   Directory Buttons in a Netscape Navigator Window

Document View

The majority of the screen is taken up by the view of the current document.

Scroll Bar

The scroll bar is on the far right of the window. You use it and the associated arrows to move through the document.

Moving Around a Document

You move around or through a document using the vertical or horizontal scroll bars on the right and bottom of the window. Use the vertical scroll bar to move up and down in the document, and use the horizontal scroll bar to move right and left. Each bar has an arrowhead on each end. You can click on these to move in the direction they indicate. Clicking on the arrowhead pointing up or down moves the window up or down one line in the document. Each scroll bar also has something called a scroll box within it. If you click on the scroll box you can move very quickly in the direction indicated. Clicking on a region of the scroll bar on one side or the other of the scroll box moves you one window in that direction.

Getting On-Line Help

The different versions of Netscape Navigator have either a button or command for on-line help. Clicking on the menu command **Help** will open a menu from which you can choose the type of help document you'll need. The items in the menu will most likely be hyperlinks to another site. When your system and your connections to the Internet are working well you'll hardly notice where these documents are located. Two choices you're likely to see are the **Netscape Handbook**, a complete guide to using Netscape Navigator, and **FAQ Page**, a list of frequently asked questions and answers about Netscape Navigator.

Following Hyperlinks

The general rule for following a link is to move the mouse pointer or hand to the item and click on it. The links are represented in all sorts of forms: underlined text, images, icons representing sound files, or portions of larger objects such as maps. The links represent URLs, or pointers to other items. The items can be in the same document, somewhere on your system, or anywhere on the Internet. When you click on an icon representing a sound file, you'll hear the sound recorded in that file. If you click on a hyperlink representing a still image, animation, or movie, you'll see it displayed. Whether these are completely successful depends on whether the computer you're using is equipped to play audio files or display images. Not all images in a document represent a hyperlink, just as not all text represents a link. You'll be able to tell when you've come across a hyperlink by watching the pointer. When it turns to a hand you know you've moved it to a hyperlink. Click and follow the link!

Saving, Printing, and Mailing a Document

Choose the **File** command menu from the top line. You'll see items to choose for saving the current document to a file on disk, printing the document, or sending a copy of the document by e-mail to any Internet address. When you choose any of these a dialog box opens and you fill in the appropriate information: to save a file, name the file the document will be saved to; to print a document, click the item that starts the printing; to e-mail the document, fill in the address to which the document will be sent. You'll be able to choose how you want to save, print, or mail the document—either as a hypertext document with all the information about the links, or as a plain file that doesn't contain any information about links. In the latter case, only the text is saved, printed, or sent by e-mail. Saving it as a hypertext document allows it to be used by Netscape Navigator in the same form it appeared on the screen.

Here's an example of a saving a document to a file: If icons aren't present, click on the command menu **File** and then, depending on the version of Netscape Navigator you're using, choose an item such as **Save to a local file**, **Save**, or **Save As ..**, and fill in the name of the file in the appropriate region of the dialog box. For versions with icons, click on the one for saving the document to a file. If you're using the version of Netscape Navigator for Microsoft Windows and you choose **Save As..** you'll see a dialog box similar to Figure B.4. We've filled in the name **goodpage.htm**. Click on the **OK** button to save the document in the file named **goodpage.htm**.

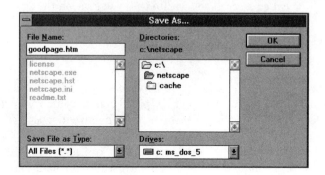

Figure B.4   Dialog Box for Saving a File

In this case the file is saved in hypertext or hypermedia form so it can be called up by Netscape Navigator and displayed just as it appeared in the window.

Searching a Document

There will be times when you'll want to search a document for a word or phrase. The steps you go through on all systems are:

❑   Choose **Find** from the **Edit** command menu or the **Find** (binoculars) icon from the toolbar.

❑   Fill in the dialog box: Type the string to use for the search and press Enter.

If the string is in the document, you'll be taken to the first occurrence of the string. To find the next one, press Enter again (if the dialog box is still open). If you've closed the dialog box, repeat the process.

Keeping Track of Where You've Been

As you use Netscape Navigator you'll be following hyperlinks to all sorts of places. You're likely to be following many links and not be keeping track of how you arrived at a document or image. You will, however, want to know how to get to some documents or images so you can return. Netscape Navigator, like other WWW browsers, does keep track of where you've been. It has to do so to let you use the arrow icons to go backward and forward. Versions of Netscape Navigator without icons have boxes labeled **Forward** and **Back** to let you move through the documents you've seen. To see where you've been you can look at the History list. This is the list of the links you've followed to get to the present document. To view it, click on the menu item labeled **Go**, and then choose the item **View History**. The history list will appear on the screen and you can choose to jump to any of the items listed. If you change your mind about going to an item on the history list, click on the button labeled **Close**. The history list contains only items you've seen in the current session.

Keeping Track of Favorite Places

When you find a document you want to return to in the future, even in a different Netscape Navigator session, you can save the URL to the item in a Bookmark list, a list of important, interesting, or favorite places to refer to at any time. It's easy to add an item to a Bookmark list. Click on the **Bookmarks** command menu and then choose the **Add Bookmark** item from the menu. The item is added to the Bookmark list!

To jump to an item on the Bookmark list click on the command menu **Bookmarks** and choose **View Bookmarks** from the menu. A dialog box will appear showing your bookmarks. (If you have a long Bookmark list, you'll want to use the portion of the dialog box that lets you enter a word or phrase to search though your Bookmark list.) Use your mouse to select any bookmark on the list, click on it, and Navigator will take you to that item on the WWW.

Viewing Local Files

Netscape Navigator can be used to browse the Internet, and it can also be used to view files, with some restrictions, on your system. First of all you have to have permission to read the file. On some types of systems, Unix for example, not all files can be read by everyone. Also, some versions of Netscape Navigator allow you to view only files whose names end with the suffixes **.htm** or **.html**. To view a file on your computer system, choose the menu command **File** and then choose the item **Open File ...** A dialog box will pop up so you can enter the name of the file to open.

Opening a URL

A URL gives Netscape Navigator and other WWW browsers all the information they need to jump to a document or item. In fact, all the hyperlinks within a document are written as URLs; you don't necessarily see them, but they are there. There will be times you'll want to supply Netscape Navigator with a URL, one you've read or heard about somewhere else, rather than follow the hyperlinks in a page. The phrase *open a URL* means just that. You type the URL into a dialog box, and Netscape Navigator interprets it and gets the information or resource. A URL can represent any form of Internet resource.

Here are two ways to open a URL: Click on the command menu item **File** and then choose **Open Location**, or click on the toolbar icon labeled **Open**. In any case a dialog box, as shown in Figure B.5, pops up and you type the URL in the text box. After it's typed, press Enter or click on the button labeled **Open**.

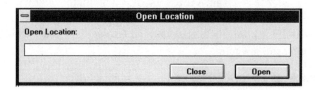

Figure B.5   Dialog Box for Opening URL

A Few Starting Points

All versions of Netscape Navigator come with a list of starting points. They're interesting, nicely constructed, and usually lead to other services and resources. They really are good places to start. You just click on the directory button **What's New!**, **What's Cool!**, or **Net Directory**, and then follow hyperlinks. There's enough there to keep you occupied for days!

Searching the World Wide Web

The WWW, with its easy-to-use browsers, makes many of the services and resources of the Internet accessible. You've seen in this book different tools or services to help you find information you can access on the Internet. Some examples are Hytelnet to help you find sites you can access through Telnet, Archie to help find files available by anonymous FTP, and Veronica to help search Gopher servers. Of all those mentioned, the WWW has been around for the shortest amount of time. Lynx, Mosaic, Netscape Navigator, and browsers like them have made the WWW very popular, and the number of sites offering WWW documents and other items has grown at an astounding rate. There are a number of tools for searching the World Wide Web and the Internet. Many of them are available by clicking on the directory button labeled **Net Search**. When you do that you'll see a page or document that lists several different tools for searching the World Wide Web and the Internet. That page also includes examples of how to use them. When you need to find something on the Internet, this is a great place to start.

Summary

Netscape Navigator is a very popular World Wide Web browser. It displays the images and text on WWW pages quickly, it allows for the possibility of making secure commercial and financial transactions on the Internet using encryption, and it provides the menus, icons, and directory buttons to make accessing the World Wide Web easy. As with any WWW browser, it lets you retrieve documents or web pages using Uniform Resource Locators or URLs. Each page contains links to other information sources or Internet services. The sources are accessible by WWW, FTP, Telnet, Gopher, WAIS, etc. The information can be text, it can be binary, still images, videos, audio, or any combination of these.

The Netscape Communications Corporation developed Netscape Navigator and offers it as a commercial product. However, it is free to students, and faculty and staff of educational or non-profit organizations. Versions are available for Unix (X-Windows), Microsoft Windows, and Macintosh systems. You can retrieve a copy of Netscape Navigator by anonymous FTP from **ftp.netscape.com** in the directory **netscape** (URL **ftp://ftp.netscape.com/netscape/**).

Glossary

Acceptable use policy A policy statement from a network or organization giving the acceptable uses of the network for local use and accessing the Internet.

Administrative address The address to use to join a Listserv or interest group, and to send requests for services.

Anonymous FTP A means of using FTP (File Transfer Protocol) in which a user starts an FTP session with a remote host, gives the log-in or user name *anonymous*, and her e-mail address as a password.

Archie An information service that helps to locate a file, which can then retrieved by anonymous FTP.

Article A message or file that is part of a Usenet newsgroup.

ASCII American Standard Code for Information Interchange. A code for representing characters in a numeric form. An ASCII file usually contains characters that can be displayed on a screen or printed without formatting or using another program.

BBS Bulletin Board System. A computer and software that provide an electronic forum, message center, and archives of files to its members. Traditionally these have been run by hobbyists through dial-up modem lines. Recently some of these have been connected to the Internet for a variety of organizations.

Binary file A file containing information such as a compressed archive, an image, a program, a spreadsheet, or a word processor document. The items in the file usually cannot be displayed on a screen or printed without using some program.

Bookmark list A list of links to items on the Internet. Usually created by an individual as he uses Gopher or Lynx. A good way to keep track of favorite or important sites, these are saved and can be used at any time. Note that Gopher and Lynx keep separate bookmark lists. Some WWW browsers, e.g., Mosaic, use the term *hotlist* for this list of links.

Client A program or Internet service that sends commands to and receives information from a corresponding program (often) at a remote site called a server. Most Internet services run as client/server programs. Gopher, for example, works this way. A user starts a client program on her computer, which contacts a Gopher server.

Compression An algorithm or scheme used to compress or shrink a file. A file in compressed form must first be uncompressed or transformed before it can be read, displayed, or used. Files available through anonymous FTP are often stored in compressed form, and must be treated as binary files.

CWIS Campus Wide Information System. An information system for making information available to a campus or organization.

Dial-up access Access to the Internet through a phone line and a modem. Typically gives the user a log-in name and shell account to another computer, which has a full IP Internet connection. The user usually has access to only text-based Internet services.

Digest A collection of messages from a Listserv or interest group sent at regular intervals such as daily or weekly.

Discussion list A form of group discussion and sharing information carried on by electronic mail. A discussion list focuses on a single topic.

Domain name The Internet name for a network or computer system. The name consists of a sequence of characters separated by periods such as **s850.mwc.edu**.

Download Transfer a file from a remote computer to the computer used by an individual.

E-mail Electronic mail. A basic Internet service that allows users to exchange messages electronically.

Electronic Communications Privacy Act (ECPA) A 1986 federal law protecting the privacy of electronic communications, providing civil remedies for those whose e-mail has been read, and providing exceptions to system administrators and court-authorized actions.

Encryption A procedure to convert a file from its original form to one that can be read only by the intended recipient.

FAQ Frequently Asked Questions. A list, often associated with Usenet newsgroups, of commonly asked questions and answers on a specific topic. These are usually the first place users should look to find answers to questions or to get information on a topic.

Flame An e-mail message or article in a Usenet newsgroup that's meant to insult someone or provoke controversy. This term is also applied to messages that contain strong criticism of or disagreement with a previous message or article.

Free-Net A community-based network, allowing access to the Internet for no or a small membership fee.

FTP File Transfer Protocol, which allows computers on the Internet to exchange files. One of the three basic Internet services.

FTP Archive A collection of files available by using anonymous FTP.

Gateway A device or program that transfers information between different types of networks. The networks may have similar functions, but in most cases use different technologies for handling information.

Gopher A menu-oriented system that gives access to documents, files, and other Internet services, regardless of where they are on the Internet. The software for Gopher was created and developed at the University of Minnesota to allow users to browse and retrieve documents in a campus environment.

GUI Graphical User Interface. Uses icons and images in addition to text to represent information, input, and output.

Header A portion of an e-mail message containing information pertinent to the transmission of the message such as the address of the sender, the address of the recipient, and when the message was sent.

History list A list of Internet sites, services, and resources that have been accessed through a WWW browser to arrive at the current item.

Home page The first screen or page of a site accessible through a WWW browser.

Host A computer on the Internet that allows users to communicate with other computers.

Hotlist A list of favorite or important links to sites, resources, and services compiled during WWW sessions using a browser such as Mosaic. The hotlist can be saved for future use. Similar to a bookmark list used with Gopher, Lynx, or Netscape Navigator.

HTML Hypertext Markup Language. The format used for writing documents to be viewed with a WWW browser. Items in the document can be text, images, sounds, and links to other HTML documents or sites, services, and resources on the Internet.

Hypermedia An extension to hypertext to include graphics and audio.

Hypertext A way of viewing or working with a document in text format that allows cross-references to be followed and then return. This presents a nonlinear means of dealing with text, and is accomplished through a computer interface to text.

Hytelnet A guide and a tool for working with resources accessible by Telnet. It presents a hypertext interface to an organized list of Telnet sites. The sites are arranged in categories by the type of service such as a library catalog, database, bulletin board, electronic book, network information, and includes a glossary.

Interest group Group discussion and sharing information carried on by electronic mail. An interest group focuses on a single topic. An individual subscribes or joins an interest group electronically and all messages sent to the group are distributed by e-mail to the members.

Internet protocol (IP) The basic protocol used for the Internet. Information is put into a single packet; the packet contains the address of the sender and the recipient and is then sent out. The receiving system removes the information from the packet.

InterNIC Internet Network Information Center. A National Science Foundation (NSF) funded organization to provide information, registration, and database services to NSFNET (a major portion of the Internet in the U.S.).

IP address An Internet address in numeric form. Consists of four numerals, each in the range of 2 through 255 separated by periods. An example is **192.65.245.76**.

IP connection A connection to the Internet that provides access to all services, resources, and tools. A computer system with an IP connection has an IP address.

Jughead A tool (software) used to search for items listed in Gopher menus (usually) at a specific site. Veronica is used to search for Gopher menus throughout the Internet.

Kermit A protocol or program used to exchange (upload and download) files between computer systems. Often used to exchange files between a personal computer and another system via a modem.

List address The address to use to send e-mail to be distributed to each member of a discussion list, interest group, Listserv list, or mailing list.

Listproc One of the several types of software used to manage and administer a discussion list, interest group, or mailing list.

Listserv The type of software used to manage a Listserv list, a form of a discussion list, interest group, or mailing list.

Lurking Reading the e-mail or articles in a discussion group or newsgroup without contributing or posting messages.

Lynx A text-based World Wide Web browser (software) used for accessing information in a hypertext manner on the Internet.

Mail user agent The software used to access and manage a user's electronic mail. Two examples are Pine and Mailx.

Mailbase One of the several types of software used to manage and administer a discussion list, interest group, or mailing list.

Mailing list Group discussion and sharing information carried on by electronic mail. A mailing list focuses on a single topic. An individual subscribes or joins a mailing list electronically and all messages sent to the group are distributed by e-mail to the members.

Mailserve One of the several types of software used to manage and administer a discussion list, interest group, or mailing list.

Mailx An electronic mail program or user mail agent. Used by individuals to read, send, and process their e-mail. Common on computers using the Unix operating system.

Majordomo One of the several types of software used to manage and administer a discussion list, interest group, or mailing list.

Message body The text portion of an e-mail message.

MIME Multipurpose Internet Mail Extensions. Extensions to standard e-mail programs making it easy to send, receive, and include nontext files.

Moderator A person who manages or administers a discussion list, interest group, Listserv list, mailing list, or Usenet newsgroup. In most cases the moderator is a volunteer. Messages sent to the group are first read by the moderator, who then passes appropriate messages to the group.

Mosaic A World Wide Web browser (software) used for accessing information in a hypertext or hypermedia manner on the Internet. It gives the user a graphical interface (GUI) to Internet services and resources.

National Public Telecommunications Network (NPTN) A confederation of Free-Nets, community-based networks. Its purpose is to help establish community networks, to link those systems into a common network, and to supplement their services with networkwide services and resources.

Netiquette A collection of rules for behavior on the Internet and/or Usenet.

NetFind An Internet service used to find e-mail addresses based on information, such as a person's name, location, or domain name, provided by the user.

Netnews An alternative term for Usenet News; usually refers to Usenet News carried on the Internet.

Newsreader Software used by an individual to read, reply to, and manage Usenet News.

Packet The basic unit of information sent across the Internet. Packets contain information (data), the address of the sender, and the address of the recipient.

Pico Pine Composer. The full-screen text editor commonly used with the Pine e-mail program.

Pine Program for Internet News and E-mail. A mail user agent for reading, sending, and managing electronic messages. On-line help is always available and it includes MIME and an address book.

Port number Some Internet services have a unique number assigned to them, which refers to a logical channel in a communications system. Using a port number with a Telnet session, such as **telnet madlab.sprl.umich.edu 3000**, allows for a connection without providing a log-in name.

Posting An article or message sent to a Usenet newsgroup; sending an article or message to a newsgroup.

Protocols A set of rules or procedures for exchanging information between networks or computer systems.

Rn A newsreader (software) used with Usenet News. Newsgroups and articles are presented one at a time in sequential order. A user selects a newsgroup and then works with the articles in that group.

Router A device (hardware) that transfers information between networks.

Server A computer that shares resources with other computers on the Internet. In the context of Internet services a server is a computer system or program that provides information to other programs called clients. When a user starts a Gopher session she starts a client Gopher program, which contacts a Gopher server program.

Signature An optional portion of an e-mail message consisting of information about the sender such as his full name, mailing address, phone number, etc. The signature is usually in a file named *.signature*, *signature*, or *.sig* and is automatically included with each message.

Signoff A term used in a command to leave, quit, or unsubscribe from a discussion list, interest group, Listserv list, or mailing list.

SLIP Serial Line Internet Protocol. Software allowing the use of the Internet protocol (IP) over a serial line or through a serial port. Commonly used with a modem connection to a service providing Internet services.

SMTP Simple Mail Transfer Protocol. The Internet standard protocol used to transfer electronic mail from one computer system to another.

Subscribe A term used in a command to join or become part of a discussion list, interest group, Listserv list, or mailing list. This term is also used when choosing to make a Usenet newsgroup one of those listed when you use a newsreader.

System Administrator An individual whose responsibility is to manage and maintain a computer system.

TCP/IP Transmission Control Protocol/Internet Protocol. A collection of protocols the Internet uses to provide for services such as e-mail, FTP, and Telnet.

Telnet Allows for remote log-in capabilities on the Internet. One of the three basic Internet services. A user on one computer on the Internet can access and log in to another computer.

Text file A file that contains characters in a plain human-readable format. There are no formatting commands such as underlining or displaying characters in boldface or in different fonts. Also called an ASCII file.

Thread A collection of articles all dealing with a single posting or e-mail message.

Tin A newsreader (software) used with Usenet News. Newsgroups and articles are presented in a full-screen menu format. Articles within a newsgroup are threaded; articles on the same topic are grouped together.

Transmission Control Protocol (TCP) A protocol used as the basis of most Internet services. It is used in conjunction (actually on top of) the Internet Protocol. It allows for reliable communication oriented to process-to-process communication. Used to create virtual terminal sessions; packets are passed so it appears a dedicated, constant connection exists between computer systems.

Unsubscribe A term used in a command to leave, sign off, or quit a discussion list, interest group, Listserv list, or mailing list. The term is also used to remove a Usenet newsgroup from the list of those you would regularly read.

Upload Transfer a file from the computer system being used to a remote system.

URL Uniform Resource Locator. A way of describing the location of an item (document, service, resource) on the Internet and also specifying the means to access that item.

Usenet A system for exchanging messages called articles arranged according to specific categories called newsgroups. The articles (messages) are passed from one system to another, not as e-mail between individuals.

Uudecode A program to recreate binary files from the ASCII or text form to which they were converted by uuencode. Used by someone who has received a file or e-mail in uuencode form.

Uuencode A program to convert binary data into ASCII form. Necessary to use to send binary files with some e-mail systems. Used to send binary files on e-mail systems without MIME.

Veronica A tool (software) for searching for items on Gopher menus throughout the Internet.

VT100 A specific type of terminal, most commonly used with Internet services and programs such as Hytelnet, Lynx, and Pine. Many programs work in full-screen mode and need to know the type of terminal they'll be using.

WAIS Wide Area Information Server. A system for searching and retrieving items from databases. The databases can be anywhere on the Internet.

Web browser A program (software) used to access the Internet services and resources available through the World Wide Web.

World Wide Web (WWW) The World Wide Web is a way of thinking about and working with the Internet as a collection of different services, resources, and protocols, which can be accessed in a uniform manner.

Zmodem A protocol used to transfer files, usually by modem, between computer systems. This allows for relatively high-speed transfers in a reliable and convenient manner.

Index